D1561257

University Success

READING

Success

TRANSITION LEVEL

Lawrence Zwier and Maggie Vosters

Series Editor: Lawrence Zwier

Authentic Content Contributors: Ronnie Alan Hess II and Victoria Solomon

University Success Reading, Transition Level

Pearson Education, 221 River Street, Hoboken, NJ 07030

Staff credits: The people who made up the *University Success Reading, Transition Level* team, representing content creation, design, manufacturing, marketing, multimedia, project management, publishing, rights management, and testing, are Pietro Alongi, Rhea Banker, Stephanie Bullard, Tracey Cataldo, Sara Davila, Mindy DePalma, Dave Dickey, Warren Fischbach, Nancy Flaggman, Gosia Jaros-White, Niki Lee, Amy McCormick, Jennifer Raspiller, Paula Van Ells, and Joseph Vella.

Project supervision: Debbie Sistino

Contributing editors: Eleanor Barnes, Andrea Bryant, Nancy Matsunaga, and Leigh Stolle

Cover image: Nassau Hall, Princeton University, Clock Tower © P. Spiro / Alamy Stock Photo

Text and cover design: Yin Ling Wong

Video research: Constance Rylance

Video production: Kristine Stolakis

Text composition: MPS Limited

Library of Congress Cataloging-in-Publication Data

A catalog record for the print edition is available from the Library of Congress.

ISBN-10: 0-13-440078-X

ISBN-13: 978-0-13-440078-5

Printed in the United States of America

3 18

Contents

PART 1: FUNDAMENTAL READING SKILLS

PART 2: CRITICAL THINKING SKILLS

PART 3: EXTENDED READING

Welcome to
University Success

INTRODUCTION

University Success is a new academic skills series designed to equip transitioning English learners with the reading, writing, and oral communication skills necessary to succeed in courses in an English-speaking university setting. The blended instructional model provides students with an inspiring collection of extensive authentic content, expertly developed in cooperation with five subject matter experts, all "thought leaders" in their fields. By utilizing both online and in-class instructional materials, *University Success* models the type of "real life" learning expected of students studying for a degree. Unlike a developmental textbook, *University Success* recognizes the unique linguistic needs of English language learners. The course carefully scaffolds skill development to help students successfully work with challenging and engaging authentic content provided by top professors in their academic fields.

SERIES ORGANIZATION: *THREE STRANDS*

This three-strand series, **Reading**, **Writing**, and **Oral Communication**, includes five distinct content areas: the Human Experience, Money and Commerce, the Science of Nature, Arts and Letters, and Structural Science, all popular fields of study among English language learners. The three strands are fully aligned across content areas and skills, allowing teachers to utilize material from different strands to support learning. Teachers can delve deeply into skill development in a single skill area, or provide additional support materials from other skill areas for richer development across the four skills.

THE *UNIVERSITY SUCCESS* APPROACH: *AN AUTHENTIC EXPERIENCE*

This blended program combines the utility of an interactive student book, online learner lab, and print course to create a flexible approach that adjusts to the needs of teachers and learners. The skill-based and step-by-step instruction helps students master essential skills and become confident and successful in their ability to perform in academic-degree-bearing courses taught in English. Students at this level need to engage with content that provides the same challenges faced by native speakers in a university setting. Many English language learners are not prepared for the quantity of reading and writing required in college-level courses, nor are they properly prepared to listen to full-length lectures that have not been scaffolded for them. These learners, away from the safety of an ESL classroom, must keep up with the rigors of a class led by a professor who may be unaware of the challenges a second-language learner faces. *University Success* steps up to the podium to represent academic content realistically with the appropriate skill development and scaffolding essential for English language learners to be successful.

The program features the following:

- **Rigorous academic preparation** that allows students to build on their strengths and prior knowledge, develop language and study skills, and increase their knowledge of academic content related to the STEAM areas of study
- **Systematic skill development**, from strategies to critical thinking to application and assessment, that explicitly teaches students to notice, understand, and employ English language features in the comprehension and synthesis of new information
- **A fluency driven approach** designed to help learners with fluency, accuracy, and automaticity allowing them to process linguistically complex texts of significant length
- **Flexible three-part developmental English approach** that includes intensive skill development and extensive practice
- **Extensive work with authentic texts** and videotaped **lectures** created by dynamic Stanford University professors providing a challenging experience that replicates the authentic experience of studying in a mainstream university classroom
- **Flexible format** and sophisticated design for students who are looking for authentic academic content, comprehensive practice, and a true college experience
- **Global Scale of English for Academic Learners** alignment with content tied to outcomes designed to challenge students who have achieved a B2+ level of proficiency or higher
- **Content and fluency vocabulary approach** that develops learner ability to read words as multiword units and to process text more quickly and with greater ease
- **Strategies for academic success**, delivered via online videos, including how to talk to professors during office hours and time management techniques, that help increase students' confidence and ability to cope with the challenges of academic study and college culture
- **Continuous formative assessment** and extensive formative assessment built into the series, offering multiple points of feedback, in class or online, assessing the ability of students to transfer and apply skills with rigorous academic challenges

TEACHER SUPPORT
Each of the three strands is supported with:

- **Comprehensive downloadable teaching notes** in MyEnglishLab that detail key points for all of the specialized academic content in addition to tips and suggestions for teaching skills and strategies
- **An easy-to-use online learning management system** offering a flexible gradebook and tools for monitoring student progress
- **Audioscripts, videoscripts, answer keys, and word lists** to help in lesson planning and follow-up

BOOK ORGANIZATION: *THREE PARTS*

University Success is designed with a part structure that allows for maximum flexibility for teachers. The series is "horizontally" aligned allowing teachers to teach across a specific content area and "vertically" aligned allowing a teacher to gradually build skills. Each part is a self-contained module, offering teachers the ability to customize a nonlinear program that will best address the needs of students. The skills, like the content areas, are aligned, giving teachers and students the opportunity to explore the differences in application based on the type of study experience the students need.

In Part 1 and Part 2 students work with comprehensive skills that include:

- Working with and developing complex ideas reflecting areas of academic interest
- Using, creating, and interpreting visuals from data, experiments, and research
- Distinguishing facts and opinions and hedging when presenting, reviewing, or writing academic research
- Recognizing and using inference and implications in academic fields
- Identifying, outlining, and describing complex processes in research, lab work, and experiments

Part 3 provides a truly authentic experience for students with an extended essay (Reading strand), lecture (Oral Communication strand), and interview about the writing process (Writing strand) provided by the thought leader. Part 3 functions as a final formative assessment of a student's ability to apply skills with mainstream academic content. Part 3 content includes:

- Subject matter to which students can find personal connections
- Topics with interdisciplinary appeal
- Material that draws students into the most current debates in academia
- Topics that strengthen the cultural and historical literacy of students

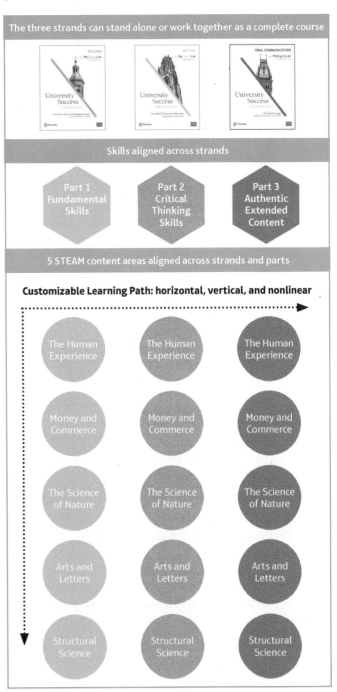

The three strands can stand alone or work together as a complete course

Skills aligned across strands

Part 1 Fundamental Skills

Part 2 Critical Thinking Skills

Part 3 Authentic Extended Content

5 STEAM content areas aligned across strands and parts

Customizable Learning Path: horizontal, vertical, and nonlinear

The Human Experience

Money and Commerce

The Science of Nature

Arts and Letters

Structural Science

SUBJECT MATTER EXPERTS

Marcelo Clerici-Arias teaches undergraduate courses at Stanford University's Department of Economics, from principles of micro- and macroeconomics to upper-level courses in computational economics, behavioral economics, and economic policy. He has researched innovative pedagogies used in economics and other social and natural sciences. His main research areas are game theory, computational economics, and teaching and learning. Professor Clerici-Arias is a popular speaker and presenter, has participated in NSF-sponsored projects, and has co-edited an economics textbook.

Jonathan D. Greenberg is a lecturer in law at Stanford Law School; teaching fellow for the school's advanced degree program in International Economic Law, Business and Policy; and scholar-in-residence at the school's Gould Center for Conflict Resolution. He has published scholarly articles and chapters in a broad range of interdisciplinary journals and books.

Robert Pogue Harrison is a professor of French and Italian literature at Stanford University and author of six books, the most recent of which is *Juvenescence: A Cultural History of Our Age* (2014). He writes regularly for the *New York Review of Books* and hosts the radio podcast *Entitled Opinions*. He is a member of the American Academy of Arts and Sciences, and in 2014 he was knighted Chevalier of the French Republic.

Lynn Hildemann is a professor of civil and environmental engineering at Stanford University and currently is serving as department chair. She is an author on over 80 peer-reviewed publications. Her research areas include the sources and dispersion of airborne particulate matter in indoor environments and assessment of human exposure to air pollutants. She has served on advisory committees for the Bay Area Air Quality Management District and the California Air Resources Board and as an associate editor for *Environmental Science & Technology*.

Robert Siegel is a professor in the Department of Microbiology and Immunology at Stanford University. He holds secondary appointments in the Program in Human Biology, the Center for African Studies, and the Woods Institute for the Environment. He is the recipient of numerous teaching awards including Stanford's highest teaching accolade, the Walter Gores Award. Dr. Siegel's courses cover a wide range of topics including virology, infectious disease, and global health, as well as molecular biology, Darwin and evolution and island biogeography, and photography. He is an avid hiker, photographer, and dromomaniac.

SERIES EDITORS

 Robyn Brinks Lockwood teaches courses in spoken and written English at Stanford University in the English for Foreign Students graduate program and is the program education coordinator of the American Language and Culture undergraduate summer program. She is an active member of the international TESOL organization, serves as chairperson of the Publishing Professional Council, and is a past chair of the Materials Writers Interest Section. She is a frequent presenter at TESOL regional and international conferences. She has edited and written numerous textbooks, online courses, and ancillary components for ESL courses and TOEFL preparation.

 Maggie Sokolik holds a BA in anthropology from Reed College, and an MA in romance linguistics and a PhD in applied linguistics from UCLA. She is the author of over 20 ESL and composition textbooks. She has taught at MIT, Harvard, Texas A&M, and currently UC Berkeley, where she is director of College Writing Programs. She has developed and taught several popular MOOC courses in English language writing and literature. She is the founding editor of *TESL-EJ*, a peer-reviewed journal for ESL/EFL professionals, one of the first online journals. She travels frequently to speak about grammar, writing, and instructor education. She lives in the San Francisco Bay area, where she and her husband play bluegrass music.

 Lawrence J. Zwier is an associate director of the English Language Center, Michigan State University. He holds a bachelor's degree in English literature from Aquinas College, Grand Rapids, MI, and an MA in TESL from the University of Minnesota. He has taught ESL/EFL at universities in Saudi Arabia, Malaysia, Japan, Singapore, and the United States. He is the author of numerous ELT textbooks, mostly about reading and vocabulary, and also writes nonfiction books about history and geography for middle school and high school students. He is married with two children and lives in Okemos, Michigan.

Key Features of
University Success Reading

UNIQUE PART STRUCTURE

University Success employs a unique three-part structure, providing maximum flexibility and multiple opportunities to customize the flow of content.

Each part is a self-contained module allowing teachers to focus on the highest value skills and content. Parts are aligned around science, technology, engineering, arts, and mathematic (STEAM) content relevant to mainstream academic areas of study.

Part 1 and Part 2 focus on the fundamental and critical thinking skills most relevant for students preparing for university degrees. **Part 3** introduces students to extended practice with the skills. Students work directly with the authentic content created by top professors in their academic fields.

PART 1 AND PART 2

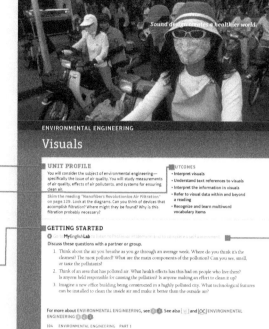

A **Unit Profile** outlines the content.

Outcomes aligned with the Global Scale of English (GSE) are clearly stated to ensure student awareness of skills.

Getting Started questions explore the content, develop context, and engage students' prior knowledge.

An **online self-assessment** identifies students' confidence with skills and helps them create personal learning objectives.

Professors greet students at the beginning and end of each part, providing a preview and a wrap-up of the content.

Why It's Useful highlights the purpose for developing the **Fundamental Skill** or **Critical Thinking Skill** and supports transfer of the skill to mainstream class content.

A **detailed presentation** contextualizes the skill's value in academic study.

A **Noticing Activity** allows students to see the skill demonstrated within the context of an authentic academic reading.

Online activities encourage students to personalize content with collaborative research activities.

Each skill is divided into discreet **Supporting Skills**.

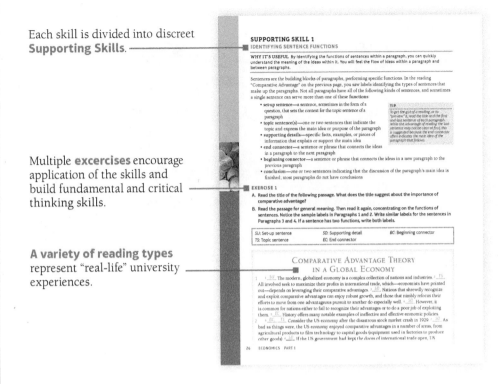

SUPPORTING SKILL 1
IDENTIFYING SENTENCE FUNCTIONS

WHY IT'S USEFUL By identifying the functions of sentences within a paragraph, you can quickly understand the meaning of the ideas within it. You will feel the flow of ideas within a paragraph and between paragraphs.

Sentences are the building blocks of paragraphs, performing specific functions. In the reading "Comparative Advantage" on the previous page, you saw labels identifying the types of sentences that make up the paragraphs. Not all paragraphs have all of the following kinds of sentences, and sometimes a single sentence can serve more than one of these functions:

- **set-up sentence**—a sentence, sometimes in the form of a question, that sets the context for the topic sentence of a paragraph
- **topic sentence(s)**—one or two sentences that indicate the topic and express the main idea or purpose of the paragraph
- **supporting details**—specific facts, examples, or pieces of information that explain or support the main idea
- **end connector**—a sentence or phrase that connects the ideas in a paragraph to the next paragraph
- **beginning connector**—a sentence or phrase that connects the ideas in a new paragraph to the previous paragraph
- **conclusion**—one or two sentences indicating that the discussion of the paragraph's main idea is finished; most paragraphs do not have conclusions

TIP
To get the gist of a reading, or to "pre-view" it, read the title and the first and last sentence of each paragraph. While the advantage of reading the last sentence may not be clear at first, this is suggested because the end connector often indicates the main idea of the paragraph that follows.

EXERCISE 1

A. Read the title of the following passage. What does the title suggest about the importance of comparative advantage?

B. Read the passage for general meaning. Then read it again, concentrating on the functions of sentences. Notice the sample labels in Paragraphs 1 and 2. Write similar labels for the sentences in Paragraphs 3 and 4. If a sentence has two functions, write both labels.

| SU: Set-up sentence | SD: Supporting detail | BC: Beginning connector |
| TS: Topic sentence | EC: End connector | |

COMPARATIVE ADVANTAGE THEORY
IN A GLOBAL ECONOMY

1   *SU* The modern, globalized economy is a complex collection of nations and industries. *TS* All involved seek to maximize their profits in international trade, which—economists have pointed out—depends on leveraging their comparative advantages. *SD* Nations that shrewdly recognize and exploit comparative advantages can enjoy robust growth, and those that nimbly refocus their efforts to move from one advantageous pursuit to another do especially well. *SD* However, it is common for nations either to fail to recognize their advantages or to do a poor job of exploiting them. *EC* History offers many notable examples of ineffective and effective economic policies.

2   *BC TS* Consider the US economy after the disastrous stock market crash in 1929. *SD* As bad as things were, the US economy enjoyed comparative advantages in a number of areas, from agricultural products to film technology to capital goods (equipment used in factories to produce other goods). *SD* If the US government had kept the doors of international trade open, US

26   ECONOMICS   PART 1

Multiple **excercises** encourage application of the skills and build fundamental and critical thinking skills.

A variety of reading types represent "real-life" university experiences.

READING-WRITING CONNECTION
SUMMARIZING

WHY IT'S USEFUL By writing a summary after you have read something, you are creating a study tool that you can refer back to, discovering what you did and did not understand about the text, and consolidating your memory of information from the text.

A summary is a short version of an original text that gives the most important information. As a student, you will frequently be as... understanding of its main idea(s) and in a much shorter form.

The most important aspects of a w... idea(s) of the original text in a con... read and understood it. Most sent... summary. Here are some suggestio...

- Notice the title. Note the to... (Or make an outline to hel...
- Use your own words.
- Brevity is a central feature... of the original.
- Avoid words or phrases tha... already know, after all, acco...
- Avoid repeated words, phr...
- Use pronouns (it, this, they,...
- Shorten or leave out most e...
- Shorten or avoid stylistic e... strange enough, and so on.
- Shorten or leave out paren... comments about an idea... or commas: (xxx) —xxx—

EXERCISE 4

A. Read the title and the passag...

GIFT EXCH...

Economies come in many... sizes, not all of them involving... based trading. Some theorists... the French sociologist and ant... Marcel Mauss, have concentra... economies." These involve exc... as money-oriented economies... interaction is less direct. The l... is that I help you meet your n... though you don't have anythin... me in return—not yet, anywa... that at some point in the futu... your relatives will give somethi... to balance things out. Althou...

34   ECONOMICS   PART 1

LANGUAGE SKILL
USING DICTIONARIES TO STRENGTHEN VOCABULARY

WHY IT'S USEFUL By familiarizing yourself with three features of dictionary entries, you can work to further develop and strengthen your vocabulary.

In building your English vocabulary, being able to make full use of a dictionary and its features is key. Understanding the components of a dictionary entry will help take your vocabulary to the next level. Three critical parts of dictionary entries and subentries are **multiple definitions** listed for some words, **collocations**, and **multiword units**.

- If you are relatively familiar with dictionaries, you will know from experience that one word often has **multiple definitions**. To find the one you need, first quickly scan all of the definitions, as well as the example phrases and sentences provided. If you cannot find the right definition by scanning, slow down and read each definition (plus examples) more carefully. Then return to the original context where you found the word and determine which definition best fits that context.

Example
Original context: The **geography** of the countryside near my home is mountainous and replete with valleys.
Dictionary entry:

| Dictionary | Thesaurus | Topic Vocabulary | Study Center | Exam Practice | Writing Skills |

geography
1. the study of the countries, oceans, rivers, mountains, cities, etc., as well as populations, industry, agriculture, and economies of different areas of the world
2. the way the parts of a place are arranged, such as the location of streets, mountains, rivers, etc.
3. the way that the buildings, streets, etc., within an area are arranged

Here, the second definition best explains geography as it is used in the original context. In order to build your existing vocabulary, it is essential to develop the skill of determining the best definition from a multiple-definition entry.

- **Collocations**—the way in which some words are often used together, or a particular combination of words—may be indicated in a dictionary by being set in bold, italics, or within example sentences. Some dictionaries even highlight collocations in special boxes. Identifying collocations for a given word will help you with comprehension and writing. For example, the adjective *strong* collates with the word *principles* in this sentence: *The man has strong principles, always demonstrating honesty and truthfulness.* Strong cannot be replaced with a word that has a similar meaning, like *muscular*.

- A **multiword unit** is a vocabulary item made of two or more words that are very tightly bound to each other. Some familiar kinds of multiword units are phrasal verbs (*pass out, see [something] through, clean up*), compound nouns (*brass knuckles, space shuttle, USB port*), and idioms, in whole or in part (*odd man out, the last straw, a stitch in time*).

TIP
Research An online corpus—a large collection of written and/or spoken language—can be very helpful in developing your knowledge of collocations. Most corpora have a "collocations" feature, where you can enter the word you want to use and then a word you think might collocate with it. If a list of sentences containing the words you entered appears, it means that those two words collocate with each other. If only a few sentences appear, the collocation is probably weak. If no sentences appear in the results, you can assume that the two words do not collocate.

If there is a word you want to use but you do not know what other words collocate with it, you can find out by simply entering the word into the search box for your online corpus and then analyzing the results to determine which co-occurrences are common.

16   SOCIOLOGY   PART 1

Reading-Writing Connection aligns the Reading and Writing strands establishing how strategies apply across language skills and using authentic academic content relevant to mainstream study.

The **Language Skill** study provides support for complex lexical and grammatical skills.

An **Apply Your Skills** section at the end of Part 1 and Part 2 functions as a formative assessment.

An extended **Reading** aligned with the academic content allows students to apply skills practiced in the unit.

Critical Thinking and **Language** activities challenge students to dig deeper.

READ

A. Read the passage. Annotate and take notes as necessary.

Nanofibers
Revolution
Air Filtrati

Urban areas around th
particle pollution and
some cities engulfed i
exceeds the guideline
Health Organization (
of nanofiber technolog
allowed engineers to b
air-filtration devices t
pollutants. Electrospu
are both comfortable t
and efficient at blockir
pollution, and researc
develop advanced air
people breathe safely
Nanofibers can be use
well as in other enviro
such as water filtratio
air purification system

Nanofiber

Fine particulate and
pollution from substan
and industrial emissio
breathe and have been
respiratory disease, ca
risks. Disturbingly, WF
particulate air pollutio
urban areas around th
power plants, increase

vehicles, inefficient heating systems, and the
burning of biomass for heat and cooking. WHO

THINKING VISUALLY

The graph and its accompanying notes give essential data about cervical cancer in the United States. Using the information in the graph, follow these steps:

1. Summarize the overall trends in cervical cancer incidence and mortality over the time period covered by the graph.
2. What do you expect the future to hold, regarding the incidence and mortality of the disease?
3. Briefly state what you think has been the impact of HPV vaccines.

NUMBER OF NEW CERVICAL CANCER CASES AND DEATHS AMONGST US FEMALES, FROM 1992 TO 2012

■ New Cases   ■ Deaths

Estimated Data for 2015	Three HPV vaccines have been approved for use in the United States:
·Number of new cases per 100,000 females: 5.2	·Gardasil (approved in 2006; trialed with more than 15,000 patients
·Estimated number of deaths per 100,000 females: 1.85	before release)
·Percent of women surviving at least 5 years after	·Cervarix (approved in 2009; trialed with >30,000)
first diagnosis: 67.8%	·Gardasil 9 (approved in 2014)

Facts about cervical cancer in the United States

THINKING ABOUT LANGUAGE

The reading "Vaccinating Against Cancer" contains a substantial amount of language that conveys function and purpose. Follow these steps:

1. Identify and underline such language in each of the excerpts on the following pages.
2. Use an online corpus (such as Corpus of Contemporary American English) to find one authentic example of the language you underlined in each excerpt.
3. Write the example sentence you find as well as the frequency of the phrase (e.g., the number of instances in which this language appeared in the corpus).
4. If the corpus you use has a "context" or "genre" filter, write whether the phrase appears to be frequently used in scientific speech or publications.
5. Write down as many of the following facts as possible about the source of the example—year, title, author, and journal.

Evidence and Argumentation   203

PART 3

Students read an **authentic essay** written by a professor working in a specific STEAM field.

Thinking Critically activities ask learners to engage at a deep level with the content, using information from the essay to address specific real-world applications.

Thinking Visually provides an opportunity for students to analyze charts, graphs, and other visuals.

Thinking About Language reviews language skills developed in Part 1 and Part 2, using the source content from the professor to provide final examples.

A final **Research Project** encourages in-class and online project collaboration, mirroring real-world expectations of project learning.

READ

Read the passage. Then answer the questions after each section.

Thinking
About Str

INTRODUCTION
What is strategy and
about it? How can thi
strategy enable you
effective strategies f
you belong?
This essay ventu
providing a brief intr
of intellectual and m
surprising to talk abo
this way since we im
develop and implem
For example, we take
y approach to solving
this essay suggests t
in greater depth ope
field of analysis and
intellectual history. I
strategy is a moral l
for first designing ef
then implementing t
make a better world.
a better world is a m
that each person mu

The author of the essay
A History (Oxford 2013),
FRAMEWORK #3: The Me

THINKING CRITICALLY

Consider each situation in light of what you have read in "Markets, Prices, and Price Controls." By yourself or with a partner, apply what you know about competitive markets to address each situation.

Situation 1 You are the mayor of San Francisco—a beautiful, highly desirable city with scores of top-quality employers who pay their high-level employees very well. These highly paid workers have been buying up or renting all the desirable housing at high prices. People with lower-income jobs (e.g., salespeople in stores, restaurant workers, taxi drivers, maintenance workers, low-level medical workers) are being priced out of the city. Their pay is not high enough for them to compete for good housing. In turn, they now have to live in outlying communities far from their jobs and have to spend huge amounts of time commuting to work. It is also bad for the city in many ways. For example, it is in danger of becoming less interesting and vibrant as its cultural diversity is being weakened and low-paid creative people (artists, writers, thinkers, etc.) have to flee to more affordable locations. In what ways should you, the mayor, respond to this situation?

Situation 2 You are the head of an airline company. Of course your company is the producer of a service sold to general consumers—a service considered a necessity by some and therefore possibly subject to price controls. Make a list of some of the factors you have to consider in setting ticket prices—not only your costs but also factors that affect consumer demand for your services. Is there anything your company can do to reduce volatility in pricing?

Go to **MyEnglishLab** to complete a critical thinking exercise.

290   ECONOMICS PART 3

TEACHER SUPPORT

Each of the three strands is supported with comprehensive **downloadable teaching notes** in MyEnglishLab that detail key points for all of the specialized, academic content in addition to tips and suggestions for how to teach skills and strategies.

Assessments on selected topics provide extra opportunities for students to demonstrate learning. Flexible design allows assessments to be used as unit reviews, mid-terms, or finals. Test bank presents multiple test versions for easy test proctoring.

An easy to use online learning management system offering a **Flexible Gradebook** and tools for monitoring student progress, such as audioscripts, videoscripts, answer keys, and word lists to help in lesson planning and follow up.

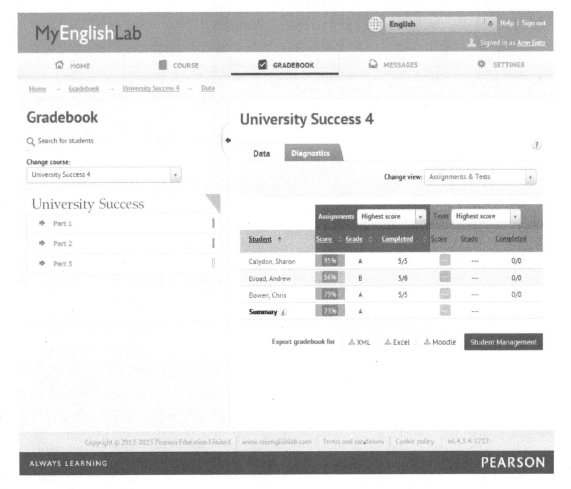

Scope and Sequence

PART 1

Fundamental Reading Skills is designed to build fundamental skills step by step through exploration of rigorous academic content.

	FUNDAMENTAL READING SKILLS	SUPPORTING SKILLS	READING-WRITING CONNECTION	LANGUAGE SKILLS	APPLY YOUR SKILLS
SOCIOLOGY **Active Reading**	Read actively	Skim for gist Scan for details	Annotate and take notes	Use dictionaries to strengthen vocabulary	Read "Sports as the Moral Equivalent of War" Explain and defend your position on political expression in sports Draw conclusions about a map of Olympic Game boycotts
ECONOMICS **Main Ideas and Supporting Details**	Recognize main ideas and supporting details	Identify sentence functions Identify topics and main ideas Identify supporting details	Summarize	Analyze meaning using word parts	Read "World Trade Problems and Their Resolutions" Evaluate the fairness of trade agreements Analyze and interpret a graph showing WTO disputes
BIOLOGY **Cohesion**	Understand cohesion	Recognize patterns of cohesion: cause / effect, compare / contrast, problem / solution Understand cohesion in descriptions	Use outlines and graphic organizers	Recognize collocations	Read "DNA Vaccines" Infer findings about the approval process for a vaccination Evaluate a graph showing a trend in the DNA vaccine market
HUMANITIES **Fluency and Accuracy**	Develop reading fluency	Increase fluency Tolerate ambiguity	Recognize and use rhetorical techniques	Understand nominalization	Read "Confucius's Influence" Imagine and discuss factors that influence the accuracy of undocumented teachings Theorize about changes in Chinese education, based on a chart
ENVIRONMENTAL ENGINEERING **Visuals**	Interpret visuals	Understand text references to visuals Interpret the information in visuals	Refer to visual data within and beyond a reading	Recognize and learn multiword vocabulary items	Read "Nanofibers Revolutionize Air Filtration" Choose and defend a position in the air pollution policy debate Interpret and formulate statements about an emissions graph

PART 2
Critical Thinking Skills moves from skill building to application of the skills that require critical thinking.

	CRITICAL THINKING SKILLS	SUPPORTING SKILLS	READING-WRITING CONNECTION	LANGUAGE SKILLS	APPLY YOUR SKILLS
SOCIOLOGY **Fact and Opinion**	Distinguish fact from opinion	Recognize and interpret statements of opinion Recognize and interpret statements of fact	Understand and produce critiques	Understand signpost expressions that limit or define	Read "Henry David Thoreau's Civil Disobedience" Explain how punishment for tax evasion has changed Assess events on a timeline to predict future events
ECONOMICS **Implication and Inference**	Understand implication and inference	Make strong inferences and avoid weak ones Distinguish between deliberate implications and direct statements	Paraphrase	Identify and use equivalent and near-equivalent expressions	Read "Public Goods vs. Private Gain" Analyze the duality of some public and private goods Elaborate on a chart featuring public and private goods
BIOLOGY **Evidence and Argumentation**	Evaluate evidence and argumentation	Identify and evaluate evidence Recognize and deal with faulty rhetoric	Understand extended metaphor	Identify and use expressions of function and purpose	Read "Vaccinating Against Cancer" Explore and support your position on animal testing Make predictions about trends in cervical cancer, based on statistics
HUMANITIES **Synthesis of Information**	Synthesize information from several sources	Understand multiple perspectives Evaluate the credibility and motives of sources	Understand and use direct and indirect quotations	Appreciate hedging	Read "The Hero's Journey" Identify the 7 stages of a hero's journey Categorize characters within a chart of archetypes
ENVIRONMENTAL ENGINEERING **Definitions and Classifications**	Understand definitions and classifications	Recognize and understand definitions within a text Work with classifications	Understand and produce references to other sources	Understand and use clarifiers	Read "The Impact of Energy-Saving Devices on Indoor Air Quality" Explain and support your position on clean air technology Theorize about energy consumption trends, based on a graph

PART 3

Extended Reading presents authentic content written by university professors. Academically rigorous application and assessment activities allow for a synthesis of the skills developed in Part 1 and Part 2.

	READINGS	RESEARCH
SOCIOLOGY The Art of Strategy	Thinking About Strategy The 1963 Birmingham Campaign: The Turning Point in the American Civil Rights Movement	Choose and research a figure who is notable for his or her "investment" in a change movement.
ECONOMICS Supply and Demand in the Marketplace	Markets, Prices, and Price Controls Minimum Wages	Choose and research a product or service that has been subject to government price controls or government attempts to control supply.
BIOLOGY A Study of Deadly Diseases	Cows. Cannibals, and Crystals – Explaining the Mechanism of Prion Diseases Vaccines That Prevent Virally-Induced Cancer	Choose and research a prion disease.
HUMANITIES Cultivation of the Educated Person	The Cultivation of Higher Learning The Golden Bough	Choose and research a notable educational philosopher or theorist.
ENVIRONMENTAL ENGINEERING In Pursuit of Clean Air	Sources of Indoor Pollutants Increasing Energy Efficiency vs. Maintaining Indoor Air Quality	Choose and research a major indoor pollutant or category of pollutant.

A Note from Lawrence Zwier

Series Editor for *University Success Reading*

My high-level EAP reading students at Michigan State University are typical transition-level learners of English. They are torn between a desire to get on with their academic lives beyond ESL and a fear that they cannot compete in college classes. They don't need much basic instruction in reading skills, vocabulary, or structure, but they are not really ready to fly solo. They need practice with serious, substantive material. They need to round out their vocabularies with multiword items and to handle college-level twists of vocabulary. Fluency is vital, for they won't be able to handle course reading loads unless they build it. Their command of discourse markers and "signposts" has to solidify, to help them move easily from one thought group to another.

However, there's no point in simply throwing large amounts of difficult material at them. Practice is a staged, reiterative process. It has to include short pieces as well as long, because readers need the reward of completion every now and then. And when they do work with longer, more difficult material, they need outside hands—those of the textbook writer as well as those of the teacher—to help point the way.

The transition level of *University Success Reading* is perfect for them. It aims to offer serious, informative, expertly calibrated texts with which to practice. There is instruction in reading skills, but it serves more to remind than to reveal. This volume has a personality—direct, mature, eager to explore difficult topic realms, high-level, and proud of it.

PART 1 – FUNDAMENTAL READING SKILLS

In the first five units of *University Success Reading* each of the five main subject areas (Sociology, Economics, Biology, Humanities, Environmental Engineering) is introduced. The most fundamental aspects of structure and approach in academic texts—such as main ideas, cohesive patterns, fluency-building strategies, and the role of visuals—are featured and practiced in ways appropriate for transition-level readers. The Stanford University professors who are the thought leaders for all three strands introduce themselves and their fields. This part of the text amps up the discourse in accessible yet challenging ways, providing thematically related yet diverse reading passages that demonstrate fundamental text features and encourage transition-level readers to tackle the passage with some scaffolding.

PART 2 – CRITICAL THINKING SKILLS

In these units each main subject area is explored in greater depth, with reading passages that demand more sophisticated processing and analysis. Critical thinking is more directly elicited so that transition-level students engage in such processes as evaluating the quality of evidence, refining the inferences they draw, and watching out for shaky rhetorical ploys. As in the Part 1 units, the Stanford thought leaders have informed the content so that reading passages are accessible and appealing yet rock-solid in their factuality and field-specific relevance.

PART 3 – EXTENDED READING

University Success Reading opens up and brings the Stanford thought leaders front and center. Each of the readings in this part is long, serious, and substantive—penned by the professor and testing the frontiers of thought in his or her academic specialization. The Part 3 questions posed to our transition-level students are not simple, but they are high-interest and meant to promote lively discussion among readers. In Part 3, *University Success* does something no other high-level ELT reading text does. It dives deep into the work of high-prestige professors and researchers; it offers unique academic rigor as students step over the threshold into their life beyond ESL.

Acknowledgments

We would like to thank Amy McCormick and Gosia Jaros-White at Pearson for tirelessly nurturing this project, championing its mission, and taking the long view of what's good for students and teachers. Sara Davila, who can make anything, deserves thanks for fashioning fresh ideas for format, topics, and approaches. The always-realistic Debbie Sistino helped keep the trains running on time, which was not easy to do. Our development editor Leigh Stolle was always encouraging. We were continuously impressed by her attention to detail in combination with her ability to see the big picture.

We also wish to extend our thanks to Victoria Solomon—an amazing writer who wrangled technical material into tight spaces. Professional, fast, and smart, Victoria was a pleasure to work with. Laura Eickhoff also deserves thanks for her involvement and contributions, which added value to this book. Thanks as well to the thought leaders at Stanford University for their expert direction and understanding of what nonspecialists can learn. — *Larry Zwier and Maggie Vosters*

Special thanks to my wife, Jean, who once again rearranged the life of our family to accommodate an 800-pound book. As usual, deep gratitude for your patience and encouragement. — *Larry Zwier*

I would like to especially thank Eduardo Mello for his encouragement throughout the process of writing this book. It would not be what it is without your unfailing support. — *Maggie Vosters*

Reviewers

We would like to thank the following reviewers for their many helpful comments and suggestions:

Jamila Barton, North Seattle Community College, Seattle, WA; **Joan Chamberlin**, Iowa State University, Ames IA; **Lyam Christopher**, Palm Beach State College, Boynton Beach, FL; **Robin Corcos**, University of California, Santa Barbara, Goleta, CA; **Tanya Davis**, University of California, San Diego, CA; **Brendan DeCoster**, University of Oregon, Eugene, OR; **Thomas Dougherty**, University of St. Mary of the Lake, Mundelein, IL; **Bina Dugan**, Bergen County Community College, Hackensack, NJ; **Priscilla Faucette**, University of Hawaii at Manoa, Honolulu, HI; **Lisa Fischer**, St. Louis University, St. Louis, MO; **Kathleen Flynn**, Glendale Community College, Glendale, CA; **Mary Gawienowski**, William Rainey Harper College, Palatine, IL; **Sally Gearhart**, Santa Rosa Junior College, Santa Rosa, CA; **Carl Guerriere**, Capital Community College, Hartford, CT; **Vera Guillen**, Eastfield College, Mesquite, TX; **Angela Hakim**, St. Louis University, St. Louis, MO; **Pamela Hartmann**, Evans Community Adult School, Los Angeles Unified School District, Los Angeles, CA; **Shelly Hedstrom**, Palm Beach State University, Lake Worth, FL; **Sherie Henderson**, University of Oregon, Eugene, OR; **Lisse Hildebrandt**, English Language Program, Virginia Commonwealth University, Richmond, VA; **Barbara Inerfeld**, Rutgers University, Piscataway, NJ; **Zaimah Khan**, Northern Virginia Community College, Loudoun Campus, Sterling, VA; **Tricia Kinman**, St. Louis University, St. Louis, MO; **Kathleen Klaiber**, Genesee Community College, Batavia, NY; **Kevin Lamkins**, Capital Community College, Hartford, CT; **Mayetta Lee**, Palm Beach State College, Lake Worth, FL; **Kirsten Lillegard**, English Language Institute, Divine Word College, Epworth, IA; **Craig Machado**, Norwalk Community College, Norwalk, CT; **Cheryl Madrid**, Spring International Language Center, Denver, CO; **Ann Meechai**, St. Louis University, St. Louis, MO; **Melissa Mendelson**, Department of Linguistics, University of Utah, Salt Lake City, UT; **Tamara Milbourn**, University of Colorado, Boulder, CO; **Debbie Ockey**, Fresno City College, Fresno, CA; **Diana Pascoe-Chavez**, St. Louis University, St. Louis, MO; **Kathleen Reynolds**, William Rainey Harper College, Palatine, IL; **Linda Roth**, Vanderbilt University ELC, Greensboro, NC; **Minati Roychoudhuri**, Capital Community College, Hartford, CT; **Bruce Rubin**, California State University, Fullerton, CA; **Margo Sampson**, Syracuse University, Syracuse, NY; **Sarah Saxer**, Howard Community College, Ellicott City, MD; **Anne-Marie Schlender**, Austin Community College, Austin, TX; **Susan Shields**, Santa Barbara Community College, Santa Barbara, CA; **Barbara Smith-Palinkas**, Hillsborough Community College, Dale Mabry Campus, Tampa, FL; **Sara Stapleton**, North Seattle Community College, Seattle, WA; **Lisa Stelle**, Northern Virginia Community College Loudoun, Sterling, VA; **Jamie Tanzman**, Northern Kentucky University, Highland Heights, KY; **Jeffrey Welliver**, Soka University of America, Aliso Viejo, CA; **Mark Wolfersberger**, Brigham Young University Hawaii, Laie, HI; **May Youn**, California State University, Fullerton, CA.

Fundamental Reading Skills

Part 1 is designed to build fundamental skills step by step through the exploration of rigorous, academic content. Practice activities tied to specific learning outcomes in each unit focus on understanding the function and application of the skills.

Struggle influences social change.

Active Reading

UNIT PROFILE

You will consider the subject of sociology—specifically, the ideas of identity, goals, and strategy. As you read about topics such as games, sports, and war, you will see that identity plays a significant role in which "battles" individuals engage in.

Preview the reading "Sports as the Moral Equivalent of War" on page 21. Skim the whole reading. What is the gist? Scan Paragraph 4. Which two countries were in a dispute about an island—a dispute that led to a demonstration at a soccer game?

OUTCOMES

• Read actively
• Skim for the gist
• Scan for details
• Annotate and take notes
• Use dictionaries to strengthen vocabulary

GETTING STARTED

▶ Go to **MyEnglishLab** to listen to Professor Greenberg and to complete a self-assessment.

Discuss these questions with a partner or group.

1. Think of a time when you were part of a group trying to accomplish a task or produce a result—for example, a group doing a class project, a club trying to reach a goal, or even an organization trying to help your community. What strategies did your group use to work together effectively? How were those strategies different from what you might have done individually?

2. Think about sports in your home country or some other country you know well. Is there a sport that is considered the "national sport"? Why are so many people interested in that sport? Do people think the sport somehow relates to the strengths and virtues of that country?

3. What are examples of different "teams" that people play on and "battles" that they engage in?

For more about **SOCIOLOGY**, see ② ③. See also Ⓦ and Ⓞ**C** **SOCIOLOGY** ① ② ③.

FUNDAMENTAL SKILL
READING ACTIVELY

WHY IT'S USEFUL By reading actively—using high-level mental activities such as questioning, evaluating an author's claims, and keeping track of ideas to explore further—you create a deeper understanding of a passage.

Reading is an active, not passive, process. A reader does more than simply receive information that a writer has laid out. Good readers begin forming ideas about the topic as soon as they see the simplest features of a reading, such as the title and any images. Before they read, active readers skim the reading to get a general idea of its main ideas. While they read, they continually ask themselves questions about what they read, and many of them take notes either in the margins, in a notebook, or on a computer. After they read, readers review their notes and perhaps do classroom exercises that require scanning back for facts or even rereading certain sections.

This unit breaks **active reading** down into two supporting skills:

- skimming for gist
- scanning for details

NOTICING ACTIVITY

As you read the following passage, be aware of questions that form in your mind about the topic. Write five questions that you asked yourself about the topic. Use these lists of words to help you express your thoughts.

Question Words / Phrases			Topic Words		
How	Who	How many / How much	advantage	Japanese	strategy
When	Why	What does X mean	competition	lateral thinking	tactical
Where		What is an example of	domination	market	

THE GAME OF *GO*

1   The ancient Chinese game *Go* is comparable to the classic Western game of chess in terms of the games' long histories, labyrinthine techniques, ardent fan bases, and seemingly infinite possibilities for winning. *Go*, however, teaches a manner of strategic thinking different from chess that might offer a particular advantage in the sphere of business. Where chess is a game of strategy with tactical threats, attacks, and eventual domination over the other player's pieces, *Go* seeks to control territory on a board through a combination of patience, balance, and lateral thinking that leads to an eventual comparative advantage over the opposing player.

2   In fact, many Japanese business executives compare the vast number of possibilities on the board of *Go* to the international market, and find *Go* board-placement strategy akin to resource allocation. In addition, players in *Go* may concede tactical losses in the interest of presenting a strategic advantage, and parallels may be drawn between this aspect of the game and competitive business behavior. For example, Nissan settled for a 30 percent share of the Japanese economy car market, yielding a 40 percent share to competitor Toyota in order to strengthen its hold on particular target markets, including the sale of luxury vehicles, sports cars, and minivans.

How is it possible to lose in a tactical area but still gain a strategic advantage?

TIP

As you read, open a notebook or note-taking software and jot down ideas, questions, etc., like the question in the margin, above.

Go to **MyEnglishLab** to complete a vocabulary exercise and skill practice, and to join in collaborative activities.

SUPPORTING SKILL 1
SKIMMING FOR GIST

WHY IT'S USEFUL A good first step in active reading is to **skim for the gist**—that is, look briefly at the whole passage to formulate a guess about its overall meaning. With the gist in mind, you can put other ideas into perspective and mentally organize them into a whole.

Skimming is the act of running your eyes quickly over a reading to get a basic mental picture of the main ideas. Skimming (unlike **scanning**; see Supporting Skill 2, p. 7) does not target individual pieces of information. Instead, it is meant to pick up general meaning, creating a basic overview.

Skimming is a prereading activity; you are not yet trying to read the piece. As you skim, keep going at a steady pace, though you might slow down for certain features (see list below). A steady, fast skimming process will ensure that you avoid getting caught on small ideas. Remember: Your goal is to pick up the gist.

The skimming process should involve the whole reading. Make sure you skim the entire text, with special attention to these elements:

- the title and any subheadings
- the first one or two sentences of each paragraph
- pictures and their captions (the words under or next to them)
- graphics (tables, graphs, etc.)
- words in bold type
- words that begin with capital letters (e.g., names of people and places, titles of books)

Since skimming goes very fast, you can do more than one pass through a short reading without wasting too much time. If you like, you can organize your efforts by skimming in stages. For example, focus on one set of features (headings, pictures, etc.) during one pass. Then focus on others (first sentences of paragraphs, capitalized words, etc.) in another.

Some readers skim quickly and take only mental notes. Others make written notes. Taking notes can help you clarify your expectations before you read. You may also want to compare your prereading notes with notes you took while reading. This can show you how your ideas have evolved.

EXERCISE 1

A. Do not read the following passage yet. To organize your efforts, skim it in two stages, as described here:

Stage 1

- Run your eyes quickly over
  - the title
  - subheadings
  - the heading of the sidebar
  - the photograph and its caption
- Take notes about the thoughts that come to you. What main ideas do you expect in the reading? Discuss your ideas with a partner.

Stage 2

- Run your eyes quickly over
  - the first two sentences of every paragraph
  - the first sentences of the sidebar
  - any words with capital letters
  - any numbers
- Take notes about *additional* ideas that have come to you. Discuss these with a partner.

Memories That Define the Self

1   A sense of self-identity allows an individual to distinguish himself or herself from others, both individually and en masse. The realization of self-identity begins in childhood and is first demonstrated when toddlers exuberantly explore new abilities. It progresses through adolescence when young adults experience life-shaping events that lead to the refinement of the self. Through all of this personality formation, one takes on markers of self-identity, including biological features such as being female or male, old or young, and social status features such as being married or single, employed or unemployed, and so forth. Significant events in a person's life—times of great joy, sorrow, accomplishment, disappointment—also shape identity by yielding self-defining memories, which are vivid, intense recollections that an individual associates with his or her personality.

2   These self-defining memories are the autobiographical coding of a person, and researchers have found that when measured objectively, these memories correspond to aspects of an individual's personality. Through clinical studies conducted at the end of the 20th century, psychologist Jefferson Singer, Professor of Psychology at Connecticut College, and his colleagues created a method for measuring self-defining memories and a system of categorization. Singer's schema involves listing approximately ten self-defining memories and then breaking each one down according to the following categories: specificity, meaning, and emotions.

Specificity

3   Specificity of memory in this context refers to the time period of the memory. There are three levels of specificity. A *highly specific* memory is a memory clearly defined in time, such as a particular day, week, or even single event, such as a car crash or a week at a summer camp. A *nonspecific* memory is an episodic recollection of events that fit into a single, lengthy time period, such as a semester abroad, a war, or a period of illness. Finally, a *generic* memory is a memory that occurs repeatedly in time, when the settings, characters, and emotions are the constant factors. Examples of generic memories include an annual family vacation and helping with a yearly crop harvest.

Meaning

4   In terms of meaning, there are two kinds of self-defining memories: integrative and nonintegrative. An *integrative* memory is a memory from which a person draws significant meaning. Singer's study cites an example of a person who remembers a friend who tried to commit suicide and what it was

Continued

Memories of the Old, Memories of the Young

Psychological studies show that adults over the age of 50 recall self-defining memories quite differently from young adults.

1. Older adults tend to
   - view remembered events more positively.
   - remember things in a more abridged, nonspecific fashion.
   - have memories that are integrative—meaning that they involve considerations of personal growth.

2. In contrast, college students tend to
   - view remembered events more negatively.
   - remember things in greater detail.
   - have memories that are nonintegrative.

Brain image studies show significant neural changes, depending on one's age, in the hippocampal region of the brain, which is associated with the recall capacity of specific memory. Interestingly, no difference in brain image scans shows up between the old and the young when recalling semantic memories, such as the names of colors and other basic facts, as opposed to memories drawn from personal experience.

like to visit that friend in the hospital every day. The recognition of personal growth as a result of the episode makes the memory integrative. The second type of memory is a *nonintegrative* memory, which is a memory that may be significant but has not been interpreted or defined as promoting self-growth.

Emotions

5   The emotions of self-defining memories can be positive or negative. A positive memory is associated with positive emotions like pride, happiness, and love. A negative memory is associated with adverse emotions like disgust, shame, fear, and sadness.

6   Among self-defining memories, most people have in common certain experiences, including relationships, life-threatening events, and achievements. Notably, however, when Singer and other psychologists compared memories of older adults to those of college students (see sidebar), they found significant differences in meaning and emotion. These findings suggest that self-identity is somewhat fluid, depending on your age and life conditions.

Dr. Jefferson Singer

B. Now read the entire passage. Discuss the questions with a partner.

Look back at the notes you took in Part A, just after skimming. How accurate were your impressions? Which main ideas did you anticipate from skimming?

....

C. Answer the questions. Use information and examples from the passage to support your answers.

1. In skimming, you saw a picture of Jefferson Singer, so you knew he would be important in the reading. Now that you've completed the reading, describe Dr. Singer's importance in the area of self-defining memories.

....

2. In skimming, you saw a sidebar about age and memories. How does Singer's schema—involving specificity, meaning, and emotions—apply differently to older and younger adults?

....

D. Compare your answers to the notes you took after skimming.

Go to **MyEnglishLab** to complete a vocabulary exercise and skill practice, and to join in collaborative activities.

SUPPORTING SKILL 2
SCANNING FOR DETAILS

WHY IT'S USEFUL By scanning for details, you can quickly find necessary information without wasting time on sentence-by-sentence reading (or on rereading). This is valuable, for example, when taking tests or trying to find the best hits found by a search engine.

Sometimes your purpose in reading is to find very specific pieces of information. You might be trying to answer questions on a test, find a specific fact to use in writing, or check your understanding of specific points in a reading. You don't need to read, or reread, an entire passage. You only need to **scan for details**—very specific pieces of information. Your eyes should zero in on the essential information and filter out all the rest.

BASIC SCANNING TECHNIQUES
- **For the name of a place, person, or organization, scan for capital letters.** Many organizations are referred to first by their whole names (the United Nations, the American Cancer Society) and later by an abbreviation or acronym (the UN, the ACS). Scanning for the abbreviation or acronym is a good strategy, but also scan backwards after the first abbreviation for the full name of the organization.
- **For the name of a book, movie, game, song, and so on, scan for both capital letters and a typographical clue, such as quotation marks or italics.**
- **For a year, date, amount, proportion, and so on, scan for numerals.** When you scan for numbers, keep the following in mind:
  - Numerals are the figures 1, 2, 3, and so on. However, numbers less than 11 are usually spelled out as words, although different publications use different style rules.
  - Very large numbers (hundreds of thousands and higher) may be expressed in a combination of words and numerals, e.g., *345 thousand* or *345,000*, *12 million* or *12,000,000*. Scan for both kinds of expressions.
- **For information that is not signaled by unusual type or by numerals, select keywords or phrases to scan for.** Imagine you are scanning to try to answer the question "Which of the following subject areas fall under 'liberal arts'?" The most important keywords in this question are *subject areas* and *liberal arts*, so you should scan for these keywords to find the answer.
- **Use your skills at annotation or taking notes (see Reading-Writing Connection, p. 11) to keep track of the information you find as you scan.**

> **TIP**
> **Work forwards and backwards.** Many readers can scan more efficiently if they go in two directions. They scan through a passage once in the normal way, from the beginning of the reading to the end. If they still haven't found their target, they scan again, but they start at the end and work toward the beginning. A piece of information that was hard to see when scanning forwards might become obvious when seen from the opposite direction.

In this example, notice how with a quick scan, key information such as dates, names, and titles stand out: *at the end of the 20th century*, *Jefferson Singer*, and *Professor of Psychology*.

Excerpt from MEMORIES THAT DEFINE THE SELF

These self-defining memories are the autobiographical coding of a person, and researchers have found that when measured objectively, these memories correspond to aspects of an individual's personality. Through clinical studies conducted at the end of the 20th century, psychologist Jefferson Singer, Professor of Psychology at Connecticut Colleague, and his colleagues created a method for measuring self-defining memories and a system of categorization. Singer's schema involves listing approximately ten self-defining memories and then breaking each one down according to the following categories …

EXERCISE 2

A. Read each question. Choose the kind of information you need to scan for to answer the question. Then answer the questions by scanning the passage "Nationalism and Sports" on the next page for the information you need.

1. In 1988, what did South Korea host? ....
   a. Name of an event
   b. Name of a person
   c. Name of a place
   d. Name of an organization

2. Which has sought to revive its national character? ....
   a. Name of an organization
   b. Name of a place
   c. A year
   d. An amount

3. During what period did the Canadian government increase funding for sports threefold?

   ....

   a. Years
   b. People
   c. Proportions
   d. Amounts

> **TIP**
> One of the keys to scanning is the ability to do it quickly. Periodically time yourself to see that you're refining your scanning skills. For example, before you start Part B, set a timer or use the stopwatch function on your cell phone to mark your starting time. Then turn off the timer / stopwatch when you finish. Note how long it took you to complete the scanning. Divide the number of seconds by the number of questions to get a per-question time.

Nationalism and Sports

1   Athletic games can buoy patriotism and nationalism, particularly when territorial disputes exist within a nation or with an opposing nation. Sports also have the dual effect of aiding a nation in unification and projecting that unity and identity outward to gain recognition in the world. This phenomenon is common among many nations, including South Korea, which is still technically at war with North Korea; Canada, which has faced domestic tensions; and Britain, which has sought to redefine its national character.

TIP

Read questions first. One of the best strategies for finding the information you need in a passage is reading the questions before you read the text. Once you determine the information you must search for, locating and identifying the information you need—and disregarding that which you don't—is much easier.

2   Nations define themselves by a number of methods, including the establishment of state symbols, such as a flag, a currency, an anthem, and an armed force. In addition, leaders of nations engage in relational activities by taking up membership in international organizations and international sporting events, all of which invigorate nationalistic pride. Since World War II, both industrialized nations and developing nations have increased funding for sports at a rate faster than other services, and some researchers believe that this is for the express purpose of fostering nationalism and asserting nations' identities in an increasingly globalized world.

3   Territory-defining behavior plays a symbolic role in such sporting contests. For example, South Korea's 1988 hosting of the Olympic Games achieved, among many objectives, the reinforcement of the division of territory between South Korea and North Korea. Similarly, in 1990, shortly after the fall of the Berlin Wall, a national marathon crisscrossed the line of demarcation between the two Germanys, purposely using the sporting event to highlight the new territory of the country.

4   Athletics serve not only to define territory among nations but also to unite disparate peoples within a nation. The Canadian government increased funding for sports threefold between 1978 and 1987 as a way to promote unification between many of the nation's disparate peoples in the diverse country. For example, ice hockey served as a shared symbol of identity among the divided English Canadians and French Canadians in the mid-20th century. That Canada's national identity is tied up in ice hockey was never more evident than in the uproar over star hockey player Wayne Gretzky's move to Los Angeles in the late 1980s, which provoked accusations of Gretzky defecting from his country.

5   Some social scientists argue that sports act as a metaphor for culture, revealing the character of a nation, its value system, and elements of its social structure. Undoubtedly, sports foster a sense of loyalty and purpose among citizens. Britain, in contrast to South Korea, Germany, and Canada, has had little need to seek international definition for itself. As a nation, Britain comprehensively achieved recognition during its centuries as a political superpower. However, the policies of the government of the United Kingdom from 1990 to 1997 reveal efforts to try to redefine the country's national identity through the promotion of sports. One aim was to focus on traditional English sports, such as soccer, cricket, and swimming, in order to reinforce a sense of national identity and pride, particularly during a time of decline in Britain's economic and diplomatic status. National policymakers redesigned school physical education curricula to emphasize the playing of traditional team sports, rather than the study of physical education, as another way of infusing the programs with moral values and strengthening ties to the nation's past. The establishment of the Department of National Heritage in 1992—renamed the Department for Culture, Media, and Sport in 1997—and the restructuring of the Sports Councils that took place at the time also sought to bring more emphasis to the nation's traditional sports.

C. Scan "Nationalism and Sports" for the information in the categories. Check (√) the categories you find and mark the information as indicated. Then, with another student, discuss the information you found from each category that you scanned for.

Categories of Information:

☐ name of a person, place, event, or organization (Circle each.)

☐ name of a book, movie, game, song (Underline each.)

☐ year, date, amount, proportion (Draw a box around each.)

D. Answer the questions. Then discuss your answers with another student. Use information and examples from the passage to explain and support your answers.

1. Scan for a symbol that some countries use to display their identity.
   a. Relational activities
   b. National marathons
   c. A currency
   d. Value system

2. Why might countries have increased their funding in sports since World War II?
   a. To put themselves on the political stage
   b. To promote national pride and character
   c. To help develop their athletes' skills
   d. To compete with other countries

3. What indication of identity united English Canadians and French Canadians?
   a. Sports funding
   b. Ice hockey
   c. Wayne Gretzky
   d. Domestic tensions

4. What was the end result of South Korea's hosting of the Olympic Games in 1988?

   ....

5. Which country is NOT characterized as having a great need to define itself internationally?
   a. Canada
   b. Germany
   c. South Korea
   d. Britain

6. Scan for the original name of an organization founded by the British government.
   a. Department of National Heritage
   b. The Olympic Games
   c. Department for Culture, Media, and Sport
   d. Prime Minister

Go to **MyEnglishLab** to complete a vocabulary exercise and skill practice, and to join in collaborative activities.

READING-WRITING CONNECTION
ANNOTATING AND TAKING NOTES

WHY IT'S USEFUL Note-taking helps you keep actively engaged with a text and strengthens your ability to write about what you read. The notes you take are often a first attempt at summarizing and paraphrasing, capturing the ideas of a text in words that are partially your own.

There are many ways to produce notes as you read. You can mark or highlight important parts of a reading. You can keep track of key vocabulary. You can write down questions that enter your mind as you read.

If you write or highlight directly on the page you are reading, you are **annotating.** If you are reading a print version, your annotations will probably go in the margins or maybe between lines. If you are reading an e-book, check whether your reader software has an annotation feature and learn how to use it. The advantage of annotating is that you don't have to copy pieces of text into your notes. The text is right there. The biggest disadvantage is that the annotations mar the book. If you've borrowed your book from a library or a friend, annotations may not be an option.

Taking separate notes is the act of writing things like main ideas, questions, and definitions in a notebook or some other place outside the text. Sometimes you cannot annotate, so separate notes will be your only choice. At other times, you may choose to keep separate notes as well as to annotate in the text.

> **CULTURE NOTE**
> *Annotations: Readers' Reflections*
> Some of the most expensive used books in the world owe their value to annotations written by a previous owner. Thomas Jefferson, who was an architect as well as one of the founders of the United States, sometimes wrote numbers and measurements in the margins of his technical books. The brilliant scientist and mathematician Sir Isaac Newton sometimes made annotations about whether he thought a device described in a text would really work. Countless readers who have picked up books of philosophy and science fiction have annotated these works of thought with additional ideas and questions of their own. The annotations are prized because they show what the reader was thinking as he or she actively engaged with the reading passage.

WHAT SHOULD YOU TAKE NOTES ABOUT?

Your annotations or separate notes depend on your relationship to the text you read. What will you have to remember from the text? What parts of the text do you have questions about? Are there any words you should look up? Will you have to integrate ideas from this text with ideas from somewhere else? Typical features of annotations and note-taking include

- highlighting, underlining, and circling vocabulary that needs to be looked up.
- marking points in the text that a reader disagrees with. A question mark or the word "no" might be used.
- using symbols and abbreviations to save space.
- using lines, arrows, and numbers to show relationships. For example, in the reading "Voting in the Jim Crow South" on the following page, all the points about Jim Crow laws in the United States might be marked with a circled *JC*, an asterisk (*), or another feature that shows commonality.
- marking similarities to material in other sources with comments like *See also Jefferson, p. 162.*
- writing separate notes, which often involves copying bits of text. However, this can be time-consuming. It's more efficient to just refer to a page in the book instead.

> **TIP**
> **Note-Taking Style** *Just as everyone's study methods are different, so the style and content of everyone's notes will be very personal. Your teacher may recommend certain note-taking techniques, and some of these recommendations may be helpful for you. However, the most important thing is to find note-taking materials (a notebook, cards, a tablet app, a computer program, etc.) and a note-taking system that works for you personally. Find what works and use it often.*

In the following example, notice the annotations.

VOTING IN THE JIM CROW SOUTH

commonly existing

Does this mean it WAS illegal some places?

Which pp? Look up.

???

Contrary to <u>prevailing</u> modern belief, voting by blacks was not illegal in <u>most of the South</u> during the Jim Crow era (1877–1954). Opponents of black voting did not need to outlaw it. They needed only to erect so many obstacles that voting was practically impossible, despite being legal. Some of the mechanisms for this suppression are well known. We have already seen how literacy tests were used to exclude blacks from the polls and how the tests were manipulated so that whites could pass whether they were literate or not. There were at least five other common practices that <u>stunted</u> political participation by blacks in many areas of the rural South (and often in cities as well).

The threat of violence—accompanied by the possibility of death—was a major deterrent. If blacks dared to vote, segregationists might make an example of them by beating, torturing, raping, or even lynching them as a warning to others who might get similar ideas. In the 21st century, readers casually concoct images of white-robed members of the Ku Klux Klan as the agents of such horrors, but in truth, the KKK's actions were only the most extreme, highly institutionalized form of violent suppression. In many localities, a black voter's own neighbors, or someone he or she had frequent commerce with, would be the ones committing the violence.

Also mentioned in NYT article. Check!!

EXERCISE 3

A. Read the title and paragraph. Notice the annotations.

Excerpt from ATHLETICS IN
(CLASSICAL) TIMES

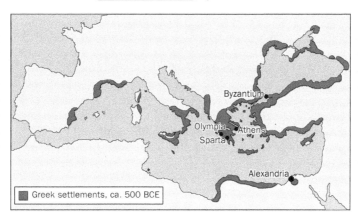

Byzantium
Olympia Athens
Sparta
Alexandria

■ Greek settlements, ca. 500 BCE

The Roman Empire
in 117 AD, at its greatest extent

Athletics held a place of indisputable importance in (ancient)
(Greece and the Roman world,) though the way citizens engaged in
the games and how they viewed their purpose varied considerably.
The Greeks imbued their culture with a **competitive spirit** that
extended not just to sports but to other *agons,* or contests, in art,
music, law, and nearly all areas of life. They are, famously, the
originators of the Olympics, first held in 776 BCE on the Plain of
Olympia on the Peloponnese Peninsula. Likewise, in the Roman   *main difference !!*
Empire, **war and sport** stand as defining aspects of the culture.
??   Some of the games of antiquity, including boxing, wrestling, and
look up   discus, are still popular in the modern-day Olympics.

B. **Answer the questions. Then discuss your answers with a partner.**

1. Notice the blank oval with two arrows near the start of the paragraph. Fill the oval with a word or phrase that would make a good annotation relating the word *classical* to the phrase *ancient Greece and the Roman world*.

2. Notice the annotation *main difference!!* What does this annotation refer to? What two things are different, and what is that difference?

   ....

3. Notice that the word *discus* is underlined, and notice the annotation near it. Why is *discus* underlined?

   ....

4. What does the circle on the map probably indicate? Can you think of any other annotations you'd like to make to the map?

   ....

> **CULTURE NOTE**
> **Academic Culture** *Most students know that when they use information from an outside source in their academic writing, some form of a citation must be given. Types of information that should always be cited include books, journal articles, newspapers, and magazines. However, one exception to that rule is dictionaries. Because dictionaries are considered a basic tool that most students need for their academic writing, professors do not typically like when students quote dictionary entries in their papers. A second reason why professors often discourage students from citing dictionaries is that the information found in them is generally not unique; in other words, definitions for the same words can be found in myriad other dictionaries.*

EXERCISE 4

A. **Read the passage. Annotate (or take notes in a separate place) as you go.**

ATHLETICS IN CLASSICAL TIMES

1   Athletics held a place of indisputable importance in ancient Greece and the Roman world, though the way citizens engaged in the games and how they viewed their purpose varied considerably. The Greeks imbued their culture with a competitive spirit that extended not just to sports but to other *agons,* or contests, in art, music, law, and nearly all areas of life. They are, famously, the originators of the Olympics, first held in 776 BCE on the Plain of Olympia on the Peloponnese

Peninsula. Likewise, in the Roman Empire, war and sport stand as defining aspects of the culture. Some of the games of antiquity, including boxing, wrestling, and discus, are still popular in the modern-day Olympics.

2   Greek culture, which was at its peak from the 8th to the 6th centuries BCE, and the Roman Republic / Empire, which existed from 509 BCE to 476 CE, are considered the cradles of Western civilization. Though many features are common between Greek and Roman cultures, especially in the area of sports, there are major differences between them, most notably who participated in athletics. Free Greek citizens took part in sporting events and earned honor for their participation. Roman citizens, on the other hand, were nearly exclusively spectators; lower-class residents, foreigners, and slaves engaged in the games. The gladiators of the Roman playing arenas almost

never joined the ranks of the army. While the Greeks extended their competitive spirit to nearly all areas of society and viewed athletics as character-building, the Romans wrote that the Greeks placed too heavy an emphasis on athletics and not enough on the practice of arms; they believed this led to the downfall of Greek society.

3　Though neither the Greeks nor the Romans used sports as specific wartime training, elements of the sports themselves mimicked warlike behavior in both cultures. Wars resembled prearranged athletic contests in Greece, with heavily armed, opposing armies made up of privileged citizens wealthy enough to arm themselves. Citizens earned status for participation in both wars and games, and often fought hand-to-hand until one side ceded victory. An example of a war that was very much like a Greek game is the prearranged conflict between Sparta and Argos in 546 BCE, when an equal number of evenly matched warriors—three hundred for each side—were sent to fight each other. (Both sides claimed victory.)

4　The most popular Greek athletics were often individualistic and combat-based. They included races, wrestling, fencing, jousting, archery, spear throwing, discus, and boxing. Many of these sports were also popular in Rome, especially boxing, which featured two competitors fighting until one boxer either ceded or was knocked out. Boxers in Greece wore leather on their knuckles to protect their own hands and increase the effects of their hits on the opponent, á la modern brass knuckles. The Romans similarly enjoyed boxing, and it was a favored sport of the Emperor Augustus. They held both Greek-style boxing matches and Roman-style, in which the boxers wore heavier gloves. The purpose of the heavier gloves was not to protect either the hitter or the opponent, however. Rather, iron and lead were sewn into the gloves, and unsurprisingly, bouts often concluded with the death of a player. Another sport that was even rougher and also occasionally led to death was *pankration,* a Greek game consisting of an unarmed fight between two men, with scarcely any rules.

5　Not all ancient Greek city-states participated in the bloodiest of the traditional athletic sports. Legendary Greek generals, including Alexander the Great, discouraged or even forbade soldiers from taking part in popular games. Similarly, Sparta, the most militaristic state in ancient Greece, discouraged boxing and pankration. Instead, games that promoted even more military efficacy were encouraged. Spartans regularly held team-based combative contests in which groups of young men fought each other on an island until one of the teams pushed the other into the water. Spartans also played team sports that centered on a ball. These Spartan sports are the only known occurrence of ball-oriented games in either ancient Greek or Roman cultures. In his book *Combat Sports in the Ancient World: Competition, Violence, and Culture,* Michael B. Poliakoff says, "It of course makes perfect sense that if play is to be at all useful for war, it should include corporate activity like that of a battle squadron." His argument is that Sparta's team sports had the underlying purpose of offering military training.

6　Team sports today, though they do not involve pushing players off an island, require physical strength and skill, as well as teamwork and strong group dynamics. By and large, modern sports do not resemble ancient sports, yet some parallels can be drawn between the Olympic Games of Greece and the modern Olympics. Thousands of years after the Greek originals, today's Olympics still feature many of the same events, including long jump, foot races, shot put, and boxing.

B. Review your annotations and notes. Are any of them hard to understand? If so, look again at the reading and improve them. As you review, make additional annotations or notes that come to mind.

C. Compare annotations and notes with a partner.

Go to **MyEnglishLab** to complete a vocabulary exercise and skill practice, and to join in collaborative activities.

For more about TAKING NOTES, see |OC| SOCIOLOGY ❶.

LANGUAGE SKILL
USING DICTIONARIES TO STRENGTHEN VOCABULARY

WHY IT'S USEFUL By familiarizing yourself with three features of dictionary entries, you can work to further develop and strengthen your vocabulary.

In building your English vocabulary, being able to make full use of a dictionary and its features is key. Understanding the components of a dictionary entry will help take your vocabulary to the next level. Three critical parts of dictionary entries and subentries are **multiple definitions** listed for some words, **collocations**, and **multiword units**.

- If you are relatively familiar with dictionaries, you will know from experience that one word often has **multiple definitions**. To find the one you need, first quickly scan all of the definitions, as well as the example phrases and sentences provided. If you cannot find the right definition by scanning, slow down and read each definition (plus examples) more carefully. Then return to the original context where you found the word and determine which definition best fits that context.

Example
Original context: The **geography** of the countryside near my home is mountainous and replete with valleys.

Dictionary entry:

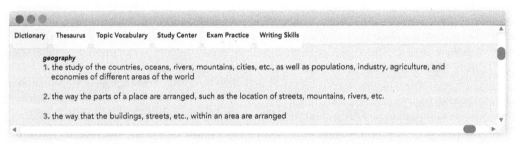

Here, the second definition best explains *geography* as it is used in the original context. In order to build your existing vocabulary, it is essential to develop the skill of determining the best definition from a multiple-definition entry.

- **Collocations**—the way in which some words are often used together, or a particular combination of words—may be indicated in a dictionary by being set in bold, italics, or within example sentences. Some dictionaries even highlight collocations in special boxes. Identifying collocations for a given word will help you with comprehension and writing. For example, the adjective *strong* collates with the word *principles* in this sentence: *The man has strong principles, always demonstrating honesty and truthfulness. Strong* cannot be replaced with a word that has a similar meaning, like *muscular.*

- A **multiword unit** is a vocabulary item made of two or more words that are very tightly bound to each other. Some familiar kinds of multiword units are phrasal verbs (*pass out, see [something] through, clean up*), compound nouns (*brass knuckles, space shuttle, USB port*), and idioms, in whole or in part (*odd man out, the last straw, a stitch in time*).

> **TIP**
>
> *Research* An online corpus—a large collection of written and / or spoken language—can be very helpful in developing your knowledge of collocations. Most corpora have a "collocations" feature, where you can enter the word you want to use and then a word you think might collocate with it. If a list of sentences containing the words you entered appears, it means that those two words collocate with each other. If only a few sentences appear, the collocation is probably weak. If no sentences appear in the results, you can assume that the two words do not collocate.
>
> If there is a word you want to use but you do not know what other words collocate with it, you can find out by simply entering the word into the search box for your online corpus and then analyzing the results to determine which co-occurrences are common.

EXERCISE 5

A. Work alone or with a group. Use the dictionary entries to decide which collocation best completes each sentence. There may be more than one correct answer.

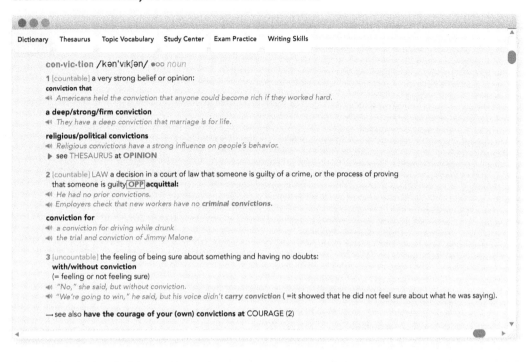

Dictionary   Thesaurus   Topic Vocabulary   Study Center   Exam Practice   Writing Skills

con·vic·tion /kən'vɪkʃən/ ●○○ *noun*

1 [countable] a very strong belief or opinion:
conviction that
◀) *Americans held the conviction that anyone could become rich if they worked hard.*

a deep/strong/firm conviction
◀) *They have a deep conviction that marriage is for life.*

religious/political convictions
◀) *Religious convictions have a strong influence on people's behavior.*
▶ see THESAURUS at **OPINION**

2 [countable] LAW a decision in a court of law that someone is guilty of a crime, or the process of proving that someone is guilty [OPP] **acquittal:**
◀) *He had no prior convictions.*
◀) *Employers check that new workers have no **criminal convictions**.*

conviction for
◀) *a conviction for driving while drunk*
◀) *the trial and conviction of Jimmy Malone*

3 [uncountable] the feeling of being sure about something and having no doubts:
with/without conviction
(= feeling or not feeling sure)
◀) *"No," she said, but without conviction.*
◀) *"We're going to win," he said, but his voice didn't **carry conviction** (=it showed that he did not feel sure about what he was saying).*

→ see also **have the courage of your (own) convictions** at COURAGE (2)

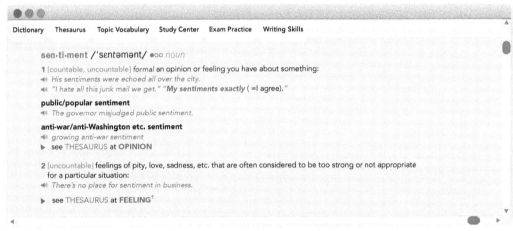

Dictionary   Thesaurus   Topic Vocabulary   Study Center   Exam Practice   Writing Skills

sen·ti·ment /'sɛntəmənt/ ●○○ *noun*

1 [countable, uncountable] formal an opinion or feeling you have about something:
◀) *His sentiments were echoed all over the city.*
◀) *"I hate all this junk mail we get." "My sentiments exactly (=I agree)."*

public/popular sentiment
◀) *The governor misjudged public sentiment.*

anti-war/anti-Washington etc. sentiment
◀) *growing anti-war sentiment*
▶ see THESAURUS at **OPINION**

2 [uncountable] feelings of pity, love, sadness, etc. that are often considered to be too strong or not appropriate for a particular situation:
◀) *There's no place for sentiment in business.*
▶ see THESAURUS at **FEELING**[1]

1. She has a .... conviction that all children should have equal opportunities in life.

2. Human Resources always checks to make sure that applicants do not have convictions .... misdemeanors or felonies before they are considered for a position.

3. "I will fight until I find my daughter," the mother said .... conviction.

4. His spiritual beliefs led him to have strong .... convictions.

5. .... sentiment favors spending more money on road maintenance.

6. A(n) .... sentiment was felt throughout college campuses when war broke out.

B. Some dictionaries have separate sections below an entry with a list of collocations for a certain word. Decide which of the collocations listed below best completes each sentence. There may be more than one correct answer.

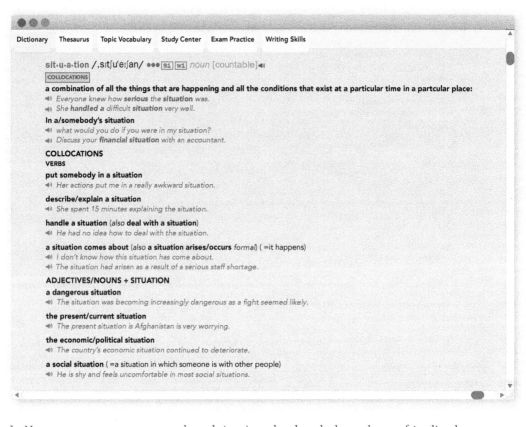

Dictionary   Thesaurus   Topic Vocabulary   Study Center   Exam Practice   Writing Skills

sit·u·a·tion /ˌsɪtʃuˈeɪʃən/ ●●● S1 W1 *noun* [countable]

COLLOCATIONS

a combination of all the things that are happening and all the conditions that exist at a particular time in a partcular place:
- Everyone knew how **serious** the **situation** was.
- She **handled** a difficult **situation** very well.

In a/somebody's situation
- what would you do if you were in my situation?
- Discuss your **financial situation** with an accountant.

COLLOCATIONS
VERBS
put somebody in a situation
- Her actions put me in a really awkward situation.

describe/explain a situation
- She spent 15 minutes explaining the situation.

handle a situation (also **deal with a situation**)
- He had no idea how to deal with the situation.

a situation comes about (also **a situation arises/occurs** *formal*) (=it happens)
- I don't know how this situation has come about.
- The situation had arisen as a result of a serious staff shortage.

ADJECTIVES/NOUNS + SITUATION
a dangerous situation
- The situation was becoming increasingly dangerous as a fight seemed likely.

the present/current situation
- The present situation is Afghanistan is very worrying.

the economic/political situation
- The country's economic situation continued to deteriorate.

a social situation (=a situation in which someone is with other people)
- He is shy and feels uncomfortable in most social situations.

1. He .... a very awkward situation when he asked me what my friend's salary was.

2. The situation became quite .... when riots broke out and people began to fight.

3. The .... situation in several war-torn countries is extremely distressing.

4. My boss knew exactly how to .... the situation when a customer complained.

5. She tried to .... the situation to her employer, but he did not seem to understand.

6. The nation's .... situation worsened when the stock market crashed.

7. She is very outgoing and feels at home in .... situations.

8. The situation .... after a number of soldiers defected.

EXERCISE 6

A. Find multiword units in these excerpts from readings in this unit. Then write the words on the lines. Each item contains more than one multiword unit.

1. A *highly specific* memory is a memory clearly defined in time, such as a particular day, week, or even single event, such as a car crash or a week at a summer camp.

   car crash; summer camp

2. Among self-defining memories, most people have in common certain experiences, including relationships, life-threatening events, and achievements.

3. Sports also have the dual effect of aiding a nation in unification and projecting that unity and identity outward to gain recognition in the world.

4. This phenomenon is common among many nations, including South Korea, which is still technically at war with North Korea; Canada, which has faced domestic tensions; and Britain, which has sought to redefine its national character.

5. Since World War II, both industrialized nations and developing nations have increased funding for sports at a rate faster than other services, and some researchers believe that this is for the express purpose of fostering nationalism and asserting nations' identities in an increasingly globalized world.

6. Similarly, in 1990, shortly after the fall of the Berlin Wall, a national marathon crisscrossed the line of demarcation between the two Germanys, purposely using the sporting event to highlight the new territory of the country.

7. Some social scientists argue that sports act as a metaphor for culture, revealing the character of a nation, its value system, and elements of its social structure.

8. James could not have known that his essay stood upon a ledge of history, overlooking two world wars that would shape the landscape of war and peace. Nor did James offer an activity he believed could fill the supposed void war would leave behind, were it eradicated.

9. There is no clear answer for why the world has fallen on such comparatively harmonious times, though scholars cite several theories, including the nuclear deterrent, increased international trade, and the interconnectedness of the world in the digital age.

B. Compare answers with a partner.

Go to **MyEnglishLab** to complete a skill practice.

APPLY YOUR SKILLS

WHY IT'S USEFUL By applying the skills you have learned in this unit, you can successfully read this challenging text and learn about the relationship between sports and war, and how identity both informs and manifests in each.

BEFORE YOU READ

A. Discuss these questions with one or more students.

1. Think of sports events you have watched in person, on TV, or online. Have you ever noticed the warlike language that is often used in sportscasting? What are some examples? Why do you think such language is used in sports?

2. Can you think of any situations in which an athlete used his or her role on the world stage to promote a personal political or nationalistic viewpoint? Share what you know.

3. Do you know of any efforts to implement a sports program with the aim of reducing violence among youth? Has it been successful in achieving that objective?

B. Imagine that you will be participating in a small group discussion about the passage "Sports as the Moral Equivalent of War," which begins on the next page. Your group will be discussing the following questions. Keep these questions in mind as you read the passage.

1. What qualities do sports and war have in common?

2. What war themes do sportscasters often focus on in sports stories?

3. What are some examples of specific events in history where sports were used to promote nationalism?

4. What is the relationship between civil unrest and sports in a given society?

5. Within sports, which group of people tends to be the most violent?

C. Review the Unit Skills Summary. As you read the passage, apply the skills you learned in this unit.

UNIT SKILLS SUMMARY

Be an active reader.
• Evaluate your understanding, question the author's claims, and record ideas to investigate further.

Skim for gist.
• Move your eyes quickly over the reading to get a general mental image of the main points.

Scan for details.
• Use the strategies you learned to quickly identify details—like names of people, places, organizations, years, and dates—without reading every sentence.

Annotate and take notes.
• Write or highlight on the printed page or use the annotation feature in an e-book. Another option is writing notes, such as questions and definitions, in a notebook.

Use dictionaries well to strengthen your vocabulary.
• When faced with a word entry that has multiple definitions, analyze the text you are reading to choose the most appropriate definition. In dictionary entries, look for highlighted words to find common collocations, and read example phrases to identify multiword units.

READ

A. Read the passage. Annotate and take notes as necessary.

Sports as the Moral Equivalent of War

1   In the early 1900s, renowned philosopher and psychologist William James posited that war was, as he somberly lamented, the "romance of history," insofar as it stimulates the human psyche and gives some a sense of purpose and nobility. James, a self-described pacifist, argued that war cannot simply disappear and that it must have a "moral equivalent," or an activity that could, as he put it, "redeem life from flat degeneration." James could not have known that his essay stood upon a ledge of history, overlooking two world wars that would shape the landscape of war and peace. Nor did James offer an activity he believed could fill the supposed void war would leave behind, were it eradicated. Other experts, however, theorize that sports could perhaps fill this vacuum and offer a moral equivalent. Furthermore, evidence shows that the introduction of sports into societies plagued by violence may help curb warlike behavior.

2   Sports and war undeniably share common characteristics. Sports, by definition, are types of physical activity that are usually competitive, or even combative, by nature. Sporting events and wars typically arouse intense feelings and emotions among invested parties—spectators and players as well as civilians and soldiers. Stamina, courage, discipline, and team spirit are characteristics lauded in participants of both sports and war. Athletes together with war heroes are distinguished and celebrated. In addition, both sports and war, until more recent times, have existed as predominantly male activities.

3   Sports commentary abounds with battle-like language. Sports writers choose words analogous to war reporting, such as *tragedy, massacre, punishment, defeat, tactics,* and *defense.* Commentary ranges from stories of injury, loss, and defeat, to victory and heroic transformation. Bill Shankly, former manager of the Liverpool Football Club, was famously quoted as saying, "Football is not a matter of life and death; it's much more serious than that." Shankly's quote, whether intended to be humorous or not, is a prime example of the comparison of sports to war and the equation of the two activities' importance in society.

4   Likewise, individual sporting games can become a mirror for a battle between nations with a history of actual war, with individual players' actions the attacks. For example, in a 2012 Olympic soccer match between South Korea and Japan, two countries with an extremely acrimonious relationship and a long history of conflict, Korean soccer player Park Jongwoo held up a sign that asserted that a disputed island territory belonged to South Korea. It is important to note that actual statements or actions related to political quarrels between nations are strictly forbidden in modern international games. Park was suspended by the Disciplinary Committee of FIFA (Fédération Internationale de Football Association) for two matches and initially had his bronze medal withheld for his overtly political display.

5   The idea of sports fostering a sense of nationalism also comes into play when considering the concept of games replacing battle tactics. In 1884, Ireland successfully formed the Gaelic Athletic Association, which was closely tied to both the militant nationalist group called the Irish Republican Brotherhood and the Irish resistance movement. The Association formed as a way to promote nationalism and distinguish itself from England. The purpose of the organization was not only to resuscitate purely Irish games, such as hurling and Gaelic football, but also to separate itself from English games, such as football, rugby, and cricket. The Association also prohibited contact with English sport clubs, symbolizing political resistance.

6   The parallel of games and battles is not only drawn between opposing nations, but also within single societies plagued by warring factions within their borders. Such civil unrest is often prevented when sports are introduced, lending credence to

Continued

the theory that games can become a stand-in for battle. In Manchester, England, gang warfare and knife crimes seized the city at the turn of the 19th century. In the 1890s, philanthropists founded clubs for the youth to provide them access to sports, which in part led to British football's rise in popularity and the eventual establishment of the teams Manchester United and Manchester City. After the introduction of the sports clubs, gang violence abated. Arguably, group aggression was redirected to organized games and dispensed on the soccer field rather than on the streets. It is important to note that though conflict may be displaced by sports, violence among sports fans, whether in the form of brawls between fans of opposing teams or in the form of looting or victory riots, is still prevalent.

7   The movement to help at-risk youth in England in the 1890s set a precedent for future similar efforts. In recent years, Mercy Corps, an American aid agency, has worked to provide alternatives to youth violence and to deter children from joining armed movements. Mercy Corps has employed a program called Sport for Change in communities rife with violence, including South Sudan, Kenya, Colombia, and the West Bank and Gaza. The organization states that soccer is not simply a sport, but a "transformative force in the lives of young people, teaching them leadership skills and healthy ways to handle conflict." The statement elevates a game to an activity that goes beyond simple play and functions to prevent larger conflict in society.

8   Arguably, allegiance to a country as its troops march to war has been replaced with allegiance to a team as players compete on the playing field. Since the conclusion of World War II, the number of deaths due to group conflict in the world as a whole has been steadily declining. The past 25 years in particular, despite many violent conflicts, has been a time of relatively great peace, with fewer wars overall. There is no clear answer for why the world has fallen on such comparatively harmonious times, though scholars cite several theories, including the nuclear deterrent, increased international trade, and the interconnectedness of the world in the digital age. As violence has fallen, sports have grown correspondingly, supporting the theory of sports being the moral equivalent of war.

B. Reread the questions in Before You Read, Part B. Is there anything you cannot answer? What reading skills can you use to help you find the answers?

Go to **MyEnglishLab** to read the passage again and answer critical thinking questions.

THINKING CRITICALLY

In "Sports as the Moral Equivalent of War," you read about an instance in which a soccer player openly displayed his nationalistic views during a game. He was later disciplined for doing so, as actions and statements associated with political disputes between countries are prohibited in modern international games. Why do you think political expression in sports is taboo? What problems could such displays cause? Currently, some nationalistic displays—for example, flags, national anthems—are allowed, but others are not. Where should the dividing line be for what is and is not permitted?

THINKING VISUALLY

Look at the map and map key, which show different countries that boycotted the Olympic Games in three different years. Based on the countries and years indicated and what you know about what was happening in the world during those years, what do you think may have been the reasons for each boycott?

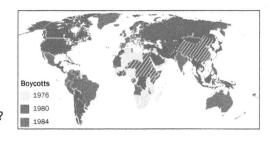

Boycotts
1976
1980
1984

THINKING ABOUT LANGUAGE

Read these excerpts from "Sports as the Moral Equivalent of War." Use a dictionary to determine the best definition for
each underlined word. Write the definition.

1. Other experts, however, theorize that sports could perhaps fill this <u>vacuum</u> and offer a moral equivalent.

   ....

2. Furthermore, evidence shows that the introduction of sports into societies plagued by violence may help <u>curb</u> warlike behavior.

   ....

3. For example, in a 2012 Olympic soccer <u>match</u> between South Korea and Japan, two countries with an extremely acrimonious relationship and a long history of conflict, Korean soccer player Park Jongwoo held up a sign that asserted that a disputed island territory belonged to South Korea.

   ....

4. Stamina, courage, <u>discipline</u>, and team spirit are characteristics lauded in participants of both sports and war.

   ....

5. Such <u>civil</u> unrest is often prevented when sports are introduced, lending credence to the theory that games can become a stand-in for battle.

   ....

6. The <u>parallel</u> of games and battles is not only drawn between opposing nations, but also within single societies plagued by warring factions within their borders.

   ....

7. James could not have known that his essay stood upon a ledge of history, overlooking two world wars that would <u>shape</u> the landscape of war and peace. Nor did James offer an activity he believed could fill the supposed void war would leave behind, were it eradicated.

   ....

8. Sports by definition are types of physical activity that are usually competitive, or even combative, by <u>nature</u>.

   ....

9. Bill Shankly, former manager of the Liverpool Football Club, was famously quoted as saying, "Football is not a <u>matter</u> of life and death; it's much more serious than that."

   ....

▶ Go to MyEnglishLab to listen to Professor Greenberg and to complete a self-assessment.

Individual choices impact
the global economy.

ECONOMICS

Main Ideas and Supporting Details

UNIT PROFILE

You will consider the subject of economics—specifically the issue of international trade. Some topics you will read about include the concepts of comparative advantage, free trade versus protectionism, and public good.

Preview the second paragraph of the reading "World Trade Problems and Their Resolutions" on page 42. Can you identify the main idea? The supporting details? The sentence functions?

OUTCOMES

- Recognize main ideas and supporting details
- Identify sentence functions
- Identify topics and main ideas
- Identify supporting details
- Summarize
- Analyze meaning using word parts

GETTING STARTED

▶ Go to MyEnglishLab to listen to Professor Clerici-Arias and to complete a self-assessment.

Discuss these questions with a partner or group.

1. Choose five countries that you know something about. What is each country's strongest product or service? Does it trade that product or service internationally? Why or why not?

2. Think of a country that is facing international competition. How should it respond to this situation?

3. Many of the big businesses you have heard of began as small start-ups. Which fields are rich terrain for start-ups today? Are they different from those in the past? Which fields will offer start-ups opportunities in the future?

For more about **ECONOMICS**, see ② ③. See also Ⓦ and ⓄⒸ **ECONOMICS** ① ② ③.

FUNDAMENTAL SKILL

RECOGNIZING MAIN IDEAS AND SUPPORTING DETAILS

WHY IT'S USEFUL Seeing the main ideas helps you appreciate the interrelationships among thoughts and claims. Supporting details—the real pattern of evidence for the main idea—may be hidden among unimportant sentences. Finding this evidence is the key to understanding a writer's reasoning.

Well-structured paragraphs are the backbone of a good reading. Collectively, paragraphs organize and advance the ideas in a reading, with each paragraph serving a particular purpose. Individually, most paragraphs convey a topic, a main idea, and support for that idea.

The skill of **recognizing and understanding the main idea and supporting details** in a paragraph is essential to understanding a text. This unit breaks the skill down into three supporting skills:

- identifying sentence functions
- identifying topics and main ideas
- identifying supporting details

NOTICING ACTIVITY

Notice the basic elements of a paragraph, identified in the passage.

COMPARATIVE ADVANTAGE

Set-up sentence — [1] The classical economist David Ricardo developed a theory that remains critical to our understanding of international trade. *Main idea: how comparative advantage explains trade relations*

Topic sentence — [2] His <u>comparative advantage</u> theory argued against protectionist legislation and neatly illustrated the benefits of free trade.

Topic — [3] The theory of comparative advantage demonstrates that rather than trying to remain isolated from other countries, a nation's businesses can profit by specializing in their most efficient industries. [4] Ricardo, whose exposition of the concept was published in 1817, tackled the question of trade advantages in an illuminating way.

Topic sentence / Beginning connector — [5] What was so brilliant about it? [6] Comparative advantage theory recognizes subtleties of trade that are not dealt with in the more straightforward theory of absolute advantage by legendary political economist Adam Smith. [7] According to absolute advantage theory, if one country can produce all commodities more efficiently than another, trade activity between the two is never profitable. [8] Comparative advantage theory, however, says it is better to specialize in one product—that in which a country has the greatest production advantage—and buy other products from elsewhere. [9] This is true even if the country could produce all of the products more efficiently. [10] This strikes some students of economics as counterintuitive. [11] However, Ricardo's theory has proven useful over and over, even in circumstances far more complex than the idealized two-country trading grid that he used to illustrate its principles. [12] Let us look at some of those complexities. *Supporting details*

End connector

Go to **MyEnglishLab** to complete a vocabulary exercise and skill practice, and to join in collaborative activities.

SUPPORTING SKILL 1
IDENTIFYING SENTENCE FUNCTIONS

WHY IT'S USEFUL By identifying the functions of sentences within a paragraph, you can quickly understand the meaning of the ideas within it. You will feel the flow of ideas within a paragraph and between paragraphs.

Sentences are the building blocks of paragraphs, performing specific functions. In the reading "Comparative Advantage" on the previous page, you saw labels identifying the types of sentences that make up the paragraphs. Not all paragraphs have all of the following kinds of sentences, and sometimes a single sentence can serve more than one of these **functions**:

- **set-up sentence**—a sentence, sometimes in the form of a question, that sets the context for the topic sentence of a paragraph
- **topic sentence(s)**—one or two sentences that indicate the topic and express the main idea or purpose of the paragraph
- **supporting details**—specific facts, examples, or pieces of information that explain or support the main idea
- **end connector**—a sentence or phrase that connects the ideas in a paragraph to the next paragraph
- **beginning connector**—a sentence or phrase that connects the ideas in a new paragraph to the previous paragraph
- **conclusion**—one or two sentences indicating that the discussion of the paragraph's main idea is finished; most paragraphs do not have conclusions

> **TIP**
> To get the gist of a reading, or to "preview" it, read the title and the first and last sentence of each paragraph. While the advantage of reading the last sentence may not be clear at first, this is suggested because the end connector often indicates the main idea of the paragraph that follows.

EXERCISE 1

A. Read the title of the following passage. What does the title suggest about the importance of comparative advantage?

B. Read the passage for general meaning. Then read it again, concentrating on the functions of sentences. Notice the sample labels in Paragraphs 1 and 2. Write similar labels for the sentences in Paragraphs 3 and 4. If a sentence has two functions, write both labels.

SU: Set-up sentence	*SD*: Supporting detail	*BC*: Beginning connector
TS: Topic sentence	*EC*: End connector	

COMPARATIVE ADVANTAGE THEORY IN A GLOBAL ECONOMY

1   ¹ _SU_ The modern, globalized economy is a complex collection of nations and industries. ² _TS_ All involved seek to maximize their profits in international trade, which—economists have pointed out—depends on leveraging their comparative advantages. ³ _SD_ Nations that shrewdly recognize and exploit comparative advantages can enjoy robust growth, and those that nimbly refocus their efforts to move from one advantageous pursuit to another do especially well. ⁴ _SD_ However, it is common for nations either to fail to recognize their advantages or to do a poor job of exploiting them. ⁵ _EC_ History offers many notable examples of ineffective and effective economic policies.

2   ⁶ _BC, TS_ Consider the US economy after the disastrous stock market crash in 1929. ⁷ _SD_ As bad as things were, the US economy enjoyed comparative advantages in a number of areas, from agricultural products to film technology to capital goods (equipment used in factories to produce other goods). ⁸ _SD_ If the US government had kept the doors of international trade open, US

businesses probably would have been able to rebound after a couple of trying years. [9] _SD_ Instead, Congress passed, and President Herbert Hoover signed in 1930, an infamously restrictive tariff usually known as the Smoot-Hawley Tariff. [10] _SD_ While the aim was to encourage both citizens and industry to "Buy American" as a way of bringing money back into the national economy, things went awry. [11] _SD_ The tariff wrongheadedly pinned most hopes for growth on economic activity within the country, a foolish notion considering the far greater pool of potential earnings from international trade. [12] _SD_ Setting off a series of sanctions and countermeasures from US trading partners, the tariff worsened the crisis and led to the worldwide Great Depression. [13] _EC_ It seemed to many that government could not formulate effective economic policies.

3   [14] Though not the only economic misstep in history, the Smoot-Hawley Tariff and others like it have fortunately given way to wiser trade decision-making. [15] Nations that have opted for freer trade have historically been rewarded with economic growth. [16] For example, for several decades in the mid-20th century, China chose not to maintain trading relationships with many of the world's foremost economies. [17] Then, after opening up to foreign investment and producing goods for export, the waking giant found a comparative advantage in many types of manufacturing. [18] China quickly became dominant in a variety of industrial and manufacturing sectors. [19] It is a rare country that remains an autarky (a self-contained economy) in an age of wide-ranging trade and hard-to-thwart digital communications. [20] The few present-day examples, such as North Korea, tend to rank low in nearly every measure of economic health, demonstrating just why a relatively free international market coupled with the pursuit of a nation's comparative advantage within that market results in a superior choice for growth and development.

4   [21] Given the ever-changing landscape of international trade today, no nation or industry can afford to rest on its advantages. [22] In the 1970s, US automakers, who had previously held comparative advantages over those of nearly all other nations, suddenly found themselves unable to compete with an innovative Japanese automobile industry, which operated more efficiently and analyzed more effectively the wishes of consumers. [23] Subsequently, auto firms in other countries, notably South Korea, entered the fray and exploited certain comparative advantages (namely related to price and labor). [24] While attempts by US automakers to regain some of their market advantages have been somewhat successful, the car market deserves more attention.

C. Discuss these questions with another student. Use information and examples from the passage to support your answers.

1. What idea is introduced by the end connector in Paragraph 2?
2. In Paragraph 3, what idea is introduced by the beginning connector?
3. In Paragraph 3, how is the topic sentence different from the beginning-connector sentence?
4. Does Paragraph 4 end with a conclusion? Why or why not?

Go to **MyEnglishLab** to complete a vocabulary exercise and skill practice, and to join in collaborative activities.

SUPPORTING SKILL 2
IDENTIFYING TOPICS AND MAIN IDEAS

WHY IT'S USEFUL By identifying the topic and main idea of a text, you will be able to recognize and pinpoint the most important information that you should take away from a reading.

The **topic** of a text is essentially *what the text is about.* One of the simplest ways to determine this is by reading the title, which nearly always indicates something about information in the text. This way, readers have an idea of what they are going to read about before actually beginning to read.

After previewing the title, you can mine further information about the topic by scanning the **headings** within a reading. These short phrases, statements, or questions, which separate a reading into sections, indicate the **subtopics**—or smaller topics that support the main topic. These headings are often boldfaced or italicized, making it clear to readers that the text beneath one heading, for example, contains information that differs from the text beneath another heading. That said, information associated with each heading always contributes to the main topic of the text.

Once the topic of a text has been identified, the **main idea** can be determined by considering *what the author is attempting to express* about the topic. A topic cannot stand in isolation; authors always provide a variety of ideas associated with a given topic in order to communicate their main point.

The topic and main idea of the following paragraph, excerpted from "Comparative Advantage Theory in a Global Economy" (p. 26), can be determined by reading it and analyzing its components.

SUCCESS AND FAILURE IN THE GLOBAL ECONOMY

[1]The modern, globalized economy is a complex collection of nations and industries. [2]All involved seek to maximize their profits in international trade, which—economists have pointed out—depends on leveraging their comparative advantages. [3]Nations that shrewdly recognize and exploit comparative advantages can enjoy robust growth, and those that nimbly refocus their efforts to move from one advantageous pursuit to another do especially well. [4]However, it is common for nations either to fail to recognize their advantages or to do a poor job of exploiting them. [5]History offers many notable examples of ineffective and effective economic policies.

The topic—success and failure in the global economy—can be easily identified by reading the title of the excerpt. A reader can only determine the main idea, however, after reading the entire paragraph. In this excerpt, the main idea is as follows: whether a nation recognizes and takes advantage of what sets it apart from others leads to its success or failure in the global economy.

EXERCISE 2

A. Preview the passage. What topics and main ideas do you think will be expressed?

B. Now read the full passage. As you read, identify the topic of each paragraph and make notes about what you think the main ideas are.

PATRIOTIC PURCHASING

1   As international trade becomes freer, a nation's workers may regard unprecedented levels of competition from low-wage workers abroad as a major threat to their livelihood. Various types of protectionist measures have been implemented in some countries in an attempt to shelter citizens from the supposedly negative effects of the global exchange of goods. Some examples of such measures are trade restrictions like tariffs (a tax on goods coming into or going out of a country) and import quotas (an official limit on the amount of a particular product allowed into a country). Certain groups of Americans are concerned that, should such trade restrictions *not* be passed, foreign competitors could, for example, drive the American automotive industry over a cliff. Similarly, some Canadians wonder whether they would be in a better position if they purchased only domestically manufactured products. However, most mainstream economists steadfastly maintain that free trade benefits all consumers and boosts financial prosperity worldwide. If this is accepted as truth, is it ever to a country's economic advantage to encourage its citizens to solely buy products made in-country?

Who Benefits?

2   It may be beneficial to some businesses in the short term to convince citizens to purchase goods produced in their own country. However, that nation's *economy* does not always benefit in the same manner. Businesses within a country frequently seek governmental restrictions on trade for the sake of avoiding both competition and the expense of innovating to maintain market superiority. Politicians, who must ingratiate themselves to special interests within their districts, often justify their support of protectionist policies by claiming that their objective is to bolster the country's economy. In the long term, however, these safeguards nearly always hurt the national economy. In turn, other countries pass retaliatory legislation, which results in the slowdown of international trade and, accordingly, the worldwide economy. Paradoxically, this slowdown will eventually have a detrimental effect on those same businesses that sought those tariffs and quotas in the first place.

3   A nation's workers might be correct in asserting that in the very short term, buying domestically produced goods slows the rate of job losses in a certain industry. However, while protectionist policies may help them maintain job security for a limited time, the economic problems caused by these policies will ultimately

Continued

hurt them. Under a protectionist umbrella, workers may actually lose their ability to weather economic crosswinds as they cling to skills that become increasingly obsolete. If businesses and workers adapt to changing circumstances early on, they will be better off than if they adapt only when forced to do so by dire economic circumstances.

Should You Buy Local?

4   Buying products manufactured in one's own country may confer a sense of patriotism on the consumer, which is perfectly understandable. Local manufacturers may even enjoy a comparative advantage by having an ability to appeal to local consumers' tastes in ways international companies cannot. But subscribing to a campaign like "Buy American" or "Buy Canadian"—which urges the purchase of only domestic products—is unlikely to have any positive effect on the long-term health of local producers and certainly not on that of the nation's economy as a whole. By the time a business even starts trying to rally consumers against international competition, the battle is probably lost. More often than not, the most patriotic thing a consumer can do is to provide home-country businesses with the incentives they need to outcompete their international rivals.

C. Answer the questions.

1. What is the main idea of Paragraph 1?

   a. Consumers and the world economy overall gain substantially from free trade.
   b. Protectionist measures safeguard domestic businesses from excess outside competition.
   c. There is controversy over whether a country should promote the purchase of domestically produced goods.
   d. Increases in international competition have caused workers to be concerned about keeping their jobs.

2. What is the main idea of Paragraph 2?

   a. Businesses might benefit more from products being purchased in-country than the economy does.
   b. Politicians support governmental restrictions because they believe the economy will benefit from them.
   c. In order to make more money, businesses often advocate for the passing of trade restrictions.
   d. The global economy is adversely affected by retaliatory legislation passed in certain countries.

3. Which two sentences work together to express the topic of Paragraph 2?

....

....

....

4. What is the main idea of Paragraph 3?

    a. Citizens would benefit significantly from purchasing goods made in their country.

    b. It is advantageous for workers to adapt swiftly to dynamic economic conditions.

    c. Workers should change their circumstances as soon as the economy is hit with problems.

    d. Protectionist policies serve to help workers in certain industries keep their jobs.

5. What is the main idea of Paragraph 4?

    a. Small businesses have a unique advantage because they cater to the preferences of citizens in their country.

    b. Customers should recognize that the impact they can make on the global economy by "buying local" is limited.

    c. As a result of economic downturns, local companies are often forced to take different business approaches.

    d. Companies do everything in their power to inform consumers of the drawbacks of foreign competition.

6. What is the topic of Paragraph 4? Write it in your own words.

....

....

....

D. Now discuss your answers in Part C with another student. Use information and examples from the passage to explain and support your answers.

Go to **MyEnglishLab** to complete a vocabulary exercise and skill practice, and to join in collaborative activities.

SUPPORTING SKILL 3

IDENTIFYING SUPPORTING DETAILS

WHY IT'S USEFUL Academic texts contain different levels of detail. By distinguishing supporting details from less important details, you can read more efficiently and focus on the relevant information.

Supporting details in a paragraph add information about the topic and main idea. Most paragraphs contain more than one supporting detail sentence, but shorter paragraphs may offer only one. Details can support the main idea in many different ways.

Types of Supporting Details
- facts (historical, scientific, etc.)
- statistics
- causes / effects
- explanations
- opinions
- examples
- descriptions

Not every sentence in the interior of a paragraph provides a supporting detail. Some sentences serve other functions. The author might include a certain sentence to set up another point, to be entertaining, to refer to some other part of the reading, or to fill any number of other roles. Here is an example of a paragraph that includes both support and nonsupport sentences.

[1] One of the most enduring—and controversial—concepts to come out of the financial crisis of 2008–2009 is that some companies are too big to fail. [2] The argument is that some companies are so essential to the national economy (or even the world economy) that government has to step in and save them from failure. [3] Of course, any such judgment is inherently anti-competitive, as we explain in Chapter 6. [4] **Initially, the concept was applied to banks and financial institutions as the US government stepped in to prop some of them up.** [5] **For example, the US government sank $85 billion into a bailout plan for AIG Insurance in 2008.** [6] It's notable that a month or so earlier, Lehman Brothers had been allowed to go bankrupt and break up; one wonders why. [7] **Later, the focus was on the automobile industry as loans and equity purchases by the US government kept General Motors and Chrysler afloat and managed their bankruptcies.** [8] Here's a toast to Ford Motor Company for having the backbone to emerge from the crisis without any such help. [9] The chorus of complaints following this round of government largesse, which was called the "Troubled Asset Relief Program" (TARP), was huge.

Topic sentence

Not a support sentence. Introduces an unimportant extra point and refers to another part of the text.

Support sentence. Introduces a new kind of company (car companies) that got support.

Support sentences. Gives an example of "some companies ..."

Not a support sentence. Expresses a point of view about a situation that doesn't support the "some companies ..." point.

Not a support sentence. Expresses an extraneous point of view about a situation (praising Ford) that doesn't support the idea of government bailing out companies.

End connector sentence

EXERCISE 3

A. In the following excerpts, notice the supporting details in bold. Then identify the type of support: *fact, statistic, cause / effect, explanation, opinion, example, description*. More than one type may be correct.

If the US government had kept the doors of international trade open, US businesses probably would have been able to rebound after a couple of trying years. **(1) Instead, Congress passed, and President Herbert Hoover signed in 1930, an infamously restrictive tariff usually**

known as the Smoot-Hawley Tariff. While the aim was to encourage both citizens and industry to "Buy American" as a way of bringing money back into the national economy, things went awry. **(2) The tariff wrongheadedly pinned most hopes for growth on economic activity within the country, a foolish notion considering the far greater pool of potential earnings from international trade. (3) Setting off a series of sanctions and countermeasures from US trading partners, the tariff worsened the crisis and led to the worldwide Great Depression.** It seemed to many that government could not formulate effective economic policies. (From "Comparative Advantage Theory in a Global Economy" Paragraph 2, p. 26)

(1) ....

(2) ....

(3) ....

The lessons of comparative advantage theory extend beyond the realm of the job search. There is also the matter of the worker's own comparative advantages in terms of skills, a calculus that looks very much like what economists do in figuring a nation's comparative advantage. **(4) Imagine someone looking for web-development work in a job market where many applicants are competing for every available position.** Our web developer is good at coding in Java and C++, and she has two years of web-development experience. Not bad, but nearly every other job-seeker in that field can say the same. It is best for her to avoid competing for jobs based on those skills alone even though she may feel that she's better than most competitors. (From "Comparative Advantage and Job-Hunting" Paragraph 4, p. 36)

(4) ....

Perhaps the clearest focus provided by comparative advantage theory is on the phenomenon of opportunity cost (OC). **(5) If a job-hunter spends time applying for jobs that do not suit him or her very well, an OC is incurred.** He or she cannot spend that time applying for more appropriate positions. The costs might not be measured in money (unless you assign a certain dollar value to an applicant's time) but could be quantified in terms of some other unit you might invent to measure success or satisfaction, some sort of "fruitfulness factor." (From "Comparative Advantage and Job-Hunting" Paragraph 2, p. 36)

(5) ....

Economies come in many shapes and sizes, not all of them involving money-based trading. Some theorists, such as the French sociologist and anthropologist Marcel Mauss, have concentrated on "gift economies." These involve exchange, just as money-oriented economies do, but the interaction is less direct. **(6) The basic idea is that I help you meet your needs even though you don't have anything to give me in return—not yet, anyway.** I trust that at some point in the future, you or your relatives will give something to me to balance things out. (From "Gift Exchanges as an Economic System," p. 34)

(6) ....

B. Compare answers with another student and explain the reasons for your answers.

Go to **MyEnglishLab** to complete a skill practice.

READING-WRITING CONNECTION

WHY IT'S USEFUL By writing a summary after you have read something, you are creating a study tool that you can refer back to, discovering what you did and did not understand about the text, and consolidating your memory of information from the text.

A **summary** is a short version of an original text that gives the most important information. As a student, you will frequently be asked to summarize a text in order to demonstrate (1) your understanding of its main idea(s) and (2) your ability to express the information in your own words and in a much shorter form.

The most important aspects of a summary are its brevity and its accuracy. It has to clearly capture the main idea(s) of the original text in a condensed form. Before you summarize a text, make sure you have carefully read and understood it. Most sentences contain words or phrases that are not necessary to include in a summary. Here are some suggestions to help you keep your summaries short and focused:

- Notice the title. Note the topic, main idea(s), your questions, and important supporting details. (Or make an outline to help you see important elements and plan your summary.)
- Use your own words.
- Brevity is a central feature of a good summary. The best summaries are about one-third the length of the original.
- Avoid words or phrases that do not contain important information—for example: *as most readers already know, after all, according to several sources.*
- Avoid repeated words, phrases, and ideas.
- Use pronouns (*it, this, they,* etc.) to replace repeated or long sequences of words.
- Shorten or leave out most examples and minor supporting details.
- Shorten or avoid stylistic expressions—for example: *surprisingly, to tell the truth, as if this weren't strange enough,* and so on.
- Shorten or leave out parenthetical expressions—words or phrases that make extra, unnecessary comments about an idea. Parenthetical expressions usually appear between parentheses, dashes, or commas: *(xxx) —xxx— , xxx, .*

EXERCISE 4

A. Read the title and the passage. What is the main idea?

GIFT EXCHANGES AS AN ECONOMIC SYSTEM

Economies come in many shapes and sizes, not all of them involving money-based trading. Some theorists, such as the French sociologist and anthropologist Marcel Mauss, have concentrated on "gift economies." These involve exchange, just as money-oriented economies do, but the interaction is less direct. The basic idea is that I help you meet your needs even though you don't have anything to give me in return—not yet, anyway. I trust that at some point in the future, you or your relatives will give something to me to balance things out. Although such a

Canoes arriving for a potlatch, a gift-giving feast practiced by indigenous peoples of the Pacific Northwest coast of Canada and the United States

system sounds simple and friendly, it is very hard to maintain. Over time, the pattern of obligations gets so complicated that it's nearly impossible to outline, and balance becomes unachievable. In fact, there is some question about whether "gift economies" exist at all. Skeptics say that the gift-giving is a strong cultural trait in such systems, but it is not the basis of the real daily economy whereby people obtain food, shelter, and other necessities.

B. **Read these summaries of "Gift Exchange as an Economic System" and choose the best one.**

☐ 1. Economies come in many shapes and sizes. The French sociologist and anthropologist Marcel Mauss concentrated on "gift economies." These involve exchange, just as money-oriented economies do, but the interaction is less direct. I help you meet your needs even though you don't have anything to give me in return—not yet, anyway. At some point in the future, you or your relatives will give something to me to balance things out. This sounds simple and friendly but is very hard to maintain. The pattern of obligations gets too complicated, and balance becomes unachievable. There is some question about whether "gift economies" exist at all. The gift-giving is just a strong cultural trait, not the basis of the real daily economy.

☐ 2. Modern economies concentrate too much on money. In the past, gift economies offered a simpler, friendlier system. I gave things to you, but you didn't pay me for them. Instead, you'd eventually give me something of equal value. Though they get complicated, gift economies are supported by strong cultural traditions that ensure everyone gets the daily necessities they need.

☐ 3. The idea of "gift economies" has been explored by some theorists. In theory, such economies base their exchanges on a system of trust. If one person gives something to another, the giver will eventually be paid back in some way by a return gift. Such economies are complicated, though, and may not even really exist.

C. **Discuss these questions with one or two other students. Then explain your answers to the class.**

1. Which summary did you choose and why?

2. Approximately how many words does the original paragraph have? How many words does the best summary have, approximately?

3. Circle information in the original that is in the best summary and then notice what information was NOT included. Why was each piece of information not included? Which strategies for summarizing from the list on the previous page did the summary writer use?

4. Different readers might write different summaries of an original. This is because not all readers agree on which ideas are the most important. Would you change the best summary in any way? Would you include different information? Would you express things differently?

A. The following is an excerpt from an article that applies economic principles to personal experiences. Read the excerpt.

Comparative Advantage and Job-Hunting

1   The concept of comparative advantage is not just an abstraction. Nor is it applicable only to entire national economies. A job-hunter would do well to recognize his or her personal comparative advantages and use this recognition both to choose the best jobs to apply for and to stand out among other job-seekers. The savvy person looking for a job will look at the galaxy of employment possibilities through the lens of global economics.

2   Perhaps the clearest focus provided by comparative advantage theory is on the phenomenon of opportunity cost (OC). If a job-hunter spends time applying for jobs that do not suit him or her very well, an OC is incurred. He or she cannot spend that time applying for more appropriate positions. The costs might not be measured in money (unless you assign a certain dollar value to an applicant's time) but could be quantified in terms of some other unit you might invent to measure success or satisfaction, some sort of "fruitfulness factor." Potential employment that has a high fruitfulness factor, that is, a strong chance of being offered to a candidate and a strong chance of being accepted, is far better for a job-seeker to pursue than employment with a low fruitfulness factor. Such a job would be unlikely to be offered or unlikely to be accepted, or both. So a candidate would incur higher OC by spending time applying for low-fruitfulness positions rather than jobs that are better suited to him or her.

3   Of course, in calling a position "better suited" and assigning a fruitfulness factor, we have to consider a number of attributes, most of which are only indirectly about money. Some relate to the likelihood that an offer will be made. Others relate to the likelihood that an offer will be accepted. The job-seeker's skills and experience are the main criteria for appropriateness to the stated requirements of the job—a given level of education or training, an ability to do certain tasks, prior work in the field, and so on. The candidate presents such qualifications, and in return the prospective employer assigns a certain salary to the position (plus a package of other money-related benefits, such as health insurance). But other factors also figure into the calculus, such as location, corporate culture, the character of one's fellow workers, and innumerable other features of the job. Without such nonmonetary enticements, the position's fruitfulness factor would decrease, and the OC of applying for it would increase.

4   The lessons of comparative advantage theory extend beyond the realm of the job search. There is also the matter of the worker's own comparative advantages in terms of skills, a calculus that looks very much like what economists do in figuring a nation's comparative advantage. Imagine someone looking for web-development work in a job market where many applicants are competing for every available position. Our web developer is good at coding in Java and C++, and she has two years of web-development experience. Not bad, but nearly every other job-seeker in that field can say the same. It is best for her to avoid competing for jobs based on those skills alone even though she may feel that she's better than most competitors. By analyzing her comparative advantages rather than absolute skills, she might recognize that she has other, less common talents she wants to leverage, something like proficiency in Spanish or a sophisticated knowledge of film production. If there are employers that value those characteristics—and if there are, she is quite likely to enjoy working there—she stands above the crowd.

5   A corollary of the theory of competitive advantage is the principle that some things are worth doing and others are worth trading for. In fact, David Ricardo's first exposition of the theory (1817) involved the question of which product(s) Britain and Portugal should produce and which they should trade for—wine, cloth, both, or neither. Ricardo concluded that even if a country—he postulated Portugal—were more efficient at producing both, it made economic sense for it to concentrate on the product where its advantage is greatest (wine, in Ricardo's example) and to buy the other product from elsewhere. A job-seeker has to recognize that a full exploitation of comparative advantage in the search for employment involves analogous judgments.

6   Some of these judgments are obvious. In almost no case is it to a job-seeker's advantage to cut his or her own hair or sew clothes for the interview. However, the principle is helpful in less obvious cases as well. Should the job-seeker compose his or her own résumé? Most do, and many of them do well enough that the time spent in this writing has a low OC—that is, it is a sufficiently profitable use of time that they should not pay someone else to write résumés for them. However, a job-seeker may recognize that résumé writing is not the sharpest of his or her skills. It may be worth the person's time to trade out that task—to hire one of the many professional résumé-writing companies—while concentrating time and effort on some higher-return task, like researching the histories of prospective employers or watching videos about how to behave in job interviews.

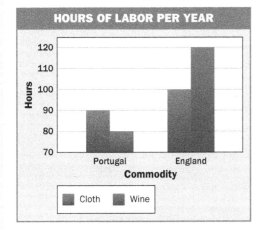

HOURS OF LABOR PER YEAR

B. **Reread and summarize Paragraphs 2, 4, and 5. Use the summarizing strategies you've learned. Note the word limit for each.**

   • Summarize Paragraph 2 in no more than 55 words.
   • Summarize Paragraph 4 in no more than 55 words.
   • Summarize Paragraph 5 in no more than 40 words.

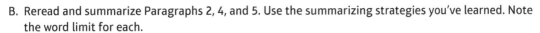

Go to **MyEnglishLab** to complete a vocabulary exercise and skill practice, and to join in collaborative activities.

For more about SUMMARIZING, see ECONOMICS ❶.

LANGUAGE SKILL

ANALYZING MEANING USING WORD PARTS

WHY IT'S USEFUL By familiarizing yourself with the meanings of the building blocks of words (roots and affixes), you can decipher unfamiliar words you encounter in your reading and build your vocabulary.

The meaning of a word is derived from its parts. The **root** of a word contains the core meaning. Words that share the same root are part of a **word family**.

We build upon the root by adding **affixes**: prefixes and suffixes. A **prefix** is placed at the beginning of a word and changes the core meaning. A **suffix** is added to the end and often changes a word's part of speech.

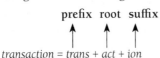

transaction = trans + act + ion

If you know that

- the root *act* means "do or act,"
- the prefix *trans-* means "across or between," and
- the suffix *-ion* means "process, state, or quality," and changes a verb to a noun,

then you can determine that the word *transaction* means "action across or between." For example, in the following sentence, you can determine that *transactions* refers to the trade or exchange of money or goods between people:

> If only a few people consider a thing valuable, it can't be used for many **transactions**.

You can apply this knowledge to other words with the same root: *react–reaction, counteract–counteraction, activate–activation*, and so on.

GREEK AND LATIN ORIGINS

Many words in English have origins in Latin or Greek words. Studying the meanings of Latin and Greek roots and affixes is especially helpful for analyzing the meaning of unknown words. The following charts list examples of Greek and Latin roots and affixes commonly found in English words.

ROOTS			
Root	Meaning	Root	Meaning
alter	other (Lat.)	poli / polit	city, state (Gr.)
anthro	human (Gr.)	port	carry (Lat.)
cep / cip	take (Lat.)	prim	first (Lat.)
critic	discern, judge (Gr.)	sens / sent	feel (Lat.)
dur	hard (Lat.)	sign	mean, meaning (Lat.)
gener	people, birth (Gr.)	simil	like, resembling (Lat.)
labor	work (Lat.)	sist	stand, stay (Lat.)
mis, mit	send, put (Lat.)	tract	pull, drag (Lat.)
mons / mont	show (Lat.)	trib / tribut	pay, give, bestow (Lat.)
not	letter, note (Lat.)	uni	one, together (Lat.)
plic	fold (Lat.)		

AFFIXES				
Prefix	**Meaning**	**Suffix**	**Meaning**	**Part of Speech**
a-, an-	without, not	-able, -ible	able to be …	adj.
con-	together, with	-al	relating to …	adj.
de-	remove, reduce	-ant, -ent	a person who … a thing that … state or quality	n. adj.
dis-	not, apart, away	-ate	make, do	v.
ex-	out	-ist	a person who …	n.
in-, im-	in, into	-ity	state, condition, quality	n.
in-, im-	not	-ive	inclined to, having the quality of …	adj.
per-	through	-tion / -ion	process, state, or quality	n.

EXERCISE 6

A. List one word you know for each root. Then compare lists with another student and talk about how the meaning of the root relates to your words.

	Root	Word		Root	Word
1	alter	*alternative*	12	poli / polit	
2	anthro		13	port	
3	cep / cip		14	prim	
4	critic		15	sens / sent	
5	dur		16	sign	
6	gener		17	simil	
7	labor		18	sist	
8	mis / mit		19	tract	
9	mons / mont		20	trib / tribut	
10	not		21	uni	
11	plic				

B. With your partner, combine roots and affixes from the Roots and Affixes charts to create words. Then isolate each word's root and affix(es). Finally, write the word's meaning, using your own words.

Word	Root / Affix(es)	Meaning
dismissive:	dis + mis + ive	inclined to send away

EXERCISE 7

A. Each item contains a definition followed by an excerpt from a reading in this unit. Read each definition. In each excerpt, circle and then write the word that corresponds with the definition. Then write another word with the same root.

	Definition + Word	Excerpt	New Word
1	Word that means "to gradually go from an advanced state to a less advanced state": *devolve*	This makes it all the more frustrating when trade talks break down and (devolve) into arguments and threats of retaliatory action.	*involvement*
2	Word that means "to think about or work on a particular subject, group, etc., especially because you think it is more important than others":	Ricardo concluded that even if a country—he postulated Portugal—were more efficient at producing both, it made economic sense for it to concentrate on the product where its advantage is greatest (wine, in Ricardo's example) and to buy the other product from elsewhere.	
3	Word that means "a serious argument or disagreement":	The WTO can function as an excellent mediator at early stages of a dispute, helping to solve many problems before they spiral out of control.	
4	Word that means "the action or business of bringing goods into one country from another to be sold:"	In the late 1960s and early 1970s, a Japan that had only recently found its economic footing enacted voluntary export restraints in deals with the United States, an arrangement that limited the import of Japanese vehicles to the United States.	
5	Word that means "to stretch, reach, or continue":	The lessons of comparative advantage theory extend beyond the realm of the job search.	
6	Word that means "not directly caused by or related to something":	Of course, in calling a position "better suited" and assigning a fruitfulness factor, we have to consider a number of attributes, most of which are only indirectly about money.	
7	Word that means "to become less in number, size, or amount, or to make something do this":	Without such nonmonetary enticements, the position's fruitfulness factor would decrease, and the OC of applying for it would increase.	
8	Word that means "the process of traveling through a place in order to find out about it or find something such as oil or gold in it":	In Brazil, rules for oil and gas exploration require that the national oil company, Petrobras, have a 30 percent stake or higher in any exploration activity.	

B. Compare answers with another student. Talk about how you can use this strategy to understand unfamiliar words you encounter in academic texts.

Go to **MyEnglishLab** to complete a skill practice.

APPLY YOUR SKILLS

WHY IT'S USEFUL By applying the skills you have learned in this unit, you can successfully read this challenging text and learn how global trade problems are typically addressed and resolved.

BEFORE YOU READ

A. Discuss these questions with one or more students.

1. Who do you think are the main players when it comes to making decisions about trade between countries? Who do you think is affected most by these decisions?

2. What do you know about your home country's position on global trade? Is free trade widely supported, or are there many sanctions on it? Give examples.

3. Have you heard or read about anything in the news lately related to trade agreements between particular countries? Summarize what you've heard.

B. Imagine that you will be participating in a small group discussion about the passage "World Trade Problems and Their Resolutions," which begins on the next page. Your group will be discussing the following questions. Keep these questions in mind as you read the passage.

1. What is the main responsibility of the World Trade Organization?

2. Why do countries often threaten to enact sanctions against other countries?

3. Usually, how successful are sanctions in forcing a change of behavior in the targeted country?

4. The free-trade system is built on the philosophy of countries "working things out." Who tends to gain from this? Who suffers?

5. Who does the WTO generally give preference to: nations with strong economies or economically disadvantaged ones? Why?

C. Review the Unit Skills Summary. As you read the passage, apply the skills you learned in this unit.

UNIT SKILLS SUMMARY

Recognize main ideas and supporting details.
- Identify main ideas and supporting details to focus on the most important information in a reading.

Identify sentence functions.
- Recognize and understand the functions of certain sentence types—such as topic sentences, supporting details, and end connectors—in order to quickly understand the meaning of paragraphs.

Identify topics and main ideas.
- Pinpoint the topic and main idea of a reading to understand the most important content.

Identify supporting details.
- Separate supporting details from less important details to focus on relevant information.

Summarize.
- Write a short version of a text to determine what you do and do not understand about its main ideas.

Analyze meaning using word parts.
- Study common roots and affixes to determine the meaning of unfamiliar words.

World Trade Problems and Their Resolutions

1 It is late 2014, and the leaders of the G20—a trade group comprising the world's biggest economies—are meeting in Australia. The gathered nations, ostensibly discussing free trade, debate the implementation of trade sanctions against one member, Russia, to express displeasure over actions in the Crimean Peninsula. It seems like an outright contradiction: A group meant to promote free trade is contemplating measures to choke it off. But when economics and politics meet, free trade and sanctions can counterintuitively exist together in a patchwork of policy measures. It is all part of how international trade agreements are enforced through a byzantine process that attempts to hold nations to the agreements they sign. It involves a lot of behind-the-scenes diplomacy, but also more open mechanisms such as trade courts invoked when a government refuses to play by the rules.

SANCTIONS AND PROTECTIONISM IN CONTEXT

2 The General Agreement on Tariffs and Trade (GATT) was enacted following World War II to avoid a reprise of the disastrous domino effect of protectionist policies adopted before and during the Great Depression of the 1930s. Since then, the nations of the world have, with a few exceptions, steadily, continuously moved toward greater freedom in international trade. By the time the World Trade Organization (WTO) was formed in 1995, most nations already had skills for working out problems among themselves. Despite all the nationalistic bluster of worldwide politicians, most leaders now go along with economists on the benefits of free trade. This makes it all the more frustrating when trade talks break down and devolve into arguments and threats of retaliatory action. In theory, this is when the WTO steps in with a solution everyone can accept. In practice, however, things may not go so smoothly.

3 The most common hiccup in the process is a nation's kneejerk response to institute sanctions on its own—for example, the 19 non-Russian members of the G20 threatening to enact sanctions against Russia over Russian actions in Crimea, or the United States enacting sanctions against Iran over a long list of disagreements, or nearly everyone enacting sanctions against North Korea. Presently, the United States has sanctions in place against 20 or so nations to protest political stances, and against dozens more for reasons related to drugs, terrorism, trade in illegal diamonds, and so on.

4 The natural question is whether this vast skein of sanctions—or sometimes merely the threat of them—actually causes nations to mend their ways. The answer is: sometimes, but not often. Proponents of sanctions point to South Africa, which did finally end its racially discriminatory apartheid system partly because of pressure from its trading partners. However, there are few such clear-cut successes in the history of trade sanctions. The threat of sanctions can often motivate a struggling country, but actually enacting them does little to change things. Economist Daniel Drezner points out that enacting sanctions tends to both hurt the targeted nation and depress the economy of the sanctioning nation. Usually the targeted countries remain unchanged and simply blame outsiders while tolerating a period of economic distress. Iran, for example, was the target of US trade sanctions for nearly 40 years, but despite the hardship these caused, the Iranian government and much of its population remained unmoved. Furthermore, the economic distress that sanctions generate tends to disproportionately harm poorer citizens while letting political elites claim that they are standing firm against foreign economic aggression.

HOW ARE PROBLEMS ACTUALLY RESOLVED?

5 Fortunately, most strong economies have responsible governments that recognize how important it is to mind one's p's and q's when

guiding world economics. However, especially in large, diverse nations like the United States, Brazil, and Russia, local governments and even well-organized private citizens can impede that careful work. Local politicians may oppose the building of, say, a Japanese-owned auto plant in some US state, stirring up enough support to impose state or local regulations that would kill the project. In Brazil, rules for oil and gas exploration require that the national oil company, Petrobras, have a 30 percent stake or higher in any exploration activity. International agreements often have anti-quota provisions, such "local-content" or "local participation" requirements—essentially de facto quotas—that are beloved by politicians and typically play very well with voters. Not surprisingly, complaints about such practices are often brought to the WTO (see Fig. 1.1).

6   In the rare instances where a modern, economically connected nation suddenly passes an obvious bit of protectionist legislation, international partners usually respond in a predictable way. Retaliatory sanctions are threatened, then enacted, and the WTO is petitioned for intervention. The offending nation offers a heartfelt shrug. The contentious piece of legislation may or may not be withdrawn. The world economy and the economies of the disputants are ever so slightly worsened. The whole drawn-out process can easily hurt

consumers, but the good news is that it rarely leads to a truly debilitating trade war.

WORKING THINGS OUT

7 These troubling trade issues rarely progress beyond complaints and WTO adjudication because all the parties have a stake in maintaining the status quo. The WTO can function as an excellent mediator at early stages of a dispute, helping to solve many problems before they spiral out of control. When the system fails to work, the failure might be catastrophic, but this is often due to a heated political history between the involved nations, such as countries with longstanding territorial disputes. The system works well enough, frequently enough, that most economists are genuinely surprised when nations actually appear to be heading toward real trouble that might destabilize the price of oil, for example.

8   Pragmatic leaders recognize that in the final analysis, the system depends on the parties "working things out." This may not always result in an even-handed resolution. In the late 1960s and early 1970s, a Japan that had only recently found its economic footing enacted voluntary export restraints in deals with the United States, an arrangement that limited the import of Japanese vehicles to the United States. This was essentially a quota by another name—technically absolving the United States of any accusations of breaking any rules. Those measures

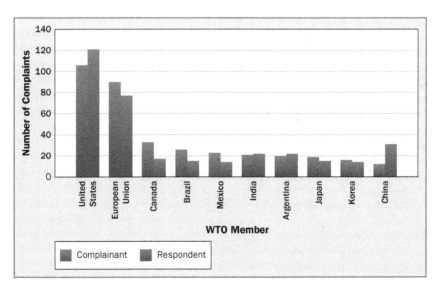

Figure 1.1 Ranking of top ten WTO members involved in complaints, 1995–2013   *Continued*

were enacted by Japan. In this situation, an economically recovering nation was forced to limit trade to avoid possible economic retaliation. In the long term, Japan fared well and grew to become a leading automotive manufacturer. The earlier deals with the United States were replaced by such practices as Japanese auto-making plants being located in the United States. The WTO has gotten involved occasionally, but "working things out" has generally sufficed for relations between Japan and the United States.

[9] Despite its authority, the WTO does not singularly have the leverage to prevent economically powerful nations from uniting their interests in a way that all but forces other nations to comply. At the other end of the spectrum, the truth is that sometimes there is no enforcement of the rules or only the weakest of responses. Still, while it may at times seem to offer an imperfect model of enforcement, arguably, the system has so far kept the gears of the global economy turning.

B. Reread the questions in Before You Read, Part B. Is there anything you cannot answer? What reading skills can you use to help you find the answers?

Go to **MyEnglishLab** to read the passage again and answer critical thinking questions.

THINKING CRITICALLY

Based on the information in Paragraphs 8 and 9 of "World Trade Problems and Their Resolutions," do international trade agreements prevent strong economies from pushing weaker ones around? Is the international trading system equal and fair for all members of the WTO? Explain your answers and support them with evidence from the reading.

THINKING VISUALLY

Look at Figure 1.1 in "World Trade Problems and Their Resolutions" and consider these questions:

1. Is there a correlation between the size of an economy and the number of disputes it is involved in?
2. Do you notice any other patterns in the data? Support your claims with specifics from the graph.

THINKING ABOUT LANGUAGE

Read these excerpts from "World Trade Problems and Their Resolutions." Underline the indicated part(s) of the words in bold. Then write definitions, using your knowledge about word parts and their meanings.

1. Underline the prefix:

   The gathered nations, ostensibly discussing free trade, debate the implementation of trade sanctions against one member, Russia, to express **displeasure** over actions in the Crimean Peninsula.

   Definition: *the feeling of being unhappy and fairly angry with someone or something*

2. Underline the root of *exceptions*. Underline the prefix of *continuously*. Underline the prefix and two suffixes of *international*.

   Since then, the nations of the world have, with a few **exceptions**, steadily, **continuously** moved toward greater freedom in **international** trade.

   Definition: ....

   Definition: ....

   Definition: ....

3. Underline the prefix.

   In the rare instances where a modern, economically **connected** nation suddenly passes an obvious bit of protectionist legislation, international partners usually respond in a predictable way.

   Definition: ....

4. Underline the prefix and root.

   Furthermore, the economic distress that sanctions generate tends to **disproportionately** harm poorer citizens while letting political elites claim that they are standing firm against foreign economic aggression.

   Definition: ....

5. Underline the root.

   Despite its authority, the WTO does not singularly have the leverage to prevent economically powerful nations from **uniting** their interests in a way that all but forces other nations to comply.

   Definition: ....

6. Underline the suffixes of *sanctions* and *political*.

   Presently, the United States has **sanctions** in place against 20 or so nations to protest **political** stances, and against dozens more for reasons related to drugs, terrorism, trade in illegal diamonds, and so on.

   Definition: ....

   Definition: ....

7. Underline the suffix.

   In the long term, Japan fared well and grew to become a leading **automotive** manufacturer.

   Definition: ....

▶ Go to **MyEnglishLab** to listen to Professor Clerici-Arias and to complete a self-assessment.

Exploring the secret lives of viruses

BIOLOGY

Cohesion

UNIT PROFILE

You will consider the subject of biology—specifically, the topic of vaccines. You will read about highly specialized vaccines and science's challenge of staying ahead of rapidly evolving pathogens (organisms that cause disease).

Preview the reading "DNA Vaccines" on page 72. Skim the reading. Do you notice any comparisons? Cause / effect relationships? Solutions to problems? Description language? Common collocations?

OUTCOMES

- **Understand cohesion**
- **Recognize patterns of cohesion: cause / effect, compare / contrast, problem / solution**
- **Understand cohesion in descriptions**
- **Use outlines and graphic organizers**
- **Recognize collocations**

GETTING STARTED

⏵ Go to **MyEnglishLab** to listen to Professor Siegel and to complete a self-assessment.

Discuss these questions with a partner or group.

1. What is a disease in your home country or another country that was once rampant but is now controlled by vaccine? What were the symptoms of the disease? How exactly was the situation brought under control?

2. Have the vaccines you have received been effective? Have you or anyone you know ever experienced any negative side effects as a result of being vaccinated? Has anyone you know ever contracted an illness after having received the vaccination against it?

3. If you currently reside outside your home country, were any vaccinations required prior to moving? If so, which? Is it justifiable for governments to require that foreign visitors be immunized against certain diseases? Why or why not?

For more about **BIOLOGY**, see ②③. See also Ⓦ and ⓄⒸ **BIOLOGY** ①②③.

FUNDAMENTAL SKILL
UNDERSTANDING COHESION

WHY IT'S USEFUL *Cohesion* means "staying together." By recognizing patterns of cohesion, you can understand how ideas in a reading relate to one another, which can help you organize the material mentally as you read it.

Academic reading involves processing complicated collections of information. Successful academic writers arrange their data, descriptions, and analyses in a form that promotes comprehension for most readers. A reading passage has **cohesion** if the author has effectively pieced the information together. Many cohesive devices—tools for creating cohesion—are obvious and easily recognized. You may know them as "transition words and phrases" (also called "signposts").

Common Transition Words and Phrases	
After this	On the other hand
Consequently	The problem is
However	Therefore
Most importantly	When

Other cohesive devices may be less obvious but are no less important:

- pronouns
  - personal pronouns (*he, it, they*, etc.)
  - demonstrative pronouns (*this, that, these, those*)
  - relative pronouns (*which, who, that*, etc.)
  - quantitative pronouns (*some, all, any, most*, etc.)
- specialized nouns, verbs, or adjectives (*puzzles, resolves, similar, outermost*, etc.)
- comparative or superlative adjectives and adverbs (*faster, more efficiently*, etc.)
- text-locator signals (*as we saw in Chapter 2, in the next section*, etc.)
- patterns of synonyms / near synonyms (*effort / initiative; quandary / dilemma*, etc.)

Understanding cohesion will enable you to connect ideas presented in a passage. This unit breaks the skill down into two supporting skills:

- recognizing patterns of cohesion: cause / effect, compare / contrast, and problem / solution
- understanding cohesion in descriptions

TIP

Grammar We have named many types of pronouns because 1) they are extremely important cohesive devices, and 2) it is important to recognize how many pronouns there are. People often think only of personal pronouns and dismiss them as having little meaning—and as therefore being unimportant. This is untrue. Pronouns may be "little," but they pack a lot of important information and a lot of cohesive power.

A. As you read the following passage, be aware of questions that form in your mind about relationships among ideas. After reading, write five of the questions that you asked yourself. You may want to use words from the box to help you express your thoughts.

Relationship Words			Topic Words		
after	cause	similar	active / inactive	immune	toxin
among	different	solution	antigen	pathogen	virus
before	problem		DNA	recognize	
between	result				

WHAT IS A VACCINE?

1   A vaccine is a biological substance that trains the body to fight off dangerous pathogens. The material in a vaccine contains antigens, which are the molecules found on the surface of pathogens. Typically injected into the body, the antigens in the vaccine mimic the real disease in the system. The antigens first trigger an immune system response that causes a wide array of cells, known collectively as antibodies, to fight them. The body then develops memory cells specific to recognizing those antigens in the vaccine. After developing this memory of the disease, the body will have the defenses to fight the real pathogen if it is exposed to it in the future. This encounter with a vaccine is often termed a "primary response." When the vaccinated person undergoes what is known as a "secondary response," or an encounter with the real pathogen, the immune system is able to respond to the pathogen quickly and more effectively than during the first episode. In much the same way an athlete might run through moves before a real competition, the vaccinated body practices its defenses before becoming infected with the bona fide disease.

2   Depending on the virus or bacteria they protect against, vaccines are made with different substances. Some are developed with live but attenuated viruses, which means that the virus has been weakened to the point of being, in effect, disarmed—unlikely to cause disease. Other vaccines are made with dead, or inactive, viruses. In addition, some vaccines, such as those termed "subunit," contain specific antigens but no viral particles. The vaccines that help ward off bacterial illnesses like diphtheria and tetanus contain toxoids, which are toxins rendered inactive. The body misinterprets exposure to toxoids as a threat, and it solves the perceived problem by producing antibodies to block the related toxin that would have been released by actual bacteria. Finally, there are new types of vaccines that are mostly still in the experimental stage, such as DNA-based vaccines—that is, vaccines that use DNA (deoxyribonucleic acid), which is a complex molecule that carries genetic information and is found in the nucleus of nearly every cell. As we will see in a later reading ("The MMR Vaccine and Anti-Vaxxers," p. 56), significant numbers of Americans have been misled

TIP

The description of processes is vital to scientific writing. More will be said about cohesion in process descriptions in Supporting Skill 2: Understanding Cohesion in Descriptions (p. 56). Before wrestling with their cohesive patterns, you have to recognize that a process is being described. In "What Is a Vaccine?" several processes are mentioned in connection with the extended definition. The first, most basic, is the process of injecting antigens into a body. The last is that the body produces antigens in response to toxoids. Between these two there are several more.

into seeing vaccines as a greater threat than the diseases they prevent. This is unfortunate. No matter what their type, vaccines are considered safe by medical professionals and help prevent crippling and potentially fatal illnesses.

B. Read each excerpt from the passage. Then choose the item that correctly identifies the cohesive device in the excerpt.

Excerpt

When the vaccinated person undergoes what is known as a "secondary response," or an encounter with the real pathogen, the immune system is able to respond to the pathogen quickly and more effectively than during the first episode.

In much the same way an athlete might run through moves before a real competition, the vaccinated body practices its defenses before becoming infected with the bona fide disease.

The antigens first trigger an immune system response that causes a wide array of cells, known collectively as antibodies, to fight them. The body then develops memory cells specific to recognizing those antigens in the vaccine.

Some are developed with live but attenuated viruses, which means that the virus has been weakened to the point of being, in effect, disarmed—unlikely to cause disease. Other vaccines are made with dead, or inactive, viruses.

The body misinterprets exposure to toxoids as a threat, and it solves the perceived problem by producing antibodies to block the related toxin that would have been released by actual bacteria.

As we will see in a later reading ("The MMR Vaccine and Anti-Vaxxers," p. 56), significant numbers of Americans have been misled into seeing vaccines as a greater threat than the diseases they prevent. This is unfortunate. No matter what their type, vaccines are considered safe by medical professionals and help prevent crippling and potentially fatal illnesses.

Cohesive Device

1. A pair of synonyms:
   a. *vaccinated / real*
   b. *undergoes / respond*
   c. *encounter / episode*
   d. *pathogen / system*

2. A signpost indicating a "comparison" cohesive relationship:
   a. *in much the same way*
   b. *before a real competition*
   c. *the vaccinated body*
   d. *before becoming infected*

3. A personal pronoun:
   a. *that*
   b. *them*
   c. *those*
   d. *the*

4. A quantitative pronoun:
   a. *some*
   b. *which*
   c. *to*
   d. *other*

5. A specialized noun, verb, or adjective that indicates a solution-to-a-problem cohesive relationship:
   a. *exposure*
   b. *solves*
   c. *perceived*
   d. *actual*

6. A text-locator signal:
   a. *as we will see in a later reading*
   b. *into seeing vaccines as a greater threat*
   c. *this is unfortunate*
   d. *no matter what their type*

Go to **MyEnglishLab** to complete a vocabulary exercise and skill practice, and to join in collaborative activities.

Cohesion 49

SUPPORTING SKILL 1
RECOGNIZING PATTERNS OF COHESION: CAUSE / EFFECT, COMPARE / CONTRAST, PROBLEM / SOLUTION

WHY IT'S USEFUL By learning to recognize three frequently employed patterns of cohesion, you will further develop your understanding of how authors produce unified ideas.

Writers employ a variety of **patterns of cohesion** to ensure that ideas in their articles, research papers, and other texts are unified and logically organized, both within paragraphs and throughout an entire reading. Three types of cohesion that are consistently used to achieve this end are **cause / effect, compare / contrast,** and **problem / solution**. Each type is characterized by unique words and phrases that serve to make these types of relationships clear.

CAUSE / EFFECT
The intent of the language used to achieve **cause / effect** cohesion is to demonstrate to a reader the reason, source, or event that brought about a particular result, outcome, or consequence.

Language Used with Causes	Language Used with Effects
As	As a result
As a result / consequence of [X cause],	As the aforementioned facts show / indicate, …
Because	Consequently
Because of [X cause],	One effect / result / offshoot / consequence of this is …
Due to [X cause], …	
For this reason,	So
Once	Therefore
Since	Thus
Taking [X cause] into consideration,	
The reason for [Y effect] is … [X cause]	
When	
Language Linking Causes and Effects	
[X cause] brings about [Y effect].	[Y effect] can be attributed to [X cause].
[X cause] contributes to [Y effect].	[Y effect] is caused by [X cause].
[X cause] creates [Y effect].	[Y effect] is the consequence / result of [X cause].
[X cause] generates [Y effect].	
[X cause] is responsible for [Y effect].	
[X cause] leads to [Y effect].	
[X cause] produces [Y effect].	
[X cause] results in [Y effect].	

In the following example, the "cause" marker in bold indicates the cause / effect relationship between the two ideas.

> **As a result of** receiving the vaccination against yellow fever, she was not concerned that she would contract the disease during her travels.

Another way of writing the sentence, while maintaining the original meaning, is with an "effect" marker:

> She received the vaccination against yellow fever; **therefore**, she was not concerned that she would contract the disease during her travels.

COMPARE / CONTRAST

A second type of cohesion often used by writers is **compare / contrast** cohesion. This category of cohesive patterns is employed to convey and highlight the similarities and differences between objects, ideas, people, places, and concepts.

The linguistic cues that typify compare / contrast cohesion include the following:

Compare		Contrast	
Also, …	Alternatively	In contrast	Though
As … as	Although	In contrast to / with, …	Unlike
Both X and Y …	But	In spite of	When comparing X to / with Y, …
Each	Compared to	Instead of	Whereas
In the same way, …	Despite	Is different	While
Like	Differ with respect to	Nevertheless, …	X and Y differ from each other
Likewise, …	Dissimilar	On the contrary …	Yet
Similar	Even though	On the other hand, …	
Similar to	However, …	Rather than	
Similarly, …	In comparison to / with, …	Than	
While			
X and Y are alike			

Study this example of some of the aforementioned compare / contrast phrases:

> **While** both the MMR (measles, mumps, rubella) and chickenpox vaccines are live attenuated vaccines, they **differ with respect to** the number of diseases they provide protection against. The former protects individuals from three, **whereas** the latter only offers defense against one.

In addition to the cues above, another very common way to discuss similarities and differences between entities is through the use of comparative and superlative adjectives and adverbs. This includes language such as *most virulent, stronger, least important, more quickly,* and *less intensely.* For example:

> Inactivated vaccines tend to be **safer** than live vaccines as they are **less potent** than live ones.

> In regions where a disease is spreading quickly, live attenuated vaccines are used **more frequently** than inactivated vaccines.

TIP

Think about the reading that you do in English for your classes. 1) Is one type of cohesive pattern especially common in readings about a particular topic? 2) Is one type of cohesive pattern easier for you to notice in English than other patterns? 3) Do you often notice the signposts we have been discussing? Which seem the most common? 4) Have you noticed other devices for signaling cause / effect, compare / contrast, or problem / solution cohesion?

PROBLEM / SOLUTION

Problem / solution cohesion is a third commonly used pattern. This type of cohesive language is used when a writer is discussing a situation, the problem(s) associated with that situation, solution(s) to the problem(s), and an evaluation of the solution(s). This chart contains phrases that are frequently employed to identify a problem and offer a solution:

Problem	Solution
A barrier to overcoming the problem is …	However, scientists found that if they [Y solution], then [Z good result].
Due to the aforementioned issue …	One solution was …
One obstacle [biologists] encountered was …	The answer to the problem was [Y solution].
One problem / issue is …	The key to solving the problem was …
[Scientists] are battling against …	They achieved this goal by …
Some of the complications associated with this include …	To solve this …
The biggest hurdle was …	[Y solution] serves as a solution to [X problem] …
The challenge was …	
The difficulty in / of [X problem] was …	
There were several drawbacks …	
This is ineffective because …	
Unfortunately, …	

Here is an example of "problem" language:

> **There were several drawbacks** to the plan, one of them being that it did not outline the specific methods scientists would use to research how individuals contract the disease.

Look at this example of "solution" language:

> **One solution** for safeguarding an individual who cannot be vaccinated against a disease **is** to prevent contact with others who have not been vaccinated.

Problem / solution cohesive phrases are not always separate from each other; in fact, you will often see them within one sentence. For example:

> **The challenge was** convincing college students to get the flu vaccine, and public health officials **achieved this goal by** opening up flu vaccine clinics in popular hangout areas on campus.

Sometimes, more than one cohesive pattern may be at work in a passage. Here's an example of compare / contrast, problem / solution language, and cause / effect within one sentence:

Compare / Contrast ————————————————————————— *Problem / Solution*

> **Despite** the **difficulty of** administering vaccines to young children, health officials maintain that neglecting these efforts would almost certainly **lead to** outbreaks of diseases that were thought to have been eradicated.

Link Cause / Effect ————

Cause / effect and problem / solution language are especially likely to interrelate. For example, language that demonstrates a "problem" can also represent a "cause." Study this example:

> **One issue** with the newly developed vaccine is its **relatively low level of immunogenicity**, and **because of this**, researchers are tirelessly working to increase this in clinical trials.

In this situation, *One issue* represents "problem" language, as it refers to the problem of the vaccine having a relatively low level of immunogenicity. *One issue* also serves as the "cause" for why researchers are working to increase the level of immunogenicity in the vaccine.

EXERCISE 1

A. As you read, highlight words and phrases that are examples of the cause / effect, compare / contrast, and problem / solution cohesion that you just read about. Consider how these examples contribute to the cohesiveness of the reading.

Live Attenuated Vaccines and Inactivated Vaccines

1   A vaccine's overall success in combating disease is an equation of many variables, including how effective, safe, durable, and cost-effective the vaccine is to produce. Of the many different types of vaccines, the two most basic forms are made from living, weakened viruses and from dead viruses. These primary forms are both used regularly for protection against dangerous diseases like polio, measles, and influenza, and the two forms have advantages and disadvantages. While both live attenuated (weakened) vaccines as well as inactivated (dead) vaccines work to safeguard individuals against illness, the former is generally more effective than the latter.

2   Live attenuated virus vaccines, such as those that protect against measles, mumps, and rubella, are produced in two ways. The first way is to use a nonpathogenic virus related to the real pathogen. The earliest smallpox vaccines were created in this manner, when physicians inoculated patients against the disease by exposing them to the cowpox virus—a close relative of the lethal smallpox virus. In contrast to this antiquated method of producing an attenuated vaccine, the second method is a step more complex, involving physicians weakening the virus in a laboratory, purifying the vaccination solution, and administering the vaccine orally or by injection. A challenge associated with these lab-produced live attenuated vaccines is that they must be refrigerated or they are rendered unstable. For this reason, they unfortunately are not easy to provide to lower-income nations where refrigeration devices are not abundant. Unlike live attenuated vaccines, inactivated vaccines are not produced with a living virus. Scientists use chemicals, heat, or radiation to render a pathogenic virus harmless, or "fixed." Inactivated vaccines, in contrast to perishable live-virus vaccines, can be reconstituted and easily stored. Inactivated vaccines include those against hepatitis A and rabies.

3   Live attenuated virus vaccines also create a stronger immunity to a disease than inactivated vaccines because the attenuated virus triggers a strong response of lymphocytes, which causes the body to produce more memory T and B cells that circulate in the blood and fight against the virus if it ever appears in the body again. In many cases, one or two doses of the vaccine confer a lifelong immunity on individuals. A live attenuated vaccine is the nearest thing to contracting the actual disease, so it provides the most resistance against the disease. Whereas live attenuated vaccines are quite potent, inactivated vaccines deliver a much weaker immune system response. As a result, they require several additional doses, known as boosters, to ensure that an individual's immune system is able to fight off the actual infection.

4   While live attenuated vaccines typically provide better protection against illnesses, a problem with these vaccines is that their strength tends to lead to a lower level of safety when compared with fixed-virus vaccines. When a vaccine's virus is alive, it can, on rare occasions, mutate back to its original, virulent form and cause a true infection. For this reason, live attenuated vaccines are not recommended for individuals with compromised immune systems, such as pregnant women or those who have undergone immune-system suppressing treatments like chemotherapy. Because attenuated vaccines can, though rarely do, mutate into virulence, inactivated vaccines are considered safer because the dead viruses cannot mutate. However, in the case of the polio vaccine, which comes in both forms, medical officials in parts of the world where polio is still endemic recommend using the live attenuated virus to inoculate against polio because it offers a stronger defense for both the individual and the region. The inactivated vaccine is typically used by health officials in the United States to attempt to solve the problem of accidental contraction of polio from the vaccine.

B. Read each excerpt from the passage and determine which cohesive device is used. Then write the item number in the correct category in the chart below.

1. These primary forms are both used regularly for protection against dangerous diseases like polio, measles, and influenza, and the two forms have advantages and disadvantages.

2. In contrast to this antiquated method of producing an attenuated vaccine, the second method is a step more complex, involving physicians weakening the virus in a laboratory, purifying the vaccination solution, and administering the vaccine orally or by injection.

3. A challenge associated with these lab-produced live attenuated vaccines is that they must be refrigerated or they are rendered unstable.

4. Unlike live attenuated vaccines, inactivated vaccines are not produced with a living virus.

5. As a result, they require several additional doses, known as boosters, to ensure that an individual's immune system is able to fight off the actual infection.

6. When a vaccine's virus is alive, it can, on rare occasions, mutate back to its original, virulent form and cause a true infection.

Cause / Effect	Compare / Contrast	Problem / Solution

C. Rewrite each sentence in Part B, replacing the cohesive device language with another word or phrase related to the given pattern of cohesion. Do not change the meaning of the sentence. It may be necessary to change the sentence structure.

1. ....

....

....

2. ....

....

....

3. ....

....

4. ....

....

5. ....

....

6. ....

....

D. Each of the following excerpts from the passage contains more than one cohesive device. Mark the sentences: Underline cause / effect language, circle compare / contrast language, and put brackets around problem / solution language.

1. For this reason, they unfortunately are not easy to provide to lower-income nations where refrigeration devices are not abundant.

   ....

2. Live attenuated virus vaccines also create a stronger immunity to a disease than inactivated vaccines because the attenuated virus triggers a strong response of lymphocytes, which causes the body to produce more memory T and B cells that circulate in the blood and fight against the virus if it ever appears in the body again.

   ....

3. Whereas live attenuated vaccines are quite potent, inactivated vaccines deliver a much weaker immune system response.

   ....

4. While live attenuated vaccines typically provide better protection against illnesses, a problem with these vaccines is that their strength tends to lead to a lower level of safety when compared with fixed-virus vaccines.

   ....

5. Because attenuated vaccines can, though rarely do, mutate into virulence, inactivated vaccines are considered safer because the dead viruses cannot mutate.

   ....

6. However, in the case of the polio vaccine, which comes in both forms, medical officials in parts of the world where polio is still endemic recommend using the live attenuated virus to inoculate against polio because it offers a stronger defense for both the individual and the region.

   ....

7. The inactivated vaccine is typically used by health officials in the United States to attempt to solve the problem of accidental contraction of polio from the vaccine.

   ....

Go to **MyEnglishLab** to complete a vocabulary exercise and skill practice, and to join in collaborative activities.

SUPPORTING SKILL 2
UNDERSTANDING COHESION IN DESCRIPTIONS

WHY IT'S USEFUL By recognizing the pattern of information in a description, you can develop a more accurate mental image of an object, person, place, or process.

Some patterns of cohesion are **spatio-temporal**. That means they reflect the way something exists in space or time. These cohesive patterns usually work with other cohesive devices, mixing in with the cause / effect, compare / contrast, and problem / solution cohesive patterns we have already seen.

> **TIP**
>
> **Nonlinear Cohesion** *An author might try to create spatio-temporal descriptions that "skip around." Rather than arranging information in a linear way, the author might move unpredictably in space or time. However, this nonlinear movement is very difficult to do successfully. If you ever see it, it will probably be in artistic writing like fiction, poetry, or drama—not in factual writing.*

Descriptions of physical entities—things, people, places—usually have **spatial cohesion**. The author organizes the presentation of information according to the position of things in relation to one another. Some examples of patterns are left-to-right (or right-to-left), top-to-bottom, and inside-to-outside. These arrangements are usually linear—that is, they start at one point and move continuously in one direction until the pattern is complete. If the description is complex, two or more spatial sequences might be combined. Look at this example:

> At the top of the device is a steel tube containing a lens, below which is a tray for holding the specimen. The entire device rests on a heavy base that contains springs to minimize vibration. A knob on the left side allows adjustment of the lens, while a hand rest on the right helps the observer steady himself or herself during observation.

In the example, a top-to-bottom cohesive pattern comes first. Then there is a left-to-right pattern.

Descriptions of processes usually have **temporal cohesion**. The author organizes information according to what happened first in time and then progresses until the last stage in time has been reached. Sometimes an author may begin to tell things in real-time order and then temporarily shift back in time—as in the technique called a "flashback," which is sometimes used in fiction to communicate memories. Temporary shifts to the future are also possible—a technique called "fast forward," which may communicate predictions. However, these techniques are mostly artistic (see the TIP). They are unusual in fact-based writing.

One last type of cohesion in descriptions is to arrange things according to a characteristic that can be charted on a **continuum**—for example, from largest to smallest, from cheapest to most expensive, from most harmful to least harmful, and so on.

EXERCISE 2

A. Read the passage, which is an excerpt from a much larger text about anti-vaccination sentiment in the United States. This excerpt—which only begins to introduce the reasons why some people oppose vaccination—focuses on some of the basics of the vaccination process. Consequently, this excerpt concentrates on some descriptions organized in a spatio-temporal way. As you read, highlight all instances of spatially cohesive physical descriptions and temporally cohesive process descriptions.

THE MMR VACCINE AND ANTI-VAXXERS

1 The measles virus, a microscopic, circular particle, contains a nucleic acid that is housed inside a protein coating. Along the surface of the protein are tiny receptors, also called antigens, that can latch onto the surface of a cell. Once the virus enters the body and attaches itself to human cells, it begins to replicate. After about a week of incubation, the first symptoms appear, which include a cough, a runny nose, and a fever. This early stage is followed by a rash, which starts as

tiny white spots inside the mouth. The illness then flares into a full-blown measles rash, with red spots that begin on the face and hairline and slowly travel down over the neck, chest, and arms. Finally, the rash spreads all the way to a person's legs and feet. One in four cases of measles requires hospitalization, and one in one thousand cases ends in encephalitis (swelling of the brain) or death from complications. The measles vaccine—which is typically given as part of the MMR vaccine (measles, mumps, and rubella)—prevents the illness by teaching the immune system to fight off the virus. But a rising tide of parents are refusing to vaccinate their children.

2   This refusal is not out of fear that the inoculation process is, in itself, traumatic. Granted, the apparatus used in vaccination can be a bit daunting in appearance to a child, especially the needle. Imagine a syringe held vertically, with its tip pointing upward. The kind typically used to vaccinate children has a needle that is 1 inch long and has a 25- to 27-gauge thickness (meaning an outer diameter of about 0.02 inch). On the inside, the needle is hollow (the hollow interior is called the *lumen*), and the outside surface is almost always made of shiny stainless steel. The needle consists of three parts. At the tip is the *bevel*, a slanted crosscut that forms the sharp end of the needle. The long body of the needle is called the *shaft*, and the base of the needle fits into a fixture called the *hub*, which holds the needle secure in the barrel of the syringe (the large tubular body with volume markings on it). Inside the hub, the base of a typical modern needle ends in a cone-shaped fitting that forms part of a connection called a *Luer lock*. The cone-shaped base of the needle may screw tightly onto a threaded projection on the barrel, or the needle may be pressed onto a pressure fitting of the barrel. Either way, the Luer lock ensures that the connection between needle and barrel is watertight and airtight, secure against any ambient contaminants. Fitting within the tube of the syringe is a movable plastic rod—the plunger—that terminates at the bottom of the whole assembly, in a flat plastic disk against which one's thumb is pressed while administering the injection.

3   Despite the use of scary-looking needles, vaccinating a child against measles, mumps, and rubella is simple. The first dose is administered within about three months after a child's first birthday, the second at the age of four or five years. The doctor finds a site on the child's thigh muscle—or the deltoid muscle at the shoulder for the second dose—that is thick enough to accommodate the needle. Stretching the skin flat, the doctor places the tip of the needle against the muscular area. The doctor holds the syringe with two fingers—typically the index finger and middle finger—just forward of the flange, which is like a flat plastic collar at the base of the barrel. His or her thumb is on the flat disk of the plunger. The shaft of the needle is held at an angle of 90 degrees to the skin surface. The needle tip penetrates the child's skin and travels through the subcutaneous fat and into muscle, but not so far into the muscle as to cause injury. After pressing the plunger of the syringe forward for a few seconds, the doctor withdraws the needle. The whole procedure takes perhaps 60 to 90 seconds, if the child holds still. No child likes it, but it causes lasting physical trauma for almost no one, and the value of the vaccine far outweighs any unpleasantness.

4   The real difficulty faced by vaccination programs is rejection not because of the pain of inoculation but because of the pernicious belief, increasingly common among American parents, that vaccines like the MMR cause health problems, most particularly, that they can cause autism. These falsehoods have dire consequences. If a parent chooses not to vaccinate a child, how could it affect others in the community?

5   This question accurately implies that a continuum of selfishness exists in this situation. At the least-selfish end of the spectrum are public health officials who work in the face of great criticism and irrational rancor from some parents to guard the herd immunity conferred by vaccination. Also unselfish, though not so much on the firing line, are parents who heed evidence-based advice and make sure their children get vaccinated. On the selfish end of the spectrum, the most

Continued

tainted persons include the author of the fallacious article linking vaccination to autism (see sidebar) and some of the publicity-seeking medical doctors who fell into line behind it. Not quite so far on the selfish end—but close—are the "anti-vaxxer" parents. Anti-vaxxer parents have made a calculation about relative harm—obviously acting in the (misguided) belief that measles poses less a threat to their children than autism. There is also a calculation based on self-interest that whatever harm may befall society as a whole, it is less than the potential harm to their child. The parents may be following their most basic, and honorable, instincts to protect their children, but we other members of the herd have a right to expect that this protection be informed by a thoughtful weighing of evidence, not credulous, knee-jerk iconoclasm. The twisted anti-vaxxer calculation and its unintended consequences have set back a number of public health efforts in the United States. Indeed, anomalously among developed nations, the United States has seen a troubling increase in the incidence of diseases previously thought to be under control, such as measles.

6   In 2000, the Centers for Disease Control (CDC) declared that measles was no longer endemic to the United States. However, since that time, there have been several major outbreaks of the illness due to flagging vaccination rates. In 2014, the CDC reported 634 measles cases for the year. Then in early 2015, a contagious person with measles passed the illness around while at a theme park in California, and the outbreak that followed affected more than 100 people in California alone. These outbreaks are troubling because of the severity of measles. The virus is highly contagious and infects up to 90 percent of unprotected individuals exposed to the bug.

Misleading Article, Troubling Reactions

Parents who decline vaccines for their children typically reject the vaccines because they fear that the biological substance in a vaccine contains harmful chemicals that cause neurological disorders. This erroneous belief originated with an article about the connection between autism spectrum disorder and vaccines that was published in 1998 in a medical journal. The author of the article claimed a link between the vaccines and the disorder, but the study was deemed to be flawed, and the journal later retracted the article. The scientist who authored the paper was subsequently discredited and barred from practicing medicine. Despite medical professionals finding the study and the doctor's methods fraudulent, the panic the article induced was widespread and enduring. People began to follow the ideas that were touted in the bogus study as a way to explain the frightening increase in the rate of autism cases in the United States. The people who choose not to vaccinate are now numerous enough to be considered a movement.

In an effort to encourage parents to vaccinate their children, health officials have conducted several studies on vaccines and autism since the publication of the article and have found absolutely no link between the two. Along with the medical community, state governments have also gotten involved and have begun taking legal action to protect citizens. In response to a law passed in 2015, for example, California and Vermont will no longer permit unvaccinated children to attend public school without a valid medical reason for not being vaccinated. Whether because of the law or the recent measles outbreak (or other causes), childhood vaccination rates rose in most counties of California in 2015, according to information released by the California Department of Public Health.

B. Read the questions and choose the best answers.

1. Which occurs last, after someone has contracted the measles virus?

   a. A rash on one's toes
   b. Flulike symptoms
   c. An oral rash
   d. A rash on one's torso

2. What is true about the hub of a syringe?

   a. It is inside the base of the needle.
   b. It is the material inside the barrel.
   c. It is where the base of the needle connects to the syringe.
   d. It is crosscut to make a sharp point.

3. Which description of "anti-vaxxer" demonstrates a greater harm to the safety of a society?

    a. Those who are more concerned with autism than measles

    b. Those who prioritize protecting their child over protecting a society in its entirety

    c. Both categories are equally threatening to a society.

4. Which statements are true of a syringe if it is held vertically with the point at the top? Choose TWO.

    a. The sharpest part faces the doctor.

    b. The flange is at the lowest part of the barrel.

    c. The lumen is inside the barrel.

    d. The plastic disk of the plunger is at the bottom.

    e. The top inch is made of stainless steel.

5. When administering a vaccination, what should a doctor do?

    a. Target the thigh for the second dose

    b. Insert the needle at the proper angle

    c. Get the needle deep into the muscle

    d. Apply pressure to the plunger for at least one minute

6. Which event happened first?

    a. More than 100 Californians contracted measles.

    b. More than 500 Americans were diagnosed with measles.

    c. A person infected with measles went to a US amusement park.

    d. Measles was deemed to be low risk and not widespread in the United States.

C. Below is a list of features described in the reading. Match each feature with the pattern of cohesion used to describe it in the reading.

Features	Pattern of Cohesion
.... 1. The symptoms of the measles virus	a. spatial — top / bottom
.... 2. The entire syringe for the measles vaccination	b. characteristics on a continuum
.... 3. The needle on the syringe	c. temporal — process
.... 4. How a doctor provides the vaccine to a child	d. both temporal and spatial
.... 5. The point of insertion of the vaccination needle	e. temporal — time
.... 6. The variation in "anti-vaxxers"	f. spatial — both inside / outside and top / bottom
.... 7. The prevalence of measles in the United States	g. spatial —outside / inside

Go to **MyEnglishLab** to complete a vocabulary exercise and skill practice, and to join in collaborative activities.

READING-WRITING CONNECTION
USING OUTLINES AND GRAPHIC ORGANIZERS

WHY IT'S USEFUL Using an outline or a graphic organizer while you read can be a useful way to help you process what you have read and organize your thoughts for future reading, writing, or study. This is particularly useful when reading a piece that contains many cohesive patterns.

When reading complex academic texts, it is easy to get bogged down in the details. Creating a visual representation of the ideas in the text is a useful strategy. Specifically, utilizing an **outline** or **graphic organizer** can aid in clarifying the nuances and complexities of such a reading, especially one that employs a diverse set of cohesive devices and writing patterns.

Recording information in visual form also creates a shorter, more approachable and personalized documentation of the reading, for future reference. Whether it be to help with writing a paper, studying for an exam, or synthesizing information from a variety of sources, creating a strong outline or graphic organizer makes a task more manageable.

SELECTING A STYLE OF VISUAL ORGANIZER
While the exact style of organizer you use is largely contingent on the type of text you are reading and your personal preference, the first step is to determine the information that it will contain.

Information
- What is your purpose? That is, what will you be doing with your notes, and how much information will you be recording in the visual organizer?
- How familiar are you with the information? The less familiar you are, the more necessary it may be to record information in order to help you understand and remember it.
- What is the most important information to record? It is impossible and impractical to reproduce an entire text in an outline or graphic organizer, so figure out what information is relevant and pertinent and what is extraneous.
- Which type(s) of cohesive devices seem to dominate the text? This may determine the type of organizer that is most appropriate.

Outlines
Outlines are useful because they typically replicate a text in its original order and are a familiar format that can be easily understood. They also demonstrate clear levels of the most important details, their subparts, and so on. However, they are often best suited for recreating readings that do not contain complex structures, such as time sequences, which may not be presented in a whole-and-subparts fashion.

Also it can sometimes be difficult to add more information after a section of an outline has been written—if you are writing by hand. This is not so much of an issue if you are creating your outline using a word processor.

The most important information in an outline should be left aligned, often with a Roman numeral, and each subordinate detail should be indented according to that same hierarchy. For each subsequent level, a new counting system is often used, such as letters and Arabic numerals:

I. Important Point 1
   A. Information set 1 about Point 1
      1. Further detail 1
      2. Further detail 2
   B. Information set 2 about Point 1
II. Important Point 2
   A. Information set 1 about Point 2
      1. Further detail 1
         a. Even further detail 1
         b. Even further detail 2
      2. Further detail 2
   B. Information set 2 about Point 2

GRAPHIC ORGANIZERS

Graphic organizers, often called mind maps, can be used as a more visual way of representing information. An advantage of graphic organizers is that it is usually fairly easy to go back and add information as new information comes about in the text. There are many different styles of graphic organizers, some of which may work especially well with a given structure. In most cases, however, multiple types of organizers could work for a given reading. Some special cases:

- **Temporal Description:** When organizing a reading that has a temporal cohesive pattern, it is often helpful to create a visual that reflects that process. For example, a timeline can be used to show a sequence of events that happen over time. The following is another example of a kind of visual that could be used to detail a process:

- **Spatial Description:** If a text is describing the physical arrangement of something—say, inside-to-outside or left-to-right—it may be useful to create a graphic organizer that mimics that spatial description. This is also true for other types of description that include a lot of detail but do not present a strong temporal component. With some spatial descriptions, it may be even more beneficial to draw a simple picture of the thing or scene being described, rather than trying to represent it with a graphic organizer.

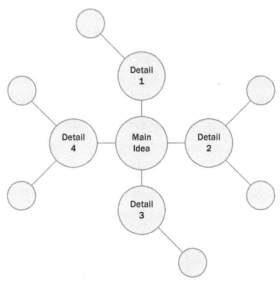

- **Compare / Contrast:** A Venn diagram is a very common graphic organizer used to demonstrate how two (or more) things are similar to and different from one another. Differences are included in the portion of the circles that do not overlap, and similarities are contained in the circles' intersection.

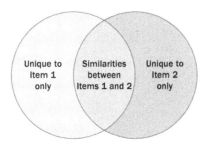

EXERCISE 3

A. Read the following paragraph. Then create an outline in the box to the right.

Similar to the hepatitis B vaccination, the vaccination for chickenpox also contains a small amount of the actual virus. The vaccination is designed to build immunity in those who receive the shot and to prevent them from contracting the disease. If someone who was not vaccinated contracts the virus, the symptoms, while not pleasant, typically run their course in less than ten days and are not incredibly severe. However, the disease is much worse for certain groups of people. This usually includes those with weakened immune systems, very young children, and older adults.

B. Read the following paragraph. Then complete the graphic organizer.

While there is little debate that getting the chickenpox vaccination is better than contracting the actual disease, there are still some side effects of the vaccination of which people should be aware. Some minor side effects include a fever, a rash, fatigue, and a headache. If these occur, they will not likely last long. In more extreme cases, side effects may include seizures, breathing problems, and a change in behavior. If any of these latter symptoms do appear, a doctor should be contacted immediately.

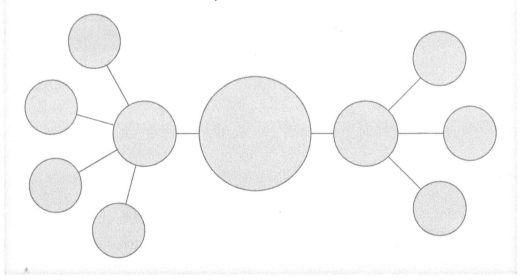

C. **Read the passage.**

POLIOVIRUS

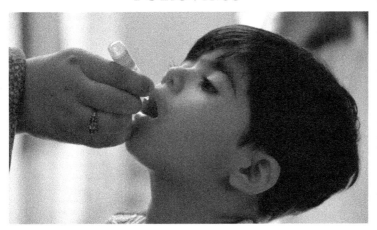

1   In the early 1950s in the United States, an epidemic swept through cities and towns, leaving more than 20,000 individuals paralyzed and more than three thousand dead. The crippling disease was caused by the poliomyelitis virus, a type of enterovirus that inhabits the gastrointestinal tract and spreads through droplets from coughing and sneezing, and through feces. A few years after the outbreak reached its peak in 1952, doctors developed a polio vaccine that very quickly made the disease rare in the United States, and in the late 1980s, health officials made a plan to do the same for the entire globe. Nearly 30 years later, however, physicians are still fighting to vaccinate vulnerable population groups in the nations of Pakistan and Afghanistan. An examination of polio eradication endeavors reveals that though health officials have made enormous progress, they still face obstacles in regions of the world plagued by violence, poverty, and endemic polio.

2   Polio, which mainly affects children, can cause a rapid onset of paralysis in approximately 1 out of every 200 cases of the illness. In addition, 5 to 10 percent of people who experience these paralytic symptoms will die from complications of the disease. If polio patients are lucky enough to recover their mobility and avoid permanent paralysis, the disease still causes neurological problems later in life. In 1988, 350,000 cases of polio in 125 nations were reported. That year, health officials formed an international Global Polio Eradication Initiative and began an aggressive campaign to rid the world of polio. Nearly three decades later, the statistics reveal incredible success. Cases of polio worldwide have decreased by 99 percent, and the World Health Organization (WHO) estimates that the eradication efforts have prevented paralysis in 13 million people and saved the lives of 1.5 million children.

Continued

3   While the force leading this feat is made up of international partners, the key tool against the virus is the vaccine for polio. Known as the oral polio vaccine, the vaccine uses a weakened form of the virus to build antibodies in the body and create an immune response that lingers in the mucous membranes. This live attenuated (weakened) vaccine provides protection, but it also carries risk. In rare cases, the attenuated pathogen in the oral polio vaccine could revert to its virulent form and cause the disease, which is known as vaccine-associated paralytic polio (VAPP) and occurs in approximately 1 in every 2.7 million first doses of the vaccine. The virus might then travel throughout a community, particularly if the community has unvaccinated individuals. This mutation and infection, known as circulating vaccine-derived poliovirus (cVDPV), has occurred approximately 24 times since 2005, and it has caused more than 750 cases of polio. cVDPV is considered a risk not only to individuals but also to eradication efforts because even if "wild" polio strains are eradicated, the vaccine itself could continue to cause the spread of polio.

4   Neither VAPP nor cVDPV can occur if the inactivated polio vaccine, which does not contain live viruses, is the agent of inoculation. Nations in which polio is no longer endemic, such as the United States, use this inactivated polio vaccine despite its somewhat lower level of protection because the risk associated with the oral vaccine outweighs the benefits. However, in nations where wild polio strains are still common, the use of the oral polio vaccine is considered the best choice epidemiologically because it protects against all types of polio, gives long-lasting immunity, and provides passive immunization within a community, according to the Global Polio Eradication Initiative. Once wild polio strains are no longer endemic to a nation, health officials recommend switching to the inactive vaccine.

5   In the two remaining nations with endemic polio, Pakistan and Afghanistan, more challenges exist against eradicating polio than simply combating the virus. Health workers continually face violent threats and attacks from members of the community who believe the vaccine causes harm to the community. For example, in January 2016, a suicide bomber blew up an eradication center, citing the common fear that the vaccination effort is a secret plan to sterilize children or to infiltrate the countryside with Western spies. Medical aid workers in Nigeria have faced similar attacks, but the campaign workers remained heroically persistent, and Nigeria was removed from WHO's list of polio-endemic nations in 2015.

6   That persistence will be necessary to finally rid the world of polio since even a few cases of the disease can lead to worldwide outbreaks. To attain eradication of an illness, particularly in nations destabilized by political fragility and poverty, it will be important for health care workers to make vaccinations part of routine health care programs and find community-based allies who will take ownership of the eradication initiatives, be it for polio, measles, or any other infectious disease. In the case of polio eradication, once the human-created problems are resolved, the polio vaccine can be given to everyone, and then health care workers can switch the vaccine type to the inactivated vaccine, which will prevent the rare incidence of vaccine-derived poliovirus. In closing, it is worthwhile to note that despite the difficulties that health officials face, the Global Polio Eradication Initiative has helped millions of children avoid polio. In addition, the initiative has trained local epidemiologists and put into place disease surveillance systems that can alert officials to other infectious diseases in the future.

D. Complete the following steps, based on the reading.

1. Create a graphic organizer that depicts the chronology of polio-related events described in the article. Be sure to include the following years and time periods: 1950s, 1952, 1980s, 1988, 2015, 2016.

2. Create an outline that includes the most important facts about polio described in Paragraph 2.

3. Use a graphic organizer to present the most important information about the oral polio vaccination discussed in Paragraph 3.

4. Make an outline or graphic organizer based on Paragraph 4 that contrasts nations with and without widespread cases of polio.

5. Using an outline or graphic organizer, demonstrate your understanding of modern attempts to eradicate the polio virus, as described in Paragraph 6.

Go to **MyEnglishLab** to complete a vocabulary exercise and skill practice, and to join in collaborative activities.

LANGUAGE SKILL
RECOGNIZING COLLOCATIONS

WHY IT'S USEFUL To really know a vocabulary item, you have to recognize and understand the collocations in which it commonly occurs. If you understand collocational groups as you read, you will be far more efficient than if you read word by word.

Collocations are common combinations of vocabulary items. If two items occur together often, they strongly **collocate** with each other. (*Collocation* comes from Latin words meaning "being located together.") Native speakers and other proficient speakers of English have strong intuitions about which items strongly collocate. They also have strong intuitions about which vocabulary items do *not* strongly collocate with each other.

That is why, for example, when they want to speak of the action of producing homework, native and proficient speakers of English are very likely to use the verb *do* and very likely to think that the verb *make* "sounds weird." These intuitions can be confirmed by looking at large databases of language (called *corpora*; singular *corpus*). In fact, computer analysis of a corpus of several hundred million words shows that forms of the verb *do* are the most likely words to occur with the word *homework*—more than twice as likely as any other verb.

Consider this example. The strong collocations appear in bold.

> Edward Jenner, a young British physician, established in 1796 that cowpox inoculations can **confer immunity against** the **dreaded disease** smallpox—for which the **death rate** was typically 35 percent. Jenner was certainly not the first person to **come up with the idea** of inoculating against smallpox, nor was he even the first to use cowpox to do so. However, by **conducting a simple experiment**, he **made it crystal clear** that there was a **causal relationship** between exposure to cowpox and **immunity to** smallpox. Jenner's experiment was simple but **posed a huge risk** to **someone else**, an eight-year-old boy named James Phipps. It's **hard to believe**, but James's father allowed Jenner to inject the boy with cowpox serum from an infected milkmaid and then two months later, to **give him injections**, one in each arm, of actual smallpox material. James did not **come down with the disease** because he had **developed immunity to it. There is no way that** any physician today could do what Jenner did. It would **violate every standard**, ethical and legal, that **governs the behavior** of medical researchers in **modern times**.

The many strong collocations in this paragraph hint at the degree to which English is strongly patterned into vocabulary chunks. You can *give* or *confer* immunity. This immunity can be *to* or *against* a disease. Diseases are often *dreaded*. You can *pose* a risk, *come down with* a disease, *violate* a standard, and *govern* behavior.

How do you strengthen your knowledge of collocations? The most effective way is to read a lot so that you often see collocational groups in action. After enough exposure, certain combinations just seem "right" or seem to "go together." At that point, you will have begun to develop the same instincts that guide native and proficient English speakers.

Also, as we note in the section Using Dictionaries to Strengthen Vocabulary (p. 16), your dictionary can help you learn collocations. Collocations may be indicated in the dictionary by being set in bold, in italics, or within example sentences. Consider the entry for *disease* from the *Longman Advanced American Dictionary*.

---

dis·ease/dɪˈziz/ S3 W1 *noun*

1 [countable, uncountable] MEDICINE an illness of the body or mind, that affects a person, animal, or plant:

*Thousands of people are **dying of** hunger and **disease**.*
***Heart disease** is a leading cause of death in the U.S.*
*Tina **suffers from a** rare brain **disease**.*
*The viruses **cause disease**.*
*She **contracted the disease** (=became infected with the disease) through a mosquito bite.*
*Unclean drinking water can **spread disease** (=cause other people to become infected).*
*There is no known **cure for the disease**.*

⎱ Some collocations shown in example sentences

2 [countable] something that is seriously wrong with society, or with someone's mind, behavior, etc.:

Loneliness is a disease of our urban communities.

[**Origin**: 1300–1400 Old French *desaise*, from *aise* **relaxed feeling, comfort**]

Other collocations noted in related vocabulary items

—diseased *adjective*

→see also HEART DISEASE, ILLNESS, SOCIAL DISEASE, VENEREAL DISEASE

COLLOCATIONS
VERBS
have a disease (*also* **suffer from a disease** *formal*)
*How long **have** you had the **disease**?*
*About three million people **suffer from** the disease.*

catch/get a disease (*also* **contract a disease** *formal*)
*He **contracted the disease** while traveling in Africa.*

develop a disease
*A few years ago, she **developed a** serious lung **disease**.*

carry a disease (=be able to pass it on)
*They tried to kill the insects that **carried the disease**.*

spread a disease/pass on a disease (*also* **transmit a disease** *formal*)
*Parents may **transmit the disease** to their children.*

die of/from (a) disease
*He was hospitalized and nearly **died from a** mysterious **disease**.*

cause a disease
*Smoking is probably the major factor **causing** heart **disease**.*

diagnose a disease (*also* **diagnose somebody with a disease**) (=say what a disease is)
*The **disease** is difficult to **diagnose**.*
*He was **diagnosed with** the disease 10 years ago.*

prevent a disease
*It has been claimed that fiber in the diet can help **prevent** many serious **diseases**.*

treat a disease
*The **disease can be treated** with antibiotics.*

cure a disease
*The plant was believed to **cure diseases**.*

fight (a) disease (=try to stop it continuing)
*Some bacteria help the human body **fight disease**.*

a disease spreads
*The government has no idea how far the **disease** has **spread**.*

EXERCISE 4

A. Reread "The MMR Vaccine and Anti-Vaxxers" on page 56. The following target vocabulary words appear in that reading in acceptable collocations. The dictionary entries here illustrate other acceptable collocations. Which example sentences (a, b, c, d) feature the target word in a collocation that is found in the reading or the dictionary entry? Choose TWO or more.

1.

> **cal·cu·la·tion** /ˌkælkyə ˈleɪʃən/ *noun* [countable usually plural, uncountable]
>
> **1** MATH the act of adding, multiplying, dividing, etc. numbers in order to find out an amount, price, or value:
> *Ellie looked at the report and **did** some quick **calculations**.*
> **by somebody's calculations/according to somebody's calculations**
> ***By our calculations,** it will cost about $12 million to build.*
>
> **2** careful planning in order to get what you want:
> *He defeated his opponent with **cold** political **calculation**.*
>
> **3** when you think carefully about what the probable results will be if you do something

   a. To estimate how long his hike would take, he made a quick **calculation based** on his experience.
   b. **By my calculations**, this dinner is going to cost us more than we paid for groceries for the entire week.
   c. It is easy to predict how the stock market will change over the next year with one **calculation at** recent trends.
   d. The bank robbers plotted their scheme with **cold calculation**.

2.

> **con·se·quence** /ˈkɑnsə kwɛns, -kwəns/ W3 AWL *noun*
>
> **1** [countable usually plural] something that happens as a result of a particular action or situation:
> *Ignoring safety procedures can have potentially tragic consequences.*
> **consequence of**
> *The economic consequences of vandalism are enormous.*
> *You should be aware of the **consequences of** your actions.*
> **suffer/face the consequences** (=accept and deal with bad results of something you did)
> *He broke the law, and now he must face the consequences.*
>
> **2 as a consequence (of something)** as a result of something:
> *Tyler rarely paid for anything and, **as a consequence,** had no idea what things cost.*
>
> **3 of little/no/any consequence** without much importance or value:
> *Your opinion is **of little consequence** to me.*

   a. Because she wanted to see the movie so badly, the long line outside the theater was **of little consequence** to her.
   b. Meeting her favorite musician was a **resulting consequence** of getting backstage passes to the concert.
   c. Failing his final exam was an **unintended consequence** of a late night hanging out with friends and not studying.
   d. When the boy lied to his parents, he had to **suffer the consequences** of his poor choice after his parents found out what he had done.

3.

> **fight¹** /faɪt/ `s1` `w1` *verb* (*past tense and past participle* **fought** /fɔt/)
>
> **1** `HIT PEOPLE` [intransitive, transitive] to use physical force, for example hitting or kicking, or weapons to try to hurt someone:
> *The children fought and pushed in line.*
> **fight with**
> *The two boys are always **fighting with** each other.*
> **fight about/over/for**
> *They were **fighting over** a woman.*
> *She and her brother used to **fight like cats and dogs** (=fight violently).*

a. The woman and her husband sometimes **fight on** the best politician for which to vote.

b. The siblings have always **fought like cats and dogs**, even though they really do love each other.

c. The doctor prescribed antibiotics to help **fight off** the infection the patient got from the cut.

d. Her immature attitude caused her to constantly **fight with** her friends over insignificant issues.

4.

> **nose¹** /noʊz/ `s1` `w2` *noun*
>
> **1** `ON YOUR FACE` [countable] the part of a person's or animal's face used for smelling or breathing:
> *He broke his nose playing football.*
> *the guy with the big nose*
> *Here's a Kleenex–**blow your nose** (=clear it by blowing).*
> *Robin has a sore throat and a **runny nose** (=liquid is coming out of her nose because she has a cold).*
> *Davey, don't **pick your nose** (=clean it with your finger)!*
> *Her eyes were red and her **nose was running** (=liquid was coming out of it).*
>
> **2 (right) under somebody's nose** so close to someone that he or she should notice something, but does not:
> *The drugs were smuggled in **under the noses** of customs officers.*
>
> **3 stick/poke your nose into something** to show too much interest in private matters that do not concern you:
> *No one wants the government **sticking its nose into** the personal business of citizens.*
> → see also NOSY

a. Even though she got over her cold, she is still suffering from a **runny nose**.

b. He was extremely nosy, so his friends needed to tell him to stop **sticking his nose into** places it didn't belong.

c. The mother always keeps her **nose at** her kids' business because she wants to make sure they stay out of trouble.

d. Because he just had surgery for his broken nose, the doctors warned him to not **blow his nose** until it begins to heal.

5.

> **pro·cess¹** /'prasɛs, 'proʊ-/ `s1` `w1` `AWL` *noun* [countable]
>
> **1** `DEVELOPMENTS` SCIENCE a series of things that happen naturally and result in gradual change:
> *The aging process is natural and unavoidable.*
> *Listening is an improtant **part of the** learning **process**.*
>
> **2** `ACTIONS` a series of actions that someone takes in order to achieve a particular result:
> *Some rebel groups oppose the **peace process**.*
> *The American **political process** can be confusing to foreigners.*
> **a process of (doing) something**
> *It's time to **start the process of** applying to colleges.*
> **a process for (doing) something**
> *The airline has tried to **improve the process for** checking in passengers.*
> *Making the cheese was a **slow process**.*
> *What's the next **step in the process.***
>
> **3 be in the process of doing something** to have started doing something and not yet be finished:
> • *Our office is **in the process of** upgrading all the computers.*
>
> **4 process of elimination** a way of discovering the cause of something, a right answer, or the truth by carefully examining each possibility until only the correct one is left:
> • *A **process of elimination** may help you find out why your child can't sleep.*

a. Even though they were finished baking the cake, they still had to complete the most important **step in the process**: frosting it.

b. Although not the standard way of doing things, her **process for** preparing for exams worked well for her personal studying style.

c. Through the **process of elimination**, they found the one wire that was broken and preventing the lights from working.

d. As a professor in military sciences, he is responsible for delivering many lectures on the complex **war process.**

6.

val·ue¹ /'vælyu/ [s2] [w1] *noun*

1 MONEY
a) [countable, uncountable] the amount of money that something is worth, or the qualities that something has that make it worth the money that it costs:
   Real estate ***values are rising*** *once again.*
value of
   The exact ***value of*** *the painting is not known.*
   We have seen a rapid ***increase in the value of*** *technology stocks.*
   The dollar has ***fallen in value*** *against the yen.*
of value
(=worth a lot of money)
   The only item ***of value*** *was a small bronze statue.*
→ see also MARKET VALUE, STREET VALUE
b) [countable, uncountable] used to talk about whether something is worth the amount of money that you paid for it:
value for your money/dollars
   Customers are demanding more ***value for their money.***
something is a good/great/poor etc. value (for the money)
   The software ***is a great value*** *and easy to use.*
c) [countable] used in advertising to mean a price that is lower than usual

a. Because the children had been spoiled their whole lives, their parents were worried that they had never learned the **value of** a dollar.

b. Thanks to the excellent real estate market, the house the young couple just bought was **a great value** based on its size and condition.

c. Even though he thought the figurines would be good collectors' items and that he would become rich off of them in a few years, it turns out that they had significantly **fallen in value** over the past five years.

d. She decided to buy the car immediately because of its excellent **value at the money.**

B. Compare answers with a partner.

Go to **MyEnglishLab** to complete a skill practice.

APPLY YOUR SKILLS

WHY IT'S USEFUL By applying the skills you have learned in this unit, you can successfully read this thought-provoking reading about the latest type of vaccinations.

BEFORE YOU READ

A. Discuss these questions with one or more students.

1. If you could create a vaccination for any disease that exists today, what would it be and why? Do you think it is scientifically possible to eradicate all serious diseases on Earth?

2. Do you think companies that create vaccinations should be able to become rich off of selling their drug? Why or why not?

3. Would you consider trying a vaccination that is still in the clinical trial phase or is allowed in other countries but not your own? Where would you draw the line? Explain.

B. Imagine that you will be participating in a small group discussion about the passage "DNA Vaccines," which begins on the next page. Your group will be discussing the following questions. Keep these questions in mind as you read the passage.

1. When did DNA vaccines first begin being developed? Are they widely available today?

2. How are DNA vaccines created?

3. What occurs on a cellular level when DNA vaccines enter the body? What is the end result?

4. Why are DNA vaccines considered safer than attenuated vaccines?

5. What is one reason why DNA vaccines remain in clinical trials?

C. Review the Unit Skills Summary. As you read the passage, apply skills you learned in this unit.

UNIT SKILLS SUMMARY

Understand cohesion.
• Recognize patterns of cohesion to understand how ideas relate to one other.

Recognize cause / effect, compare / contrast, and problem / solution cohesion.
• Develop your understanding of how an author produces unified ideas through three types of cohesion.

Understand cohesion in descriptions.
• Recognize the pattern of information in a description to develop accurate mental images of an object, person, place, or process.

Use outlines and graphic organizers.
• Use an outline or graphic organizer to help you organize your thoughts and understand what you read.

Recognize collocations.
• Recognize and understand the collocations in which a vocabulary item commonly occurs.

A. Read the passage. Annotate and take notes as necessary.

DNA Vaccines

1 In the more than two centuries since vaccination became a mainstream medical approach, medical researchers have struggled to stay ahead in the contest with mutating microbes and to create vaccines that are safer and more directly targeted. The established home territory of vaccination involves live attenuated and inactive vaccines (see "Live Attenuated Vaccines and Inactivated Vaccines," p. 53). A little further out from the medical home country are subunit and conjugate vaccines, which were actually not possible before modern technological advances. The outer frontier of vaccines is now in the realm of DNA vaccines, which research first began to test only in the 1990s. Though the vast majority of DNA vaccines are still in clinical trials, the global market for research and development for the vaccines has grown tremendously over the past several years. Given DNA vaccines' ability to elicit strong immune responses, as well as their relative safety, they could eventually achieve the goal of inoculating patients against the most devastating maladies of our age, including malaria, HIV, and cancer.

2 When compared with more-established methods, DNA vaccines have an altogether different approach. Neither attenuated nor killed pathogens are involved, nor are pathogen subunits isolated. Instead, DNA vaccines utilize the genetic material from the virus or bacteria to elicit an immune response. To create a DNA vaccine, scientists first isolate a gene from the target pathogen. They then splice the viral gene into a double-stranded DNA vector. This vector, also known as a bacterial plasmid, is a circular genetic structure that can be replicated and purified in a laboratory. Once the plasmid is established, the vaccine is ready to be injected. In some cases, plasmid is layered on the outside of gold beads or particles. It is then shot directly into tissue through a "gene gun," which uses high-pressure gas to insert particles into living tissue. Research indicates that scientists are also attempting to convert the DNA vaccine into a liquid form that could be used as nasal spray.

3 After the DNA vaccine is injected into the body, it accomplishes two goals: creating a strong cellular response and building a potent humoral, or antibody, response. Once injected, DNA vaccinations prompt helper T cells and B cells to multiply and produce memory cells, as well as activate cytotoxic "killer" T cells, which are the toughest pathogen fighters. This type of dual cellular and humoral response gives long-lasting immunity, similar to what most live attenuated vaccines achieve; however, they are much safer than a live-virus vaccine. Attenuated vaccines, though very effective, are capable of occasionally causing the illness they are meant to provide protection against. Because DNA vaccine plasmids are not living, and thus nonreplicating, there is no risk that they may cause an illness. For these reasons, DNA vaccines hold enormous promise in the development of both prophylactic vaccines, such as those that target a pathogen, as well as therapeutic vaccinations, which fight cancer.

4 Because of the advantages of DNA vaccines, their release to the public is highly anticipated. However, unfortunately, virtually all remain in clinical trials. So far, in clinical trials with human patients, DNA vaccines have shown mixed results. While they are both cost effective and well tolerated by patients, some concerns hamper their advancement. In particular, these are related to their ability to disrupt cellular processes and produce anti-DNA antibodies, resulting in too low a level of immunogenicity. This essentially means that they are not effective enough. It is worthwhile to note, however, that the technology for improving the vaccines' efficacy has advanced by leaps and bounds since the 1990s.

5 Though DNA vaccines are not yet established in a vaccination schedule or routinely given to HIV or cancer patients, it is likely that this will change in the relatively near future. If global market reports are any indication, scientists foresee continued breakthroughs in the vaccines

sooner rather than later. The global DNA vaccine market was valued at nearly $244 million in 2013 but is expected to grow to $2.7 billion by 2019, according to some market research. In addition, new biotechnologies and nanotechnologies are helping to improve the vaccines. Scientists are in uncharted waters with the development of DNA vaccines, but they are hopeful that in the not-so-distant future, advancements will lead to the eradication of currently incurable illnesses.

B. Reread the questions in Before You Read, Part B. Is there anything you cannot answer? What reading skills can you use to help you find the answers?

Go to **MyEnglishLab** to read the passage again and answer critical thinking questions.

THINKING CRITICALLY

In "DNA Vaccines," you read that DNA vaccines have levels of immunogenicity that are lower than they should be, which is why essentially all of them remain in clinical trials. Research the vaccine used against one of these illnesses: typhoid fever, yellow fever, or rotavirus. Then answer the following questions:

- Did this vaccine encounter the same problem as DNA vaccines do (too low a level of immunogenicity) when it was in clinical trials? If so, what steps were taken for it to be approved for use?
- If it did not, were there any other issues during clinical trials, such as participants experiencing adverse side effects? If so, what were those issues?
- What steps were taken to get this vaccine past clinical trials and approved for use? How long did the entire vaccine development and approval process take?
- Are there any attempts to develop DNA vaccines for the disease you chose?
- Based on your findings and answers, what conclusions can you draw about the disease and vaccine you researched?

THINKING VISUALLY

Study the graph. Based on what you read in "DNA Vaccines" as well as what you read earlier in the unit about other more established vaccine types, what do you think might account for projections shown in the graph? Consider specific features of DNA vaccines, including but not limited to the following: the process through which they are created, their method of inoculation, their effectiveness, and any known advantages and disadvantages.

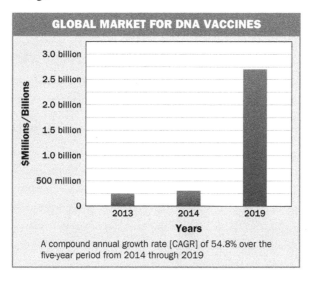

GLOBAL MARKET FOR DNA VACCINES

A compound annual growth rate [CAGR] of 54.8% over the five-year period from 2014 through 2019

THINKING ABOUT LANGUAGE

Read these excerpts from "DNA Vaccines" and notice the collocations in bold. Use the collocation feature of a print or online dictionary, an online corpus, or an Internet browser to search for each collocation. For each collocation, choose two example sentences that use the collocation and write them on the lines. Remember to cite your sources.

1. In the more than two centuries since vaccination became a mainstream medical approach, medical researchers have struggled to **stay ahead** in the contest with mutating microbes and to create vaccines that are safer and more directly targeted.

   Sentence 1: ....

   Source: ....

   Sentence 2: ....

   Source: ....

2. Though the vast majority of DNA vaccines are still in clinical trials, the **global market** for **research and development** for the vaccines has grown tremendously over the past several years.

   Sentence 1: ....

   Source: ....

   Sentence 2: ....

   Source: ....

   Sentence 1: ....

   Source: ....

   Sentence 2: ....

   Source: ....

3. For these reasons, DNA vaccines **hold** enormous **promise** in the development of both prophylactic vaccines, such as those that target a pathogen, as well as therapeutic vaccinations, which fight cancer.

   Sentence 1: ....

   Source: ....

   Sentence 2: ....

   Source: ....

4. So far, in clinical trials with human patients, DNA vaccines have shown **mixed results**.

   Sentence 1: ....

   Source: ....

   Sentence 2: ....

   Source: ....

5. It is worthwhile to note, however, that the technology for improving the vaccines' efficacy has advanced by **leaps and bounds** since the 1990s.

Sentence 1: ....

Source: ....

Sentence 2: ....

Source: ....

6. If global market reports are any indication, scientists foresee continued breakthroughs in the vaccines **sooner rather than later**.

Sentence 1: ....

Source: ....

Sentence 2: ....

Source: ....

7. The global DNA vaccine market was valued at nearly $244 million in 2013 but is **expected to grow** to $2.7 billion by 2019, according to some market research.

Sentence 1: ....

Source: ....

Sentence 2: ....

Source: ....

8. Scientists are in **uncharted waters** with the development of DNA vaccines, and they are hopeful that in the not-so-distant future, advancements will lead to the eradication of currently incurable illnesses.

Sentence 1: ....

Source: ....

Sentence 2: ....

Source: ....

▶ Go to **MyEnglishLab** to listen to Professor Siegel and to complete a self-assessment.

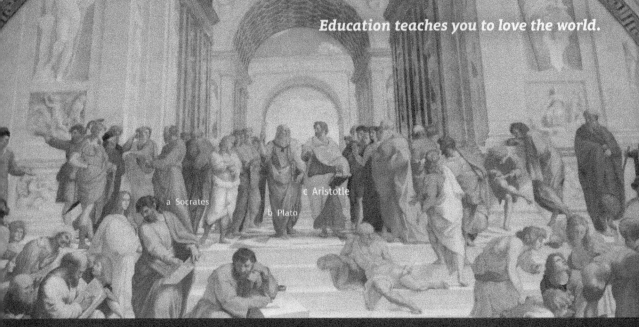

Education teaches you to love the world.

a Socrates

b Plato

c Aristotle

HUMANITIES

Fluency and Accuracy

UNIT PROFILE

In this unit, you will consider the subject of education and values—specifically, classical philosophers' thoughts about education. You will study Socrates's influence, Plato's Academy, and Confucius's thoughts.

Look at the reading "Confucius's Influence" on page 100. Set a timer and read through once as smoothly as you can. Don't stop to reread parts, to look up words, or for any other reason. Stop the timer. How long did it take you? How much did you understand?

OUTCOMES

• Develop reading fluency

• Increase fluency

• Tolerate ambiguity

• Recognize and use rhetorical techniques

• Understand nominalization

GETTING STARTED

▶ Go to **MyEnglishLab** to listen to Professor Harrison and to complete a self-assessment.

Discuss these questions with a partner or group.

1. What is your personal definition of *education*? Is it something that happens only in an academic setting like a high school or university? Does it mean students listening and taking notes as their professor speaks, or does it involve discussion with the teacher and among students? If you could change your current educational system, what would that entail?

2. Consider the moral doctrines and codes, approaches to education and the concept of knowledge, and political views of some philosophers you are familiar with.

3. What do you already know about the Greek philosophers Socrates, Plato, and Aristotle? What do you already know about the Eastern philosopher Confucius?

For more about **HUMANITIES**, see ② ③. See also W and OC **HUMANITIES** ① ② ③.

FUNDAMENTAL SKILL
DEVELOPING READING FLUENCY

WHY IT'S USEFUL Most readers of academic English must handle large volumes of text, so they have to be efficient. They have so much to read that they cannot afford to spend too much time on any single reading passage. Developing greater fluency is the key to accurate reading at the necessary pace.

The word *fluency* comes from the same root as the word *flow*. Someone who is fluent in a language can deal with words and ideas as they flow during communication. A fluent reader can move at a steady, almost native-like pace while understanding enough of a reading passage to get the main points. In fluent reading, one moves steadily through a passage as it progresses from one topic to another. There is very little stopping, going back over parts, or word-by-word reading.

This unit breaks **fluency development** down into two supporting skills:

- increasing fluency
- tolerating ambiguity

NOTICING ACTIVITY

A. To work on building fluency, read the passage on the next page three times, following these instructions:

1. First time: Set a timer for 2 minutes. Read the whole piece in that time, without stopping or going back over any parts of the reading. Then answer the True / False questions that appear after the reading.

2. Second time: Set a timer for 1 minute 30 seconds. Read the whole piece again in that time. Check your answers to the True / False questions, and change any that you think are incorrect.

3. Third time: Set a timer for 1 minute. Read the whole piece again in that time, or as close to that time as possible. Once again, check the True / False questions and change any answers you think are incorrect.

4. Reflect on this experience. How did you feel during each reading iteration? Did you feel equally comfortable each of the three times you read? If not, when did you feel most comfortable? Did you increase your understanding with each reading? Did you change any answers even after the third reading? Do you think your reading was most fluent the third time through? Discuss your answers with a partner.

> **TIP**
>
> *Reading fluency involves the concept of **automaticity**, the understanding of words and structures so automatically that you are not even aware that you are doing so. Naturally, automaticity takes a long time to develop, but if you are an advanced student, you have probably experienced it at some point: You do some reading in English, the ideas come through to you, and only afterwards do you realize, "I understood that without even thinking about the words or structures."*

> **VOCABULARY TIP**
>
> *Fluency improves as your comprehension of multiword vocabulary items grows. (See the section Recognizing and Learning Multiword Vocabulary Items, p. 125.) The efficiency of knowing and using multiword items contributes to both speed and accuracy.*

WHAT DOES *EDUCATION* MEAN?

[1] The etymology of the word *education* implies much more than learning, and encompasses both the personal development and academic training of an individual. *Education* is derived proximately from the Latin verb *educare*, "to bring up," and more distantly from the Latin verb *educere*, "to bring forth." *Educere* can be further dissected into the prefix *e-*, meaning "out," and the verb *ducere*, meaning "to lead." As evidenced by the historical etymology of the word, education is more than just schooling. Some education theorists reference the Latin roots and argue that the purpose of education is to draw out the inherent abilities of young people to hone their intellectual thought and moral reasoning. Others see something else in the etymology—that when you educate someone, you draw the person forth from his or her limited individual circumstances into a wider community. An educated person expands and is concerned with matters beyond the family, the neighborhood, or the hometown.

[2] The modern usage of the word *education* stretches beyond formal schooling to encompass countless avenues of mentorship and personal growth. As presently conceived, *education* can refer to an adult's job-training and to self-directed study of a topic of personal interest, and it is of increasingly less consequence whether it happens within the physical walls of a classroom or the virtual walls of online programs. Whereas the terms *academy* and *academia*, both derived from the location of Plato's lectures in ancient Greece, refer to a physical space and an institution, *education* is less spatially constrained. It's a process that can play out nearly anywhere and is perhaps most effective at drawing a person out of the parochial if it proceeds along many dimensions at once.

B. Read the statements about the passage. Then mark each statement as *T* (True) or *F* (False).

.... 1. The word *educate* comes from two Latin verbs, *educare* and *educere*.

.... 2. Education is an inherent part of learning.

.... 3. The word *educere* makes some people see education as a process of drawing out a young person's talents.

.... 4. The word *educere* makes some people think of education as drawing a person beyond his or her home setting.

.... 5. Since Plato's Academy existed before Latin was spoken, most experts do not consider its activities real education.

.... 6. If you teach yourself how to do something, it is learning but not education.

.... 7. Some education takes place online, without any face-to-face interaction between teacher and learner.

.... 8. The term *academy* implies a place more strongly than the term *education* does.

Go to **MyEnglishLab** to complete a vocabulary exercise and skill practice, and to join in collaborative activities.

SUPPORTING SKILL 1
INCREASING FLUENCY

WHY IT'S USEFUL By effectively recognizing words and correctly interpreting their meanings, you will increase your reading fluency, ultimately becoming a more successful academic reader.

Fluency, or the ability to read a text at a good pace, automatically, and with solid comprehension, is essential to academic proficiency. Reading speed is part of it, but fluency is much more than that. We will consider speed, automaticity, and accuracy—three of the main aspects of fluent reading.

One obvious factor in fluency is **pace**, or reading speed. Reading speed is typically measured as the number of words that a reader can read within a minute (WPM). The formula for measuring this is:

> **CULTURE NOTE**
> *Some typical—and not-so-typical—reading speeds:*
> *Average third-grade students = 150 WPM*
> *Average college students = 450*
> *Average "high-level execs" = 575*
> *Speed readers = 1,500*
> *World speed reading champion = 4,700*

Number of words ÷ Time in seconds	= X words per second	x 60 seconds	= **WPM**
For example, if you are reading a 750-word text and you complete it in 1 minute 34 seconds, you would first convert the time to seconds: 60 seconds + 34 seconds = 94 seconds. The equation would look like this:			
750 ÷ 94	= 7.98	x 60 seconds	= **479 WPM**

At the heart of fluency is **automaticity**. The term refers to a reader's ability to rapidly recognize thought groups and decode their meanings without being consciously aware of doing so. Dysfluent readers tend to pause at each word they encounter to determine its meaning before moving on. They spend so much time translating and rereading that the result is often poor comprehension of the overall meaning of the text. However, a more fluent reader will automatically recognize groups of words and their meanings, allowing the reader to move through the reading at a steady pace. The reader is then able to make connections between ideas, which ultimately leads to strong comprehension of a text. When a text is read aloud, this processing of thought groups results in good prosody—that is, stress, intonation, and elision between structures. In silent reading, there is a kind of mental prosody that characterizes smooth progress through the text. The key characteristic of automaticity is that it involves unconscious processing; your mind is not focused on the code—the language itself—but on the meaning, and you realize only after you have finished that you have been reading with automaticity.

> **TIP**
> ***Extensive Reading and Fluency***
> *Researchers say that extensive reading—enhancing reading skills through reading large amounts of material—is key when working to become a more fluent reader. By regularly reading texts at your reading level, over time you will begin to spend less time decoding meanings of individual words, eventually automatically accessing their meanings. As a result, you will be better able to build bridges between groups of words and phrases and thus see a significant improvement in your overall understanding of a text. In order to make strides in your reading fluency, it is important to set aside time for extensive reading, as only with a significant amount of exposure to reading material will you make progress. Note that this material does not have to be academic material; actually, you will likely advance more quickly if you choose material that you are interested in.*

Accuracy, a third element of fluency, is a reader's ability to adequately comprehend what he or she is reading. Accurate comprehension is the real test of whether a reader is fluent or just fast. A fast reader who understands very little has not developed much real reading proficiency.

The following passage is an excerpt from the upcoming reading "Aristotle and Alexander the Great." Set a timer for 30 seconds and read until that point. Mark where you ended. Read the passage a second time and do the same. Did you get any further in your reading?

TIP

One way to increase reading accuracy is by listening to a voice reading a comprehensible text. This could be any native speaker or proficient speaker of English—your professor, a friend, or even an actor reading the text of an audiobook. Then practice reading the same text out loud to a partner, recording your voice. After you have finished, listen to the model voice again and compare it against your recording. Ask yourself these questions and then ask your partner to give you additional feedback:

1. Do you know the meanings of most of the words that you read? Were you able to put them together into thought groups, rather than process them as individual words?
2. Did you stop or backtrack at any point while reading? Why? Was it because of grammar? Unfamiliar vocabulary? Difficult content?
3. After you finished reading, were there any parts of the reading that still didn't make sense to you? Try reading those parts again more slowly.
4. At which parts in the reading process did you feel most fluent? Why?

Alexander the Great (356–323 BCE) was arguably the most famous pupil of the legendary philosopher Aristotle—and the most infamous. When Alexander was in his early teens, his father, King Philip II of Macedonia, undertook an extensive search for a suitable tutor for his son and selected Aristotle, who tutored Alexander from age 13 to 16. The significance of Aristotle's mentorship of the prince cannot be overstated since Alexander highly respected Aristotle, and Aristotle's teachings had significant influence on Alexander. While Alexander ushered in the Hellenistic period, an age of cultural pluralism and artistic expression in ancient Greece and Persia, he did so ruthlessly, causing death, displacement, and upheaval throughout the 10,000-mile stretch of Europe and Asia that he conquered. The young Alexander was likely not taught such excessive, savage behavior by his teacher. Aristotle advocated what is known as the golden mean, a gentle philosophical principle whereby the individual can achieve virtue, or excellence, through balance and moderation. Alexander, however, either failed to understand or renounced outright Aristotle's theory of virtue and balance. The reasons for this are unclear, though they were probably due to Alexander's hubristic adherence to an ethic of heroism that twisted Aristotle's ideas about courage.

EXERCISE 1

A. Read the passage, which contains 528 words. Time yourself reading it and then calculate your words per minute. Read it a second time and do the same. Did your words per minute increase after the second reading?

Aristotle and Alexander the Great

1   Alexander the Great (356–323 BCE) was arguably the most famous pupil of the legendary philosopher Aristotle—and the most **infamous**. When Alexander was in his early teens, his father, King Philip II of Macedonia, undertook an extensive search for a suitable tutor for his son and selected Aristotle, who tutored Alexander from age 13 to 16. The significance of Aristotle's mentorship of the prince cannot be overstated since Alexander highly respected Aristotle, and Aristotle's teachings had significant influence on Alexander. While Alexander ushered in the Hellenistic period, an age of cultural pluralism and artistic expression in ancient Greece and Persia, he did so **ruthlessly**, causing death, **displacement**, and upheaval throughout the 10,000-mile stretch of Europe and Asia that he conquered. The young Alexander was likely not taught such excessive, savage behavior by his teacher. Aristotle advocated what is known as

the golden mean, a gentle philosophical principle whereby the individual can achieve virtue, or excellence, through balance and moderation. Alexander, however, either failed to understand or **renounced** outright Aristotle's theory of virtue and balance. The reasons for this are unclear, though they were probably due to Alexander's hubristic **adherence** to an ethic of heroism that twisted Aristotle's ideas about courage.

2   The precise instruction Aristotle gave Alexander cannot be known since none of the philosopher's extant texts mention his student, but it is likely that Aristotle **infused** his lessons of logic, rhetoric, botany, zoology, and other classical subjects with the ethics of moderation. Under Aristotelian philosophy, excess in behavior and character leads to failures of a person to develop virtue, and thus happiness, while the person who exercises self-control and respect cultivates virtue and harmony. However, Aristotle essentially limited his ideas of who could achieve this virtue to Greek male citizens. He **unequivocally** accepted slavery and was blatantly ethnocentric, a discrimination that had far-reaching consequences when he taught his pupil to deal with foreigners in the same manner as animals or plants. Aristotle also indulged Alexander's love of the heroic virtue in Homer's *Iliad*, which Alexander sought to emulate by achieving greatness through battle and heroic conquest. Alexander's **lofty** goal to conquer the world and his inability or unwillingness to moderate his behavior may have also been **bolstered** by the oracle at Delphi, a priestess in an ancient temple who prophesied that Alexander was unbeatable.

3   Regardless of his reasons, Alexander followed an **unwaveringly** opposite path from Aristotle's ideals of a balanced life of virtue. A few years after Aristotle tutored Alexander, the young prince inherited a kingdom that faced uprisings from the city-states of ancient Greece as well as the possibility of annihilation by the enormous Persian Empire, which had repeatedly attacked Greece. Alexander's father had planned to conquer Persia, and Alexander carried out those intentions. His troops preemptively attacked Persia, and despite being outnumbered, he defeated the Persians. He then marched victoriously through Asia Minor, Persia, the Levant, and Egypt on his journey to seek greatness. Alexander turned back in his conquest only at the northern edges of India after his men refused to follow him any further. Alexander died before ever returning to his native land.

B. Read the statements about the passage. Then circle *T* (True) or *F* (False).

T / F   1. Alexander the Great was infamous for being a student of Aristotle's.

T / F   2. Alexander the Great was unintentionally violent in his efforts to conquer a huge amount of land in Europe and Asia.

T / F   3. Alexander the Great rejected Aristotle's theory of virtue and balance because he believed that it was invalid.

T / F   4. Aristotle taught that a result of an individual's lack of self-control and moderation in comportment is the inability to cultivate integrity.

T / F   5. Alexander the Great had strong beliefs in the righteousness of slavery.

T / F   6. Alexander the Great and his army triumphed over the people of Persia, following the wishes of his father.

C. Discuss with a partner how many words per minute you read when you went through the passage the first time and the second time. Were the times different? What might have caused the difference?

D. Work with a partner to develop speed in scanning. One student chooses List A and the other List B. Set a timer for 3 minutes 30 seconds. Without using a dictionary and to the best of your ability, write definitions for the words on your list. These words are in bold in the reading. Were you able to complete the task in the time allowed? How was this "speed-scanning" different from fluent reading? Discuss with your partner.

List A

1. infamous ....

2. ruthlessly ....

3. displacement ....

4. renounced ....

5. adherence ....

List B

1. infused ....

2. unequivocally ....

3. lofty ....

4. bolstered ....

5. unwaveringly ....

Go to **MyEnglishLab** to complete a vocabulary exercise and skill practice, and to join in collaborative activities.

SUPPORTING SKILL 2
TOLERATING AMBIGUITY

WHY IT'S USEFUL An **ambiguous** part of a reading is a part that seems to have several possible meanings, and you may not be able to decide exactly which possibility is best. In most reading situations, you have only limited time to complete the passage and move on. You simply have to tolerate the ambiguity—accept it and go forward. If you do well at tolerating ambiguity, you can read effectively and understand much of what you read despite a few unclear parts. You will remain calm despite the occasional lack of clarity, and you will maximize your understanding of the parts that are accessible to you.

Every reader—even one with a lot of experience—encounters some reading passages that are difficult or even impossible to understand.

Some Possible Causes of Ambiguity

- The reading is about a very complicated or specialized topic of which the reader has little knowledge.
- Many words or phrases in the difficult passage are unknown to the reader, and it is impossible to look them up or get their meanings from context.
- The grammar of the difficult passage is complex or unusual; this is especially a problem with passages that were written long ago or are in a nonstandard variety of English.
- The difficult part of the passage contains cultural or historical references unfamiliar to the reader.
- In an effort to be entertaining or artistic, the author states ideas indirectly, metaphorically, or in an otherwise unusual way.

> **TIP**
>
> *Study Skill Psychologists and cognitive scientists point out that tolerance of ambiguity in everyday life is essential in becoming a stable, well-adjusted adult. Many situations in life are complex, poorly explained, or uncertain in other ways. The most practical response to this uncertainty is to accept a certain amount of it without getting anxious.*
>
> *Research into language learning shows that a high tolerance for ambiguity correlates strongly with effective study skills and higher second-language proficiency overall. Your task as an academic reader is to transfer your everyday ambiguity-tolerance skills to your reading behavior. Interestingly, it appears that a moderate level of tolerance is best. A student who is too tolerant of ambiguity may not work hard enough to achieve understanding, while one who is too intolerant has difficulty learning because anxiety blocks the process.*

You may be thinking that you can resolve any ambiguity. You can look up unknown words. You can do some extra reading to understand difficult topics. You can ask your friends or colleagues to explain cultural references. This is probably true, if you have enough time. However, you also have to develop strategies for dealing with ambiguity that you cannot resolve.

Tolerance of ambiguity is strongly related to fluency. (See the TIP.) It is also strongly related to active-reading strategies. (See the section Reading Actively, p. 3.) Here are some characteristics of a reader who has a strong tolerance of ambiguity:

- While reading a passage for the first or second time, the reader does not stop reading to look words up in a dictionary; any reference to dictionaries comes later, if time permits.
- The reader keeps reading at a steady pace even if some grammatical structures seem unusual and hard to comprehend.
- The reader is comfortable developing guesses about the meaning of a passage, even if a lot of possible information is either not provided at all or appears later in the passage.

- In a related matter, the reader takes risks in expressing—via notes, tentative answers to questions, or discussions with other readers—his or her guesses about meaning.
- The reader remains open to the cultural and social orientation of the author and / or the presumed majority of other readers; the reader works to understand the culture, even if he or she dislikes or does not identify with it.
- The reader manages time well, recognizing limits on how much time can be spent on reading, how much on answering questions or discussion, and so on.
- The reader calmly accepts that comprehension may remain incomplete for quite a long time.

EXERCISE 2

A. Follow these steps:

1. Read the passage on the following page one time, limiting your reading time to 2 minutes 25 seconds. Then
   - answer the questions after the reading as well as you can in 3 minutes.
   - mark any parts of the reading that you find ambiguous. You can do this by underlining, highlighting, or circling the ambiguous parts.
2. Read the passage a second time. Again, limit your reading time to 2 minutes 25 seconds. Then
   - revise your answers to the questions in no more than 3 minutes.
   - mark any parts of the reading that you still find ambiguous.
   - mark any parts that you had noted as ambiguous after your first reading, but which became clear after your second reading.
3. Discuss your reading experience with one or more other students. Then compare your points of uncertainty with your partners' points of uncertainty.
   - How much of the passage was ambiguous or unclear to you after your first reading? How did you feel about having so much uncertainty?
   - How did your second reading of the passage affect the amount of ambiguity? If many parts became clearer, why did this happen? Did you notice new aspects of the reading that clarified things?
   - Did you feel rushed during your first time reading the passage?
   - Did you feel rushed during your second time reading it?
   - Do any parts of the passage remain unclear to you? Review the list of possible causes of ambiguity on the previous page. Which cause explains why a part is still unclear?
   - Are there any answers that you remain uncertain of?

FACTUAL DIGRESSIONS IN LITERATURE

1   When *Moby Dick* by Herman Melville was published in 1851, it broke ground for American literature in countless ways, which is one of the reasons it is considered by many even now, after a century and a half of competition for the title, the Great American Novel. Still, its revolutionary, unusual aspects were triggers for controversy at its outroll, through the long years of its settling into the canon, and even through questionable editorial gymnastics such as a 20th century gutting that removed all of its famous digressions about things as different as cetaceans' taxonomical zoology and the joinery of American pulpits. Yet it is in these digressions— seemingly careless wanderings away from the main plot—that *Moby Dick* is at its most modern.

2   During the mid- to late 20th century, the crystalline travel writing of Bruce Chatwin about Patagonia and Paul Theroux about central Asia, not to mention the consciously mechanistic works of Tracy Kidder (*House, The Soul of a New Machine*) and Robert Pirsig (*Zen and the Art of Motorcycle Maintenance*) attracted nonspecialist readers, particularly those primed by the "New Journalism" of such far-lesser lights as Hunter S. Thompson— readers who wanted such digressions, who thrived on the spice of verifiable fact along with narrative development. It was, in a way, a new realism, flowering at a time (the 1960s to 1980s) when other cultural streams, from Bohunk fashion to visual arts psychedelia, drenched much of American culture in a lavender-colored, patchouli-scented downpour of ideas.

B. Check (√) the statements that are true, according to the passage. If a statement is false or if the passage does not say whether a statement is true or false, do not make any marks.

☐   1. *Moby Dick* is a novel.

☐   2. *Moby Dick* was published long ago.

☐   3. *Moby Dick* is less respected now than when it was first published.

☐   4. There are parts of *Moby Dick* that do not relate to the main plot of the story.

☐   5. In parts of *Moby Dick*, scientific information about whales appears.

☐   6. Modern writers no longer use digressions like those in *Moby Dick*.

☐   7. Bruce Chatwin wrote about travel.

☐   8. Bruce Chatwin was British.

☐   9. Paul Theroux is an American.

☐ 10. Works by Tracy Kidder and Robert Pirsig are similar in that they mention mechanisms.

☐ 11. Hunter S. Thompson was a better writer than the other four mentioned in this paragraph.

☐ 12. Factual digressions in literature were unusually realistic in the culture of the era from the 1960s to the 1980s.

C. Follow these steps:

1. Read the following passage one time, limiting your reading time to 2 minutes 25 seconds. Then
   - answer the questions after the reading as well as you can in 3 minutes.
   - mark any parts of the reading that you find ambiguous. You can do this by underlining, highlighting, or circling the ambiguous parts.

2. Read the passage a second time. Again, limit your reading time to 2 minutes 25 seconds. Then
   - revise your answers to the questions in no more than 3 more minutes.
   - mark any parts of the reading that you still find ambiguous.
   - mark any parts that you had noted as ambiguous after your first reading, but which became clear after your second reading.

3. Discuss your reading experience with one or more other students. Then compare your points of uncertainty with your partners' points of uncertainty.
   - How much of the passage was ambiguous or unclear to you after your first reading? How did you feel about having so much uncertainty?
   - How did your second reading of the passage affect the amount of ambiguity? If many parts became clearer, why did they do so? Did you notice new aspects of the reading that clarified things?
   - Did you feel rushed during your first time reading the passage?
   - Did you feel rushed during your second time reading it?
   - Do any parts of the passage remain unclear to you? Review the list of possible causes of ambiguity on the previous page. Which cause explains why a part is still unclear?
   - Are there any answers that you remain uncertain of?

PLATO'S ACADEMY

1   Plato's Academy, which flourished in an ancient olive grove near Athens, served as a nonsectarian intellectual environment where pupils learned through dialectic discourse. The Academy, which Plato founded in 387 BCE, was the first school of higher learning in the Western world and continued for nearly a thousand years after the death of the philosopher. The school was secular, having no interest in tales of gods—but this did not make it unusual in Greek education. The Academy also avoided pressing any political ideology, even though Plato's personal political convictions were critical of the Athenian democracy, and in his *Republic* he envisioned a utopian society that deviated considerably from his contemporary political environment. The pupils of the Academy did not receive didactic instruction on his nontraditional political ideology but rather deliberated on and debated the tenets of Plato's doctrines and metaphysics.

2   Plato's metaphysics deal with philosophical idealism, which holds as its central principle that reality consists only of ideas or thoughts that humans bring to their consciousness. Central to Platonic idealism is his theory of Forms, in which he argues that Forms, or templates of truth, goodness, and justice, are latent within the human soul and are apprehended or made manifest to the mind through philosophical *anamnesis*, or recollection. Plato's Forms arose out of his dualistic division between the physical, visible world and the non spatiotemporal, yet intelligible, world, where he believed true reality and the Forms existed, along with the immortal soul. This

reality is only dimly hinted at in actual objects, such as a table or a turtle, which are imperfect expressions of the Forms "tableness" or "turtleness." Humans, of course, experience objects and emotions via the senses, but Forms are intelligible not by sensation but through intelligence. Like other Hellenistic period philosophers, Plato concerned himself with ideas about cultivating goodness, beauty, and justice within the individual to bring about moral virtue and the betterment of society. Plato was the first Western philosopher to discuss idealism and focus his teachings on the nature of matter, truth, the human psyche, and the origin of thought.

3   It should be noted that though Plato's Academy is remembered for housing the study of Platonic metaphysics and epistemology, its other purpose was the study of mathematics. One story, which is likely more fable than architectural record, states that an inscription above the door to the entrance to the Academy read, "Let no one who is not a geometer enter here," a play on the popular inscription found on the doors of sacred Athenian buildings, which read, "Let no unfair or unjust person enter." Plato, though not remembered as a mathematician, stressed the study of mathematics as a way to understand the universe through the development of abstract thought. This thread of mathematical education that existed in Plato's Academy has founded the modern study of the Mathematical Platonism, a term for the idea that there are abstract, true mathematical concepts that exist independent of human awareness. Like Plato's Forms, Platonism in mathematical philosophy hypothesizes that individuals discern, rather than invent, latent, universal truths of mathematics.

4   Parts of Plato's philosophy are highly criticized or wholly rejected by modern audiences, including doctrines found in the *Republic* that value hierarchical order above personal liberties. The Platonic perspective, however, is far-reaching in Western education, beginning with the etymological connection between the Academy and academics today. Plato's *Allegory of the Cave*, which illustrates his Forms and describes the liberating force of knowledge, is the clearest example of how academics attempt in some part to use Plato's dialectic to draw out knowledge and reason within students.

D. Check (√) the best word or phrase to complete each statement, according to the reading. Hint: The first and second times you answer the questions, make your checkmarks *very light*, as you may want to change answers. Then discuss your answers with another student. Use information and examples from the passage to explain and support your answers.

1. Plato's Academy was located ....

    □ a. in an area with a lot of trees   □ b. in the heart of a large city

2. The Academy .... after Plato's death.

    □ a. closed a few years   □ b. remained open for centuries

3. In most Greek schools other than the Academy, religious instruction .... emphasized.

  □ a. was   □ b. was not

4. Plato's criticisms of Athenian democracy .... part of the instruction at the Academy.

  □ a. were   □ b. were not

5. Plato's *Republic* advocated ....

  □ a. disobeying the political leaders   □ b. setting up a political system better than
     of Athens   what Athens had

6. *Anamnesis* is a way of ....

  □ a. encountering Forms   □ b. achieving justice

7. "Tableness" and "turtleness" are examples of ....

  □ a. Objects   □ b. Forms

8. The inscription "Let no one who is not a geometer enter here" is meant to indicate
   that ....

  □ a. the Academy taught mathematics   □ b. the Academy considered
     as well as philosophy   mathematics sacred

9. Plato believed that mathematical truths were similar to philosophical truths because ....

  □ a. their nature could be accessed   □ b. they were beyond the mind's ability to
     by abstract thought   understand

10. Plato did not believe that mathematics was .... by humans.

  □ a. understandable   □ b. invented

11. In modern education, Plato's ideas are not generally ....

  □ a. studied   □ b. accepted

12. Plato's *Allegory of the Cave* is now ....

  □ a. a popular play   □ b. an exercise in thought

Go to **MyEnglishLab** to complete a vocabulary exercise and skill practice, and to join in collaborative activities.

READING-WRITING CONNECTION
RECOGNIZING AND USING RHETORICAL TECHNIQUES

WHY IT'S USEFUL Reading passages, especially those written by highly skilled authors, are not just packets of information. Readings have personalities, which are defined by the techniques authors use to present information. There are many dozens of such rhetorical techniques; by recognizing a few of the most common, you can appreciate the whole character of a reading. If you learn them well enough, you can use them to add personality to your own writing in English.

Rhetoric can mean several things. The meaning we are interested in is the art of speaking or writing effectively or persuasively. Our attention will focus on effectiveness, not necessarily persuasion, because the readings in this unit are meant to inform or explain, not to persuade.

This chart names, explains, and includes examples of some rhetorical techniques:

Rhetorical Technique	Explanation	Example
Acknowledgement of opposition	The author mentions that others disagree with him or her; then the author says why opponents are wrong.	Donder and her colleagues argue that the modern island of Ithaca is the island referred to in the *Odyssey*. However, that island was probably as dry and inhospitable in antiquity as it is today. An unlikely capital. The nearby island of Kefalonia is more likely what Homer called "Ithaca."
Allusion	The author mentions an outside phenomenon (cultural, historical, literary, etc.) that is relevant to a certain point in the reading. Quotes and references to other pieces of writing are a common kind of allusion. The quote in an allusion is not necessarily by an expert, so it is probably not an appeal to authority. (See Appeal to authority, below.)	"Murder will out," as the saying goes, and so will the murderous streak within Odysseus's character. But first Odysseus himself must step out of disguise—which he does by being the only one in a competition to successfully string a certain bow. When he eventually retakes his throne, he wreaks bloody vengeance within his court, like some early-day Stalin, enlisting his son and others to kill 108 suitors vying to marry his wife Penelope. **Note:** There are two allusions here: 1) A well-known phrase that appears in various English literary works and 2) a reference to Joseph Stalin, a former leader of the Soviet Union, famous for executing people by whom he felt betrayed.
Appeal to authority	The author mentions that an expert or some other highly respected person supports a certain point.	Recent work by John Bartolucci at the University of Michigan suggests that the real location of the ancient city of Troy was further south than the traditionally accepted site at the hill of Hisarlik.

Continued

Rhetorical Technique	Explanation	Example
Illustration by anecdote	The author gives a short narrative (like a miniature story), usually a true one, that helps explain a point or makes it more attractive to the reader. This technique is often used at the beginning of a reading.	It was 1928, and Dr. Alexander Fleming made a mistake that changed the world. He went on vacation and left some glass containers, called petri dishes, open to the air, and mold grew on them. He got back home, threw the mold away, and didn't think anything of it until he noticed that a certain bacterium—staphylococcus— would not grow where the mold had been. The mold somehow fought the bacterium. This marked the discovery of penicillin.
Rhetorical question	The writer poses a question that he or she then goes on to answer. It is very important to note that the author proposes one or more answers to the rhetorical question. The question by itself, with no answer, constitutes an ineffective strategy.	How could Joseph Conrad, whose native language was Polish, whose second language was French, and whose spoken English was quite poor, write with such genius in English? Cognitive linguists have some hypotheses. One is that much of Conrad's international experience, especially aboard British ships, built up an association between the English language and adventure that he learned to effectively convey in writing.
Understatement	The author presents an important point in low-key, moderate phrasing. In academic writing, understatement is widely respected. Its opposite—a highly dramatic presentation known as overstatement—is not respected.	The Aegean coast of Turkey, a rocky littoral that forms the eastern shore of the sea that separates Asia from Europe, is of some interest to Homeric scholars, to say the least. **Note:** This is understatement because that area is actually of huge interest to the scholars. The phrase "some interest" puts the situation in moderate terms. Tags such as *to say the least* and *one can say that* sometimes accompany understatement.

EXERCISE 3

A. The following passage is the first part of a much longer chapter. That is why it refers to topics that will be covered later. Notice the use of rhetorical techniques, especially in the highlighted text. Identify and label the rhetorical technique being used in each highlighted item (allusion, appeal to authority, etc.).

SOCRATIC DIALOGUE

(1) ....
....

The whole
paragraph

1   **(1) In a famous early scene** from the 1973 movie *The Paper Chase*, a new student at Harvard Law School, James Hart, has the misfortune of being called on by Professor Kingsfield, his contract law teacher. Even though Hart is obviously unprepared, the professor peppers him with questions about a legal case. It's question after question—and no answers. Kingsfield doesn't even comment about the answers Hart attempts. Are they right? The professor never says, preferring to lead the exchange in certain directions through questioning. This exchange is so well known among film buffs because the character of Kingsfield is revealed to be mercilessly extreme in his application of what the professor himself calls "the Socratic method." Hart is excruciatingly on the spot, an experience so unsettling that he becomes physically sick from the stress.

2   By "the Socratic method," the fictitious Professor Kingsfield means a form of Socratic dialogue, also known as *Socratic dialectic*—a form of exposition that originated in ancient Greece and first appeared in the texts of Plato, pupil to the enigmatic philosopher Socrates. Plato wrote the dialogues, and Socrates is a major character in them. **(2) (As Fiona Bell notes,** no writing actually done by Socrates himself is known to exist.) Though Socratic dialectic has been preserved via writing (by Plato and Xenophon), it was typically an oral art in ancient times. In his treatises, Plato describes dialectic as beginning with the posing of a question, followed by the use of logic and follow-up questions to elucidate connections and find truths through discourse. Plato claims to be emulating Socrates's dialectic style when he reveals his personal philosophy through conversations about moral, ethical, and metaphysical arguments. However scholars have a sort of **(3) "Gospel Problem"** with Platonic writings: As with sayings attributed to Jesus of Nazareth **(4), how can we know whether Socrates really said what Plato claims he said?** Most scholars have learned to tolerate ambiguity about that issue and to take Plato's writings for what we know them to be—vehicles for Plato's own thoughts.

3   Among the thinkers of the ancient Greek world, there were occasional debates about whether dialectic (in the Socratic sense) is closely related to rhetoric. One commonly held distinction between the two is **(5) illustrated by a story involving Zeno of Citium** (on Cyprus), the founder of the Stoic philosophy and a student of Plato's Academy. He famously described the difference between

(2) ....
....

(3) ....
....

(4) ....
....

(5) ....
....

The next few
sentences

Continued

dialectic and rhetoric by alternately clenching and opening his hand. Zeno held up a closed fist and said, "This is dialectic," clenching his fist to show that it is compact and narrowly directed. Opening his hand out wide, like a flower suddenly bursting into bloom, he said, "This is rhetoric," meaning that it draws on a wider set of techniques, including emotional appeals. To modern readers, the distinction is somewhat frayed, because the word *rhetoric* has diversified in meaning.

4   After the absorption of the Greek world by the Roman Empire, officials generally defined rhetoric simply as the art of speaking well. By the time Renaissance thought blossomed throughout Europe, rhetoric assimilated some of that age's focus on rationality. The 17th-century English scientist **(6)** Francis Bacon poetically portrayed rhetoric as a method used "to apply reason to imagination for the better moving of the will." **(7)** Not without reason, some theorists still conceive of rhetoric as a purely persuasive tool. Most modern scholars, however, define rhetoric more loosely and pragmatically, as a strategic communication tool used to achieve a goal. In common usage, the term *rhetoric* carries a negative connotation of manipulation, demagoguery, and speech that is void of meaning. This kind of obvious bloviation erodes the public opinion of rhetoric and has led to the expressions "just rhetoric" and "empty rhetoric," used to describe the message of a public speaker—typically a politician—who uses flowery language to persuade others.

5   This essay, however, will focus not on modern philosophical notions of dialectic and rhetoric nor on the perils of rhetoric employed for manipulation, but rather on rhetorical devices famously used since the time of Plato. These techniques include rhetorical question, allegory, allusion, understatement, an appeal to an authority, and other language-based methods that convey the author's or speaker's intentions. The first and perhaps most famous example is by Plato himself in his extended metaphor in the *Allegory of the Cave*, in which the philosopher likens being uneducated and unenlightened to being imprisoned in the darkness of a cave. Both allegory and another technique, anecdote, are narratives—short stories, if you will. The distinction between allegory and anecdote is that allegory is metaphorical fiction, a concoction that runs parallel to actual events or conditions and illustrates, in fiction, certain truths about reality. Literary classics since Plato's time have commonly employed the technique, in some cases an entire work being one long allegory. On the surface, *Animal Farm* (George Orwell 1945) is the story of some farm animals who overthrow humans and subsequently destroy their own society through vicious rule, but **(8)** it happened to come out while **(9)** Winston Churchill was shaking hands with Joseph Stalin. Anecdote, on the other hand, is usually true—or

(6) ....

....

(7) ....

....

(8) ....

....

(9) ....

....

at least believed to be true—and it illustrates rather than makes comparisons.

6   Other modern writers use rhetorical devices extensively within the text of their novels. **(10)** Professor Gordon Jones notes that Toni Morrison, for example, who is notable for depicting the experience of slavery and racism, employs rhetorical devices to great effect in her Pulitzer Prize–winning book *Beloved*. "'Here,' she said, 'in this here place, we flesh; flesh that weeps, laughs; flesh that dances on bare feet in grass. Love it. Love it hard. Yonder they do not love your flesh. They despise it.'" By metaphorically breaking the human body into pieces of flesh, a clear symbol of what the system of slavery did, Morrison uses the lyrical passage, which is dotted with repetition and understatement, to convey themes of both fragmentation and reclamation.

(10) ....
....

7   Political leaders as well as writers have a history of charming crowds through the use of rhetorical devices in oratory. The quote attributed to Julius Caesar, "I came. I saw. I conquered," which is also powerfully alliterative in the original Latin ("*Veni, vidi, vici*"), uses *anaphora*, a type of repetition, to convey a powerful and swift military victory. The technique passes the test of time. Martin Luther King Jr.'s "I Have a Dream" speech, lauded as one of the greatest speeches in modern history, repeats the speech's eponymous phrase in eight consecutive sentences. **(11)** Some eyewitness historical accounts say that President John F. Kennedy, **(12)** a pretty good speaker in his own right, was watching King's speech on TV at the White House. As King hit his famous cadences (which other reports say were almost not included in his speech), Kennedy reportedly expressed, in somewhat colorful language, awe at King's oratory skills. US President Barack Obama, who is generally considered an excellent orator, used the word *grace* more than 30 times in a eulogy he gave in 2015. He has notably used other rhetorical devices in his speeches, as well, including *syntheton*, a linking of two words closely tied together for the purpose of emphasis, such as "effort and determination," "passion and dedication," and "hazards and misfortune."

(11) ....
....
The next few sentences

(12) ....
....

8   The utility of recognizing rhetorical devices in literature and speech and of being able to employ them in self-expression has made the study of rhetoric, and even of dialectic, important to any professional communicator. But applying them unskillfully can be dangerous, opening one up to charges of—as we mentioned— "empty rhetoric." Even worse, there are, as **(13)** the rhetorician Miles Babbage has put it, "evil twins" for many rhetorical moves, devices that are widely recognized as attempts to short-circuit logic or even to deceive. It is these rhetorical faults to which we will now turn.

(13) ....
....

Some of the sources and quotations in this passage are fictional.

B. Read each item. Then write a response using the suggested rhetorical technique. To complete this task, you may have to do light online research, be creative, and supply fictitious elements—such as an anecdote, the name of an authority, and so on.

1. How do we know that Socrates really did teach Plato?

   Appeal to authority: *The fact that Plato was indeed a student of Socrates has been established by researchers at Mount Partridge University.*

2. Did you get a good education or a bad education when you were in elementary school?

   Anecdote: ....

   ....

3. How would you feel if suddenly you won a lottery totaling more than $100 million?

   Understatement: ....

   ....

4. Some people would like to eliminate all jails so that no one would ever have to go to prison again. Would that be a good idea?

   Rhetorical question: ....

   ....

5. Are nuclear power plants for generating electricity a good thing or are they too dangerous to operate?

   Allusion (Try to allude to an actual event in the history of nuclear power generation.): ....

   ....

6. When a country is chosen as the host for the Olympic Games, it typically spends millions of dollars—maybe even more than a billion—on stadiums and other facilities for the games. Given the fact that every host country has poor people who can't afford the basics they need, is this building a bad thing, or are there good reasons to do it?

   Acknowledgement of opposition: ....

   ....

7. Do modern societies need philosophers? Is there really any point in having people who contribute only words and abstract ideas to society?

   Appeal to authority: ....

   ....

C. Discuss these questions with one or two other students. Then explain your answers to the class.

1. Share each of your answers in Part C.
2. Which item in Part C was hardest to do?
3. How did you come up with the fictitious elements you had to create?
4. Which of your rhetorical devices do you think would be most appealing to readers? Why?

Go to **MyEnglishLab** to complete a vocabulary exercise and skill practice, and to join in collaborative activities.

For more about RHETORICAL TECHNIQUES, see OC and W **HUMANITIES** 1

LANGUAGE SKILLS
UNDERSTANDING NOMINALIZATION

WHY IT'S USEFUL Higher-level reading passages in English are often characterized by higher levels of nominalization. This creates text complexity in several ways. By learning to deal with this higher-level text, you will understand academic writing as it naturally occurs when writers are not making allowances for nonnative speakers of the language. You will also be exposed to good models for making your own writing more sophisticated.

Research shows that one major characteristic of higher-level English writing is **nominalization**. The word has a simple meaning: "making things into nouns and noun phrases." However, it encompasses a wide variety of processes, including

- reducing the number of verb-centered structures and expressing them as noun-centered structures.
- often increasing the number of words that appear before a sentence's main verb.
- often "compressing" a sentence by increasing the number of modifiers in noun phrases.
- increasing the instances in which nouns modify other nouns.

Researchers who study nominalization have found that it often increases the density of information in a reading passage—that is, it helps a writer say more in fewer words. Some of this research involves the opinions of raters on big tests (like the TOEFL). It is very clear that highly nominalized writing is viewed more positively by raters in these situations. This may be surprising to you because so much of your English-language instruction has focused on verbs and the many difficulties of using them. Nonetheless, paying attention to nominalization is likely to pay off for you as you try to understand and use increasingly sophisticated English.

Here are some examples of passages and what they might look like if they were more highly nominalized. The passages on the left are entirely acceptable in English—there is nothing wrong with their usage of vocabulary or their grammar. The difference is that the passages on the right are more nominalized.

	Without an Effort to Increase Nominalization	More Highly Nominalized
1	A lot of people have heard of Plato's *Allegory of the Cave* and know that it has something to do with whether or not what humans experience is real. **Note:** Here 17 of 29 words (59%) are outside of noun phrases.	Plato's widely known *Allegory of the Cave* is recognizable as an inquiry into the reality of human experience. **Note:** A far smaller proportion (6 of 18 words = 33%) are outside of noun phrases.
2	Confucius based his ideas about politics on the principle that a leader needs to discipline himself, remain humble, and show compassion when he deals with those who follow him.	Self-discipline, humility, and compassionate treatment of one's followers were Confucius's conceptual bases for wise leadership.
3	Epicurus rejected Plato's claim that reason should be the prime basis for action, but he did not elevate sensation and downplay thought.	Epicurus's rejection of the Platonic reason-focused approach implies no preference in his philosophy for sensation over thought.
4	The right to vote in Athens extended only to males who were not foreigners, who were not slaves, and who were old enough to have completed the military training that was required of all Athenian men.	The Athenian voting franchise went only to native-born, military-trained free men.

Explanation

- Some of the sentences in the first column of the chart on the previous page may seem easier to read and, because of that, may seem better to you. That is a normal reaction, and different readers will have different preferences. In discussing nominalization, we are not discussing ease of reading. Instead, we are focusing on the perceived sophistication of a text—whether a text is likely to be judged as "higher-level" by a majority of proficient readers.
- The highly nominalized versions are mostly shorter. This shortening happens naturally when verb-centered structures (usually clauses) are transformed into noun phrases. Not every nominalization, however, leads to a significantly shorter sentence. (See Example 3.)
- The nominalized versions that are shorter are more dense, packing the information into a smaller space.
- Highly nominalized writing may require a large, wide-ranging vocabulary. At the very least, a writer needs to know the noun and adjective forms of familiar verbs.

> **TIP**
>
> **Grammar Reminder** *Nominalization involves increasing the number of noun phrases, not just the number of nouns. The following group of words is all one noun phrase, illustrating some possible components of a noun phrase:*

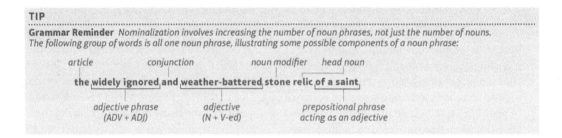

EXERCISE 5

A. The following text is about an idea often associated with Plato: that objects in our experience are just imperfect representations of "Forms." For each underlined passage, choose the replacement, a or b, that seems more sophisticated—that is, at a higher level of expression. The more sophisticated replacement may or may not be shorter than the other.

1   Plato's philosophy is famous for positing **(1)** <u>that there are certain "Forms," which are the essences of the Objects and even the emotions that we experience</u>. For example, look at a tree. You are observing a particular object that is imbued with a Form we might call "treeness"—the ideal essence of being a tree—**(2)** <u>but the Object is imperfect and only hints at the basic Form that exists beyond our experience</u>. That same Object might also be imbued with other Forms, such as "woodiness" or "branchiness" or "tallness," which it also only imperfectly represents.

2   **(3)** <u>Plato expounded much of the theory of Forms by having the character of Socrates speak of them.</u>

1. a. that there are certain essential "Forms" behind our experiences of objects and emotions
   b. that there are essential "Forms" for what we experience in objects and emotions

2. a. but the imperfection of the object is a mere hint of the Form's insensible essence
   b. but the Object is imperfect and we can only dimly sense the essence of the Form that exists with it.

3. a. Speeches supposedly by Socrates are the main way Plato expresses the theory of Forms.
   b. Plato's mouthpiece for Form theory is the character of Socrates.

Unfortunately for modern readers, this means that no coherent layout of the theory exists, and instead (4) <u>we have to piece together various statements that are widely distributed through Plato's writings into a comprehensible theory</u>. Plato portrays Socrates as saying, in various places, (5) <u>that the world of Forms is on a higher level than the world we experience</u>. Forms are even superior to time and space in the sense that they do not exist in any particular time or location. You cannot even say that they exist forever, everywhere, because their separateness from time and space makes such claims meaningless. However, (6) <u>the human mind is capable of some appreciation of the essentialness of a Form</u>—that is why we recognize the "treeness" in a tree—and the more intelligent a person is, the more he or she can appreciate the essence that is hidden from the senses.

4. a. we must comb through several passages to come up with a well-structured theory
    b. a cohesive theory emerges only from scattered passages
5. a. that Forms are superior to and separate from daily experience
    b. that Forms exist in their own world, which supersedes the world of our experience
6. a. the human mind does appreciate forms and what they imbue to Objects
    b. the human mind's appreciation of Forms can be significant

B. Compare answers with one or two other students. There are no "right" or "wrong" answers, but you will have reasons for choosing one over another. Explain these reasons to your partner(s).

EXERCISE 6

Read each Original. The highlighted words are verbs or verb phrases that may be unnecessary in a more highly nominalized version. Complete the Paraphrase to create a more highly nominalized version of the Original.

1. **Original:** If the movie directors Joel and Ethan Coen battled the Greek bard Homer, who would win?

    Paraphrase: In *a battle between movie directors Joel and Ethan Coen and the bard Homer*, who would win?

2. **Original:** You might choose the bard because, after all, his epic poem the *Odyssey* has survived for millennia and is obviously far more substantial than the movie *O Brother, Where Art Thou?*, which the Coens released in 2000.

    Paraphrase: The .... epic poem ....

    ....

    than ....

3. **Original:** The fact that the movie bears some resemblance to the epic that has so influenced Western culture actually came about quite by accident, as Joel Coen told interviewers after it was released.

    Paraphrase: The movie's resemblance ....

    ....

    .... after its release.

4. **Original:** Every Coen brothers movie is characterized by individuals who have exaggerated faults and virtues, is filled with dark humor that comes both subtly and in broad jokes, and employs epic-sounding speech even in ridiculous situations.

   Paraphrase: ....

   ....

   .... are typical for a Coen brothers film.

5. **Original:** It is that humorous slant that turns the movie into a picaresque tale that focuses on the misadventures of Ulysses Everett McGill (George Clooney), a convict who has escaped a chain gang, as he smooth talks his way through the US South during the 1930s.

   Paraphrase: Smooth-talking ex-convict Ulysses Everett McGill (George Clooney) ....

   ....

   ....

   ....

6. **Original:** The Coens have never claimed that every important incident in the film has a parallel in the *Odyssey*, but once they realized the similarities, they started playing with the idea. They put in little jokes and allusions. For example in one scene, a bust of Homer can be seen over a politician's shoulder in a restaurant.

   Paraphrase: The eventual realization of ....

   ....

   ....

   ....

Go to **MyEnglishLab** to complete a skill practice.

APPLY YOUR SKILLS

WHY IT'S USEFUL By applying the skills you have learned in this unit, you can gain a deep understanding of this challenging reading about Confucius and the influence that his philosophy had on society.

BEFORE YOU READ

A. Discuss these questions with one or more students.

1. Think about the region of the world that Socrates and Plato were from. Then consider what you already know about the philosopher Confucius. What impact, if any, do you think the place where these philosophers were born might have on their teachings?

2. Imagine that an instructor from your educational system adopted a radically different teaching style from that of the current pedagogy. What types of responses might this instructor receive from the public?

3. Consider those who have more "traditional" values in your culture, and contrast them with those who have more "progressive" beliefs. What are those different values and beliefs? Do people with these different beliefs ever clash?

B. Imagine that you will be participating in a small group discussion about the passage "Confucius's Influence," which begins on the next page. Your group will be discussing the following questions. Keep these questions in mind as you read the passage.

1. What is Confucius's ethic of *ren*?

2. Explain the different types of information about Confucius's teachings given in the *Analects*, the *Mencius*, and the *Zuozhuan*.

3. What did Socrates's and Confucius's societies have in common in terms of what was occurring at the time that each philosopher was alive?

4. What type of instruction did Confucius advocate? What belief is it founded on?

5. Explain the "higher calling" that both Socrates and Confucius thought they had.

C. Review the Unit Skills Summary. As you read the passage, apply the skills you learned in this unit.

UNIT SKILLS SUMMARY

Develop reading fluency.
• Build greater fluency to read accurately at the necessary pace.

Increase fluency.
• Read at a good pace, automatically, and with solid comprehension of a text to become a more fluent academic reader.

Tolerate ambiguity.
• Learn to accept ambiguity to read effectively and maximize your understanding of the parts that are accessible to you.

Recognize and use rhetorical techniques.
• Learn to identify some of the most common rhetorical techniques in order to appreciate the character of a reading and add personality to your own writing.

Understand nominalization.
• Learn to manage the making of things into nouns and noun phrases to understand academic writing as it naturally occurs.

A. Read the passage. Annotate and take notes as necessary.

Confucius's Influence

1   The ancient Chinese philosopher Confucius greatly influenced education systems and cultural values throughout China and East Asia. At the heart of Confucius's teachings is his ethic of *ren*, which can be loosely translated as goodness, or compassion, which Confucius urges individuals to cultivate within themselves by following precepts of humility and benevolence. Confucian doctrines also give instruction to seek harmony in relationships both in society and in the family through filial piety and obedience to elders. Though Confucius did not achieve status as a revered national leader during his lifetime, his philosophy continued to grow in popularity after his death, so much so that after the Han Dynasty came to power in 206 BCE, Confucius's ethical teachings were coded into much of the imperial rule, the education system, and the culture of China.

2   Confucius, also known as Kong Fuzi, or Master Kong, did not write down his philosophy. Rather, his teachings were passed down through extant texts that his students and disciples wrote about him posthumously, sometimes centuries following his death. Historical accuracy of aspects of Confucius's life and teachings remain as shrouded in mystery as those surrounding his contemporary, the legendary Laozi. Confucius's teachings are detailed in the *Analects*, or the *Lunyu*, and biographical information about Confucius also appears in the *Zuozhuan* and the *Mencius*. Each record provides a slightly different glimpse into his teachings. The *Analects* is the most extensive source for information on the philosopher and deals with Confucius's moral code; the *Mencius* focuses on his political influence; and the *Zuozhuan* presents a narrative history of the warring states at the time of his life. While no one knows for certain how much of a role (if any) Confucius played in authoring or editing the ancient classical books that went on to be studied for centuries as textbooks of the state, it is generally understood that Confucius was the scholar who brought them to the forefront of social and philosophical study. Beyond reviving the classical beliefs and writings of the Zhou Dynasty, Confucius broke the elitist mold of education by teaching pupils from poorer social classes, stressing the perfectibility of the individual, regardless of the person's social station.

3   Coincidentally, many other significant philosophers and religious leaders emerged during this epoch in world history from 800 to 200 BCE. This period, known as the Axial Age, saw the rise of the religious prophet Isaiah in Israel, Buddha in India, and, most notably for comparison between Eastern and Western cultures, Socrates in Greece. Confucius and Socrates both lived between the 6th and 5th centuries BCE amid periods of great political turmoil as the foundations of their societies were being rocked by savage wars, coups, and power struggles. To further analyze the striking parallels in history between Socrates and Confucius, both philosophers' doctrines were recorded by their contemporaries or disciples, and the records varied somewhat, leaving history with figures that stand as pillars of philosophical thought development, and yet remain inscrutable. Will scholars ever know, with certainty, the truth of these philosophers' beliefs, or does the lack of record of their writings and the imponderable expanse of years between ancient and modern times prevent such certainty? Regardless of the limited amount of documentation about Confucius's life, scholars search and continue to make archeological discoveries that reveal small truths about his existence.

4   Historical records about Confucius show that at approximately 30 years of age, he founded a school to teach the precepts of the religious and ethical code of the earlier Zhou Dynasty, which emphasized traditional values and the importance of education. The prevailing trend during Confucius's life was for only the children of the elite to receive education, but Confucius did not adhere to this particular tradition. In fact, he taught anyone who wanted to learn. His style quickly gained traction, and in his mid-30s, he began to receive recognition as an

important scholar. In addition to teaching a wide range of people, he also advocated differentiated instruction and is widely quoted as saying that a teacher should "teach according to the student's ability." While he taught his pupils a core doctrine of ritual, music, archery, chariot riding, calligraphy, and computation, his broader, liberal arts emphasis on morality and scholarship is the hallmark of his educational influence. Confucius famously stated that for true scholars, loyalty and faith replace gold and jade as precious treasures. Confucius instructed about three thousand people during his lifetime.

5   In examining the effects that Confucius's teaching had on society during his lifetime, another comparison of Confucius and Socrates is warranted, for the similarities between the two philosophers' pedagogical styles are striking. Both philosophers approached teaching in a dialectical, or conversational, manner. Confucius generally preferred not to spend endless hours preaching his doctrinal principles to his disciples, instead favoring a more engaging approach of exchanging information. Like Socrates and his follower Plato, who founded the Academy, Confucius posed questions, referenced classical works, and provided analogies to students to lead them to self-realization of knowledge. Both Confucius and Socrates focused on the development of civic virtue as the highest goal and the pursuit of knowledge as the highest ambition. Both men believed they had a higher calling. Confucius maintained that he knew the will of heaven, as he termed it, and Socrates believed that his teaching was fulfilling the will of the gods, as he stated at his trial.

6   The comparison between the two scholars only holds for so long before unraveling, however. Socrates's moral doctrines were not tied to consanguineous relationships and patriarchal institutions. Confucius revered order in society and advocated a fundamental hierarchy of the sovereign and the subject, be it a husband and wife, a parent and child, or a teacher and student. Modern Western scholars argue that it is this particular distinction that reveals itself so plainly in modern times. Education scholars have studied how this difference manifests itself in the classroom, for example. Students from Confucian cultures often take a more passive approach to classroom behavior that is more deferential to an instructor, whereas Western students are more likely to behave in a way that involves engagement with a teacher or older students, such as speaking out or presenting alternative points of view.

7   Despite Confucius's failure at influencing broad political and social change during his lifetime, after his death and the swift fall of the harsh Qin Dynasty, the Han Dynasty made the study of Confucian texts part of the imperial examination that individuals were required to pass in order to hold public office. As a result, Confucian doctrine was linked to education and public ideology for more than two thousand years. The philosophy has, scholars note, waxed and waned in popularity through the centuries. Though Confucianism fell out of favor in the early 1900s with the disestablishment of Imperial China and was further purged during the Cultural Revolution, Confucian institutes continue to grow in popularity worldwide. As recently as 2015, famous Western newspaper headlines have noted China's "turning back" to Confucius. If this is indeed the case, it will certainly not be the first time the philosophy has found favor among political leaders.

B. Read the discussion questions in Before You Read, Part B. Is there anything you cannot answer? What reading skills can you use to help you find the answers?

Go to **MyEnglishLab** to read the passage again and answer critical thinking questions.

THINKING CRITICALLY

In "Confucius's Influence," you read about how fragmented versions of Confucius's teachings were written and passed down by his students and followers. Because of the varied accounts of his teachings, it is unclear whether information is distorted or left out altogether. Think about someone who you consider to be a great mind or thought leader of today. Imagine if like Confucius's teachings, this individual's ideas and beliefs were only recorded by supporters and followers, and not by this person himself or herself. What effect do you think this might have on the accuracy and comprehensive documentation of the person's ideas? Explain your ideas to another student.

THINKING VISUALLY

In "Confucius's Influence," you read that as recently as 2015, newspaper headlines indicated a return to Confucianism. This return extends beyond politics to Chinese educational institutions. The following chart depicts the components of the Chinese Education Curriculum during two time periods. Examine the chart. After years of students being taught antitraditional concepts, what do you think may result from this return of traditionalism? Consider the generations who were taught one curriculum and the next generation of students who will be taught Confucian values. Explain your thoughts to another student.

COMPONENTS OF CHINESE EDUCATION CURRICULUM	
Period of Antitraditionalism	**Present-Day Confucianism**
• Little traditional culture, including classical literature • Few ancient texts advocating respect for elders and moral values • Western art, religion, science, and politics • European languages • Highly specialized education • Technical skills	• Traditional culture, including classical literature (such as the use of traditional-culture textbooks in some places) • Ancient texts that advocate respect for elders and moral values • Study of Chinese festivals • For high schoolers: encouragement to take up a traditional Chinese sport, do calligraphy, and recite ancient poetry • Belief that students should "know they are part of the Chinese nation"

THINKING ABOUT LANGUAGE

Read these excerpts from "Confucius's Influence." Then paraphrase them, increasing nominalization as much as possible.

1. The ancient Chinese philosopher Confucius greatly influenced education systems and cultural values throughout China and East Asia.

   ....

   ....

2. Confucian doctrines also give instruction to seek harmony in relationships both in society and in the family through filial piety and obedience to elders.

   ....

   ....

3. Rather, his teachings were passed down through extant texts that his students and disciples wrote about him posthumously, sometimes centuries following his death.

....

....

4. Coincidentally, many other significant philosophers and religious leaders emerged during this epoch in world history from 800 to 200 BCE.

....

....

5. Regardless of the limited amount of documentation about Confucius's life, scholars search and continue to make archeological discoveries that reveal small truths about his existence.

....

....

6. The prevailing trend during Confucius's life was for only the children of the elite to receive education, but Confucius did not adhere to this particular tradition.

....

....

7. Confucius generally preferred not to spend endless hours preaching his doctrinal principles to his disciples, instead favoring a more engaging approach of exchanging of information.

....

....

8. Confucius revered order in society and advocated a fundamental hierarchy of the sovereign and the subject, be it a husband and wife, a parent and child, or a teacher and student.

....

....

▶ Go to MyEnglishLab to listen to Professor Harrison and to complete a self-assessment.

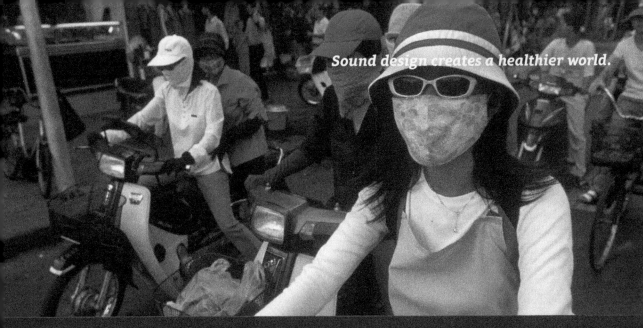

Sound design creates a healthier world.

ENVIRONMENTAL ENGINEERING

Visuals

UNIT PROFILE

You will consider the subject of environmental engineering—specifically the issue of air quality. You will study measurements of air quality, effects of air pollutants, and systems for ensuring clean air.

Skim the reading "Nanofibers Revolutionize Air Filtration" on page 129. Look at the diagrams. Can you think of devices that accomplish filtration? Where might they be found? Why is this filtration probably necessary?

OUTCOMES

- Interpret visuals
- Understand text references to visuals
- Interpret the information in visuals
- Refer to visual data within and beyond a reading
- Recognize and learn multiword vocabulary items

GETTING STARTED

▶ Go to **MyEnglishLab** to listen to Professor Hildemann and to complete a self-assessment.

Discuss these questions with a partner or group.

1. Think about the air you breathe as you go through an average week. Where do you think it's the cleanest? The most polluted? What are the main components of the pollution? Can you see, smell, or taste the pollutants?

2. Think of an area that has polluted air. What health effects has this had on people who live there? Is anyone held responsible for causing the pollution? Is anyone making an effort to clean it up?

3. Imagine a new office building being constructed in a highly polluted city. What technological features can be installed to clean the inside air and make it better than the outside air?

For more about **ENVIRONMENTAL ENGINEERING**, see 2 3. See also W and OC **ENVIRONMENTAL ENGINEERING** 1 2 3.

FUNDAMENTAL SKILL
INTERPRETING VISUALS

WHY IT'S USEFUL By interrelating visuals (graphs, diagrams, tables, etc.) with the text in a reading, you can deepen your understanding and appreciation of an author's entire explanation. This is especially important in technical readings, where a lot of information is too complex to be detailed in words and is presented in visuals instead.

Readings with visuals are the norm in many fields, including scientific and technical disciplines. Even in nontechnical fields, visuals such as tables, photographs, diagrams, and maps are common. Authors use them to support the ideas that they detail in the text, and often the visuals give a full treatment of information that can only be briefly summarized in the words of a reading.

Besides **photographs** and **maps**, here are some other terms for visuals:

- **Graphs** The word can refer to many kinds of visuals that use lines, bars, dots, or other design features to represent data. Many graphs have an *x*-axis at the bottom (a horizontal scale) showing one set of numbers and a *y*-axis at the left (a vertical scale) showing another set of numbers.

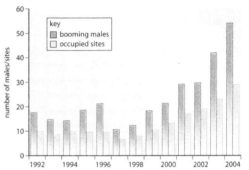

- **Diagrams** These usually depict structures or systems. They typically include shapes or drawings and often have lines or arrows showing connections or directions of movement.

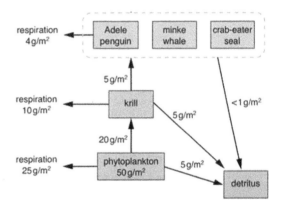

- **Tables** These are frames consisting of columns and rows. The intersections of columns and rows create spaces called *cells*. Each cell contains a piece of information.

	2014	2015	2016
Region 1	250.05	45	230
Region 2	320	784.65	25
Region 3	1560	1570	2875
Region 4	895.25	375	485
Region 5	85	125	375
Region 6	275.7	570.35	85.35
Total	**3386**	**3470**	**4075.35**

- **Illustrations** The term refers broadly to any visuals that "illustrate," or make a point clearer by means of a picture. In a more specific meaning, an illustration is a drawing of a thing, person, or situation—not a photograph but meant, like many photographs, to depict something realistically.

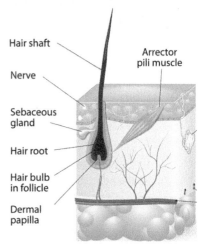

- **Charts** The word is used broadly to cover many kinds of visuals. A graph, a diagram, a table, or even a map may alternatively be called a *chart*. The only kinds not possibly referred to as charts are photographs or drawings (illustrations).
- **Figures** This is another word used broadly to cover many kinds of visuals. It is important because in readings, terms like *Figure 1* and *Figure 7.3* are used to refer to visuals of various types.

The skill of **interpreting visuals** is essential in academic reading. This unit breaks the skill down into two supporting skills:

- understanding text references to visuals
- interpreting the information in visuals

A. Look at the passage. Notice how it refers to two of the figures that appear with the reading. Also notice that various vocabulary items from the reading appear in the figures. Finally, notice that the third figure—the microscopic picture—is not mentioned in the reading but is relevant to it.

POLLUTANTS AND THE RESPIRATORY SYSTEM

1   The respiratory system, as illustrated in Figure 1, continually exchanges gases, taking in oxygen from the environment and replacing it with carbon dioxide, but as most environments are impure, pollutants, too, enter the body by way of the mouth and nose. The lung parenchyma (main tissue) and respiratory passages contain no filtering system, and once breathed in, pollutants of various sizes pass into different parts of the respiratory system. In general, larger particles land, by way of direct interception and impaction, along the upper airway passages, including in the nose, mouth, and pharynx, which Figure 1 shows. Asbestos fibers are an example of respirable particulates that become lodged in the upper airway.

2   Smaller particles, however, travel on into the lower airway passages and into the tracheobronchial and alveolar regions (see respiratory system diagram), with the smallest particles settling into the lower lung tissue (see Figure 2). In the lower passages, particles end up in the bronchial region by way of sedimentation as particles lose their buoyancy. Deeper in the lungs, particles diffuse and latch onto lung walls in a random motion similar to that of gas molecules. The smallest particles can penetrate the bloodstream, affecting the cardiovascular system, the central nervous system, the kidneys, and bone marrow.

The Respiratory System

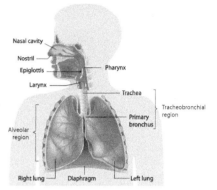

Figure 1 The human respiratory system

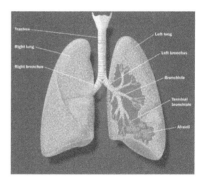

Figure 2 The structure of human lungs

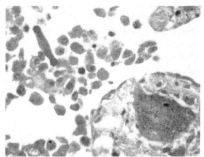

Figure 3 View through a microscope of asbestos fibers lodged in lung tissue

B. Read the questions and choose the best answers.

1. The reading uses the reference "as illustrated in Figure 1" to direct readers to information about ....

    a. the entire upper body of a human
    b. what air pollutants look like
    c. the upper part of the respiratory system
    d. how particles get into the blood

TIP

The words identifying a visual are called the caption. For example, the caption for Figure 3 in this reading is "View through a microscope of asbestos fibers lodged in lung tissue." You can use some captions to help you understand difficult vocabulary from a reading. For example, the picture in Figure 3 can help you understand fibers, lodged, *and* lung tissue.

2. What is the relationship between Figure 1 and Figure 2?

    a. Figure 1 illustrates something real, but Figure 2 doesn't.
    b. Figure 2 illustrates something that is part of Figure 1.
    c. The subject of Figure 1 causes the subject of Figure 2.
    d. The subject of Figure 2 is unhealthy, but the subject of Figure 1 is healthy.

3. Which of the following is true about Figure 2?

    a. The right side is a "cutaway," which shows the inside of something.
    b. The human lungs are "unbalanced," with structures on the left different from those on the right.
    c. The right side shows a healthy lung, but the left shows one that is "pathological," or sick.
    d. The pollution "particulates"—little pieces—are shown on the left side but not the right.

4. According to the explanation before the reading, which of the following terms could be used for only one figure in the reading?

    a. chart
    b. diagram
    c. photograph
    d. illustration

5. Which statements are true, according to the text and visuals? Choose TWO.

    a. Respiration starts with breathing in through the nose or mouth.
    b. The mouth is not part of the respiratory system.
    c. The trachea carries gases into the lungs.
    d. Larger particles like asbestos are all trapped before they can enter the lungs.
    e. The middle and lower parts of the respiratory system contain filters that keep pollutants out.

Go to **MyEnglishLab** to complete a vocabulary exercise and skill practice, and to join in collaborative activities.

SUPPORTING SKILL 1
UNDERSTANDING TEXT REFERENCES TO VISUALS

WHY IT'S USEFUL By recognizing and understanding references to visuals, you can zero in on the most important information that the visual communicates. You can also follow the thread of the author's argument, which uses details from the visual to illustrate points.

References to visuals in a text are phrases used by an author to help readers see a connection between specific information in a text and related information depicted in a visual. Technical readings reference visuals in numerous ways. By expanding your knowledge of the language often used to refer to a visual, you will be better able to

- notice when an author is working to direct readers' eyes to a particular aspect of a visual.
- understand the meanings of various visual-reference phrases.
- fully comprehend the points being made by an author.

Before reading a technical text, consider skimming for **common phrases used to reference visuals**. This can help you find key information in both the text and the visuals when you read.

Common Phrases Used to Reference Visuals	
given in the chart	represented by the figure
illustrated in Figure B	revealed by the diagram
listed in Graph 1.2	seen from the map
plotted in the chart	shown in Figure 1
presented in the illustration	summarized in Table A

EXERCISE 1

A. Skim the text for phrases used to refer to a visual. Highlight the phrases. Then look at the associated visuals to see how they may be connected to the information surrounding the phrases you underlined.

INTERNAL COMBUSTION ENGINES AND AIR QUALITY

1   Internal combustion engines in vehicles consume petroleum and other liquids such as gasoline, diesel, and fuel oil, and they produce exhaust emissions that result in environmental degradation. As shown in Figure 1, the most common internal combustion engine in automobiles is the four-stroke engine, which completes a four-part cycle of intake, compression, combustion, and exhaust. A crankshaft turns a piston to draw in an air-fuel mixture in the first step, as is illustrated in the diagram. In Step 2, the engine compresses the mixture, causing Step 3, the firing of a spark plug. Finally, as is presented in the diagram, the exhaust valve opens, resulting in the release of exhaust gases into the air through the vehicle's tailpipe.

Continued

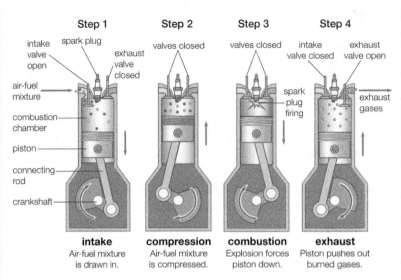

Figure 1 An internal combustion engine

2   Exhaust emissions contain the worst pollutants: carbon monoxide, unburnt hydrocarbons, and nitrogen oxides. The engines also produce toxic compounds including benzene, butadiene, aldehydes, ethers, and methanol. Pollutants from engine exhaust make up 50 percent of the total air pollution in the United States. In cities such as Mumbai and Kolkata, up to two-thirds of the pollutants in the air are caused by vehicular pollution.

3   Emissions damage lung tissue and aggravate respiratory diseases. In warmer temperatures, emissions produce the secondary pollutant ozone when hydrocarbons react with oxides of nitrogen, causing smog. Breathing in such pollution can cause headaches, asthma, kidney damage, cancer, and other serious health problems. In general, older vehicles pollute more than newer vehicles, dumping toxic respirable particles into the air. Therefore, such vehicles should be retrofitted with emission controls—such as oil filters—and subjected to engine tune-ups and emission checks, or replaced altogether. This is an especially pressing problem in developing nations because of the prevalence of older, poorly maintained vehicles.

4   Changing the engine design, using cleaner fuels, and installing postcombustion control devices are some of the possible solutions for reducing pollution from transportation engines. A hybrid-electric vehicle (shown in Figure 2) combines a conventional internal combustion engine with an electric propulsion system that increases fuel efficiency and lowers emissions. As illustrated in the diagram, the hybrid-electric engine employs regenerative braking, which is the use of kinetic energy from the spinning wheels to turn the electric motor. As illustrated in the figure, the turning of the motor creates resistance that slows the wheels down while at the same time creating electricity to be stored in the battery. The electric motor uses this stored energy to assist the engine in powering the vehicle while it is accelerating.

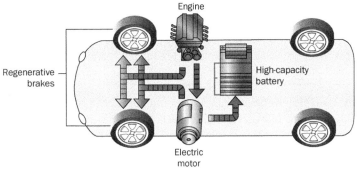

Figure 2 A hybrid-electric vehicle

5   In a hybrid system, the electric motor runs the engine entirely when the vehicle is stationary or almost stationary, such as when it's stopped for a traffic light or inching along in heavy traffic. The combustion engine does not run at all in such circumstances. Hybrids also use automatic start and shutoff features, which save energy. According to some studies, a stationary vehicle with its engine running emits seven times more exhaust than a moving vehicle.

6   Hybrid-electric engines have advantages over older internal combustion engines but do not entirely eliminate the need to burn fossil fuels. Switching to an all-electric engine vehicle that is powered by renewable resources obviates the need for fossil fuels and a plethora of fuel-related products and processes that tax the environment. Electric vehicles, however, are not entirely free of environmental concerns due to battery production and disposal issues.

B. Answer the questions. Use your own words and what you learned from the reading and the associated visuals.

1. According to Figure 1, what occurs in the second step of an internal combustion engine's operation? ....

2. According to Figure 1, what happens in the last step of an internal combustion engine's operation? ....

3. Regenerative braking is referenced both in the text and in Figure 2. How does it work?

    ....

4. Which part of a hybrid-electric vehicle assists the engine when the vehicle is accelerating?

    ....

Go to **MyEnglishLab** to complete a vocabulary exercise and skill practice, and to join in collaborative activities.

SUPPORTING SKILL 2
INTERPRETING THE INFORMATION IN VISUALS

WHY IT'S USEFUL By learning to read information that has been organized into visuals, you can gain knowledge and insights the text does not offer. Also, visuals often suggest related topics that you may want to learn more about.

In some ways, **interpreting a visual** can be easier than reading the words of an article or a chapter in a book. The visual will probably contain a mix of words and images, and the images help you understand the words. Also, there are fewer words to read in a visual than in a full text. There may be a lot of new vocabulary in the visual, but probably not any difficult grammatical structures.

However, reading visuals can be challenging in other ways:

- The large amount of information in some visuals can stretch your comprehension skills.
- A visual may contain numbers or even mathematical formulas; these may seem threatening to people who are not comfortable with numbers.
- A visual may show relationships among pieces of information without providing words for such relationships. This could leave some relationships unclear. (Does X cause Y? Does X simply happen at the same time as Y?) You may have to figure them out without any explanation from the author of the article.
- This lack of "relationship vocabulary" may make your job more difficult if you are assigned to explain the information in the visual. You may not find the relationship vocabulary and grammar you need in the visual itself. You will have to depend on your own vocabulary and grammatical knowledge to "tell the story"—to create descriptions of the relationships.

TECHNIQUES FOR INTERPRETING VISUALS

As you try to interpret a visual, do the following:

- Read titles and labels.
- Read captions.
- Read any notes (including source notes).
- Look for large trends.
- Look for extremes.
- Take notes about surprises.
- Summarize it in a few sentences.

Regardless of the kind of visual you are analyzing, certain parts—such as titles, labels, captions, and any notes—require attention. Also, if you are reading actively (see the section Reading Actively, p. 3), you should interact with the visuals by taking notes about obvious data extremes and trends, especially any that may surprise you. Finally, a helpful exercise is to write a short summary—three or four sentences at most—of what you have learned from the visual. This will help you to start putting the graphic or nonverbal information that you gathered into words.

Consider the line graph and caption on the following page, which present fictional information for the purposes of our discussion—not real data from an actual study. Look at the labeled parts of the visual. Then read the explanation.

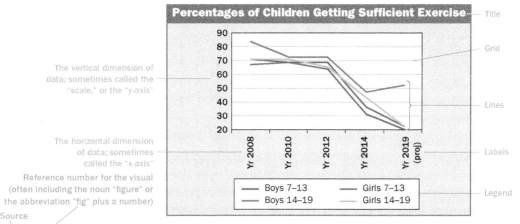

The vertical dimension of data; sometimes called the "scale," or the "y-axis"

The horizontal dimension of data; sometimes called the "x-axis"

Reference number for the visual (often including the noun "figure" or the abbreviation "fig" plus a number)

Source

Title

Grid

Lines

Labels

Legend

Caption

Figure 8.3 Comparison of children in the UK (by sex and age band) before and after the London 2012 Olympics. From Barker, et al. (2015) "Did Britain See an 'Olympic Effect' on Childhood Exercise?" (For demonstration purposes only. Not a real study.)

EXPLANATION OF THE EXAMPLE VISUAL

Title, Labels, Lines, and Legend

It is clear from the title, labels, lines, and legend that the visual communicates the following:

- Its main idea is to show whether certain percentages rise and fall over the course of time.
- The extent of the rise or fall is measured by a scale of percentage levels at the left.
- The time is specified by years at the bottom.
- These percentages are for four groups—boys and girls, and within those categories, a younger group (7–13 years old) and an older one (14–19). Each group is indicated by a colored line.

Caption (Including Source Note)

The caption reveals important information that may not be obvious from the graph itself.

- The data are limited to one nation (the United Kingdom).
- There were Olympic Games in London in 2012, and that is somehow significant to this data. The exact nature of that significance is not yet clear.
- The source is an article that asks about a possible "Olympic Effect" in Britain. Even if you have never heard of an "Olympic Effect" before, you can infer that it somehow relates to whether children get sufficient exercise.

Information Not Expressed in Words and Numbers

The graph communicates points and trends. For an assignment or in a discussion, you may have to express them in your own words. Here are examples of what could be said from the data:

> In all four groups, the percentages of children getting enough exercise dropped from 2012 to 2014.

> The declines are expected to continue until 2019 for all groups except the older boys, for whom a slight rise is projected. (*Proj* means "projected" or "predicted.")

> In all four groups, declines from 2012 to 2014 were steeper than those before 2012. If the Olympic Effect means "a decrease in sufficient exercise," then this chart shows there was one. However, if the Olympic Effect means "an increase in sufficient exercise," then this chart shows there was no such thing in the UK after the London 2012 Olympics.

A. Review the Techniques for Interpreting Visuals and the example graph on pages 112–113. Then skim the following reading and the accompanying visuals.

B. Now read the full passage. As you read, pay special attention to textual references to the visuals.

AIR QUALITY AND ATHLETIC EVENTS

1   Athletic events have a complicated relationship with air quality conditions at any given location. For one thing, just as air pollution and smog pose particular health threats to the very young and the elderly, they also threaten athletes, whose respiration rates during training and competition are typically quite high. For another, prestigious athletic competitions tend to draw intense national and international scrutiny to poor air quality wherever the contests are held. That is, while unhealthy air may receive little attention from authorities during normal times, the advent of elite athletes may force governments to improve their environments. Regarding the latter effect, the International Olympic Committee, for one, boasts that it requires host nations to provide a healthy environment for athletes, including meeting basic air quality standards.

2   Research shows that the claim by the Olympic Committee has merit. Leading up to the 2008 Olympics in Beijing, the Chinese government closed coal-burning factories and restricted vehicles from roads, and reports by the Olympic Committee noted that the government either replaced or scrapped 300,000 high-emitting vehicles, relocated polluting factories, and employed nitrogen oxide abatement and dust control measures at thermal power stations. Consequently, air quality measures improved dramatically in Beijing, at least until after the Olympics. (See Fig. 1.) Other international sporting events have also drawn the public eye to environmental issues. In June 2015, news agencies published photos of Santiago, Chile, blanketed in smog prior to the Copa América soccer tournament. Air conditions were so deplorable that Chilean authorities declared a national emergency, closed 3,000 factories, and banned many cars from the roads. They did not, however, cancel the tournament.

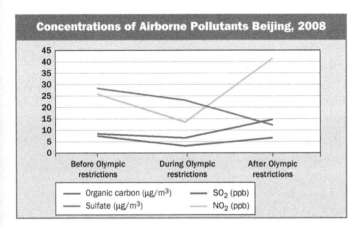

Figure 1 Concentrations of select airborne pollutants before, during, and after a period of restrictions on activities, such as coal-burning, surrounding the 2008 Olympics

3   Some studies have highlighted the particular threat that dirty air poses to athletes because of their overall higher rates of respiration. The human respiratory system absorbs particulates as the body exchanges carbon dioxide for oxygen, and the smaller the particles, the farther into the lungs they travel. While a normal, resting adult takes in 3 to 5 liters of oxygen per minute,

a strenuously exercising athlete takes in ten to twenty times that amount. In some cases, as observed in studies of South African runners in the 1980s, an athlete's increased respiration rate can have extremely toxic consequences. (See Fig. 2.) In this case, the average athlete who ran one of the two marathons or practiced for one in an urban setting had ultra-high blood-lead levels. They were so high that, if found in a child today, the US Centers for Disease Control and Prevention would call for urgent blood-cleansing treatments. Routine inhalation by athletes in any city of ground-level particulates, ozone, and other gases such as nitrogen dioxide restricts the airways and can tax the respiratory and cardiovascular systems. It can damage the tissues of the lungs and aggravate conditions such as asthma, chronic lung disease, and heart disease. Air quality standards vary from country to country,

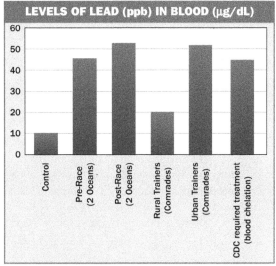

Figure 2 Blood lead levels of runners from two South African marathons (the 2 Oceans Marathon and the Comrades Marathon) in 1984. "Urban trainers" trained in cities for the Comrades Marathon, and "rural trainers" in the countryside. "Control" subjects are nonrunners. Only the "control" group and the "rural trainers" had blood-lead levels below 45, the point at which the US CDC recommends that a child undergo emergency treatment to chelate (chemically cleanse) the blood.

though the World Health Organization's guidelines call for levels of the smallest particulate matter ($PM_{2.5}$ or smaller) to be limited to 10 micrograms per cubic meter ($\mu g/m^3$) as an annual average. Some cities far exceed that rate, and the burden of poor air quality tends to fall disproportionately on low- and middle-income nations.

4   Still, cities in high-income nations, such as London, England, do not escape scrutiny over air quality for athletic games. In the lead-up to the 2012 Olympic games, London's nitrogen dioxide pollution was similar to the levels seen in Beijing before 2008 Olympic restrictions. This prompted a public outcry. The British government used air quality–control measures similar to those employed by other nations and met target levels by the start of the games. The government also met some of its goals to build a sustainable Olympics by using low-carbon efforts when creating and operating structures for the games.

C. Read the questions and choose the best answers.

1. Which statement is true about the data shown in Figure 1?

   a. During all three time periods, there was more NO_2 in the air than any other pollutant.

   b. Of all four pollutants, SO_2 is the least dangerous.

   c. The amount of sulfates in the air was not lowest during the period of Olympic restrictions.

   d. The Olympic restrictions had no effect on the amount of organic carbon in the air.

VOCABULARY TIP

The data in Figures 1 and 2 are stated in measurement units you may not recognize such as $\mu g/m^3$ (micrograms per cubic meter) and ppb (parts per billion). This will be true of many visuals you encounter. Usually, it is not necessary to know exactly what these units mean; you can understand the trends and extremes of the data in the visual without such specialized knowledge.

2. Which statement from the reading does Figure 1 support?

    a. … Just as air pollution and smog pose particular health threats to the very young and the elderly, they also threaten athletes …

    b. … The International Olympic Committee, for one, boasts that it requires host nations to provide a healthy environment for athletes …

    c. … Air quality measures improved dramatically in Beijing, at least until after the Olympics.

    d. Leading up to the 2008 Olympics in Beijing, the Chinese government closed coal-burning factories and restricted vehicles from roads …

3. Look carefully at Figure 1 to consider what it does and doesn't show. Which of the following points is shown in Figure 1 but not explicitly stated in the text of the reading?

    a. During the Olympics, air quality improved in all parts of China, not just Beijing.

    b. Before the Olympics, organic carbon was not a problem in the air of Beijing.

    c. Some airborne pollutants in the graph failed to decrease during the period of Olympic restrictions.

    d. Most airborne pollutants in the graph increased after the period of Olympic restrictions.

4. Why do athletes typically have a different relationship with air quality than most people do?

    a. Most athletes are healthier than most people.

    b. Most athletes breathe in more air.

    c. Most athletes are typically younger.

    d. Most athletes are from poorer countries.

5. Which statement from the reading does Figure 2 support?

    a. News agencies published photos of Santiago, Chile, blanketed in smog prior to the Copa América soccer tournament.

    b. In this case, the average athlete who ran one of the two marathons or practiced for one in an urban setting had ultra-high blood-lead levels.

    c. Air quality standards vary from country to country, though the World Health Organization's guidelines call for levels of the smallest particulate matter ($PM_{2.5}$ or smaller) to be limited to 10 micrograms per cubic meter ($\mu g/m^3$) as an annual average.

    d. In the lead-up to the 2012 Olympic games, London's nitrogen dioxide pollution was similar to the levels seen in Beijing before 2008 Olympic restrictions.

6. Look carefully at Figure 2 to consider what it does and doesn't show. Which of the following points is shown in Figure 2 but not mentioned in the text of the reading?

    a. Every category of runner had blood-lead levels at least twice as high as the nonrunners (the control group).

    b. No category of runner had dangerously high levels of lead in their blood.

    c. Even nonrunners in 1984 in South Africa had dangerously high blood-lead levels.

    d. The worst blood-lead levels came from training in the countryside.

D. **Discuss your answers with another student. Use information and examples from the passage to explain and support your answers.**

Go to **MyEnglishLab** to complete a vocabulary exercise and skill practice, and to join in collaborative activities.

READING-WRITING CONNECTION
REFERRING TO VISUAL DATA WITHIN AND BEYOND A READING

WHY IT'S USEFUL By learning expressions to refer to data in several sources—both within a reading and elsewhere—you can appreciate references that a writer or speaker makes. You can also successfully detail your own thoughts about technical material you have read and express its relevance to other ideas in your own writing.

Technical readings are the most common setting for visual data such as graphs, tables, maps, and diagrams. However, you will likely also encounter these visuals outside of textbooks, in places like slide presentations, technical videos explaining structures or processes, and product specifications.

TIP

Multiword Engineering Vocabulary *Many expressions for describing information from a visual are multiword vocabulary items. (See the section Recognizing and Learning Multiword Vocabulary Items [p. 125].) The list on this page give only a sampling of useful multiword items. Research on the language typical of engineering texts has shown that these multiword expressions are especially valuable in the field..*

Expressions for Referring to or Interpreting a Visual			
a function of (time)	determined by the	is expected to	parameters such as
a significant effect on	diagram of the	is obtained by	proportional to the
assumed to be	for a given	is proportional to the	remain relatively stable
at room temperature	for different values	is shown in	results obtained from
be attributed to	for each test	it is evident	the experimental data
by a factor of	in this design	it is observed that	the experimental results
can be described	indicate that	it should be noted	the relationship between
can be determined	is assumed that	limited by the	the results show (that)
can be expressed as	is considered to	noted that (the)	with respect to
can be observed	is defined as the	number of samples	

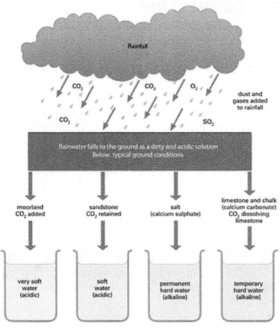

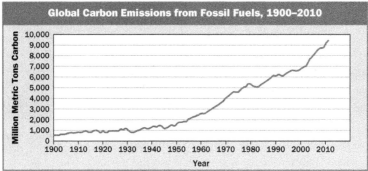

The following statements are examples of references that could be made to the two visuals above:

The figure is a **diagram of the** impact of air quality and soil types on the pH levels in water.

Together air quality and soil type can have **a significant effect on** the acidity or alkalinity of groundwater.

Very soft water—water derived from rainwater and moorland soil—**is defined as the** least acidic water type of the four categories.

It should be noted that global carbon emissions from fossil fuels remained relatively stable from 1900 to 1940.

The diagram **indicates that** global carbon emissions from fossil fuels began to increase dramatically around 1950.

By becoming more familiar with these expressions—as well as recalling those you learned in the section Understanding Text References to Visuals (p. 109)—you will be better able to recognize them in a variety of contexts and understand their functions. You will also be able to use them when you are asked to complete technical homework assignments, write research reports based on your personal research, and create slide presentations about technical information.

EXERCISE 3

A. Read this excerpt from "History of Air Quality in the United States" (p. 121). Underline the expressions that refer to a visual.

   Air quality in the United States has improved dramatically in the past several decades, with fewer harmful respirable particles and airborne fumes. This is due to the adoption of federal regulations as part of the Clean Air Act of 1970. This law monitors common pollutants, and the reduction of ground-level pollution can be attributed to its enforcement over the past half-century or so, the net result being air that is cleaner to breathe and noticeably clearer in satellite images and other measurable tests. A comparison of the air quality in the eastern United States in 2005 and 2011 is shown in Figures 1 and 2. However, it can be noted that air pollution remains at toxic levels in many urban areas. More disturbingly, scientific studies indicate that other emissions, namely carbon dioxide, methane, nitrous oxide, and fluorinated gases—known as long-lived greenhouse gases—continue to increase. These atmospheric emissions are culprits in climate destabilization, which threatens humanity's health and welfare.

B. Read the slides. Identify the expressions that the speaker uses to refer to the visuals. Then circle them.

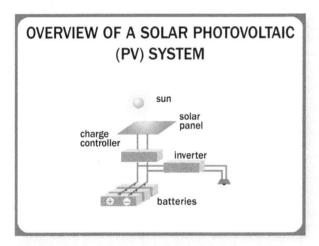

Slide 1

Presenter: I'd like to give an overview of a solar photovoltaic system. This is a diagram of the components of a solar photovoltaic system. In this design, the energy from the photovoltaic cells, or solar panels, is converted to direct current, or DC electricity, and is stored in the batteries. The DC electricity in the batteries is then typically converted into alternating current, or AC electricity.

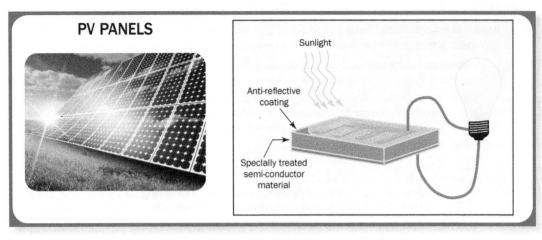

Slide 2

Presenter: A set of solar panels is shown in this image. Beside it is a diagram of the elements of a basic photovoltaic, or solar, cell. Solar cells are composed of semiconductor materials, such as silicon. A thin semiconductor layer is treated to act as an electric field, positive on one side and negative on the other. It can be observed that when sunlight hits the solar cell, electrons are released from atoms in the semiconductor material. With electrical conductors attached to the positive and negative sides, an electrical circuit is formed. And, as you can see, the diagram indicates that the electrons are then harnessed as electricity.

The amount of electricity that a solar PV system can produce and provide is limited by the number of peak sunlight hours per day, the wattage capacity of the solar panels, and the storage capacity of the batteries, among other factors. With respect to battery age and the ambient temperature of the battery box, both can have a significant effect on battery performance. A system of six 225-watt solar panels can be expected to generate up to 1,350 watts. It should be noted that this is the rate during peak sunlight hours. The total number of watts that can be transferred to a set of batteries in a day is a function of the power and number of panels in the system and the number of peak sunlight hours. For example, if there are six 225-watt panels absorbing six peak hours of sunlight per day, the battery gain for that day would 8,100 watts.

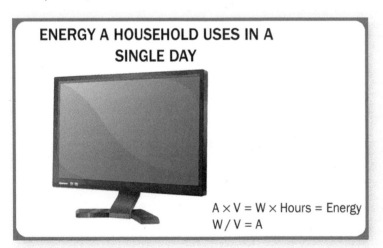

Slide 3

Presenter: With respect to household usage, standard electrical outlets and switches for most appliances in the US is 120 volts. Larger appliances such as dryers, well pumps, air conditioners, and electric furnaces require 240 volts. For a given appliance or set of appliances, the amount of watts used can be determined by the formula amps (A) times volts (V) equals watts (W). For example, a standard LCD computer monitor may be rated at 150 watts. The watts used by a single household in one day can be obtained by taking the wattage rating of each appliance times hours the appliance is in use. For example: Let's say a computer monitor that is rated at 150 watts is in use for eight hours. Watts used would equal 1,200.

EXERCISE 4

A. Read the article.

HISTORY OF AIR QUALITY IN THE UNITED STATES

1   Air quality in the United States has improved dramatically in the past several decades, with fewer harmful respirable particles and airborne fumes. This is due to the adoption of federal regulations as part of the Clean Air Act of 1970. This law monitors common pollutants, and the reduction of ground-level pollution can be attributed to its enforcement over the past half-century or so, the net result being air that is cleaner to breathe and noticeably clearer in satellite images and other measurable tests. A comparison of the air quality in the eastern United States in 2005 and 2011 is shown in Figures 1 and 2. However, it can be noted that air pollution remains at toxic levels in many urban areas. More disturbingly, scientific studies indicate that other emissions, namely carbon dioxide, methane, nitrous oxide, and fluorinated gases—known as long-lived greenhouse gases—continue to increase. These atmospheric emissions are culprits in climate destabilization, which threatens humanity's health and welfare.

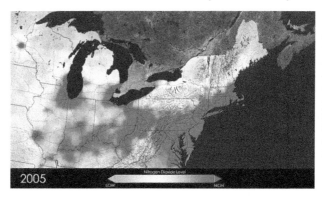

Figure 1 Satellite image of pollution buildup in the eastern United States in 2005

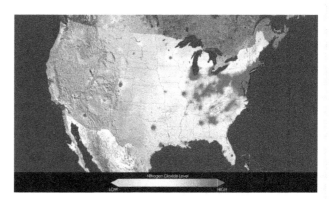

Figure 2 Satellite image of pollution buildup in the eastern United States in 2011

2   While federal regulation of the environment may seem like a relatively recent development, in fact, governmental control over air quality is an old concept. Records exist of edicts as early as the 13th century, when King Edward I ordered the execution of any person found burning sea coal, which created black bilious clouds of smog over London. In America in the 1970s, urban areas like Los Angeles had similarly notorious toxic smog. States had stubbornly failed to adopt and enforce federally recommended standards for pollution control, and growing public awareness of environmental degradation prompted Congress to pass the Clean Air Act in 1970. Since that time, air quality laws have been amended numerous times to address both implementation lags and new research that warranted changes to the

Continued

regulations. Statistics show marked improvements in American air quality in tandem with overall economic growth, a joint improvement that critics of federal regulation in the 1960s and 1970s had warned was unfeasible.

Air Quality Improvements

3   The Clean Air Act regulates six harmful pollutants: ozone, particulate matter, carbon monoxide, nitrogen oxides, sulfur dioxides, and airborne lead. These pollutants—formed primarily from human-created emission sources like combustion engines and factories without adequate emission filters—cause acute and chronic health problems including aggravated respiratory illnesses, various cancers, and an increased risk of heart failure. Overall, the United States saw an aggregate 72 percent reduction in the six pollutants from 1970 to 2012, while the economy sustained a 219 percent increase in its gross domestic product in the same time frame. Among the pollutants, for example, airborne lead pollution fell significantly after the law phased out and eventually banned lead from gasoline and other common consumer products. As a result, airborne lead pollution in 1980, at 2.64 micrograms per cubic meter of air ($\mu g/m^3$), fell to 0.63 $\mu g/m^3$ in 1990 and 0.33 $\mu g/m^3$ in 2000. This is summarized in Figure 3. The EPA recorded a level of 0.05 $\mu g/m^3$ in 2014 and found that most areas of the country fell under the air quality standard of 0.15 $\mu g/m^3$.

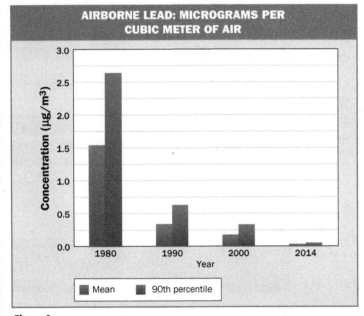

Figure 3

4   Particulate matter has also fallen due to more stringent requirements for power plants and diesel vehicles. As shown in Figure 4, fine particulate matter, which the government began distinguishing from larger particulate matter in 1996, has fallen from an average of 13.5 $\mu g/m^3$ in 2000—above the EPA's required safety threshold of 12 $\mu g/m^3$—to 8.8 $\mu g/m^3$ in 2014. Fine particulates, or those of less than 2.5 micrometers in diameter, are the smallest and most hazardous of all particles because they can settle deep within the lungs and penetrate the bloodstream.

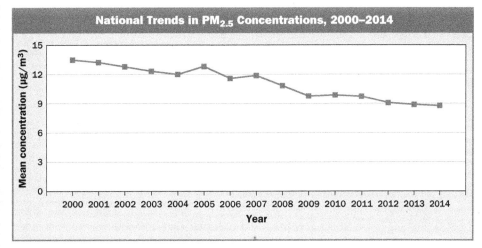

National Trends in PM$_{2.5}$ Concentrations, 2000–2014

Mean concentration (μg/m³)

Year

Figure 4

Continuing Problems and Deepening Concerns

5   Air quality improvements do not mean clean air for all. An American Lung Association report from 2015 indicates that 138.5 million people, or approximately four out of ten Americans, live in areas with harmful levels of either particulate matter or ground-level ozone. In California, ground-level ozone pollution has been greatly reduced, but many of its cities remain at the top of the list of US metropolitan areas with hazardous levels of pollution. Six US cities had a record number of days in 2015 with elevated particle pollution: Visalia, California; Fairbanks, Alaska; Phoenix, Arizona; Yakima, Washington; Reno, Nevada; and the greater San Francisco area. Drought and wildfires contributed to the air quality problems, as did burning wood as a heat source.

6   Such climate-related trends, including wildfires, intense heat waves that can wither crops, and increased airborne allergens, are symptoms that can be attributed to global warming. The results obtained from studies indicate that carbon emissions, which the government has only just begun to regulate, are expected to cause an increase in ground-level ozone and particle pollution. Scientists estimate that half of aggregate global emissions from fossil fuels have been released into the atmosphere since the mid-1970s, and levels continue to rise each year.

7   To ensure that air quality improvements continue in the future, the US government continues to update laws and regulations. In August 2015, the US government began to finalize standards that will regulate long-lived greenhouse gases like carbon dioxide and nitrous oxide, many of which had been emitted unchecked by power plants. The EPA's new standards, known as the Clean Power Plan, are part of the government's first national regulation of such pollutants. The plan calls for a firm presence of renewable energy sources as well as emissions reductions from the power sector. The target reduction is 730 million metric tons of carbon pollution by the year 2030, which equals roughly the annual emissions of two-thirds of the nation's passenger vehicles, or more than half of the nation's homes. By the same target date, sulfur dioxide levels are set to be 90 percent lower than 2005 levels and nitrogen oxide levels 72 percent lower. Public health benefits from a reduction to particle pollution, ozone, smog, and other pollution would mean fewer premature deaths, asthma attacks, and hospital admissions due to pollution exposure. Though it is evident that the US government has made great strides in controlling six main pollutants and has improved the overall air quality of the nation, these amount to only a few steps on the long road toward curbing climate-altering emissions.

B. Use what you read to complete the sentences. Note that each phrase in bold is an expression you learned about. (The completed sentences could be used to make a list of key statistics and facts reported in the reading.)

1. .... **is considered to** be a result of the government's adoption of federal regulations as part of the Clean Air Act of 1970. (Paragraph 1)

2. .... can **be attributed to** the Clean Air Act of 1970. (Paragraph 1)

3. Scientific studies **indicate that** emissions of carbon dioxide, methane, nitrous oxide, and fluorinated gases—known as .... —continue to increase. (Paragraph 1)

4. It can be **noted that** air pollution remains .... (Paragraph 1)

5. An American Lung Association figure from 2015 **indicates that** approximately four out of ten Americans live in areas with .... (Paragraph 5)

6. **The results** from studies **show that** carbon emissions will likely cause .... (Paragraph 6)

C. Create a different visual to express the relationships you read about in the reading or saw in the visuals. For example, you could create a line graph with "time" along the *x*-axis and "levels of 2.5 μm particulates" along the *y*-axis. Another possibility might be a bar graph for changes in levels of the six gases targeted by the EPA. After completing your visual, write three statements in reference to it that explain important points to a reader. Use expressions for referring to or interpreting a visual.

D. Write three sentences conveying your thoughts or observations about the visual you created in Part C. Use phrases for referring to or interpreting a visual.

Go to **MyEnglishLab** to complete a vocabulary exercise and skill practice, and to join in collaborative activities.

For more about REFERRING TO VISUAL DATA, see W and OC ENVIRONMENTAL ENGINEERING .

LANGUAGE SKILL
RECOGNIZING AND LEARNING MULTIWORD VOCABULARY ITEMS

WHY IT'S USEFUL Native speakers of English depend heavily on vocabulary items that are more than one word long. By understanding these multiword vocabulary items when you read and by using these larger chunks to express your own reactions to what you read, you can achieve greater efficiency. By learning and remembering multiword items as whole units, you can become more fluent and accurate.

You are familiar with **multiword vocabulary items** of many different types, such as
- phrasal or prepositional verbs: *give up, fall back on, pass out*
- compound nouns: *car door, transportation system*
- complex prepositions: *next to, at the front of, in terms of*
- proverbs, sayings, advice: *better safe than sorry; don't spend it all in one place; leave well enough alone*
- metaphorical idioms: *pass the buck; a fly on the wall; kick the bucket*

There are other possible categories as well, but classifying them is not really your most important task as a learner. In fact, many of them are difficult to classify grammatically; people may disagree about exactly what part of speech to call such items as these: *pay attention to, as a matter of fact, fait accompli,* and *as shown in Figure X.*

Also, trying to analyze them too much could slow down your learning. Analysis focuses your attention on the parts (for example, *pay attention to* = VERB + NOUN + PREPOSITION) when in fact you should learn and remember a multiword item as a single, whole unit.

RECOGNIZING MULTIWORD ITEMS
Your best strategy for recognizing multiword items in readings is to take note of groups of words that you see (or hear) often as tightly bound (linked together) units. For example, you have almost certainly realized that the two words *cell* and *phone* come together to make a completely separate multiword vocabulary item, *cell phone*. It is a tightly bound unit. You do not learn *cell phone* by learning the single words *cell* and *phone*, then adding them. You simply know that English vocabulary includes the item *cell phone*.

Your dictionary can be of some help in learning multiword items. Good dictionaries—both for learners of English and for general use—typically list the most common multiword items that include

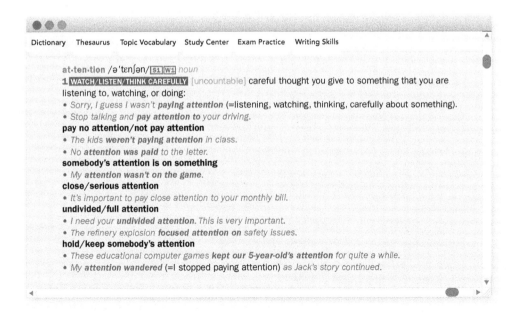

a substantial headword. For example, any good dictionary lists *pay attention to* as a subentry for the headword *attention*. Some dictionaries even list it as a subentry for the headword *pay* (although this is less common). If there is a clear headword for a phrase you have read and you are wondering whether it is part of a multiword unit, you can look in your dictionary to check.

One difficulty with the dictionary approach is that there is not always a clear headword, and many multiword units consist of very common "little" words that come together to form the multiword whole. Some examples are *get around to, make too much of,* and *a good bit of.*

MULTIWORD UNITS RELATED TO VISUALS

As we saw in the section Understanding Text References to Visuals (p. 109), there are many tightly bound multiword units for referring to visuals within a text. Research has shown that the following are among the most common:

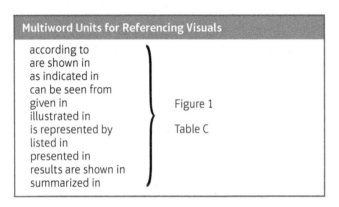

Multiword Units for Referencing Visuals

according to
are shown in
as indicated in
can be seen from
given in
illustrated in
is represented by
listed in
presented in
results are shown in
summarized in

} Figure 1

Table C

You may notice that these frequent multiword units for referring to visuals show a very strong pattern: **past participle of verb for "showing" + preposition (*by / from / in*) + noun for a kind of visual**. By mastering this one pattern, using a few appropriate verbs and a few appropriate nouns, you can more easily move through readings with such references and you can more fluently make comments about the visuals you interpret. Note that most of these units can also be stated in the active voice, such as *Figure X shows ….*

EXERCISE 5

Each multiword unit underlined in the sentences has at least one strong headword. Circle the word that you think is the headword. Some multiword units have two possible headwords. In that case, circle both.

1. I always carry a flashlight to use <u>in the event that</u> the lights go out.

2. Despite all the trouble we've had, we have <u>forged ahead</u> and have finished the project.

3. Rumors on the Internet say that the manager stole money from the company. Maybe this new report will <u>put</u> those rumors <u>to rest</u>.

   > **TIP**
   > ....
   > *To check whether your dictionary is strong, look up the headwords from Exercise 5 and see if the subentries feature multiword units. If your dictionary has no subentries, it may be a weak dictionary.*

4. The purpose of this meeting is to discuss <u>the pros and cons</u> of new regulations on power plants.

5. A: In what year did Congress pass the Clean Air Act? B: I <u>don't have the faintest idea</u>.

6. Low oil prices are a relief because consumers pay less for gas. But the situation really <u>cuts both ways</u>. There is a downside because people drive more and produce more pollution.

7. Not many people are buying the new "smart watches," which perform somewhat like cell phones. Still, that technology will <u>pave the way for</u> other types of wearable devices in the future.

8. The visibility in the city is <u>a function of</u> the amount of small dust particles in the air.

EXERCISE 6

The following sentences express information from the graph (first seen in "Air Quality and Athletic Events" on p. 114). Complete each sentence with a multiword unit that refers to the visual. For variety, use some units with the past participle and others in the active voice.

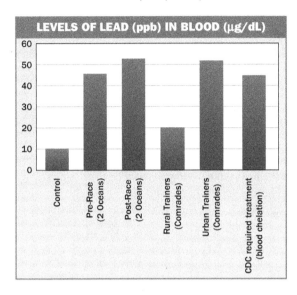

Figure 2 Blood lead levels of runners from two South African marathons (the 2 Oceans Marathon and the Comrades Marathon) in 1984. "Urban trainers" trained in cities for the Comrades Marathon, and "rural trainers" in the countryside. "Control" subjects are nonrunners. Only the "control" group and the "rural trainers" had blood-lead levels below 45, the point at which the US CDC recommends that a child undergo emergency treatment to chelate (chemically cleanse) the blood.

1. *As shown in Figure 2* _____, the CDC requires emergency blood treatment if the blood-lead level goes above 45 micrograms per deciliter.

2. _____, the highest blood-lead content was measured in runners after the Two Oceans Marathon.

3. _____, it may be healthier to train for athletic events in the country rather than in the city.

4. The high blood-lead levels that _____ may indicate that the air in South Africa in 1984 was polluted by cars burning gasoline that contained lead.

5. The control group, composed of nonathletes, had much lower blood-lead levels, _____ .

6. _____ that blood-lead levels in adults can vary quite a lot, with some athletes having about four times as much as nonathletes.

7. Even before the Two Oceans Marathon was run, _____, athletes who were planning to run it had high blood-lead levels. The figure doesn't say why, but we can infer that this was the result of high respiration during training for the race.

Go to **MyEnglishLab** to complete a skill practice.

APPLY YOUR SKILLS

WHY IT'S USEFUL By applying the skills you have learned in this unit, you can successfully read this challenging text and learn about the impact of nanofiber technology on air filtration.

BEFORE YOU READ

A. Discuss these questions with one or more students.

1. What do you know about past methods for preventing outdoor air pollution? How do you think this might have changed in recent years?

2. How do you think respirator masks and air purification systems might relate to nanofiber technology?

3. What kinds of tasks require a respirator or dust mask? Have you ever worn one, or do you know someone who has? How effective was it?

B. Imagine that you will be participating in a small group discussion about the passage "Nanofibers Revolutionize Air Filtration," which begins on the next page. Your group will be discussing the following questions. Keep these questions in mind as you read the passage.

1. What are nanofibers, and what are some applications of that technology?

2. According to a 2014 study done by the World Health Organization, particulate air pollution is worsening in many urban areas around the world. What are the causes?

3. What were some uses for filters in the recent and distant past?

4. What is the difference—in terms of protection from small particulates—between the breathable air filter developed by Hong Kong-based researchers in 2014 and the nearly transparent nanofilter developed by US-based researchers in 2015?

5. Explain the process of electrospinning.

C. Review the Unit Skills Summary. As you read the passage, apply the skills you learned in this unit.

UNIT SKILLS SUMMARY

Interpret visuals.
- Deepen your understanding of the text and gather information that may be too complex for words by making connections between visuals and the text.

Understand text references to visuals.
- Use your knowledge of phrases used to refer to visuals to take away the most important information from a visual.

Interpret the information in visuals.
- Recognize classes of data within a visual. Recognize trends, extremes, and averages.

Refer to visual data within and beyond a reading.
- Understand expressions that refer to data in a variety of sources. Detail your own thoughts about technical material you have encountered in visuals.

Recognize and learn multiword vocabulary items.
- Recognize multiword vocabulary items in the text. Add to your vocabulary useful multiword units for referring to visuals.

A. Read the passage. Annotate and take notes as necessary.

Nanofibers Revolutionize Air Filtration

1 Urban areas around the world are plagued by particle pollution and ground-level ozone, with some cities engulfed in air pollution that far exceeds the guideline limits set by the World Health Organization (WHO). Rapid development of nanofiber technology in the past decade has allowed engineers to build increasingly effective air-filtration devices that block hazardous pollutants. Electrospun polymeric nanofibers are both comfortable to wear in respirators and efficient at blocking out the worst particle pollution, and researchers are using them to develop advanced air purification devices to help people breathe safely in various environments. Nanofibers can be used in respirator masks as well as in other environmental access points, such as water filtration, vehicular air filters, and air purification systems in buildings.

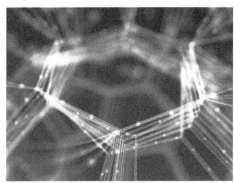

Nanofiber

2   Fine particulate and nano-sized gaseous pollution from substances like diesel fumes and industrial emissions are hazardous to breathe and have been empirically linked to respiratory disease, cancer, and other health risks. Disturbingly, WHO reported in 2014 that particulate air pollution was worsening in many urban areas around the world because of coal-fired power plants, increases in the fleet of personal vehicles, inefficient heating systems, and the burning of biomass for heat and cooking. WHO monitors 1,600 cities in 91 countries and found that of all the people living in areas of assessment, only 12 percent lived where air quality guidelines for $PM_{2.5}$ particulates were met. As studies from other organizations corroborate the notion that air pollution is cause for concern, and in the absence of effective mitigation of pollution-emitting processes, wearable respirators and home filtration devices may be the only solutions to the problem of dangerous-to-breathe air.

Figure 1 A common safety mask

3   Air purification respirators are typically associated with postindustrialized environments, but they have existed for centuries. Not unlike their modern counterparts, filters built hundreds of years ago targeted a wide range of culprits, from mold spores to dust to fumes generated by toxic weapons and mining operations. In the 1700s and 1800s, inventors dabbled in building air-purifying respirators out of materials such as fine woven cloth and moistened wool to protect miners and soldiers. Gas masks with charcoal cartridges and particulate filters were developed and used during World War I to protect soldiers from hazardous gases. In the 1970s, single-use particulate respirators with polymer fibers began to be widely used in industry in the United States. Presently, the US National Institute for Occupational Safety and Health regulates particulate matter respirators by lab testing and certifying devices that guard against 95 percent of fine particulate matter, giving such respirators a designation known as "N95" if they meet particulate matter filtration standards. These types of respirators are typically constructed of layers of polypropylene, activated carbon cotton, and sometimes nanofibers, and are in great demand worldwide in cities with high pollution levels.

4   The term *nanofibers* refers to fibers with a diameter of less than 1 micron, which is

Continued

thousands of times smaller than a human hair. Nanofibers have a broad range of applications in various fields, including in fuel cells, medicine, and the environment. Though nanofibers have been used in filtration systems for several decades, rapid development in the technology coupled with the vast potential for nano-enabled products has positioned the emerging nanotechnology as a fast-growing market. In the sector of air purification, the performance of various polymeric nanofibers as filtration material is robust due to the material's ability to provide a more efficient filter that lasts longer and catches more harmful particles. To form the nanofibers, a process called electrospinning is employed. Figures 2a and 2b show the electrospinning process whereby a polymer solution is jetted out of a syringe by a high voltage electric field and directed toward a grounded collector, where it then dries and forms a polymeric net that resembles a spider web. This web, sometimes referred to as a nanoweb, can be used in many different applications. Depending on the polymeric solution, it is possible to construct nanofibers with diameters in the range of 10 to 2,000 nanometers (nm).

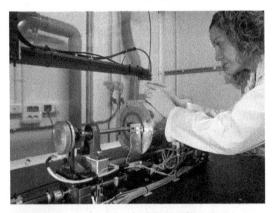

Figure 2a A technician developing nanofibers by electrospinning

5   In 2014, Hong Kong-based researchers developed effective breathe-through filters by using multilayer nanofibers with permeable layers allowing for maximal airflow. The nanofibers efficiently absorb and block 80 percent of the smallest particles. No conventional dust mask could perform that well without posing problems of great bulk and weight. Unlike heavier or thicker masks, a mask fitted with nanofiber layers is

as comfortable to wear as a conventional face mask. The technology involves coating polymeric nanofibers to a substrate medium, then sandwiching two layers of the nanofiber medium within support layers (see Figure 3). Such multilayered nanofibers make respirators practical, and could have even broader applications, including being incorporated into surgical masks, installed in air vents, or used in standing air filters in buildings to improve indoor air quality.

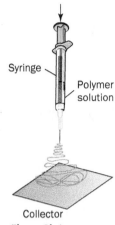

Figure 2b A representation of the electrospinning process

6   US-based researchers in 2015 used the low-cost polymeric solution polyacrylonitrile, which is used to make surgical gloves, to form a nearly transparent nanofilter that filtered out more than 95 percent of all fine particulate matter. The material also achieved high air flow, making it possible to be easily and comfortably adapted to a wearable filter. Manufacturers are excited at the prospect of filters with such great transparency—up to 90 percent—and affordability. In the electrospinning process, engineers applied the polyacrylonitrile polymer solution to a commercial metal-coated window screen mesh. The process is scalable, and nanofibers could be installed on window screens, which would maintain transparency while providing fresh, clean air to a home or business. When outdoor air conditions are poor and individuals stay indoors, eventually the indoor air also becomes unhealthy to breathe, and indoor air purification machines come with a high energy demand and prohibitive prices for many people worldwide. A nanofiber filter, however, would not require a power source and would likely be broadly affordable.

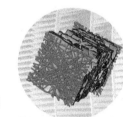

Figure 3 Multilayer nanofiber filter

7   Air pollution is a hazard for many millions of people, but air filtration capabilities and

nanotechnology advancements may be able to provide an opportunity for many to breathe a little easier. As engineers research and produce new types of nanofibers and nanofiber filtration inventions, particularly those that require no batteries and have minimal cost, more people may benefit from their incorporation into effective respirators, window screens, air vent filters, and other pollution-blocking devices.

B. Reread the discussion questions in Before You Read, Part B. Is there anything you cannot answer? Which of the reading skills you have learned in this unit can you use to find the answers?

Go to **MyEnglishLab** to read the passage again and answer critical thinking questions.

THINKING CRITICALLY

At international conferences about environmental quality, divisions often develop between wealthy countries and poorer ones. Wealthy countries often push for strong restrictions on the air pollution produced by poorer countries whose industries are not highly developed and who burn mostly coal and other high-pollution fuels to power their industries. The poorer countries then often resist these restrictions with an argument such as, "You rich countries should not try to restrict us. In earlier decades, you created a lot of air pollution while developing your industries to a high level. Now that you have succeeded, you want to stop us from catching up to you." Consider this issue from a number of standpoints. Do poor countries have a right to pollute the air in order to catch up to rich countries? Do rich countries have a right to pressure poorer countries to accept expensive limits on their development? Is some system of compensation possible—such as having rich countries pay poor countries not to pollute? Write one or two paragraphs explaining your views on the rich / poor divide in air pollution policy. Be prepared to explain your thoughts to one or more other students.

THINKING VISUALLY

The relationships shown in this visual are complex. There are categories of emissions, types of air pollutants, and levels of emissions. By taking all three things into account, we can construct statements such as, "Stationary fuel combustion accounted for more than 35 percent of direct $PM_{2.5}$ in the United States in 2010." Come up with four other combinations and construct similar statements. Be prepared to share your statements.

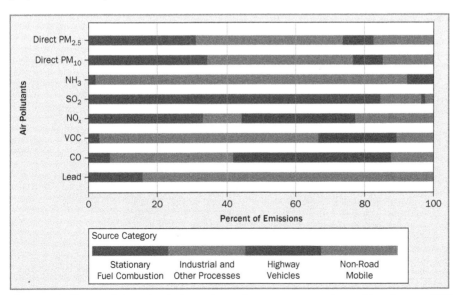

Figure 1 Distribution of US total emission estimates by source category for specific pollutants, 2010.
*Lead figures are from 2008.

THINKING ABOUT LANGUAGE

Read these excerpts from "Nanofibers Revolutionize Air Filtration." Underline the multiword item that has the meaning indicated in parentheses.

1. In the sector of air purification, the performance of various polymeric nanofibers as filtration material is robust due to the material's ability to provide a more efficient filter that lasts longer and catches more harmful particles.

   ("because of")

2. Disturbingly, WHO reported in 2014 that particulate air pollution was worsening in many urban areas around the world because of coal-fired power plants …

   ("places where electricity is generated")

3. As studies from other organizations corroborate the notion that air pollution is cause for concern, and in the absence of effective mitigation of pollution-emitting processes, wearable respirators and home filtration devices may be the only solutions to the problem of dangerous-to-breathe air.

   ("a reason to be worried")

4. Not unlike their modern counterparts, filters built hundreds of years ago also targeted a wide range of culprits, from mold spores to dust to fumes generated by toxic weapons and mining operations.

   ("many various types of")

5. These types of respirators are typically constructed of layers of polypropylene, activated carbon cotton, and sometimes nanofibers and are in great demand worldwide in cities with high pollution levels.

   ("wanted by a large number of people")

6. No conventional dust mask could perform that well without posing problems of great bulk and weight.

   ("causing difficulties")

7. Manufacturers are excited at the prospect of filters with such great transparency—up to 90 percent—and affordability.

   ("about the future possibility")

▶ Go to **MyEnglishLab** to listen to Professor Hildemann and to complete a self-assessment.

Critical Thinking Skills

Part 2 moves from skill building to application of the skills that require critical thinking. Practice activities tied to specific learning outcomes in each unit require a deeper level of understanding of the academic content.

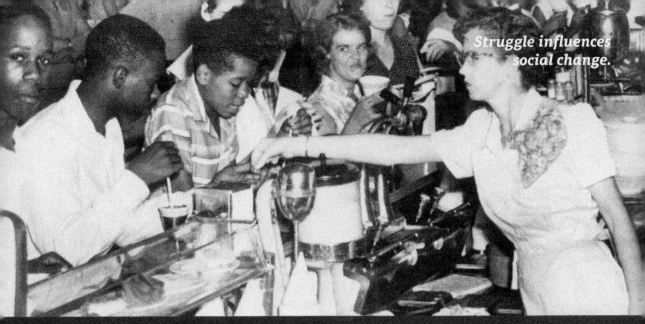

Struggle influences social change.

SOCIOLOGY

Fact and Opinion

UNIT PROFILE

You will consider the subject of sociology—specifically the issues of civil rights and race relations. Some of the topics you will study include the contributions of civil rights advocates, the history of civil rights movements, and the strategy of civil disobedience.

Preview the first paragraph of the reading "Henry David Thoreau's Civil Disobedience" on page 154. Can you identify two statements of fact in the paragraph? Can you identify two statements of opinion?

OUTCOMES

• Distinguish fact from opinion

• Recognize and interpret statements of opinion

• Recognize and interpret statements of fact

• Understand and produce critiques

• Understand signpost expressions that limit or define

GETTING STARTED

▶ Go to MyEnglishLab to listen to Professor Greenberg and to complete a self-assessment.

Discuss these questions with a partner or group.

1. Think about race relations in your home country or another country. How would you describe them in the present? In the past?

2. The image above shows African Americans being served at a soda counter in Oklahoma in 1958, after sit-ins prompted racial policy changes—though the shop removed the stools so patrons had to stand. Think of a human right you strongly believe in and feel that some members of society do not have. Would you consider participating in a nonviolent action of protest for that right? Why or why not?

3. Consider your own personal identity: student, friend, waitress, churchgoer, and so forth. How have your experiences and relationships shaped this identity? If you were to work with others to achieve a goal you believe in, what impact do you think your identity could have on this work?

For more about **SOCIOLOGY**, see 1 3 . See also W and OC **SOCIOLOGY** 1 2 3 .

CRITICAL THINKING SKILL
DISTINGUISHING FACT FROM OPINION

WHY IT'S USEFUL Distinguishing fact from opinion is necessary in recognizing the main and supporting ideas of a reading. You may discover that something presented as fact is actually opinion.

Distinguishing fact from opinion in a reading allows you to get the full meaning of the reading. This unit breaks the skill down into two supporting skills:

- recognizing and interpreting statements of opinion
- recognizing and interpreting statements of fact

NOTICING ACTIVITY

A. Read the passage.

PERCEPTIONS OF THE CIVIL RIGHTS MOVEMENT

[1] The US civil rights movement is dreamily memorialized as a virtually sacred period of moral advancement. [2] A national holiday commemorates its preeminent leader, Martin Luther King Jr., and school curricula teach children to celebrate the revolutionary ideals of the time. [3] However, during the period from 1954 to 1968—the heyday of the civil rights movement—public views of it were not nearly so sanguine. [4] Many white people throughout the United States, not just in the South, argued that antidiscrimination measures were detrimental to American society. [5] In some cases, they joined terrorist white supremacy groups such as the Ku Klux Klan. [6] Political leaders such as Alabama governor George Wallace, who ran on an openly racist platform, were reelected despite—or perhaps because of—their segregationist messages.

[7] However, the civil rights movement drew in many supporters as well. [8] National leaders, pressured in part by the global embarrassment of America's racial inequalities, increasingly supported black civil rights both legislatively and oratorically. [9] The civil rights period attracted more protesters and more white support of black people than any other time since the 1850s and the Abolitionist Movement. [10] In addition, mass media were often sympathetic, casting leaders of the civil rights movements as heroes, which helped nurture white sympathy for black struggles.

B. Look again at the passage. Notice that some sentences are mostly fact, others are mostly opinion, and others are a balance of the two.

C. Read why Sentences 1–3 are categorized as they are. Discuss why Sentences 4–11 are categorized as they are. Have they been sorted correctly?

Mostly Opinion: 1, 10: Sentence 1 includes a fact—that the civil rights period is memorialized—but the main point is that this memorialization is "virtually sacred," an opinion.

Mostly Fact: 2, 4, 5, 7, 9: Sentence 2 states that a holiday commemorates Martin Luther King Jr. and that schoolchildren learn about him. There is an element of opinion in that the author calls King "preeminent," but this is not the main idea of the sentence.

Almost Equally Fact and Opinion: 3, 6, 8: Sentence 3 factually states that 1954–1968 was the peak ("heyday") of the movement and that there is a difference in public opinion then and now, which common sense indicates is probably a fact. It also includes a statement of opinion in that it labels modern views as "sanguine" (excessively positive).

Go to **MyEnglishLab** to complete a vocabulary exercise and skill practice, and to join in collaborative activities.

SUPPORTING SKILL 1
RECOGNIZING AND INTERPRETING STATEMENTS OF OPINION

WHY IT'S USEFUL Some statements that appear to be factual may contain elements of opinion as well. By identifying the kinds of language that often accompany statements of opinion, you will be able to recognize when an author is presenting a personal idea or position.

An **opinion** is defined simply as a person's "ideas or beliefs about a particular subject."

Fact:	As of 2014, the rate of union membership had fallen 9 percent over the past 30 years.
Fact + opinion:	It's a shame that as of 2014, the rate of union membership had fallen 9 percent over the past 30 years.

The former is a pure fact because the statement is wholly neutral, containing no language that suggests an opinion provided by the author. The latter is demonstrative of a fact framed by an opinion, signaled by the phrase *It's a shame that ...*, which carries a connotation—one of the several types of language attributes to look for when attempting to recognize opinions within a text.

FEATURES OF STATEMENTS OF OPINION
- **Connotation** is a feeling or an idea that a word evokes beyond its literal meaning. Words may carry positive or negative connotations. Examples of words with positive connotations—words that indicate a favorable attitude—are *easygoing, youthful,* and *confident.* Examples of words with negative connotations include *uptight, immature,* and *arrogant.*
- **Tone** is the general feeling or attitude expressed in a piece of writing conveyed through elements such as word choice, selective use of examples and evidence, syntax, and punctuation. Categories of tone include humorous, approving, disapproving, persuasive, objective, informative, and formal. Study these two examples of tone:

Approving:	It was vitally important for the many who supported equality during the US civil rights movement to openly express their views in order to avoid disaster.
Informative:	The many who supported equality during the US civil rights movement openly expressed their views.

The first sentence approves of the movement through its use of strong language: *vitally important, avoid disaster.* The second sentence simply informs, without employing any emphatic language. By accurately identifying tone, you are better equipped to determine a writer's goal.
- **Bias** refers to a writer's partiality toward a particular perspective. The writer may either be *biased toward* a viewpoint (showing support or positive feelings toward it) or *biased against* a viewpoint (demonstrating opposition or negative feelings toward it). An example of bias is the attitude of a proud parent toward his or her child. The parent may be so biased that he or she considers the child highly gifted even when, in fact, the child's abilities are not extraordinary. Sometimes bias in a text may be very clear upon first read; however, bias is often concealed and only uncovered after a deeper reading.

In the following example, the writer demonstrates a very negative attitude toward the Ku Klux Klan. Notice the negative bias conveyed in the underlined words and phrases. For the words *values* and *ideal*, the negativity is communicated by the quotation marks, turning otherwise positive words into sarcastic remarks.

> The Ku Klux Klan—a <u>despicable organization</u> that upholds <u>"values"</u> of white supremacy and anti-immigration—<u>should be condemned</u> by all individuals who believe in equality. While this group claims to promote American and Christian values, it actually has used <u>terroristic methods</u> to instill fear in and commit violence against those it deemed <u>"impure."</u> It has gone about this in <u>inhumane and often brutal ways</u>, including burning crosses, beating and maiming people who don't fit in with <u>its "ideal" society</u>, and even going so far as to murder them. Despite what its members argue, there is <u>nothing positive or redeeming</u> about this <u>wretched organization</u>.

• **Signal phrases** are another feature of some statements of opinion. A signal phrase may indicate the author's own opinion, or it may indicate the opinion of someone else.

Author's opinion:	<u>In my opinion</u>, the current administration seems to be putting civil rights on the back burner.
Opinion reported by an author:	The current administration <u>is thought to be</u> putting civil rights on the back burner.

The mere addition of the phrase *is thought to be* in the second example tells a reader that the writer is not expressing his or her own opinion; rather, the writer is conveying an opinion held by others.

Examples of Phrases Used to Signal an Opinion	
According to X	**According to** Mahatma Gandhi, there is no better tactic for achieving goals than civil disobedience; however, many disagree.
Apparently	There was **apparently** a lot of media support of civil rights leaders, but not enough support across the population as a whole.
From my perspective	**From my perspective**, racial integration is something that still has not been achieved in US society.
In my experience	**In my experience**, protesters genuinely strive to make their desires known without resorting to violence.
In my opinion	**In my opinion**, civil disobedience is a tactic that more groups calling for change should use.
In my view	**In my view**, people do not truly support equal rights if they only state it; it must be evident through their actions.
It is the opinion of X that	**It is the opinion of** many **that** the Voting Rights Act of 1965 was only one step toward ridding American society of racism.
It is thought that	**It is thought that** the politician George Wallace was incredibly racist; however, those who supported him contest this and maintain that he fought for what he thought was right.
It may be that	**It may be that** certain high-level politicians during the civil rights movement never supported equal rights for all.
X is considered	Henry David Thoreau **is considered** to be one of the first activists in the United States to publicly advocate civil disobedience.
X suggest(s) / state(s)	Many **suggest** that it is irresponsible to intentionally violate laws in acts of civil disobedience, but others strongly endorse such actions.

- **Source and author purpose** are two other features to consider when deciding if a statement is an opinion. The information within a textbook, or in a newspaper or magazine news report, for example, is meant to inform, typically in an unbiased manner. On the other hand, the objective of blog posts, editorials, and feature articles tends to be to persuade, meaning that the information found in them is much more likely to include opinions.

EXERCISE 1

A. Circle the word in each pair that has the more negative connotation.

1. oppressive / tyrannical
2. violate / disobey
3. discard / dump
4. mutinously / defiantly
5. introduce / impose
6. barbaric / inhumane

B. Read the passage. What is the tone? How does the author set that tone? Point to specific elements of the passage (e.g., word choice, selective use of examples and evidence, syntax, and punctuation) that help you determine this.

Gandhi's Salt Strategy

Gandhi participating in the Salt March, 1930

1 Mahatma Gandhi's most successful acts of civil disobedience against Britain's oppressive rule aimed to involve people from all socioeconomic groups and bring sweeping changes to the entire society. These acts specifically employed methods of protest that were easily accessible to all. Regarded today as an exemplar of protest activism, Gandhi's so-called "khadi campaign" encouraged Indians to spin cotton into yarn, weave that yarn into cloth, and boycott British manufactured textiles. In a similar vein, Gandhi encouraged Indians to disobey British salt laws by producing their own salt. Spinning and weaving and salt-making are among the most humble of tasks, but according to Gandhi, they boosted self-respect among those viewed as the *hoi polloi*, they trained citizens to mobilize for a collective movement, and they provided people with constructive work that would eventually lead a nation to independence.

Khadi Campaign

2 Gandhi began his work as a civil rights leader not in India, but rather on the distant shores of South Africa, where he campaigned for equal rights for much of his two decades of residence there. Returning to his homeland of India in 1914 as a recognized rabble-rouser, he soon discarded Western clothing and donned the homespun cloth of India known as *khadi* as a way of symbolically casting off British rule. Britain controlled the textile market in India, and Gandhi began encouraging Indians to wear homespun cloth as a way of both

defying the British monopoly of the marketplace and increasing self-reliance. Traditional Indian clothing became not only a commodity, as it could be worn, but also a visual uniform of nationalism. The movement gained traction, and soon Gandhi's followers defiantly burned their British clothing and wore the traditional cloth.

Salt Campaign

3   The British imposed strict laws on the production and distribution of salt, which forced Indians to buy expensive, heavily taxed British salt. With meticulous care, Gandhi chose his method of protest against the British when he decided in 1930 to lead a 240-mile march to the sea to collect salt. His plan was met with disbelief when presented to the Indian authorities, but Gandhi defended his reasons, stating that salt was one of the most important necessities of life. He further called the tax inhumane and unjust, declaring that it was unconscionable to tax a commodity that millions of poor people required. Gandhi's idea, though initially met with skepticism, turned out to be ingenious because it created ripples that reached the farthest edges of the nation and spread word of the Indian independence movement throughout the world.

4   As with the khadi campaign, hundreds of thousands joined in Gandhi's Salt March. British-backed forces jailed more than 60,000 marchers and brutally beat many of them, but most marchers continued to adhere to nonviolent resistance even amidst the crackdown. The British eventually made concessions, and Gandhi's campaign gained a following abroad where his work was lauded, with *Time* magazine declaring him Man of the Year in 1930. Other civil rights leaders began to take notes for their own campaigns to come. India's victory came 17 years later in 1947, when the British succumbed to pressure and recognized India as an independent nation.

C. Read these excerpts from the passage, each of which contains biased language. Explain what language makes each excerpt biased.

1. Regarded today as an exemplar of protest activism, Gandhi's so-called "khadi campaign" encouraged Indians to spin cotton into yarn, weave that yarn into cloth, and boycott British manufactured textiles.

2. Spinning and weaving and salt-making are among the most humble of tasks, but according to Gandhi, they boosted self-respect among those viewed as the *hoi polloi*, they trained citizens to mobilize for a collective movement, and they provided people with constructive work that would eventually lead a nation to independence.

> **TIP**
> ....
> ***Biased or unbiased?*** *While it is true that news reports are intended to be informative (and thus unbiased), one part of them is often very biased: the quotes embedded in them. News reporters write their stories objectively, but the individuals who provide the quotes often give their opinions about the topic at hand.*

3. Returning to his homeland of India in 1914 as a recognized rabble-rouser, he soon discarded Western clothing and donned the homespun cloth of India known as *khadi* as a way of symbolically casting off British rule.

4. He further called the tax inhumane and unjust, declaring that it was unconscionable to tax a commodity that millions of poor people required.

5. Gandhi's idea, though initially met with skepticism, turned out to be ingenious because it created ripples that reached the farthest edges of the nation and spread word of the Indian independence movement throughout the world.

6. British-backed forces jailed more than 60,000 marchers and brutally beat many of them, but most marchers continued to adhere to nonviolent resistance even amidst the crackdown.

D. Discuss your answers with another student. Use information and examples from the passage to explain and support your answers.

Go to **MyEnglishLab** to complete a vocabulary exercise and skill practice, and to join in collaborative activities.

SUPPORTING SKILL 2

RECOGNIZING AND INTERPRETING STATEMENTS OF FACT

WHY IT'S USEFUL By considering types of language that typically characterize facts, you will be able to evaluate whether a reading excerpt is indeed a fact (versus an opinion). This will further develop your critical thinking skills and your ability to analyze and interpret what you are reading.

A **fact** is a piece of information that is known to be true. The ability to identify a statement of fact, and to distinguish that statement of fact from other types of statements—statements of opinions and statements of facts + opinions—is essential to your understanding of a reading.

Features of Factual Statements

- Phrases suggesting a citation, including:
  According to
  As reported by
  As stated in
  It is a fact that
  The author discusses / explains / writes, etc.
  The facts show that
  The results demonstrate / indicate
- Direct and indirect quotes (which often include quotation marks and in-line citations)
- Neutrality of vocabulary: This refers to an absence of connotative language and bias as well as an objective tone.
- Hedging: This is a type of cautious language that is often used in academic writing when a writer is presenting facts and wants to be as precise as possible. Examples of hedging:
  it appears
  it could be the case that
  may, might, can, could (modal verbs)
  probable / possible
  some
  tend(s) (not) to
  X indicate(s)
  X suggest(s)

> **TIP**
>
> **Be careful.** In academic writing, watch out for phrases like researchers suggest, scholars lament, and historians have established. At times, these phrases can be followed or preceded by pure facts, but they often contain a fact combined with the author's opinion about it. Facts are also frequently combined with opinions when an author reports on others' biases. Such an example of fact plus opinion is shown in this excerpt from the online reading "Distorting Effect": However, in the years since his assassination in 1968, King's slow ascension to a hero's pedestal has, **scholars lament**, frozen his character in time, thereby watering down the way in which his message speaks to continuing racial inequality today.

- Informative or enumerative tone: As mentioned earlier, an informative tone is one in which an author provides information about a topic without inserting any personal evaluation about the topic. When an author employs an enumerative tone, he or she is supplying a list of the objects, concepts, ideas, and so on that fall under a given construct, again, without adding opinions about the concept.

Informative:	A large number of legislators, state representatives, and high-level government officials now believe in providing all individuals with equal opportunities.
Enumerative:	Exactly 650 legislators, 401 state representatives, and 12 high-level government officials now believe in providing all individuals with equal opportunities.

However, the presence of an informative or enumerative tone does *not* mean that the information is necessarily purely factual. The inclusion of words that have strong connotations is often indicative of a statement of fact plus opinion. As mentioned earlier, authors sometimes interweave opinion with fact.

> Gandhi's Salt March was enormously influential, leading future civil rights leaders to adopt a tactic unparalleled by any other: civil disobedience.

While it is true that Gandhi's Salt March was influential, author bias is evident in the example above with the word "enormously." It is also a fact that future civil rights leaders adopted the tactic of civil disobedience, but it is clear that the author is inserting an opinion through the addition of the phrase "a tactic unparalleled by any other."

EXERCISE 2

A. Read this excerpt from "Gandhi's Influence" and identify the factual information. Circle the ten words and phrases in bold that are neutral. Then paraphrase five facts from the reading and write your paraphrases below.

> American civil rights movement **leader** Martin Luther King Jr. **drew heavily** upon the **strategies** of Mahatma Gandhi's campaign to combat **social injustice**, but he was not the first **civil rights leader** to draw parallels between the **oppression** of the Indian people and the injustice **inflicted upon** black people in America. In fact, King was one of many in **a long line** of leaders inspired by Gandhi's style of civil disobedience. **Decades** before King emulated Gandhi's **salt march** with his **historic march** from Selma to Montgomery, civil rights leaders were **working hard** to bring Gandhi's message **to the United States**. As early as the 1920s, **political leader** Marcus M. Garvey depended on Gandhi for intellectual legitimacy, and in 1929, **author and activist** W.E.B. Du Bois **published** a letter from Gandhi in an **influential NAACP magazine** that was widely distributed throughout **the black community**.

1. ....

2. ....

3. ....

4. ....

5. ....

B. Now read the full passage.

Gandhi's Influence

1 American civil rights movement leader Martin Luther King Jr. drew heavily upon the strategies of Mahatma Gandhi's campaign to combat social injustice, but he was not the first civil rights leader to draw parallels between the oppression of the Indian people and the injustice inflicted upon black people in America. In fact, King was one of many in a long line of leaders inspired by Gandhi's style of civil disobedience. Decades before King emulated Gandhi's Salt March with his historic march from Selma to Montgomery, civil rights leaders were working hard to bring Gandhi's message to the United States. As early as the 1920s, political leader Marcus M. Garvey depended on Gandhi for intellectual legitimacy, and in 1929, author and activist W.E.B. Du Bois

Continued

published a letter from Gandhi in an influential NAACP magazine that was widely distributed throughout the black community.

2   Gandhi's campaign targeted multiple social ills including the repressive rule of the British, the divisive "caste" system, and the pitting of Muslims against Hindus. It was Gandhi's focus on the integration of a group of people from the lowest caste, the "untouchables," that was of particular interest to many black Americans. Millions of Indians born into this caste system were marginalized and ostracized in Indian society to a degree that was almost unfathomable, and the integration Gandhi envisioned and labored for struck a chord with black Americans. In 1932, America's preeminent black newspaper, the *Atlanta Daily World*, printed a front-page article citing comments from Republican lawmaker William E. King about Gandhi's efforts to achieve integration for India's lowest class. The lawmaker compared the plight of the untouchables of India to Southern black people.

3   The message spread. In 1936, a group of leading black educators, including Howard Thurman, dean of historic Howard University, visited Gandhi in India. Gandhi asked the leaders why they had not yet adopted the approach of civil disobedience, stressing nonviolence as the only means for effective change. During and following World War II, many prominent leaders in the black community lauded Gandhi's work and prepared the way for an eventual charismatic leader of their own. Civil rights leader James Farmer studied Thurman's writings about Gandhi, and in 1942 he proposed a five-year plan of mobilization that called for acts of noncooperation, and economic boycott, both of which constituted civil disobedience. Farmer went on to become director of the Congress of Racial Equality, an organization that led a series of acts of civil disobedience in protest against segregation on buses. Another leader in the black community, Howard University president Mordecai Wyatt Johnson, visited India in 1949 and returned inspired. When Martin Luther King Jr. attended seminary, he heard a sermon by Johnson about Gandhi and soon after bought six books about the Indian leader.

4   Johnson, Thurman, and others preached of Gandhi's greatness as a leader who followed revolutionary principles while adhering to nonviolent methods. Gandhi, who referred to the untouchable caste as "children of God," was echoed by King, who spoke of a moral obligation to uphold the values of all humans, especially the oppressed. King himself visited India in 1959 and later used many of Gandhi's strategies in the US civil rights movement.

C. Answer the questions.

1. Look back at Paragraph 2. Which information do you identify as facts? Why?

....

2. Reread this sentence from Paragraph 3. Identify the neutral verb(s) and the verb(s) with connotation: Gandhi asked the leaders why they had not yet adopted the approach of civil disobedience, stressing nonviolence as the only means for effective change.

....

3. Look back at Paragraph 4. Which sentence contains the most neutral language?

....

D. Discuss the questions in Part C with another student. Use information and examples from the passage to support your answers.

Go to MyEnglishLab to complete a vocabulary exercise and skill practice, and to join in collaborative activities.

READING-WRITING CONNECTION
UNDERSTANDING AND PRODUCING CRITIQUES

WHY IT'S USEFUL In American universities and professional situations, you will very often need to understand passages that evaluate or critique something. You may also be asked to critique work you read. This involves making reasonable evaluative judgments that capture the strong and weak aspects of someone else's writing. While active reading inherently involves this critical function, in a critique, you express those value judgments and support them.

A critique is a piece of writing that examines the good and bad aspects of a work of art, a political campaign, a college course, or some other effort. Usually a critique attempts to apply reasonable criteria in its analysis, not simply offer unsupported approval or disapproval. Examples of kinds of critiques include book reports, analyses of historical events, assessments of scientific research, commentaries about political positions, and comparisons of possible solutions to problems.

Characteristics of Critiques

- Critiques make **evaluative remarks** about work, ideas, and so on. Therefore, critiques use the language of opinion along with the language of fact.
- Critiques offer **evidence** or at least explain a basis for evaluative remarks.
- The best critiques apply certain **criteria** as they judge or assess things. This lends structure to the critique and makes it seem more reasonable.
- Part of being **reasonable** is applying criteria that can reasonably be met. For example, you would not hold a high school filmmaker to the same standards as a professional.
- The best critiques attempt to be **fair**. Therefore, critiques often balance positive and negative remarks.
- Critiques may include the language of **hedging** ("X *may* be exaggerated," "*it appears that* Y happened") and the language of certainty ("X is *clearly* incompetent").
- Critiques often **speculate** about what might have happened in different circumstances. For that reason, they often include unreal conditionals ("*If* X had singled out more incidents of Klan violence, his claims *would have* carried more weight").

> **CULTURE NOTE**
> *College Culture: The Proper Persona in a Critique*
> College students are sometimes uncomfortable discussing a critique or writing their own. Young undergraduates, especially, may feel awkward making value judgments about material written by scholars more knowledgeable than they are. They feel like the persona they create in critiquing the work of others is false—only pretending to know what they're talking about. Some thoughts to keep in mind:
> - TRAIN. Assignments that require you to analyze and evaluate a piece of writing **train** you to be part of the academic discourse community. You have to start somewhere. Academics and professionals routinely go through the process of reading, considering, gathering more data, evaluating, reacting, and proposing alternate ideas. You may not have much to say yet, but you're preparing for the day when you do.
> - SEARCH. Thanks to **search** engines, it's easier than ever to fact-check the statements in a piece of writing and gather information for your own critiques.
> - LEAD. Even outside of academic writing, readers appreciate a writer who is confident. Confidence comes from knowing what you want to say and saying it in reasonable terms. In a typical reading or discussion situation, the author or the initial speaker is a leader. When delivering a critique in writing or speech, take responsibility; **lead** strongly and effectively.
> - SHOW HUMILITY. Still, no academic reader or discussion partner likes an arrogant know-it-all or sarcastic critic. You don't know it all, so be **humble** enough to admit when you are unsure of something—or avoid areas about which you are unsure. Most importantly, don't make cutting, sarcastic, or disparaging remarks about what you critique. Even if you think of something very clever to say, restrain yourself. Tell it as a joke to your friends later on, but don't use it in a critique or a discussion of a critique.

READING AND WRITING CRITIQUES

In a reading class, you could be asked to read and understand a critique that someone else has written. You may also be asked to write your own critique—to analyze and evaluate something you have read. The list of critique characteristics above can serve two purposes: 1) to help you look for certain characteristics in what you read, and 2) to guide you in writing your own critiques.

The following passages are from a critique that examines a particular political-protest tactic (organizing large marches in Washington, DC). Read each passage. Then read the questions and choose the best answers.

"Coxey's Army" is the eponymous moniker applied to a group of unemployed industrial workers who marched on Washington, DC, first in 1894 and again in 1914. Both years were times of severe economic recession. By the criterion of stamina, the 1894 march was significant, starting as it did 360 miles away in the town of Massillon, Ohio, (home of organizer Jacob S. Coxey) and involving arduous foot travel with minimal provisions. Indeed, it was the only one of several attempts that year to make it all the way to Washington.

1. What criterion is the author using to judge the significance of the marches of Coxey's Army?
   a. the time of year it occurred
   b. who led it
   c. its eventual goal
   d. its ability to tolerate hardship

2. Is the author's opinion of the 1894 march positive or negative in terms of that criterion?
   a. positive
   b. negative
   c. part positive and part negative

3. What is one piece of evidence the author gives to support his evaluation of Coxey's Army in terms of that criterion?
   a. the distance the marchers traveled
   b. the country's economic situation
   c. the message the marchers expressed
   d. the identity of the "army's" leader

The size of the crowd at Martin Luther King Jr.'s march on Washington in August 1963, officially known as the March on Washington for Jobs and Freedom, was enormous, weighing in at about a quarter of a million people. It was far better attended than any of the approximately ten similar major marches that had preceded it in US history. For comparison, note that Coxey's Army was probably no larger than 400. However, considerations of size have to grant the top prize to 1995's Million Man March. This was an effort to highlight a range of troubles in black communities—from unemployment to gang violence to police abuse— co-promoted by a motley alliance of leaders ranging from former DC mayor Marion Barry (who had served six months in prison on drug charges) to Louis Farrakhan of the Nation of Islam (infamous for his disparaging remarks about Jews). It produced no inspirational oratory or lasting pressure on lawmakers to redress wrongs. But, despite all its flaws, the Million Man March officially drew at least 400,000 black men to the capital (as estimated by the US Park Service) and probably more like 875,000 (an *après le fait* estimate by Boston University researchers). No other march comes even close in that regard.

4. What criterion does the author use to judge the marches on Washington, DC?

   a. the troubles they meant to protest
   b. the leaders who organized them
   c. the number of people in the march
   d. the degree of violence among marchers

5. Is the author's opinion of the 1995 march positive or negative in terms of that criterion?

   a. positive
   b. negative
   c. part positive and part negative

6. The author implies that the 1995 march is not admirable on some counts. What are the faults he implies? Choose TWO.

   a The problems it protested were not very serious.
   b. Some of its leaders had reputations for bad behavior.
   c. It produced no consequential outcome.
   d. It came at the wrong time in US history.

EXERCISE 4

A. Read the article.

Competing Approaches to the Civil Rights Struggle

1   Despite the 13th Amendment to the Constitution abolishing slavery, deep inequality among racial groups in the United States persisted throughout the Reconstruction Era and well into the mid-20th century. Martin Luther King Jr.'s Southern Christian Leadership Conference led one branch of the black power movement, one that preached nonviolent resistance. Leaders of more militant, revolutionary black power groups also fought against racial injustice, but they and King's branch diverged sharply in their *modi operandi*. Nonviolent resistance leaders are modern saints to mainstream America, while a pall of danger and subversiveness hangs over the memory of Malcolm X, the Black Panther Party, and other rivals of King's. One can reasonably ask whether this unbalanced retrospective is fair.

2   We can judge partly by the intellectual foundations of the various rights groups. King followed Mahatma Gandhi's advocacy of nonviolent resistance. It was a solid heritage. King built upon the work of the NAACP and other older groups, whose intellectual foundations could be traced back to W.E.B. Du Bois and the country's founders. In all cases, the emphasis was on peace. It was not so with the militant and separatist branches of the black power movement, most notably the Nation of Islam. It was headed

Continued

by Malcolm X, who invoked separatist leaders like Marcus Garvey (leader of a back-to-Africa movement) along with the principles of Islam, a faith most Americans of that era found baffling and foreign. The later black power movement sparked to life in the mid-1960s, when many black people were increasingly angry about a lack of progress even after antidiscrimination rules were signed into law. The more militant branches, notably the Black Panther Party for Self-Defense (founded in Oakland, CA), drew on black nationalist rhetoric. The Black Panthers—often pictured toting guns and quoted issuing threats to the police—urged black Americans to reclaim their racial identity and self-respect through political autonomy and force of arms. The most extreme among them argued for a new nation, the "Republic of New Africa," to be carved out of the southern United States. The Black Panthers based much of their thinking on Communist ideas about class warfare and revolution. Even in the 1960s and into the 1970s, when leftist ideology enjoyed some currency in the United States, that was a nonstarter. King clearly drew on intellectual traditions more palatable to most American thinkers.

3   By another important criterion—one's ability to speak to Americans without alienating them—King and his allies had a mammoth advantage. The peacefulness of their methods—including the gathering of some 250,000 people in Washington, DC, in 1963—lent acceptability to their message. King won a Nobel Peace Prize (1964) before his death; he would later have a national holiday named after him. King could effectively lobby white legislators, whose white constituents related better to King than to his rivals. Malcolm X (assassinated in 1965) concentrated on separating blacks from hostile whites and had no desire to influence the white-dominated government. His acceptance by mainstream white America was almost nil, although he certainly did have white sympathizers. Even support from the revered Rosa Parks could not counterbalance the Black Panther Party's openly belligerent stance, both rhetorically and pictorially—carrying automatic weapons, raising single fists in the air, calling the police "pigs," and threatening revolution. On any "alienation index" they would score high.

4   In terms of the related criterion of religion, King and his movement also triumphed. The religion of political reformers might seem an odd consideration, but America is deeply religious, at least in terms of superficial identification with one religion or another. To America as a whole, King (an ordained minister of the Southern Baptist church) was carrying on a tradition in which the black Christian church was a force for order and calm in the black community. Malcolm X was a Muslim, an identity that, as we noted, is now more mainstream but at the time seemed alien to most Americans. The Black Panther Party seemed even more alien in ignoring religion. Indeed, they identified with an anti-imperialist and anticapitalist message that implied international Socialism if not Communism. The average American heard "Communism" and thought "godless."

5   Some scholars speculate that if Malcolm X or the Panther founders had delivered oratorical wonders like King's, they might have enjoyed greater political influence. That's debatable; a more incisive question is this: What would have happened if the Nation of Islam or the Panthers had been served by wiser leaders? Though saddled with allegedly homicidal and larcenous frontmen, such groups had lasting cultural influence. Non-King branches of the black power movement bolstered black student unions, ushered in black studies programs, and raised the cultural profile of blacks. They also galvanized young black people to embrace their racial identity and set into motion a black arts renaissance, from which black theaters, art, writings, and cultural centers developed.

6   By one other criterion, King's branch of the movement may have been, ultimately, deficient. That is the ability to anticipate future conflicts. In the early battles for racial equality, the South was the battlefield, and its institutionalized racism the dragon that had to be slain. King's followers—raised in the South, taking aim at Southern mayors, sheriffs, and militias—seemed to be best poised. As it turned out, however, the Black Panther Party was probably better positioned to fight many long-term ills of the black community. Their roots were in the cities of the western and northern regions of the country. Their *cri de coeur*

was self-defense. Their leaders painted a stark scenario of continuing conflict, often armed, between black America and the law. Bobby Seale and Huey Newton of the Panthers may have had a more realistic long-term vision for America than did the far more positive King. The NAACP reports that in the early 2000s, more than 40 percent of the US prison population was black, even though African Americans comprise only about 13 percent of the US general population. An African American male has a one-in-six chance of being locked up at some point in his life. Homicide disproportionately affects blacks, who make up fully 50 percent of US murder victims. If things were tense in the 1970s between the Black Panthers and the police, current relations between blacks and urban police forces hardly seem improved. This doesn't so much vault the Panthers over King as champions of justice—for King's agenda did play out in law— but it does credit them with greater prescience, for their worldview has played out on the street.

B. Answer the questions.

1. The author states in Paragraph 1 her reason for critiquing the various approaches. What is that reason?

   a. No one has ever critiqued the approaches before.
   b. King's movement was not really successful.
   c. We should judge whether their reputations are deserved.
   d. The approaches are still competing for attention.

2. What criterion does the author use in Paragraph 2 to critique the approaches?

   ....

3. What is the most accurate restatement of the author's view of Malcolm X as expressed in Paragraph 2?

   a. His movement did not have a strong intellectual basis.
   b. The roots of his thinking seemed strange to most Americans.
   c. His effectiveness was lessened because he had been jailed for murder.
   d. He was less thoughtful than Marcus Garvey.

4. What criterion does the author use in Paragraph 3 to critique the approaches?

   ....

5. What is the most accurate restatement of the author's view of the Black Panther Party as expressed in Paragraph 3?

   a. Their militant image made them seem ominous to white people.
   b. Their willingness to use guns gave them more influence.
   c. Their use of guns and talk of revolution was only a show.
   d. Their association with Rosa Parks changed their approach.

6. What criterion does the author use in Paragraph 4 to critique the approaches?

   ....

7. What speculation about the future does the author most strongly imply in Paragraph 5?

   a. The ability to give good speeches would have made non-King activists more effective.
   b. If King had lived longer, he would have led the Panthers and Nation of Islam, too.
   c. Non-King activists would have been more successful if their leadership had been better.
   d. The Nation of Islam and the Panthers would have eventually killed each other off.

8. What is the most accurate restatement of the author's views of the Black Panther Party as expressed in Paragraph 6?

    a. The Panthers caused conditions to worsen for blacks in cities in the western and northern regions of the United States even as King improved them in the South.

    b. The Panthers were smart to cause conflicts between African Americans and the police.

    c. The Panthers were cruel to ignore the terrible conditions of African Americans in the South.

    d. The Panthers better anticipated that the longer-term racial struggles would be in the cities and would involve the police.

C. Use information from the fact sheet to write a short critique (about 150 words) about some aspect of the Black Panther Party. You may also choose to do some light research on the Internet to add material. Many different critiques are possible, including focusing on the Black Panthers' image, their accomplishments, their history, their leadership, or some other aspect of the group. In deciding how to structure your critique, be sure to choose one or two clear criteria for analysis.

FACT SHEET: THE BLACK PANTHER PARTY
- Founded in Oakland, California, 1966
- Image: Armed, dedicated to revolution, in opposition to police forces
- In 1968, Panther cofounder, Huey Newton is convicted of manslaughter in the death of a police officer, John Frey. Newton's conviction is eventually overturned.
- Ideas influence many African Americans beyond actual party members. A protest at the 1968 Olympic Games in Mexico City—the famous "Black Power" raised-fist salute by runners Tommie Smith and John Carlos—is associated in the public imagination with the party, although both men denied any Black Panther connections.
- In 1969 and 1970, Panther leader Eldridge Cleaver, along with other Panthers, visits North Korea and North Vietnam—both countries with which the United States was at war. They participate in anti-US demonstrations and meetings.
- In 1969, the Panthers and a rival California black activist organization engage in turf wars that eventually lead to a gun battle on the campus of the University of California-Los Angeles (UCLA). Two Panthers are killed in the incident in a UCLA dorm.
- Black Panther leaders Bobby Seale and Elaine Brown run for mayor and city council, respectively, in 1973 in Oakland, California. Their decisive losses led many Panthers to leave the party.
- Rumors of embezzlement and actual charges of murder follow the Panther leadership in the 1970s.
- Panther found Newton visits Communist countries China (1971) and Cuba (1974) despite US government travel bans.
- By the mid-1970s, Panther membership is down to about 25 people.
- Decades later, some former Panthers hold elective offices in various legislatures and on city councils.

Go to **MyEnglishLab** to complete a vocabulary exercise and skill practice, and to join in collaborative activities.

For more about **CRITIQUES**, see W **ECONOMICS** 2.

LANGUAGE SKILL
UNDERSTANDING SIGNPOST EXPRESSIONS THAT LIMIT OR DEFINE

WHY IT'S USEFUL Critiques and many other forms of academic writing may be careful to limit the extent of what they say. Their authors try to be very precise. Understanding certain signpost expressions will help you appreciate the true extent of what an author says. By integrating such expressions into your own vocabulary, you can express yourself more accurately.

Some vocabulary items are mostly functional. The "depth" of their lexical (word-like) meaning is not very great, but they are very useful for a certain purpose. We are interested here in those whose purpose is to **signpost** (indicate) the limits of or restrictions on an author's comments.

Most of these signposts introduce a topic area. For instance, study this sentence:

When we consider wages, African Americans fall behind most other groups.

The signpost *when we consider* is used to introduce the topic of wages, but it can do more than that. It not only introduces but also limits, as if to say "I'm not talking about all areas, but in the area of wages, African Americans fall behind." This is an important function, especially when talking about a sensitive topic like race. The author wants to make sure the reader does not think he or she is claiming that African Americans fall behind in other areas.

Signposts often indicate one limitation within a series of limitations. For example, consider the signposts in bold in this paragraph:

POLITICAL CONDITIONS FOR AFRICAN AMERICANS

The second decade of the 21st century has brought a mixed bag of political circumstances for African Americans. **By one criterion**, things have never been better. A man whose father was a black African became president of the United States. **When it comes to** future political influence, however, blacks have taken a hit, as the Supreme Court weakened some provisions of the 1965 Voting Rights Act. **When we consider** future elections, this court action will make voting harder for hundreds of thousands of blacks. **If we define** political progress to be greater participation in legislative bodies, blacks have had something to celebrate. In 2015, there were 46 black members of the House of Representatives, representing a steady rise since the 1980s. However, **in terms of** their power, they saw a reduction when the Republican Party took over the House of Representatives. The Republican leadership failed to name even one black person to a committee chair, one of the most powerful positions in the legislative branch.

The limitation signposts are especially valuable in a text like this, where the commentary swings from one issue to another, and from remarks about positive points to remarks about negative points. Notice that some limitation signposts introduce definitions.

Signposts That Indicate Limits or Defined Areas

all that matters
as far as X (goes)
by X (criterion or standard)
by way of
considering
defining X as
given X
if we define
in terms of
in the area / field / realm of
in the sense that / of
limiting ourselves / our consideration to
speaking of
the extent to which
using X
when it comes to
when we consider
within the limits of
X is defined by

SIGNPOSTS ADD PRECISION

Signposts of limitation or definition may seem unnecessary. However, their power to limit allows an author the flexibility to make several disparate, even marginally conflicting, points in a short piece of writing without causing confusion. Consider the following pairs of statements:

With a Limiter / Definer	Without a Limiter / Definer	Comment
The second decade of the 21st century has brought a mixed bag of political circumstances for African Americans. **By one criterion**, things have never been better. A man whose father was a black African became president of the United States.	The second decade of the 21st century has brought a mixed bag of political circumstances for African Americans. Things have never been better. A man whose father was a black African became president of the United States.	The passage without the limiting expression is confusing and totally inaccurate. It would have to be substantially rewritten to make up for the loss of the limiter.
When it comes to future political influence, however, blacks have taken a hit, as the Supreme Court weakened some provisions of the 1965 Voting Rights Act. **When we consider** future elections, this court action will make voting harder for hundreds of thousands of blacks.	However, blacks have taken a hit, as the Supreme Court weakened some provisions of the 1965 Voting Rights Act. This court action will make voting harder for hundreds of thousands of blacks.	The passage without the limiters makes sense and is accurate as it stands, but the concepts of political influence and future elections have been lost—a serious departure from what the author wanted to say.

EXERCISE 5

A. Reread "Political Conditions for African Americans" on the previous page. Then complete the chart.

	Signpost Expression	Topic or Area Introduced
1	By one criterion	whether an African American is president
2		
3		
4		
5		

B. The following passage draws on the "Fact Sheet: The Black Panther Party" on page 148. Complete the passage with limiting or defining expressions from the list on the previous page. Use information from the fact sheet as necessary.

THE SHORT HEYDAY OF THE BLACK PANTHERS

After a strong run in the late 1960s and early 1970s, the Black Panther Party for Self-Defense (eventually known simply as the Black Panthers) faded into irrelevance. Of all the major branches of the black power struggle, (1) .... lasting political influence, the Black Panthers come up short. (2) .... appeal to mainstream American society, the Black Panthers could not compete with peaceful resistance groups like the Southern Christian Leadership Conference. Although some branches of the Panthers had successes delivering social services such as food assistance and health care to the poor of large cities, (3) .... the party's public profile, such activities had little effect. The group

American sprinters Tommie Smith and John Carlos during the award ceremony of the 200 m race at the 1968 Olympic Games in Mexico City. In an expression of defiance, both removed their shoes, bowed their heads, and raised a black-gloved fist as the national anthem played.

cultivated an image of armed resistance, and (4) .... the minds of most Americans, that's who they were. Perhaps the least violent image of supposed Panther politics was still very controversial, the incident during the 1968 Olympics when two sprinters hung their heads and raised black-gloved fists as the US national anthem played. But (5) .... that neither athlete was a member of the party, this is not really an effective softener of the Panther ethos. (6) .... its political associations, the Panther leadership was deliberately provocative, visiting North

Continued

Korea, North Vietnam, China, and Cuba, all of which were Communist nations with which the United States had hostile relations to varying degrees. Finally, the Panther leadership made mammoth mistakes (7) .... disrespect for the law. There was a manslaughter conviction (eventually overturned) against founder Huey Newton in 1968. Later charges linked Newton to other deaths. (8) .... their efforts to seem tough, the Panthers in fact seemed little better than a street gang, shooting it out with rivals in a UCLA dorm. Even (9) .... the management of the Panthers' own internal affairs, Newton and other leaders seemed like small-time criminals, allegedly stealing money from their own organization. Even though some lower-level Panthers had political careers after separating themselves from the party, overall the organization had little influence (10) .... America's political direction.

Go to **MyEnglishLab** to complete a skill practice.

APPLY YOUR SKILLS

WHY IT'S USEFUL By applying the skills you have learned in this unit, you can successfully read this challenging text and learn about Henry David Thoreau and his approach to standing up for what he believed in.

BEFORE YOU READ

A. Discuss these questions with one or more students.

1. Do you know of anyone who has protested against a law or policy by refusing to do something required by a governing body? If so, did the person achieve his or her objective? If not, why do you think the person was unsuccessful?

2. Think about the kinds of taxes citizens in your home country pay. Has there ever been any controversy surrounding any of them? Consider whether you have heard about any protests or strikes related to taxes.

3. Would you ever refuse to pay a tax knowing that you would go to jail as a result? What do you think would happen if many people followed your lead?

B. Imagine that you will be participating in a small group discussion about the passage "Henry David Thoreau's Civil Disobedience," which begins on the next page. Your group will be discussing the following questions. Keep these questions in mind as you read the passage.

1. What was the name of the movement Thoreau was part of?

2. What were the two taxes that Thoreau did not pay, evidencing his belief in civil disobedience? What were his reasons for deciding not to pay them?

3. Why was Thoreau upset that someone paid his taxes on his behalf?

4. Why did Thoreau lose respect for the state during his time in jail?

5. How did Thoreau's relationship with friends and neighbors change after his time in jail?

C. Review the Unit Skills Summary. As you read the passage, apply the skills you learned in this unit.

UNIT SKILLS SUMMARY

Distinguish fact from opinion.
- Recognize when information is factual and when it is personal opinion.

Recognize and interpret statements of opinion.
- Consider the types of language found alongside statements of opinion and interpret them accurately.

Recognize and interpret statements of fact.
- Think about the kinds of language that fall under the category of facts and analyze them effectively.

Understand and produce critiques.
- Make reasonable evaluative judgments that capture the strong and weak aspects of a piece of writing and then be prepared to support those judgments.

Understand signpost expressions that limit or define.
- As you encounter signpost expressions, be aware of how they are limiting or defining the material they introduce.

READ

A. Read the passage. Annotate and take notes as necessary.

Henry David Thoreau's Civil Disobedience

1   ¹ When it comes to social activism, Henry David Thoreau, a classic American writer and a radical of his time, is one of history's greatest catalysts, inspiring with his 1849 essay "Civil Disobedience" several of the most renowned activists of the past century, including Mahatma Gandhi and Martin Luther King Jr. ² In the essay, Thoreau appeals to others to break laws he deems unjust, defining these as any law that "requires you to be the agent of injustice to another." ³ He also outlines the principles on which he opposed the state's taxation system, the consequences he faced for disobeying the tax law, and the profound effect his act of civil disobedience had on his perspective of his town and neighbors.

2   ⁴ Thoreau came of age during the 19th century and penned "Civil Disobedience" after completing his more widely known work, *Walden*. ⁵ Thoreau, like his contemporary Ralph Waldo Emerson, was part of the Transcendentalist movement, which placed great emphasis on the merits of nature, thought, and spiritualism. ⁶ Though best known for living in the woods, an experience he writes about extensively in *Walden*, Thoreau also details his journey to a very different space—jail. ⁷ Thoreau found himself in jail by way of deliberately disobeying the tax laws of the time, arguing that his dollars tied his allegiance to a government that enacted measures and participated in acts he reviled, including the Mexican-American War and slavery. ⁸ For his crime, he spent one night in jail.

TAX REFUSAL

3   ⁹ It was not one, but two taxes Thoreau refused to pay in the 1840s. ¹⁰ The first was a church tax, a tax that funded a clergyman in a church Thoreau did not attend, and the second was a poll tax, a state tax that went to fund multiple ventures. ¹¹ Between the two, the church tax nonpayment was a smaller indiscretion, and Thoreau questions in his essay whether the church should have the right to levy the tax. ¹² He explains that he avoids it summarily by having the town clerk remove his name from the church's register. ¹³ As for his refusal to pay the poll tax, however, Thoreau appears to be more indignant, outlining his opposition with stronger, moral reasons, stating that he wished "to refuse allegiance to the State" that sanctioned slavery and the invasion of a foreign nation. ¹⁴ Thoreau refused to pay the poll tax for six years and lobbied others to join him, arguing that "if a thousand men were not to pay their tax-bills this year, that would not be a violent and bloody measure, as it would be to pay them, and enable the State to commit violence and shed innocent blood." ¹⁵ He goes on to name such mass civil disobedience a potential "peaceable revolution," a declaration that was revolutionary in itself in the sense that pacificism was considered a "radical" approach.

4   ¹⁶ In terms of taxes in general, Thoreau did not disagree with all of them, as he happily admits in his essay when he states that he never refused to pay a highway tax because he desires to be a good neighbor, and likewise when he affirms paying taxes that fund schools because he supports educating others. ¹⁷ In the instance of his unpaid poll tax, an anonymous person paid the bill on Thoreau's behalf, which was why he spent only one night in jail instead of many. ¹⁸ Thoreau admonishes whoever paid his tax— though he does not reveal the person's name— for allowing personal feelings to interfere with the good he believed would come from his act of civil disobedience.

CONFINEMENT

5   [19] The time Thoreau served for his crime, though abbreviated, left an indelible time in jail on him. [20] When recounting his time in jail, he insists that his intellectual and moral senses remained free despite being locked inside a cell, and that the physical barriers of jail were inconsequential compared to the impervious boundaries of personhood. [21] Thoreau declares that he lost all respect for the state, which he writes has only physical strength, not wit or honesty. [22] "As they could not reach me," he writes, "they had resolved to punish my body; just as boys, if they cannot come at some person against whom they have a spite, will abuse his dog."

6   [23] According to Thoreau's reflections on his time in jail, he views himself as a person visiting a new land, which we experience by way of his descriptions of the physical dimensions of the whitewashed stone walls, iron grating, and low lighting. [24] He also details his night in jail, which passes uneventfully, beginning with getting to know his fellow jail-mate, a man whom he assumes to be innocent. [25] Thoreau writes that when asked, the man stated, "They accuse me of burning a barn; but I never did it." [26] Thoreau shrugs off the man's alleged crime, speculating that he simply fell asleep while drunk and smoking a pipe, and then benefited from what the jail had to offer: a clean room, free boarding, and decent treatment. [27] Thoreau spends the rest of the evening talking to his jail-mate, examining where others had broken out, listening to jailhouse gossip, and reading poems composed by inmates. [28] His recollections are romantic and describe the jail as giving him a new perspective entirely on his town, as though he had "never heard the town-clock strike before, nor the evening sounds of the village ... It was to see my native village in the light of the Middle Ages."

7   [29] After his release the following morning, Thoreau writes that he emerged a new man, shocked and dismayed by the reactions of his neighbors and friends, and he describes a barrier between himself and them. [30] He feels ostracized, and laments that some friendships were for the "summer weather only." [31] It is significant to note that while first recounting his sojourn in jail, Thoreau describes it as a new land, but when he is later released, he seems to have undergone a transformation, and it is his former friends and neighbors who have become the foreigners.

8   [32] Thoreau ends his jail recollections on a high note, writing that after being released, he completed his errand of retrieving his shoe from a cobbler, and following this errand, he ventured out with friends. [33] In the context of his entire essay, which is a larger examination of the individual's relationship to the state, the details of his jail stay are important because they reveal, along with his lofty philosophy of resistance and his unwavering stance on the government's involvement in war, a level of personal emotional reaction.

B. Reread the questions in Before You Read, Part B. Is there anything you cannot answer? What reading skills can you use to help you find the answers?

Go to **MyEnglishLab** to read the passage again and answer critical thinking questions.

THINKING CRITICALLY

You just read about the consequences of refusing to pay taxes in the 1840s. If an individual intentionally refused to pay a tax in the present day—citing a reason such as a strong belief against what that tax supports—do you think the consequences would differ from those Thoreau experienced for his actions? Why or why not? Consider what you know about significant events—social, religious, political—in Thoreau's time, and compare those with events happening today.

THINKING VISUALLY

The timeline shows some of the main events in the life of Henry David Thoreau, from his birth until he refused to pay his taxes. Carefully consider his life events. How do you think each event—and the combination of all of them—led to his later refusal to pay his taxes? Based on his life through 1846, what would you expect him to do in the next several years?

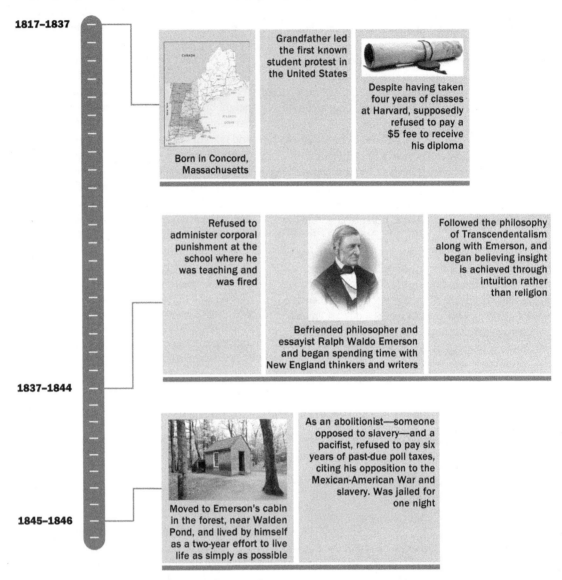

1817–1837

Born in Concord, Massachusetts

Grandfather led the first known student protest in the United States

Despite having taken four years of classes at Harvard, supposedly refused to pay a $5 fee to receive his diploma

1837–1844

Refused to administer corporal punishment at the school where he was teaching and was fired

Befriended philosopher and essayist Ralph Waldo Emerson and began spending time with New England thinkers and writers

Followed the philosophy of Transcendentalism along with Emerson, and began believing insight is achieved through intuition rather than religion

1845–1846

Moved to Emerson's cabin in the forest, near Walden Pond, and lived by himself as a two-year effort to live life as simply as possible

As an abolitionist—someone opposed to slavery—and a pacifist, refused to pay six years of past-due poll taxes, citing his opposition to the Mexican-American War and slavery. Was jailed for one night

Timeline of significant events in the first 30 years of Henry David Thoreau's life (born 1817, died 1862)

THINKING ABOUT LANGUAGE

A. Read these excerpts from "Henry David Thoreau's Civil Disobedience." Underline the signpost expressions that limit or define.

1. When it comes to social activism, Henry David Thoreau, a classic American writer and a radical of his time, is one of history's greatest catalysts, inspiring with his 1849 essay "Civil Disobedience" several of the most renowned activists of the past century, including Mahatma Gandhi and Martin Luther King Jr.

2. In the essay, Thoreau appeals to others to break laws he deems unjust, defining these as any law that "requires you to be the agent of injustice to another."

3. Thoreau found himself in jail by way of deliberately disobeying the tax laws of the time, arguing that his dollars tied his allegiance to a government that enacted measures and participated in acts he reviled, including the Mexican-American War and slavery.

4. He goes on to name such mass civil disobedience a potential "peaceable revolution," a declaration that was revolutionary in itself in the sense that pacifism was considered a "radical" approach.

5. In terms of taxes in general, Thoreau did not disagree with all of them, as he happily admits in his essay when he states that he never refused to pay a highway tax because he desires to be a good neighbor, and likewise when he affirms paying taxes that fund schools because he supports educating others.

6. According to Thoreau's reflections on his time in jail, he views himself as a person visiting a new land, which we experience by way of his descriptions of the physical dimensions of the whitewashed stone walls, iron grating, and low lighting.

B. What is the limitation or definition created by the signpost in each item? Discuss with another student.

⬤ Go to **MyEnglishLab** to listen to Professor Greenberg and to complete a self-assessment.

Individual choices impact the global economy.

Implication and Inference

UNIT PROFILE

You will consider the subject of economics—specifically how certain key terms are defined and how income, taxes, and assets relate to one another. Topics you will study include international tariffs, taxes, the definition of income, and public versus private goods.

Look at the reading on page 176. By skimming the title, the first two sentences of each paragraph, and the chart, try to infer the author's point of view about public and private goods. Will the author present one phenomenon—public or private—as being more important than the other?

OUTCOMES

• Understand implication and inference
• Make strong inferences and avoid weak ones
• Distinguish between deliberate implications and direct statements
• Paraphrase
• Identify and use equivalent and near-equivalent expressions

GETTING STARTED

▶ Go to **MyEnglishLab** to listen to Professor Clerici-Arias and to complete a self-assessment.

Discuss these questions with a partner or group.

1. Think of the last time you crossed a border from one country to another. Did you have to be careful not to bring in certain things? Which things? Why would a country prevent you from bringing such things in? Was the reason economic? Environmental? Cultural? Related to some other aspect of life?

2. Think of a country you know well. Does the government impose any extra taxes on items brought in from other countries? Why or why not? Do the taxes work as the government intends?

3. Think of the same or another a country you know well—perhaps the country where you are living now. Is there a lot of income inequality? What factors cause—or protect people against—such inequality? What signs do you see every day that show that inequality does, or doesn't, exist?

For more about **ECONOMICS**, see ❶ ❸. See also ⓦ and ⓄⒸ **ECONOMICS** ❶ ❷ ❸.

CRITICAL THINKING SKILL
UNDERSTANDING IMPLICATION AND INFERENCE

WHY IT'S USEFUL A reading passage may contain ideas that are implied (not stated directly) by the author. Readers can understand implications by making inferences—considering the information given, processing it logically, and bringing in their own knowledge of the topic and the world in general.

Understanding **implications** and your own **inferences** can allow you to get the full meaning of a reading—not just what an author explicitly states, but also what is indirectly stated. This unit breaks the skill down into two supporting skills:

- making strong inferences and avoiding weak ones
- distinguishing between deliberate implications and direct statements

NOTICING ACTIVITY

A. Read each item. Then choose the best inference about the item. Discuss your answers with another student.

1. Accounting is more than mere record-keeping. Give ten accountants the same task, and you'll get ten different results.
   a. Accounting does not have a set of rules that everyone follows.
   b. Accounting can involve personal creativity.

2. Double-entry accounting demands that each amount is recorded in at least two accounts. It has long functioned as a tool for discovering errors.
   a. Accountants sometimes make mistakes in entering amounts.
   b. Accountants suspect one another of trying to take money dishonestly.

3. Double-entry accounting is not the same as keeping two sets of books. The latter will get you thrown into jail.
   a. Double-entry accounting covers up any illegal activities among accountants.
   b. Double-entry accounting is legal, but keeping two sets of books is not.

4. Accounting is probably as old as trade itself. Without records of outflow versus income, how could a trader assess the quality of an exchange?
   a. Ancient accounting systems were not very accurate.
   b. No one knows when the first accounting system started.

5. It's only natural that the most powerful merchants of any era—medieval Arabs, Renaissance Italians, the Dutch, the British, the Americans—could impose their accounting practices internationally.
   a. The status of being the world's top traders shifts from one country to another over time.
   b. The country with the best accounting system is usually the world's top trader.

6. Paying income taxes every year unreasonably forces average Americans to become temporary accountants, a role for which they have no training.
   a. Americans should learn in school how to become accountants.
   b. The income tax system shouldn't require any accounting skills.

B. Read the following passage. What information is stated directly? What additional information can you infer? The notes in the margins show some inferences that can be drawn from the first paragraph. Look at the other numbered items (4–8). Complete each sentence with the inference that you draw. Then discuss your inferences with another student.

ACCOUNTING IN CONTEXT

Some Italian cities besides Venice and Genoa had trade during the Renaissance.

1 (1) Modern accounting developed during the Italian Renaissance and gradually insinuated itself wherever Venetians, Genoans, or others carried it to ensure predictable business practices. But that is not to say that all such trading partners were willing to manage their accounts in the Italian way. (2) Financial and legal systems varied in significant ways and were deeply rooted, not easily altered to suit foreign merchants, no matter how rich they were. And even in the 15th century, there were technological breakthroughs (Gutenberg's printing press, various advances in sailing gear) that rapidly—(3) at least in relative terms—changed the economic game and encouraged the spread of two main types of accounting: code-based accounting and common law accounting.

In some places, local traditions stayed in place despite rich foreigners.

Developments that seemed fast in the 15th century would not seem fast now.

The influence of the _____ Empire caused _____

2 (4) Common law, or case law, had developed in Britain during the 11th and 12th centuries. It was refined as trade increased during the Renaissance; later systems in colonies throughout the British Empire fell under the common law heading. (5) Accounting practices under common law emphasized adherence to voluntary conventions of transparency and accuracy. Peer pressure and potential public shame played a great role. Common law is comparatively flexible, so accounting systems based in it can be adapted to changing economic conditions with relative ease. These common law attributes are still found in the accounting practices of such former British colonies or dependencies as the United States, Australia, and India. (6) India, as it grows, is likely to benefit greatly from the common law framework; typically, as labor economies transition into service economies, they need the flexibility that common law accounting provides—as opposed to the more rigid procedures of a code-based system.

In common law accounting, a company that doesn't follow the rules is punished by _____

At present, India's economy is _____

3 The formation of a modern accounting system isn't always such a gradual process, and common law systems aren't always the result. After World War II, the United States worked to establish an American-style accounting system in Japan. (7) Within only a couple of decades, many aspects of the system took hold, and today Japan has a hybrid accounting system. It has been heavily influenced by US common law but also by prior experience with German code law and (8) a credit-focused financial system that is not inclined toward disclosures. While both India and Japan went through rapid and occasionally turbulent periods of modernization, each managed to create a system of accounting that suited its needs.

After World War II, Japan considered American accounting practices to be _____

The Japanese tendency toward some secrecy in the credit system had its origins in _____

Go to **MyEnglishLab** to complete a vocabulary exercise and skill practice, and to join in collaborative activities.

SUPPORTING SKILL 1
MAKING STRONG INFERENCES AND AVOIDING WEAK ONES

WHY IT'S USEFUL By making inferences that are strong—well supported by material in the reading and by logic—you can more accurately understand what a writer means to say. By not making weak inferences, you can keep from developing misunderstandings.

All of the **inferences** we drew from "Accounting in Context" are *strong*. A reader can find a clear statement in the reading passage that supports and leads logically to each inference. Most readers know enough about money, history, and economies to infer the information.

However, inferences—and the **implications** on which they might be based—are not always so clear. Given different background experiences, one reader may infer things that another may not. This is an important distinction. Inferences and implications are different things, and they do not always occur together:

- An author may imply something in a reading passage that a reader doesn't notice. In this case, there is an implication without an inference.
- Alternatively, a reader may infer something that the author did not intend to imply. In this case, there is an inference without an intended implication. When a reader infers things the author did not mean to imply, the inference is likely to be *weak*.

The following inferences from "Accounting in Context" are so weak that most readers would consider them wrong. They cannot be clearly supported by evidence from the reading. A reader who makes these inferences is misunderstanding the passage.

Example of a Weak Inference	Why It's Weak
During the Renaissance, Italy conquered much of the world.	The early part of the reading doesn't hint at war. In fact, the "gradually insinuated" phrase is tied to business, not war.
Common law accounting practices cause economies to become service economies.	The reading actually portrays a totally different scenario. The accounting system does not change an economy. It is available in case an economy changes.
Before World War II, Japan had no exposure to accounting systems from other countries.	The reading directly says otherwise when it uses the phrase "prior experience with Germanic code law."

EXERCISE 1

A. Read the passage actively. (See the section Reading Actively, p. 3.) Ask yourself questions and formulate guesses about possible implications.

THE EFFECTS OF TARIFFS ON RESEARCH AND DEVELOPMENT

1   In the popular imagination, an innovator is a lone genius toiling away in obscurity before stumbling upon a world-changing breakthrough. We are attracted to this image because it speaks to the kind of hard work and struggle all of us must go through to accomplish something. The less dramatic reality, however, is that innovation is more often a matter of such uninspiring factors as international trade rules, especially the taxes known as tariffs. Every country imposes some tariffs, so we have to speak of a continuum, from high-tariff to low-tariff countries. Those with high tariffs

Continued

inevitably justify them as protection for domestic inventors and producers. However true that may be in the short run, it is badly misguided as a policy for future growth. In fact, a country that supposedly protects its innovators with tariffs is probably discouraging research and development (R&D), while a country that generally pursues free trade is probably invigorating it.

2   If innovation thrives on competition—and it does—then it stands to reason that a successful monopoly whose market is guaranteed by tariffs has little reason to innovate. Tariffs reduce outside competition, and an industry "protected" by them is perversely motivated to stay out of the battle for market leadership. While a protected industry is huddling within its borders, out of the crosswinds of the world market, dozens of countries are competing in the marketplace of innovation. Even a small advancement in technology can vault an innovator nation to worldwide dominance in some particular product market. A smart leader, however, continues to innovate despite its dominance because leadership can be a fleeting thing, lasting only as long as one's technology outpaces that of competitors.

3   Meanwhile, an industry hiding in the false shelter of tariffs falls further behind. It makes no difference whether the tariff-insulated industry was the world leader when tariffs were introduced. Protected products may even continue to lead in one's domestic market for a while, but tariffs may shelter it too long, leaving it uninspired by any of the fierce innovation (and attendant R&D) that motivates market leaders. Its product line will languish, its offerings looking increasingly old-fashioned. This has been disastrous in the past. By the 1980s, for example, Soviet consumers knew that most cars produced domestically for them were dinosaurs—but the disaster can occur even faster in an age of digital communication. The products of more nimble economies are instantly on display online.

4   Pressure from outside competitors is not the only free-trade factor that jump-starts R&D. Free trade also makes it easier for a manufacturer to get intermediate goods—those materials or components needed to generate finished products. Nations that embrace free trade can typically source these midstream goods from overseas, without needing to home-grow every single component industry. The cheap importation of intermediate goods lets countries play to their strengths without building elaborate domestic industrial infrastructure. It also speeds experimentation and innovation because acquiring components with which to develop high-value end products is faster and cheaper than under a high-tariff regime.

5   Finally, free trade makes it easier for researchers to get in on the ground floor of new innovations. An aspiring computer innovator may see little room to move in a protectionist, tariff-heavy country where today's products are protected and tomorrow's R&D is stalled. Early-career innovators are more likely to thrive where cross-currents of ideas and funding for the best of them flow in from around the world. Because of this, restrictive tariffs can lead to a "brain drain" as educated professionals relocate to countries where their skills will bring them higher-paying positions. This leaves no one at home motivated to try to build such industries from scratch. If this persists, tariffs will not only inhibit R&D in the present but also place the nation at a disadvantage even if it finally opens up to free trade.

B. With another student, discuss these inferences about the passage. Rate them *Strong, Medium,* or *Weak*.

.... 1. The popular image of an innovator poorly represents how most innovation really occurs.

.... 2. Countries usually establish tariffs for unsuccessful industries but not for successful ones.

.... 3. No country that says it supports free markets would ever impose tariffs.

.... 4. The forces of competition among freely innovating companies are similar to the winds of a storm.

.... 5. Tariffs usually do not help an industry sell its products to a domestic market.

.... 6. The Soviet economy protected its auto industry with tariffs.

.... 7. Cell phones, the Internet, and other aids to communication make it easier to protect an industry with tariffs.

.... 8. Intermediate goods can sometimes be purchased from outside the country where a whole product is produced and sometimes from inside it.

.... 9. A person interested in innovating would probably want to move to a nation with a lot of tariffs.

.... 10. The international migration of highly skilled people would probably decrease if every economy in the world practiced free trade.

C. Discuss your ratings with another pair of students. Explain the reasons for your answers.

Go to **MyEnglishLab** to complete a vocabulary exercise and skill practice, and to join in collaborative activities.

SUPPORTING SKILL 2
DISTINGUISHING BETWEEN DELIBERATE IMPLICATIONS AND DIRECT STATEMENTS

WHY IT'S USEFUL You can understand an author's intentions and attitudes more clearly if you can recognize when he or she deliberately avoids saying something directly. You can develop a sense of the factors that may be motivating the author. Why does the author think such deliberate implications are necessary?

Usually, the **implications** in a reading passage are not meant to hide anything. They are simply a normal part of the pattern of meaning, said and unsaid, in a passage. However, sometimes an author may intentionally use implications to make a point that he or she does not want to state **directly**. This may occur for any of several reasons.

The author may think that

- saying something directly would cause trouble with authorities—the government, religious officials, an employer, and so on.
- being explicit would anger or embarrass certain individuals.
- using direct language would be predictable and boring, so the implication is meant to entertain.
- an implication would appeal to a subgroup of readers (an "in-group"), making them feel special because they can understand it.

EXERCISE 2

A. **Read each situation. Then discuss the questions with one or two other students.**

Situation 1: A worker at a coal company is interviewed by an environmental news website.

> **Transcript:**
>
> INTERVIEWER: The Northern Coal Company employs more than half the people in this area. Critics say the company is ruining this part of the state by cutting forests, destroying mountaintops, and polluting rivers. What do you think?
>
> COAL MINER: I've worked with the company for 20 years. That salary has allowed me to feed my family and send my daughter to college. They employ lots of folks around here, and I don't know what would happen to this economy if you took those jobs away. I'm 52 years old, and I know there's no other job for me around here except the one I have. This is a beautiful valley, and these mountains are my home.

1. What can you infer about the miner's feelings about the company? About the future?
2. Why do you think the miner avoids answering the question directly?
3. Can you think of similar situations in which a writer or speaker would avoid direct statements?

Situation 2: A British politician writes a blog post about some recent trade actions by the US government.

Blog Post:

The British people understand that US trade leaders want prosperity for American companies. It's every government's job to promote the economic interests of its people. Part of that is making sure manufacturers have access to the best materials on the market. Should our American cousins care to investigate, they will find that jet engines built by British Airfoil have outperformed all competitors for nearly half a century. I'm sure it's just an oversight that customs officials have limited the importation of 27 BA engines at the dock in Philadelphia.

1. How is the politician's motivation different from the coal miner's in Situation 1?
2. What is one implied criticism the politician makes of the US government?
3. What can you infer about the possible purpose of the US government's actions?
4. Why does the politician use the phrase "American cousins"?
5. By calling the action "an oversight," what is the politician trying to avoid?
6. Can you think of similar situations in which a writer or speaker would avoid direct statements?

B. **Read the passage. Make notes about ideas that you think are being deliberately implied because the author is reluctant to state them directly.**

SMOKING, SIN TAXES, AND CHANGING HABITS

1   Throughout the ages, authorities have tried to enforce sobriety and clean living, but their record at it has been spotty at best. Take the Ottoman Sultan Murad IV (1612–1640) who not only outlawed coffee but also imposed a penalty of execution should anyone violate the ban. (Pretty harsh moves from a man who allegedly had a taste for another oft-banned substance, fortified wine.) You can judge how well the ban worked by noting that today Turkish-style coffee is enjoyed in homes and cafes around the globe. Similarly, the earnest and well-meaning US Temperance Movement succeeded in getting Congress to establish Prohibition (a federal ban on the sale of alcoholic drinks that endured from 1920 to 1933), bringing us moonshine, the Jazz Age, and Al Capone. Parallels could conceivably be drawn to the modern US War on Drugs.

2   Governments that recognize the futility of bans often resort to taxing things instead. Declaring a "sin tax" is straightforward enough: Simply choose something you want people to avoid and impose a tax to cover whatever costs you imagine the nasty substance or activity levies on society. Writing the tax into law is, of course, the easy part. Implementing it, as history has demonstrated, leads to a multitude of difficulties, particularly black market sales and, worse, angry people who want their cigarettes, their alcoholic drink, their sugary cola, or even temporary romance.

Continued

3   Historically speaking, sin taxes have had their strongest effect on
infrequent users of the taxed substance. Research shows that taxes on
tobacco products reduce consumption the most among both younger
smokers and poorer smokers, especially those who smoke infrequently.
While advocates of the tax may be thrilled that the pool of potential
smokers is thereby reduced, the data is less promising when frequent,
heavy smokers are examined. People who already smoke more than a
pack a day seem unable or unwilling to lower their cigarette consumption
despite the tax. Given the unlikelihood that the tax will really stop
hard-core smokers, the state could be seen as taking advantage of addicts
by profiting from their dependency. That may be too cynical a conclusion.
Nothing is simple or straightforward regarding addictions or the proper
public response to them.

4   Looking through the lens of the greater good, it seems that in the
case of smoking, proponents of sin taxes have a rare set of positive data.
Smoking is far less common in the United States than it used to be, and
the smell of tobacco smoke has been nearly eliminated from indoor
environments. While the taxes will never cause some hard-core smokers
to quit, they have certainly contributed to a continuing decline in public
smoking. We just have to remember that tobacco taxes should not be given
all the credit. They coincided with massive clinical evidence of the health
hazards of smoking.

5   Taxes on other unhealthful products have had a tougher slog. Attempts
at enacting a soda tax or a "fat tax" on fast food have generally fizzled, and
such taxes are hugely unpopular where they are in effect. There is science
about the harmful effects of such products, so why hasn't there been so
great a push to tax them? A lot hinges on the scope of the harm. Cigarette
smoke is a public problem, something that wafts throughout a room or a
public bus, but sugary soda and fatty foods are private vices. My health
may suffer if I stand near you while you smoke but not while you drink
a 170-calorie glass of soda. And, at least in the United States, the public
regulation of private matters, while it certainly occurs, does not easily
survive once a media spotlight is shone on it—as happened when the state
of New York contemplated a soda tax in 2010. Some people apparently do
not want to be saved from themselves.

C. Read the questions and choose the best answers. If necessary, use a dictionary to understand difficult words in the questions.

1. What is the author implying about Murad IV in Paragraph 1?
   a. He drank a lot of coffee.
   b. His people feared him.
   c. He was a hypocrite.
   d. His government sold coffee.

2. In Paragraph 1, why does the author use the indirect phrase "could conceivably be drawn to the modern US War on Drugs"?

   a. To imply that the War on Drugs is ineffective without deeply offending antidrug readers
   b. Because it's illegal to write negative remarks about federal laws
   c. To indicate that the War on Drugs is a much more respectable policy than Prohibition
   d. Because he is not sure whether the War on Drugs is or is not a good policy

3. In Paragraph 2, why does the author use the indirect phrase "temporary romance"?

   a. To indicate that taxed substances and activities are attractive to young people
   b. To show that laws against a substance or activity cannot eliminate it
   c. To introduce the concept that taxed things are often a lot of fun
   d. To avoid saying "prostitution," which might offend some readers

4. In Paragraph 3, what does the author imply about smokers who are undeterred by the tobacco tax?

   a. They are wealthy and unconcerned about taxes.
   b. They are young and not worried about health problems.
   c. They may be addicted to tobacco and cannot stop.
   d. They could put pressure on the government to repeal the tax.

5. In Paragraph 4, what does the author imply about the effectiveness of taxes on tobacco use?

   a. They succeeded in the United States but have failed elsewhere.
   b. Their role in changing behavior may appear greater than it really was.
   c. They did not really have any effect on the incidence of smoking.
   d. It is dangerous to think that other sin taxes will be effective, too.

6. In Paragraph 5, what does the author imply about regulation of unhealthful products when he says, "while it certainly occurs, [public regulation of private matters] does not easily survive once a media spotlight is shone on it"?

   a. Taxes on unhealthful products are imposed through secret government actions, not through laws.
   b. The private lives of Americans were more regulated in the past than they are now.
   c. News media make a lot of money from ads for unhealthful products.
   d. Americans are not conscious of many ways in which their private habits are regulated.

D. **Discuss your answers with another student. Use information and examples from the passage to explain and support your answers.**

Go to **MyEnglishLab** to complete a vocabulary exercise and skill practice, and to do collaborative activities.

READING-WRITING CONNECTION
PARAPHRASING

WHY IT'S USEFUL In American universities and professional situations, you will very often need to write or speak in your own words about things you have read. Capturing an author's thoughts in your own words is therefore a crucial skill.

When authors **paraphrase**, they express someone else's statement in a different way but keep the essential meaning the same. This is not just a matter of changing a few words. It usually involves shifts in grammar as well. The most important principle for someone writing a paraphrase is this: **Work with idea groups**. When you express things in new wording, work with these groups of words, not with individual words. See the following examples. Notice, for instance, that in the first example the idea group, *According to one research firm* has been replaced by another group of words for the same idea, *Research shows*.

Original:	According to one research firm, the richest 400 people in the United States own approximately 50 percent of the country's net wealth.
Paraphrase:	Research shows that about half of the net wealth in the United States is owned by a group of only 400 people.
Original:	You might be interested to find out that the Occupy Movement was trying to draw public attention in 2011 to the fact that the richest 1 percent of earners in the United States earn nearly 20 percent of all the income.
Paraphrase:	The message of the Occupy Movement in 2011 was that almost 20 percent of all America's income is earned by the richest 1 percent.

Characteristics of Paraphrases

- Unlike a summary, a paraphrase can be about the same length as the original.
- A paraphrase conveys only the essential meaning of the original. It doesn't try to include unimportant elements like "you might be interested to find out that" in the second example above.
- A paraphrase uses equivalent expressions—such as *about half* for *approximately 50 percent*—not just individual vocabulary items. (See the section Identifying and Using Equivalent and Near-Equivalent Expressions, p. 173.)
- A paraphrase does not change technical terms or parts of the original that can't easily be expressed any other way, elements like *net wealth*, *400 people*, *the Occupy Movement*, and *research*.
- Paraphrasing is an important skill for avoiding plagiarism (copying another person's written words) when writing research papers.

> **CULTURE NOTE**
> *For more information about how US culture treats "plagiarism" and other aspects of academic honesty, see Academic Success Strategies in MyEnglishLab.*

WRITING PARAPHRASES

Even in a reading class—where your main task is comprehending what you read—you may be asked to write paraphrases. That's because a good paraphrase can show that you understand the passage. The following are some techniques for writing paraphrases:

Technique 1. Change an active clause into the passive. This usually involves switching the order of noun phrases, which helps rearrange the important parts of a sentence.

Technique 2. Break a longer sentence into two sentences.

Technique 3. Change prepositional phrases into adjectives / adverbs, or change adjectives / adverbs into prepositional phrases.

Technique 4. Change the order of ideas in your paraphrase.

EXERCISE 3

A. Read the passage. Notice the underlined sentences.

The Many Definitions of Income

1   In the rush to discuss and describe income inequality in the United States, it is crucial to make sure that everyone involved in the discussion agrees on how to define income. Each possible definition of *income* can reveal new information about the level of inequality in the United States and which segments of the country's population are most affected by it. Where the information on income is taken from is no less important. Different official government sources tabulate income within different (and mathematically crucial) parameters. Let's look at a few ways to describe income so that we can better understand what we're talking about when we examine the data in greater depth.

2   While studying the different ways to describe income, it's important to note that some have had difficulty accounting for the effects that nonsalaried forms of income and specific government benefits (also known as *transfers*) can have on determining the "real" (based on

constant prices) or "nominal" (based on market prices) income of a person or household. This is one of the reasons why there are so many approaches to what, precisely, income is. **(1)** <u>For instance, counting capital gains is deceptive because, technically, capital gains is not a source of income but rather arises from revaluation of wealth. Nonetheless, some include it, and including it makes wealth appear to be particularly concentrated in the upper percentiles of income earners. Meanwhile, counting government benefits—which is typically only taken into account when calculating disposable income along with taxes—tends to downplay the inequality.</u>

3   *Individual income* looks only at what one person earns, and this is generally lower than *family income* or *household income*, which looks at the earnings of all members of family or unrelated people sharing household resources. With a rise in single-parent households throughout the last

Continued

few decades, there has been a convergence of the figures for individual and household income. This would not necessarily be disturbing—it is possible for a single wage earner to provide quite well for an entire household. However, the wage earnings of the median US worker have been nearly stagnant, meaning that real improvements in household income almost require the addition of more earners. Depending on improvements in the income of one individual to add significantly to the household total is, arguably, somewhat tenuous. **(2)** <u>Families in more-secure income brackets—though not necessarily the very top income brackets—tend not only to report higher earnings but also to have cash coming in from multiple earners.</u>

4   Definitions of income can be *narrow* or *broad*. For example, the income being discussed might be *labor income*, a narrow measure that reflects money acquired from work, or *capital income*, a broad measure that reflects earnings in the form of dividends and retained earnings. This can be an important distinction, especially regarding earners at the top levels. For example, the value of a capital asset can accrue slowly over time, but the asset is usually sold in one transaction and is reported on a tax return as a large, sudden influx of cash. Another important distinction is between *gross income* (pretax income) and *net income* (post-tax income). **(3)** <u>Government tax policies and transfers influence household *disposable income* (see below), and thus two people with the same gross income may have vastly different net incomes, depending on their life circumstances.</u>

5   Some definitions of income are from the US Census Bureau, which has an interest in keeping track of income trends in the population. **(4)** <u>The Census Bureau's first category of income is *money income*, a term that is fairly expansive, counting all forms of income that a person receives regularly but not counting</u> <u>things like capital gains or government benefits.</u> *Market income* is the narrowest definition used by the Census Bureau; while similar to money income, market income does not count pensions and similar sources of cash. Finally, the Census Bureau's most far-ranging definition is the aforementioned *disposable income,* which includes money received from all sources. For lower-income individuals, disposable income usually means money received from various forms of government assistance such as the Earned Income Tax Credit, public housing, SNAP benefits, and so on. It's also noteworthy that capital gains and losses are included in market income and disposable income research, but not in money income.

6   The Census Bureau's income figures are interesting, but they are also very limited. **(5)** <u>They are not useful in looking at the top income earners because the bureau caps reporting at $999,999.</u> If you want to study high-earners, you'll need to use data from the US Treasury Department (which includes the Internal Revenue Service), which unfortunately doesn't do much to describe low-earners because many of them do not need to file taxes. Obviously, the definitional problems in this issue are daunting. **(6)** <u>Each definition is specifically designed by researchers to examine data in highly specific circumstances for a particular reason, but those analytical concerns are not necessarily salient to—or even recognized by—ordinary citizens who want to debate public policy.</u> Even noneconomists might have their own special income-related concerns, perhaps the way student debt affects a young person's wealth or how capital-gains tax breaks encourage so-called rent-seeking behavior (behavior in which someone gains wealth without returning anything to society). The specific definition one chooses can have an enormous influence on the argument and conclusion of a given piece of research or a given debate.

B. Refer to each underlined sentence in the reading, which corresponds with each item below. Then choose the best paraphrase.

.... **(1)** a. It is more accurate to take capital gains into account than government benefits because the latter is not really income.

b. If capital gains are included, the rich look richer, and if government benefits are included, the poor don't look so poor.

c. People who work for businesses are likely to have higher incomes than people who work for the government.

d. There are great benefits to using the same definition of income that the government uses.

.... **(2)** a. Most financially secure households have both higher incomes and more earners.

b. The larger a household is, the more likely it is to be financially secure.

c. Financially secure people usually have more income and get it from investments, not jobs.

d. Income for financially secure families is likely to be higher and to include cash.

.... **(3)** a. Wealthier people know how to take advantage of government policies to increase their net income.

b. The difference between gross income and net income is greater for wealthy people than for the poor.

c. The amount of disposable income is impacted by factors such as tax policies and government benefits.

d. The government uses tax laws to unfairly favor some earners while putting other earners at a disadvantage.

.... **(4)** a. The term *money income* does not include enough sources to be very useful because it is too broad.

b. The term *money income* includes most earnings, although not all kinds of payments.

c. The term *money income* is confusing because the things it measures are sometimes paid not in cash but by check.

d. The term *money income* works well for the purposes of the census, but it is not used for other purposes.

.... **(5)** a. The Census Bureau does not count high-earners as members of the US population.

b. The Census Bureau does not record the real income of anyone earning a million dollars or more.

c. The Census Bureau is interested in one's income only if the person receives government support payments.

d. The Census Bureau is the most reliable source for income trends among low-earners.

.... **(6)** a. The variety of definitions of *income* make it virtually impossible to discuss income inequality.

b. One definition of *income* may be too narrow, but considering them all together gives an accurate picture.

c. Different definitions of *income* emphasize different priorities, but ordinary people may not care about such details.

d. Definitions of income from government agencies reflect conflicts between various branches of government.

C. Read each excerpt from the passage. Then complete each paraphrase. When possible, use equivalent expressions and the paraphrasing techniques described in this unit.

1. Where the information on income is taken from is no less important as different official government sources tabulate income within different (and mathematically crucial) parameters.

   Measurements of income can vary because ....

   ....

2. This would not necessarily be disturbing—it is possible for a single wage earner to provide quite well for an entire household. However, the wage earnings of the median US worker have been nearly stagnant, meaning that real improvements in household income almost require the addition of more earners.

   Because US wages haven't grown very much, ...

   ....

3. Definitions of income can be narrow or broad. For example, the income being discussed might be labor income, a narrow measure that reflects money acquired from work, or capital income, a broad measure that reflects earnings in the form of dividends and retained earnings.

   One distinction among types of income is whether they are narrow or broad. For example, ...

   ....

4. For example, the value of a capital asset can accrue slowly over time, but the asset is usually sold in one transaction and is reported on a tax return as a large, sudden influx of cash.

   Although a capital asset is usually ....

   ....

5. For lower-income individuals, disposable income usually means money received from various forms of government assistance such as the Earned Income Tax Credit, public housing, SNAP benefits, and so on.

   Part of disposable income for people in lower income brackets ....

   ....

6. If you want to study high-earners, you'll need to use data from the US Treasury Department (which includes the Internal Revenue Service), which unfortunately doesn't do much to describe low-earners because many of them do not need to file taxes.

   Data from the US Treasury ....

   ....

D. Discuss these questions with one or two other students. Then explain your answers to the class.

1. Explain which paraphrases in Part B you chose and why.
2. Share your paraphrase completions from Part C. Are some more accurate than others? Which parts of some paraphrases are not accurate? How could those problems be solved? Do any paraphrases take too much wording from the original? If so, how could the borrowed parts be replaced?

Go to MyEnglishLab to complete a vocabulary exercise and skill practice, and to join in collaborative activities.

For more about PARAPHRASING, see [OC] SOCIOLOGY ①.

LANGUAGE SKILL
IDENTIFYING AND USING EQUIVALENT AND NEAR-EQUIVALENT EXPRESSIONS

WHY IT'S USEFUL Your ability to paraphrase and to understand paraphrases depends greatly on the strength of your vocabulary. By recognizing when two expressions—such as *money changing* and *currency exchange*—mean nearly the same thing, you can follow threads of cohesion in a text. By integrating such equivalents into your own vocabulary, you can express yourself more flexibly and with less repetition.

In developing your English vocabulary, size and strength are not necessarily the same thing. Of course, a large vocabulary helps a lot, but having a flexible vocabulary is just as important. Knowing **equivalent expressions** is a significant factor in developing this flexibility.

As we mentioned in the previous section, paraphrasing is more than just replacing one word with another. Instead, the best paraphrases replace one idea group—a group of words that together express an idea—with an equivalent expression. An equivalent expression is a word or group of words that means the same as another word or group of words. The equivalent expression may be a synonym—that is, a single vocabulary item with almost the same meaning. The two words *nearly* and *almost* are equivalent expressions, and they are synonyms of each other. So are the vocabulary items *nearly* and *pretty close to*—even though *pretty close to* is a multiword vocabulary item, not a single word. Dictionary definitions typically offer multiword equivalent expressions for single-word vocabulary items. For example, the single word *canyon* and its multiword definition—the phrase *deep, narrow opening in a mountain range*—are equivalent expressions.

In paraphrasing, you may not be able to find an exactly equivalent expression. Expressions that are close in meaning but not exactly the same are called **near-equivalent expressions**. Even very close synonyms—such as *occur* and *happen*—are slightly different in tone, suitability for certain contexts, and so on. For most purposes, near-equivalent phrases will accomplish what you need in paraphrases.

EXERCISE 4

Read the passage. On the next page, match the equivalent / near-equivalent expressions with expressions from the passage. Two of the expressions in the right column will not be used.

The Free Silver Movement

The first issue by the US Treasury of a paper currency, Silver Certificates, came in 1878 <u>in response to a political push</u> from the so-called "Free Silver" movement, which had begun in the early 1870s. These bills <u>were not exactly what the movement called for</u>. Instead, free-silverites wanted the government to <u>circulate silver coinage</u>, rather than paper notes, in order to increase the money supply. Advocates of free silver argued that producing more "greenbacks" (paper bills) would not <u>inflate the money supply</u> because they could be redeemed (traded in) for either gold or silver. Free-silverites said people would choose to redeem the <u>notes</u> for gold, and that was the main thing free-silverites did *not* want—<u>a continued reliance on gold to back up the value of money</u>.

Expressions from the Passage	Equivalent / Near-Equivalent Expressions
.... 1. in response to a political push	a. an ongoing wish to keep the government from issuing too much money
.... 2. were not exactly what the movement called for	b. create too many dollars, so that each dollar would become less valuable
.... 3. circulate silver coinage	c. fell short of the reforms that the group wanted
.... 4. inflate the money supply	d. issue money made of silver
.... 5. notes	e. answering questions about their political positions
.... 6. a continued reliance on gold to back up the value of money	f. pieces of paper money
	g. staying with a system where gold supports the currency
	h. because of political pressure

EXERCISE 5

Read each Original and each Paraphrase. In the Paraphrase, underline the equivalent or near-equivalent expression for the words in bold in the Original.

1. **Original:** In American English, the phrase "hiding money in your mattress" means keeping a lot of cash at home because **you don't trust banks, stock markets, or other financial institutions**.

   Paraphrase: The American English expression "hiding money in your mattress" refers to holding onto your cash because you're afraid to invest it or put it in a bank.

2. **Original:** Occasionally, an article appears in the newspaper about how someone who goes in to clean out **the house of a deceased person** discovers a hidden box, or even a real mattress, filled with tens or even hundreds of thousands of dollars in cash.

   Paraphrase: Newspapers sometimes report on the discovery of many thousands of dollars in cash stuffed into a box or mattress in the home of someone who has died.

3. **Original:** It's not unusual for the friends or relatives of the deceased to confirm that he or she believed it was unsafe to put the money to use in the markets or even to deposit it into a bank, **where any deposit up to $250,000 is covered by federal insurance.**

   Paraphrase: Typically, a cash-hoarder like that has a reputation for believing the money would disappear if it were invested or even put into a bank, where the government insures deposits up to a quarter million dollars.

4. **Original:** A Nevada man named Walter Samaszko Jr. died with a $200 balance in his bank account but about $7 million worth of gold bars and coins hidden in his house, **which workers discovered when they went to clean up his house so it could be sold.**

   Paraphrase: Walter Samaszko Jr. of Nevada had a $200 bank balance when he died, but he also had gold bars and coins valued at about $7 million hidden in his house—a stash that was found by a cleanup crew getting the house ready to be sold.

5. **Original:** An Israeli woman actually did use a mattress to hide **about $1 million in US dollars and Israeli shekels** and then mistakenly disposed of the mattress on trash-collection day.

   Paraphrase: By mistake, a woman in Israel threw into the garbage a mattress in which she had been hiding about $1 million in US and Israeli currency.

6. **Original:** Experts say that, **though your chances of finding valuables are very slim,** you should never do extensive remodeling on the walls of an old house without inspecting the space behind the old plaster or drywall because that space is a popular hoarding spot for money.

   Paraphrase: You probably won't find any money there, but always look carefully in the wall spaces if you ever do a lot of renovation on an old home.

Go to **MyEnglishLab** to complete a skill practice.

APPLY YOUR SKILLS

WHY IT'S USEFUL By applying the skills you have learned in this unit, you can successfully read this challenging text and learn about public and private goods. You can also apply your analytical and critical thinking skills to develop opinions of your own about issues raised in the reading.

BEFORE YOU READ

A. Discuss these questions with one or more students.

1. What do you know about the concept of a "public good"?

2. Are roads and sidewalks in your home country well maintained? If so, who benefits from this? Discuss where the funding for this maintenance originates.

3. Do any of your friends or family members own any real estate (a house and yard, a vacant lot, a field, etc.)? Would they allow people they know to go on their land? Strangers? Explain.

B. Imagine that you will be participating in a small group discussion about the passage "Public Goods vs. Private Gain," which begins on the next page. Your group will be discussing the following questions. Keep these questions in mind as you read the passage.

1. What is the modern-day definition of a public good?

2. What is the difference between a nonexcludable good and a nonrivalrous good? Give examples of each.

3. Economists see public goods as being various degrees of nonexcludable and nonrivalrous. Explain your understanding of this continuum. Give one example of a good that is somewhat nonexcludable and one example of a good that is somewhat nonrivalrous.

4. Why was the trade of the Apache sacred site Oak Flat controversial?

5. Name some of the reasons why discussions on public goods remain contentious.

C. Review the Unit Skills Summary. As you read the passage, apply the skills you learned in this unit.

UNIT SKILLS SUMMARY

Understand implication and inference.
- Use the information given in the text, as well as your background knowledge, to make inferences.

Make strong inferences and avoid making weak ones.
- Make inferences that are well supported by both the text and logic to accurately understand what the writer means to say.

Distinguish between deliberate implications and direct statements.
- Recognize when the author intentionally avoids saying something directly in order to better understand his or her intentions and attitudes.

Paraphrase.
- Capture the author's ideas in your own words so that you can write or speak about what you have read.

Identify and use equivalent and near-equivalent expressions.
- Recognize expressions with nearly the same meanings and apply them to your own vocabulary.

A. Read the passage. Annotate and take notes as necessary.

Public Goods vs. Private Gain

1 In July 2015, animal lovers worldwide became outraged at the death of Cecil, a famous lion and tourist attraction at Hwange National Park in Zimbabwe. It would later come to light that an American dentist had paid US $50,000 for what he said he *thought* was a legal hunt. (In fact, the lion was lured out of the park and killed by the dentist on private property, and the hunting guides were charged with poaching.) In many parts of the world, nations struggling to pay for and provide various environmental protections to help ensure the survival of endangered animals often charge high prices to hunters wishing to trail particularly unique or rare prey. Local governments insist that this money is used to help improve environmental projects aimed at protecting animals, while critics counter that it largely lines the pockets of connected individuals and does little to truly help. Some might argue that if the hunting of this famous lion had taken place at a national park—a public good—the lion's death would have been justifiable. However, from the controversy that followed, it is clear that it is not so easy to determine what constitutes a public versus a private good.

2 Governments the world over are spending increasingly less on public goods. It is one thing to expect developing nations to cut spending in tough economic times, but even developed countries like the United States are devoting less and less funding to public goods. Most spending allocations dedicated to public goods relate to hot-button political flashpoints. Reaching any sort of consensus on healthcare spending, for example, seems nearly impossible— even with the Affordable Care Act of 2010. Vast swathes of the US infrastructure are figuratively collapsing, with spending on even obvious necessities like roadways and bridges so deadlocked that literal collapse seems imminent. Even the development of a standardized educational curriculum, something many countries take for granted, has turned into a long, bitter political feud dragging in unions, publishers, teachers, parents, and politicians. Viewed through a purely capitalistic lens, public goods are a tough sell: Everyone pays for them, and nobody seems to profit, at least not in any tangible way that one can easily attach a dollar sign to. To better understand how to move forward on these issues, we must carefully examine the meaning of a public good and how it differs from a typical expenditure.

3 Public goods were originally described simply as things shared freely by all. This was until economist Paul Romer provided a more precise definition, which has since become the standard: Public goods are nonexcludable and nonrivalrous. A nonexcludable resource is something that is readily available to all. Anyone who so wishes to can make use of and exploit it. A public park, freely open to everyone, is an example. Similarly, air is available in the atmosphere, and there is no way that people can be charged for breathing. Products like cars, real estate, and aspirin sold at a pharmacy, on the other hand, are excludable goods, since someone can prevent others from using them. It's worth noting that the same product can be either excludable or nonexcludable (or partially excludable) depending on the situation. Wild strawberries growing on the side of a public road are nonexcludable, but strawberries growing on a private, fenced-in farm patrolled by security officers are excludable.

4   A nonrivalrous good is one that cannot be depleted through use. If one person makes use of it, it does not get "used up," nor are others prevented from "consuming" it at the same time. The chicken dance—an entertaining and somewhat comical dance popular in parts of the Western world—is a concept that is nonrivalrous: One partygoer dancing it does not keep another partygoer from using the *same* dance. The office stapler, on the other hand, *is* rivalrous, as only one person can utilize it at a given moment. A prime example of the difference between rivalrous and nonrivalrous goods is the classic fable of the greedy baker who tries to charge a hungry passerby for enjoying the smell of his bread. As one may anticipate, the judge in this case rules that while bread is rivalrous and excludable, the *smell* of bread is nonrivalrous and nonexcludable.

5   While many natural resources are thought to be public goods, oftentimes that is not actually the case. They frequently end up in a "Tragedy of the Commons" situation, where a shared resource is diminished because individuals pursue their own selfish interests rather than those of a larger group. These natural resources may be nonexcludable, but they are rivalrous. The inland village of two centuries ago may have believed that everyone could use the town lake for water without depleting it, but if one of their descendants built a pump system two hundred years later and drained the lake to sell bottled water at a markup, the townspeople would quickly learn just how rivalrous a lake could be.

6   It is important to note that modern economists view public goods as less of an either–or classification and more like a quality that exists on a continuum: Goods are nonrivalrous and nonexcludable to various degrees, and some can be categorized in multiple ways depending on who is making a particular argument. The distinction can get especially tricky when it comes down to specific issues and commodities, which is where arguments begin to arise; national defense may be a public good, but what about a multimillion dollar fighter jet? Healthcare in the United States, as previously discussed, is another example of a good that is partially public. While it can be excludable in the sense that the cost for it may put it beyond the reach of some people, it technically is available to all (as it is offered by the government). The issue of whether it is considered rivalrous or nonrivalrous is also sticky. It is nonrivalrous in that it cannot be completely consumed, leaving none available for others. However, others may argue that it is indeed rivalrous because not all types of plans are available to everyone due to the limits often put on it by employers. With politicians increasingly focused on the bottom line, public goods expenditures can be difficult to justify. Sometimes something that is *thought* to be a public good turns out to be quite profitable when viewed from another angle and is treated as excludable.

CULTURALLY SIGNIFICANT SITES: ALWAYS COMPLETELY PUBLIC GOODS?

7   The preservation of culturally significant sites is viewed by most as a public good, as everyone benefits from their existence and is able to experience them, even if the benefits may be difficult to quantify. The oil rights for those culturally significant places, however, are *very* easy to quantify and can certainly be treated as a saleable commodity. This clash of classifications has led to numerous controversial situations, most recently one involving an Apache sacred site in Arizona known as Oak Flat. A historically significant site, Oak Flat had been preserved through numerous exceptions made by many politicians before it was finally traded to an Australian-British mining company for land. On paper, it's quite the deal, with the US government and forestry service getting almost twice as much land in the trade. Still, the question remains as to whether the government has a duty to uphold one specific public good. It is important to consider whether being

	Nonexcludable	Excludable
Nonrivalrous	Public Goods	Partially Public Goods
	Air	Healthcare
	Public parks	National defense
Rivalrous	Shared Resources	Private Goods
	Lakes	Real estate
	Ocean swimming	Cars

Figure 1.1   *Continued*

able to incorporate a greater area of land into a national park is a "bigger" win in terms of public good than historic preservation.

8   When considering public goods, there are myriad intangible, unquantifiable issues at play. Many questions arise. Some wonder whether individuals will continue to argue the easily tallied issues as the overall infrastructure becomes more and more unstable. Others question whether healthcare is simply too immense of an issue to fix by a government built on mass consensus. Finally, a disheartening speculation is that ignoring public goods that are difficult to appraise is merely the easy choice for politicians. Opinions differ on which factor is most important to take into consideration, but it seems worryingly clear where legislators draw the line.

B. Reread the questions in Before You Read, Part B. Is there anything you cannot answer? What reading skills can you use to help you find the answers?

Go to **MyEnglishLab** to read the passage again and answer critical thinking questions.

THINKING CRITICALLY

Thinking about the information in Paragraph 7 of "Public Goods vs. Private Gain," name a few other culturally significant sites that could be considered a public good by some and a private good by others. How is this situation possible? Explain your answer using what you now know about public and private goods.

THINKING VISUALLY

Based on what you have learned about excludable, nonexcludable, rivalrous, and nonrivalrous goods, brainstorm and complete the chart with examples of goods that fit into each of the categories.

	Nonexcludable	Excludable
	Public Goods	Partially Public Goods
Nonrivalrous	Air Public parks	Healthcare National defense ....
	Shared Resources	Private Goods
Rivalrous	Lakes Ocean swimming	Real estate Cars ....

THINKING ABOUT LANGUAGE

Read these excerpts from "Public Goods vs. Private Gain." Then choose the best equivalent expression for each phrase in bold.

1. In July 2015, animal lovers worldwide **became outraged at** the death of Cecil, a famous lion and tourist attraction at Hwange National Park in Zimbabwe.
   a. expressed their annoyance about
   b. were irate upon learning of
   c. became emotionally wounded after hearing about
   d. were fearful upon hearing about

2. It would later **come to light** that an American dentist had paid US $50,000 for what he said he thought was a legal hunt.
   a. become known
   b. be illuminated
   c. be in the media
   d. be enlightened

3. Local governments insist that this money is used to help improve environmental projects aimed at protecting animals, while critics counter that it largely **lines the pockets of connected individuals** and does little to truly help.
   a. ends up in the hands of individuals in power
   b. is transferred to groups of people linked by common interests
   c. is taken from organizations made up of important citizens
   d. becomes linked to environmental protection proponents

4. Most spending allocations dedicated to public goods relate to **hot-button political flashpoints.**
   a. areas of unanimous diplomatic agreement
   b. topics of controversy among lawmakers
   c. matters considered tenacious by legislators
   d. subjects of extreme neutrality among politicians

5. Viewed through a purely capitalistic lens, public goods are a tough sell: Everyone pays for them, and nobody seems to profit, at least not in any tangible way that one can easily **attach a dollar sign to**.
   a. connect to a similar currency
   b. link to certain denominations
   c. assign a monetary value to
   d. attribute to finances

6. The inland village of two centuries ago may have believed that everyone could use the town lake for water without depleting it, but if one of their descendants built a pump system two hundred years later and drained the lake to sell bottled water **at a markup**, the townspeople would quickly learn just how rivalrous a lake could be.
   a. more inexpensively than its initial value
   b. at a price nearly equal to that of its fundamental worth
   c. at the exact same price that it is worth
   d. at a higher price than it originally would cost

7. Finally, a disheartening speculation is that ignoring public goods that are **difficult to appraise** is merely the easy choice for politicians.
   a. challenging to rate
   b. problematic to assess
   c. demanding to audit
   d. puzzling to review

▶ Go to **MyEnglishLab** to listen to Professor Clerici-Arias and to complete a self-assessment.

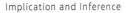

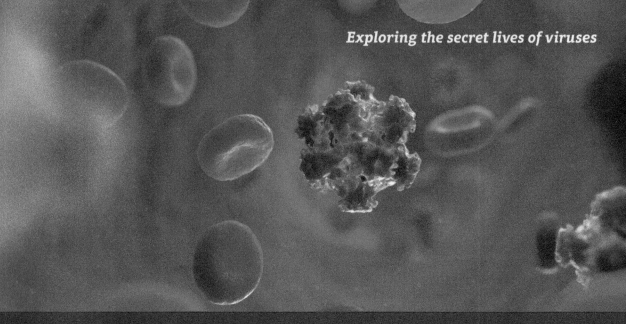
Exploring the secret lives of viruses

BIOLOGY

Evidence and Argumentation

UNIT PROFILE

You will consider the subject of biology—specifically diseases. As you read about topics such as viruses that contribute to cancer, mad cow disease, and Alzheimer's disease, you will learn about the history of the diseases, their causes, symptoms, and treatments.

Preview the reading "Vaccinating Against Cancer" on page 201. Skim the reading. What evidence can you identify? Are there any logical faults in it? Does the reading contain any extended metaphors? Also consider whether you recognize any phrases that convey function and purpose.

OUTCOMES

• Evaluate evidence and argumentation
• Identify and evaluate evidence
• Recognize and deal with faulty rhetoric
• Understand extended metaphor
• Identify and use expressions of function and purpose

GETTING STARTED

▶ Go to **MyEnglishLab** to listen to Professor Siegel and to complete a self-assessment.

Discuss these questions with a partner or group.

1. Consider how cancer has affected people you know. Do you think cancer rates are rising or falling? Think about the impact that the environment, changes in individuals' lifestyles, and advances in medicine may have on these rates.

2. What do you know about how cancer develops? Are some people more susceptible to getting cancer than others?

3. What advancements can you think of in the diagnosis and treatment of cancer? What types of advances do you think will be made in the future—both in the prevention of cancer and in the treatment of it after it has developed?

For more about **BIOLOGY**, see ① ③. See also W and OC **BIOLOGY** ① ② ③.

CRITICAL THINKING SKILL
EVALUATING EVIDENCE AND ARGUMENTATION

WHY IT'S USEFUL By learning to identify and evaluate evidence and to assess and move past misleading or faulty statements, you will strengthen your ability to think and read critically.

In the majority—if not all—of the academic courses that you take, you will read pieces of writing containing evidence and arguments. **Evidence** refers to information such as statistics, research findings, and facts. **Arguments**—also known as claims or rhetorical statements—are statements an author makes for or against something, based on the evidence.

Your professors will expect you to be able to recognize when evidence is being presented and when arguments are being made based on that evidence. This means that, as has been discussed in other units, critical thinking skills are of utmost importance. You must be able to not only read closely and recognize evidence but also evaluate it and assess its validity.

You must consider whether the evidence an author presents fully supports his or her conclusion, or if vital information is insufficient, unconvincing, or missing altogether. Misrepresentative or flawed information is innocently provided by an author more often than you may think. The author may truly believe that certain evidence is correct and valid, whereas an attentive critical reader will recognize it as misleading or faulty. Any conclusions the author may base on such evidence are unreliable..

In this unit, you will learn how to identify and evaluate evidence as well as how to recognize and deal with faulty claims. **Evaluating evidence and argumentation** will enable you to become an even more effective critical reader and will aid you in contributions you must make during class discussions as well as in written assignments. This unit breaks the skill down into two supporting skills:

- identifying and evaluating evidence
- recognizing and dealing with faulty rhetoric

NOTICING ACTIVITY

A. As you read the following passage, look for and highlight instances in which evidence is being presented. Also note the several instances of misleading or faulty rhetoric and be prepared to say why you think they are faulty.

THE TRUTH ABOUT CANCER RATES

1   [1] Statistics show that one in two individuals in America will be diagnosed with cancer—leading many to believe that the incidence of the illness is increasing. [2] Past studies have established that cancer is a disease caused by a glitch in one's own cellular replication system, and for this reason, scientists encounter insurmountable difficulty in finding a cure. [3] An analysis of the rising number of reported cases of cancer has brought to light a secondary reason for why cancer has taken the stage as a disease of epidemic proportions. [4] Research shows that this is due to our own advancements; because humans live longer, they die less from infectious illnesses that used to account for the vast majority of human mortality cases. [5] The panic about cancer is often induced by skewed studies and erroneous warnings put forth by companies that probably have a vested financial interest in alarming the public. Such panic is disproportionate

Continued

to any real threats posed by the disease. [6] Data indicates that cancer is not worsening, nor is its incidence rate increasing.

2   [7] According to a 2009 peer-reviewed scientific report in *The Journal of Cancer Research*, the rate of the incidence of cancer has remained relatively stable. [8] Statistics show that the mortality rate of cancer since that time, in fact, has fallen for every age category (Kort, et al.). [9] These findings reveal that decreases in mortality rates are due to medical advances in cancer detection and treatment. [10] This fact was also verified by a woman whose husband is a prominent cancer researcher. [11] While there are more cases of cancer, this is simply because cancer is predominantly a disease of the elderly, and thanks to vaccines and medical treatments that have extended life expectancy from about 50 years of age in 1900 to nearly 80 today, society in the United States is increasingly populated by the elderly. [12] Evidence suggests that as infectious diseases and other ailments are significantly more treatable today, cancer is what befalls many individuals.

B. Answer the questions about the passage.

1. What evidence is presented in Sentence 1? Use your own words.

   ....

2. Sentence 2 contains an instance of faulty rhetoric. Identify this language and then write why it is considered faulty.

   ....

3. What evidence is presented in Sentence 4? Paraphrase it. You may need to refer to ideas mentioned in previous sentences to do so effectively.

   ....

4. Sentence 5 contains an instance of faulty rhetoric. Identify this language and then write why it is faulty.

   ....

5. Look at the source for the evidence in Sentence 7. Do you think the evidence is trustworthy? Why or why not?

   ....

6. Sentence 10 represents a type of faulty evidence. Why do you think it is faulty?

   ....

Go to **MyEnglishLab** to complete a vocabulary exercise and skill practice, and to join in collaborative activities.

SUPPORTING SKILL 1
IDENTIFYING AND EVALUATING EVIDENCE

WHY IT'S USEFUL By recognizing evidence presented in the texts you read, you will be able to determine what a writer is basing his or her conclusion(s) on. You will learn to consider the strength of the evidence provided and decide whether it is sufficient or invalid.

In your academic courses, you will be expected to read a variety of types of texts, including journal articles, textbooks, and laboratory reports. You will also be expected to conduct your own research—typically online—and will be tasked with identifying information and evidence that is not only relevant to a given topic but also reliable and valid.

Texts provided to you by your professors, articles, and textbooks typically contain information that has been fact-checked and verified by a number of professionals before being published, so the evidence presented in such texts can generally be trusted. However, when conducting your own research, you will come across a wide variety of texts, and you are responsible for determining whether the evidence offered in these readings is sufficient, pertinent, and thoroughly explained. It is up to you to evaluate this evidence—making sure there are no holes in it—and to decide whether it effectively contributes to the conclusion an author or researcher draws.

Before you can evaluate evidence, however, you first have to identify it. The following chart contains phrases frequently used to introduce evidence or to refer to it after it has been introduced.

Phrase Used to Introduce or Refer to Evidence	Example
_____ is evidenced by [X evidence].	Scientists' determination to develop vaccines for currently incurable diseases **is evidenced by** the huge number of ongoing clinical trials.
According to evidence presented by …	**According to evidence presented by** clinical studies, carcinogens can cause cancer.
Data indicates / confirms that …	**Data indicates that** longer life expectancy plays a role in current cancer rates.
Evidence suggests that …	**Evidence suggests that** exercise could make an individual more or less likely to develop certain types of cancers.
Figures / Numbers suggest (that) …	**Numbers suggest that** cancer rates are remaining stable.
Findings indicate / reveal (that) …	**Findings reveal that** the mortality rate of cancer has decreased for people of all ages.
Past studies established that …	**Past studies established that** cancer begins with a mutation in a cell.
Research has uncovered …	**Research has uncovered** various sources of cancer over the past century.
Research shows that …	**Research shows that** the development of vaccines has resulted in a decrease in the number of cancer cases.
Statistics show that …	**Statistics show that** cancer is a leading cause of death in the United States.
The following evidence demonstrates that …	**The following evidence demonstrates that** individuals with breast cancer often benefit from hormone therapy.
The presence of [X evidence] …	**The presence of** one cancerous cell can indicate the existence of others.

Continued

Phrase Used to Introduce or Refer to Evidence	Example
The research team identified [X evidence] …	**The research team identified** chemicals in cigarettes as being toxic.
Researchers observed that [X evidence] …	**Researchers observed that** the injection of apparently cancer-free cells into otherwise healthy animals could cause cancer.
The analysis of [X evidence] …	**The analysis of** chromosome behavior in sea urchins led to Boveri's hypothesis about the origin of cancer.
What was found is that …	**What was found is that** lifestyle choices can greatly impact individuals' susceptibility to developing the disease.
[X person] concluded that …	The laboratory analyst **concluded that** the tissue contained cancerous cells.

After identifying evidence presented by an author, the next step is evaluating it. Ask yourself the following questions to decide if the evidence is valid and supports an author's conclusion(s):

Evaluative Questions

1. **Is the evidence directly related to the topic the author is discussing?** For example, if an author draws a conclusion about the effectiveness of hormone therapy in treating cancer, yet provides only evidence about chemotherapy, this evidence would not support the claims being made. Appropriate evidence would be evidence that discusses research done on hormone therapy.

2. **Is strong, sufficient evidence provided?** If a writer makes a sweeping claim about, for example, the extent to which certain toxins can cause cancer, is this claim supported by a substantial amount of meaningful evidence? The strongest evidence in this case would be studies conducted by other researchers about the same topic who drew the same or very similar conclusions. Other factors to consider are the recency of the evidence (was it published within the last couple years or 40 years ago?), as well as any criticism the evidence or the source presenting the evidence has received or withstood.

3. **Does the evidence portray some authorial bias?** Consider the source of the evidence to determine whether it is reliable or may be biased. Governmental and educational institutions are often thought to provide more credible information than organizations that have a financial stake in distributing the information. Information from nonprofit organizations is sometimes reliable and objective, but at other times, may be biased toward a particular cause.

4. **Does the author attempt to view the evidence from several angles before drawing a conclusion?** Could the significance of the evidence be interpreted in any way other than the way in which it was interpreted by the researcher?

5. **Do the author's conclusions make sense based on the evidence provided?** Are there any gaps of logic between the evidence presented and the conclusion drawn?

6. **Do you sense that anything is missing?** Should any other factor have been considered? Should any other evidence have been introduced or examined more closely?

For more information about evaluating sources, see the section Synthesizing Information from Several Sources (p. 209).

EXERCISE 1

A. Read the passage. Highlight phrases that introduce or refer to evidence.

Cancer: Research, Diagnoses, and Prognoses

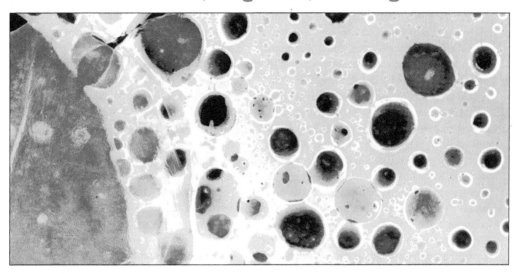

1   Cancer is not a single disease but rather a collection of more than one hundred related diseases that all begin with abnormal cell growth that results from damage to the DNA of cells. Within types of cancer there are further distinctions, including different diagnoses of particular kinds of cancerous cells. Recent research shows that even individual tumors themselves can possess heterogeneity of features. Some scientists compare cancer to a tree, with the trunk being the basic pathology of the disease, the branches the many differing types of cancer, and the leaves the millions of individual cases. A diagnosis of cancer today acts as a tripwire for a vast medical mechanism, including the delivery of potentially differing prognoses and an oncological assortment of treatments tailored to the individual patient, all evidence of the strides science has made in combatting the disease over the centuries.

2   From the time it was first recorded in ancient Egypt until the 20th century, physicians had many different—and often inaccurate—hypotheses about what caused cancer. After scientists discovered the DNA helical structure in 1962, the foundation was laid for researchers to understand cancer as a disease of genetic mutation. Clinical studies of people exposed to certain toxins, such as cigarette smoke, revealed that carcinogens cause damage to DNA, which in turn causes cancer. Similar studies have established that radiation, viruses, and certain inherited genes can all cause cancer. More recent genetic research on cancer has uncovered the "drivers" behind cancer, which are three main types of genes that affect the genetic changes that occur with cancer. These drivers, known as proto-oncogenes, tumor suppressor genes, and DNA repair genes, cause cancer when they become altered in some way. When these driver genes mutate, they cause other cells to survive when they should not and to divide in abnormal ways.

3   Diagnoses of cancer are complex, and determining the best course of action for a patient is contingent upon the specific type of cancer the individual has. Typically, the cancer is named after the organ in which it originates, as in the case of breast cancer, or the types of cells in which it forms, as in the case of squamous cell cancer or epithelial cancer. After this initial diagnosis,

Continued

pathologists delve into the particular type of tumor mass that is present. In breast cancer, for example, after pinpointing the precise location and size of the cancerous cell mass, doctors then analyze the tumor itself to determine a patient's particular type of breast cancer. Based on the type of cancerous cells in the biopsy, the breast cancer could be endocrine receptor-positive, HER2-positive, triple positive, or triple negative. This analysis of tumor tissue is essential in informing a patient's treatment program. According to clinical studies of breast cancer patients, hormone therapy is often the best choice for a person with an endocrine receptor-positive cancer, for example, as this treatment would likely result in a decrease in cancerous cells (as it does for most breast cancer cases). On the other hand, it is probable that a patient with triple-negative breast cancer—a more aggressive type—would choose chemotherapy over hormone therapy, as this type of tumor cell does not respond to common breast cancer treatment drugs that attack estrogen, progesterone, and HER-2.

4   Genetic studies in oncology have opened another door of diagnostic tools. The presence of certain inherited genes can reveal an individual's chances of getting cancer, or a clearer prognosis if he or she already has cancer. For example, after scientists discovered the tumor suppressor genes BRCA1 and BRCA2 in the early 1990s, they began clinical studies analyzing data of women who had the gene. They found that BRCA gene carriers have up to a 60 percent chance of developing breast cancer during their lifetime. If a woman has inherited this type of genetic mutation, a more aggressive form of risk assessment is generally recommended based upon the likelihood of developing cancer. Breast cancer is just one type of cancer, one branch on the malignant tree. Other cancer types have equally complex distinctions, demonstrating that cancer is certainly not a one-size-fits-all disease.

B. With a partner, compare the phrases you highlighted.

C. Now reread the passage. As you read, ask yourself the six Evaluative Questions (p. 184), making notes about sections where you see problems.

D. Share your thoughts from Part C with a partner.

Go to MyEnglishLab to complete a vocabulary exercise and skill practice, and to join in collaborative activities.

SUPPORTING SKILL 2
RECOGNIZING AND DEALING WITH FAULTY RHETORIC

WHY IT'S USEFUL By recognizing faulty attempts to argue a point, you can distinguish effective discourse from weaker attempts. This helps you avoid being misled by inadequate arguments.

Most of the readings you find in textbooks and journals are well reasoned and have been checked for validity of argument. Critical readers at prepublication stages help ensure that most of such text is free of egregious errors by the time you see it. However, you are likely to encounter quite a bit of writing that requires you to keep an eye out for faulty rhetoric.

Different types of writing present different challenges in interpreting rhetoric.

- Some logical faults are very hard to see, so even closely checked **academic writing** might have a few faulty passages that managed to make it through.
- **Journalistic writing** may contain inadequate or faulty evidence. One reason is that journalistic works are produced on short timelines and not every fault will be caught by editors. Another is that sometimes journalism presents statements by a wide range of persons, even if some of these sources have poorly reasoned or inadequately supported opinions.
- **Any account of a debate or controversy**, regardless of the source, is likely to contain some well-thought-out evidence but also a lot of poorly reasoned positions. Even if a participant in a controversy presents material that looks like solid evidence, it should be examined carefully for hard-to-spot problems.
- A great deal of material produced expressly for **online publication**—articles, blogs, chats, and so on—follows discourse rules different from those of most academic writing. In academic writing, for instance, exaggeration is considered a bad approach. Moderation is valued. However, many online outlets thrive on exaggeration, rumor, sarcasm, and so on.

This chart presents some of the most often seen **logical faults**.

Logic Problem	Example	Explanation
Ad hominem argument (sometimes called "guilt by association" argument)	Professor Blake Tomura, before being fired from Grayson University for misconduct, authored an article in which he insisted that prions could not replicate without some intermediate nucleic acid—RNA or DNA.	The author makes an issue of Tomura's personal weaknesses. He tries to make Tomura's point of view seem less respectable by mentioning the professor's "misconduct." This is not good argument. In reality, the personalities or life circumstances of the idea's proponents are irrelevant. Arguments and evidence should be evaluated on their merit, not on the likeability of their proponents or opponents.
"Conspiracy theory"	An increased gas tax, which would reduce consumption, might be good for the nation as a whole. However, Senator Twomey's personal finances are too reliant on income from gas sales for her to ever support such a tax.	Somewhat related to the ad hominem argument, "conspiracy theory" arguments dismiss someone who holds a position by implying that some sort of evil plan motivates the person.

Continued

Logic Problem	Example	Explanation
Exaggeration	Without the knowledge that genes determine the production of proteins, modern science would grind to a halt, unable to answer even the simplest questions.	The author greatly overstates the case. In reality, though knowledge about genes and proteins is extremely important, basic science would not cease to exist without it.
False certainty	Travelers to the area contract the disease by eating poorly cooked food from the informal food stalls that line the highways.	The statement makes it sound certain—or at least likely—that a traveler will get the disease. This is almost certainly not true. A more honest statement would say *Some travelers* or *may contract*.
False dilemma	The university should shift its focus away from parking enforcement. The hundreds of thousands of dollars saved would fund greatly improved health care for students.	The author portrays the situation as presenting only two alternatives, and offers a false choice. She implies that money "wasted" on enforcing parking rules would otherwise be spent on health care. In reality, money not spent on parking might be spent in dozens of different possible ways, and there is no necessary connection between less spending in the one area and more spending in the other.
Irrelevant quotation	As we consider the value of a classical education, let's remember what the biologist Stephen Jay Gould said: "We are all glorious accidents of an unpredictable process."	Without a larger context, it is hard to know, but this author appears to be dropping in a quote that has no relevance to the topic. The author is trying to exploit the name of a famous person in hopes of making the reading seem more serious.
Reasoning by anecdote	[A short anecdote about a student who became more successful after reading Confucius] This story shows the need to include Confucius in American middle school curricula.	This author is unfairly drawing a large conclusion from one instance. Anecdotes can be attractive evidence, but they do not seal an argument. Large conclusions usually cannot be drawn from one instance or even from several. Other anecdotes demonstrating exactly the opposite point can probably be found.
Reasoning by question	Protesters shut down the subway system, so the police beat them with clubs and shot them with rubber bullets. What else could the government do?	This is wrong on two counts: 1) Like the false dilemma (above), this portrays a complicated set of possibilities as an overly simple choice between two things—either the government could physically harm protesters or it could do nothing. In reality, of course, there are probably dozens of other things the government could have done. 2) A good reading states its main positions in strong declarative sentences, such as, *The government was right in doing so*—which can then be supported. This is more honest and authoritative than trying to explain or argue a position that is weakly implied through a question.

EXERCISE 2

A. Read the article, which contains several examples of faulty rhetoric. (Sentences in bold are featured in a post-reading exercise.)

MAD COW DISEASE

1   Bovine spongiform encephalopathy (BSE), commonly known as mad cow disease, is a fatal degenerative disease that attacks the central nervous systems of cows. In nearly all feedlots in modern factory farming, farmers, whether they acknowledge it or not, have supplemented food for their cattle with ground-up particles of cattle corpses. Consuming infectious deceased-cattle material can cause the living cows to contract mad cow disease. When, higher up the food chain, humans go on to consume the cows infected with the illness, they contract the human variant of the disease, known as Creutzfeldt-Jakob disease (CJD), which causes death. Consumers cannot know what farmers feed to cattle before the cattle are processed and packaged by rich multinational companies for the grocery store aisle. So meat lovers are faced with a choice they shouldn't have to make—either contract a gruesome disease or give up beef.

2   Mad cow disease originated when British farmers fed their cattle parts of sheep that were infected with a brain-wasting illness similar to mad cow. This was totally understandable. The cost of grain was high, so what else could farmers do? Humans then contracted the disease from infected beef. At its peak in the late 1980s and into the 1990s, the disease killed hundreds of innocent people. The disease is caused by an infectious agent known as a prion, which, after entering the human body, remains in an extended incubation period, sometimes for as long as five to ten years, before symptoms present. **This ticking time bomb lies dormant until it manifests with symptoms that start with depression and hallucination, and quickly progress to loss of motor control and ultimately, death.** Generally, victims only have a few months to live after receiving a diagnosis. The unpredictability of mad cow illness makes it the most appalling disease of all diseases afflicting humankind.

3   When scientists studied the effects of feeding practices in factory farms and made the correlation between mad cow disease and dead cattle particles in cattle food, the UK government intervened with regulations to stop the criticized feeding practices. To many, this was government overreach with deleterious social consequences. As Bilal Khan, president of the British South Asiatic Society, noted, "Instead of examining the contents of cow stomachs, the government should fix our crumbling roads." Other governments fell in line behind the administration of the clueless, uninformed minister of agriculture.

4   Since that time, there have been fewer cases of mad cow disease. However, a new case reported last year clearly reveals that the regulations are ineffective. A 20-year-old Exeter man became mysteriously ill and suffered rapid declines in physical and mental acuity. Reports from farms in Britain and the United States say that, while cattle farmers may have

CULTURE NOTE

Communication on the Internet has its own standards of acceptability. Many writers who post material to various sites or who participate in commentary on social media have a tendency to exaggerate or even be rude and insulting. It is important to separate the language of social media from academic English. Academic English, even if it appears on the Internet, has higher standards of civility and politeness. It never insults, it never "rants" (complains at length), and it tries to be moderate in tone while still making substantive points.

Continued

cut back on the use of sheep-derived protein to feed their herds, they have increased their use of ground-up chicken innards. No scientific reports have linked this practice to the development of mad cow disease, but it is not a leap in logic to imagine that if sheep parts could cause mad cow disease, so too could other animal parts. **Finally, there is nothing you can do to make beef safer if it has been infected, including cooking it. There is still a chance of contracting this fatal disease, and so the only responsible way to protect oneself is by avoiding meat altogether.**

5   Researcher Charles Baker, who recently authored a book on the disease, maintains that as long as regulations are in place, people need not worry about catching mad cow disease. Baker argues that beef is safe for consumption, and he sums up his book by saying the disease is a closed case. **Baker, however, has likely never witnessed a patient suffer and die from mad cow disease, so no one should trust his opinion.** Baker's book shows a blatant disregard for the perspective of victims of mad cow disease, and for this reason, he cannot be considered a reliable source when considering appropriate ways to eliminate the disease. If individuals want to eradicate mad cow disease forever, the only efficacious policy is to do away with all beef products.

6   Scientific journals also downplay the risk of the disease by using medical jargon that hides the realities of the disease from the common person. One must be careful not to be swayed by such sources. **After all, the irreducible fact about the disease remains—beef contains infectious particles. To avoid the disease, one must avoid eating meat.** How can scientists possibly expect people to think beef is safe knowing this fact? **The solution is simple and clear, though scientists and cattle industry officials would never reveal the truth of the matter to the general public because it would cost them their mansions and Ferraris.** As Mahatma Gandhi once said, "I will not let others walk through my mind with their dirty feet." No matter the regulations or insistence from some that beef is safe, it can still be contaminated. Stopping the purchase and consumption of beef is what one must do to avoid mad cow disease.

B. Read these excerpts from the article. Choose a description from the box that best characterizes the rhetorical problem in each excerpt. Some descriptions will be used more than once.

ad hominem	false dilemma
conspiracy	irrelevant quotation
exaggeration	reasoning by anecdote
false certainty	reasoning by question

.... 1. In nearly all feedlots in modern factory farming, farmers, whether they acknowledge it or not, have supplemented food for their cattle with ground-up particles of cattle corpses.

.... 2. Consumers cannot know what farmers feed to cattle before the cattle are processed and packaged by rich multinational companies for the grocery store aisle.

.... 3. So meat lovers are faced with a choice they shouldn't have to make—either contract a gruesome disease or give up beef.

.... 4. Mad cow disease originated when British farmers fed their cattle parts of sheep that were infected with a brain-wasting illness similar to mad cow. This was totally understandable. The cost of grain was high, so what else could farmers do?

.... 5. The unpredictability of mad cow illness makes it the most appalling disease of all diseases afflicting humankind.

.... 6. To many, this was government overreach with deleterious social consequences. As Bilal Khan, president of the British South Asiatic Society, noted, "Instead of examining the contents of cow stomachs, the government should fix our crumbling roads."

.... 7. Other governments fell in line behind the administration of the clueless, uninformed minister of agriculture.

.... 8. However, a new case reported last year clearly reveals that the regulations are ineffective. A 20-year-old Exeter man became mysteriously ill and suffered rapid declines in physical and mental acuity.

.... 9. As Mahatma Gandhi once said, "I will not let others walk through my mind with their dirty feet."

C. Look at the five passages in bold in the article. Work with a partner. Discuss whether each demonstrates faulty reasoning. If it does, what fault does it demonstrate? How could that part of the article be rewritten to avoid the fault?

Go to **MyEnglishLab** to complete a vocabulary exercise and skill practice, and to join in collaborative activities.

READING-WRITING CONNECTION
UNDERSTANDING EXTENDED METAPHOR

WHY IT'S USEFUL Scientific passages often deal with concepts that are complex and abstract. To help the average reader develop a mental picture of these concepts, an author might build extended metaphors. By recognizing and understanding these metaphors, you can more easily grasp explanations of scientific phenomena.

An **extended metaphor** may express similarities between a difficult scientific concept and some more familiar aspect of life. It is not just a brief statement of similarity, but rather a scenario that stretches over several sentences—or even paragraphs. Study this example:

> The process of glycolysis is like the act of putting money into a business venture in hopes of getting money back. Think of the high-energy molecule ATP (adenosine triphosphate) as the energy currency of a cell. The first part of glycolysis is called the Investment Phase because glucose (sugar derived from food) is broken down in a process that requires a lot of ATP to be used up. However, as the name indicates, the ATP is not lost but invested. It helps stabilize the rate of reactions and drives the process toward the next stage, the Pay-off Phase. A number of chemical reactions that were set up by spending some ATP are now possible, including reactions that create more ATP. Overall, the investment of some ATP in the first phase yields a net increase in ATP by the end of the second phase.

The author chose a metaphor of money and investment to describe a biological process that might otherwise be very difficult to imagine. The metaphor cannot deal with every technical aspect of the process because doing so would make it too complex. However, it does include the most important factors and stages, so it provides a general working knowledge of the technical concept.

Characteristics of Extended Metaphors
The metaphor must

- be easily accessible to most readers. It must refer to some common, nonspecialized situation or event.
- be inclusive—that is, all the crucial aspects of the scientific phenomenon being explained must have a representative in the metaphor.
- simplify. A metaphor that tries too hard to cover every small aspect of a complex process will probably be impossible to understand.
- not talk down to the reader. Although the function of the metaphor is to simplify things for average readers, the language of the metaphor has to be at the appropriate level. If the metaphor sounds like something written for children or uneducated people, it will alienate adult, well-educated readers.

READING AND WRITING EXTENDED METAPHORS

In a reading class, you could be asked to read and understand an extended metaphor that someone else has written. You may also be asked to write your own extended metaphor—to explain to non-experts some complex concept that you understand because of special experience or training. The list of characteristics of extended metaphors on the previous page can serve two purposes: 1) to help you look for metaphors in what you read, and 2) to guide you in writing your own extended metaphors.

EXERCISE 3

The following paragraphs present extended metaphors. Read each paragraph. Then read the questions and choose the best answers.

> Gravitational lensing is a process in which light is bent by high-mass objects along its path. Think of a beam of light as a bullet traveling at 186,282 miles per second. At least, that would be the bullet's speed in a vacuum, and in a vacuum it would also travel in a perfectly straight line. But if we place our bullet in a crowded space—such as our solar system, which is far from empty—we complicate things. Even if the bullet stays far away from planets and their moons as it travels through space, it will be subtly affected by them. Imagine that the bullet is shot from the Sun at its full velocity, just as a beam of light would be. As it passes the tiny planet Mercury, it feels a slight pull—not much, but enough to bend its path a little. Yet it carries on, and as it passes the somewhat larger planets Venus, Earth, and Mars, it feels slightly stronger tugs, each of which pulls it ever so slightly off its original trajectory. In fact, if we had a chart that showed its original projected path as it was shot from the Sun, and we charted where the bullet was as it passed Mars, we would notice that it was actually no longer on that original straight path. Then, as the bullet approaches the giant planet Jupiter, gravitational forces really come into play.

1. In this passage, what is the metaphorical equivalent of a light beam?
   a. A vacuum
   b. The Sun
   c. Gravity
   d. A bullet

2. Why does the author mention that the bullet travels at 186,282 miles per second?
   a. Because that is the speed necessary for anything to leave the Sun
   b. Because that is the speed that light travels in a vacuum
   c. Because that is the speed necesssary for the bullet to reach the edge of the solar system
   d. Because that is the highest speed ever recorded for a bullet

3. By inference from the paragraph, why does the metaphor include planets of different sizes?
   a. Because real gravitational lensing is affected by the mass of objects that light passes
   b. Because the author wants to make the metaphor more realistic and interesting
   c. Because light, unlike a bullet, would not be affected by the size of objects it passes
   d. Because the author wants to show that eventually the bullet will hit a large object

Communication between neurons (nerve cells) is complex—and one of the most vital processes in the human body. Where communication shuts down due to injury or disease, part of the body will cease to function. Neurons are called electro-excitable cells because they respond to electricity; however, ordinary communication among typical neurons is a matter of chemicals. Neurons are separated from each other by small spaces called synapses, in the manner of neighboring houses separated from each other by small strips of lawn. Imagine that one neighbor, the Sender, wants to communicate a simple message—such as "Wake up!"—to another, the Receiver. The Sender sends a messenger (a chemical) over to his neighbor's house. However, it's not good enough for the messenger to simply go there and start banging on the door. The Receiver is inside a bedroom far from the outside of the house and cannot receive any messages unless the messages come to exactly the right place in exactly the right form. "Receiver" neurons require that messenger chemicals fit into special receptor spaces that can accommodate only those chemicals. So the Sender neighbor equips his messenger with a very specific key. The messenger goes to one very specific slot that accommodates the key, which, when turned, rings a bell. If all steps are followed properly, the key turns, a bell rings next to the Receiver neighbor's bed, and he wakes up.

4. In the paragraph, what is the metaphorical equivalent of a neuron?

   a. A neighbor

   b. A chemical

   c. A space

   d. A bell

5. Why does the author mention that the Receiver is deep inside the house?

   a. To explain why the Sender needs to wake him up

   b. To explain why a wrongly placed message won't reach him

   c. To emphasize that neurons are very hard to communicate with

   d. To show why a chemical, not electricity, is necessary

6. Why does the metaphor include mention of a key?

   a. To demonstrate that the messenger has to go inside the Receiver's house

   b. To explain that the Receiver cannot send a message back to the Sender

   c. To show that the Sender cannot communicate with any other neighbors

   d. To emphasize that only a special-shaped thing can be received

EXERCISE 4

A. Read the article.

Alzheimer's Disease and Prion Diseases

1   Alzheimer's disease, a neurodegenerative illness that afflicts more than five million Americans, cannot be prevented, cured, or significantly slowed. The disease generally strikes those 65 years and older. To relatives watching a family member succumb to Alzheimer's, it may seem as if a magnificent structure—the loved one—is slowly being dismantled by invisible termites. Some of the destructive bugs take away motor function, while others slowly eat away at intellectual abilities. Most disturbingly, there are malign vermin eating away at temperament and causing neuropsychiatric changes like increased aggression. It is not at all uncommon for the relatives of someone with advanced Alzheimer's to comment that the person who used to be in the body is no longer there. The edifice has been stripped to the studs, abandoned, and then taken over by some stranger.

2   The disease is a riddle, and scientists have few answers for why it occurs and how it might be prevented. There are some similarities between the pathogenesis of Alzheimer's and a much rarer group of neurodegenerative infectious diseases known as prion diseases, and the patterns of development of Alzheimer's and the prion group have been studied closely in recent years. Like any brain research, it's frustratingly tricky. It is as if the human brain stands behind an iron gate, delicate yet robust, configured in filigree of daunting complexity. The gate allows glimpses of what is inside, but it resists access. Even when researchers believe they have a key, either the lock holds, or another gate is discovered just inside the outer one. True as this is for understanding the unimpaired brain, it is even worse for discerning that of the Alzheimer's patient. The lock is rusted shut, and deadening vines have grown up all over the wrought iron.

3   However, a pick for the Alzheimer's lock may have been found by researchers examining the brain tissue of deceased patients who had a disease not previously considered similar to Alzheimer's—the group of maladies called prion diseases. In particular, researchers have found evidence that suggests that amyloid-beta peptides (chemical groupings smaller than proteins), which are associated with brain plaque formation in Alzheimer's disease, may be infectious in a few circumstances—just as prions are. If borne out, this speculation would upend our conception of Alzheimer's, which has always been understood as genetically inherited or caused by environmental factors—not transmissible from the outside. The startling findings, if proven true, would have broad implications for health officials.

4   Prion diseases, part of a class of illnesses known as transmissible spongiform encephalopathies (TSEs), can afflict humans and animals. The symptoms associated with prion diseases are strikingly similar to those of Alzheimer's—loss of coordination, behavioral changes, and dementia. One difference is that they are usually fatal, whereas Alzheimer's itself can kill but usually does not because patients die of something else first. Prion diseases have a long incubation period but a rapid progression, often ending in death 12 months after symptoms first develop, or even sooner. Relatively little is understood about prion diseases, but they quite clearly develop because of malign structural features in proteins. Most proteins are long molecules, like chains with chemical groups as their links. They are only chemical compounds, not living organisms. The chain can pivot on its links and bend into a huge variety of complex shapes such as corkscrews, bows, balls of tangled string, and countless other trickier configurations. It may look as if someone grabbed the protein molecule and scrunched it up in her hand, yet this folding is not random. Each protein has a natural (sometimes called "native") shape that is its default formation. In fact, proteins that do not fold properly do not function properly. That is what a prion is: a misfolded protein.

Continued

5   Prions can be introduced both exogenously, as an infectious agent, or endogenously, via an inherited PRNP gene—which causes the normal prion protein on the surface of cells to change its shape. When the misfolded prion enters the central nervous system, it adheres to other proteins and causes them to become misshapen. Eventually, these sticky proteins cause plaque buildup in the brain. Areas of plaque are like sticky spots of spilled syrup that have hardened between nerve cells in the brain blocking the normal passage of nerve signals. They tend to grow by accumulating other pieces of broken or misshapen proteins, as a sticky syrup spill would accumulate crumbs on a table.

6   A similar process happens in Alzheimer's disease, in which the characteristic plaques are caused by amyloid-ß (pronounced as "amyloid beta") peptides. Both Alzheimer's and prion diseases are classified as "misfolding protein diseases"—even though the amyloid-ß chains in Alzheimer's are so short they are more like pieces of proteins. In all misfolding protein diseases, which include Parkinson's disease and Huntington's disease, the protein accumulations in the brain begin with a single "bad seed," ready to propagate its problematic form to other proteins or even break others apart. The bad seed, in the case of prion diseases, begins when the misfolded prion infects other proteins. It now appears that Alzheimer's, once not considered infectious in any way, might bear out the "bad seed" comparison after all, in its amyloid-ß peptides.

7   In several 2015 and 2016 studies, researchers examined the brains of cadavers of patients who had Creutzfeldt-Jakob disease (CJD), a prion disease that causes rapid brain degeneration, to look for signs of amyloid-ß infection. The CJD disease in the subjects was acquired through iatrogenic means (in the course of medical treatment), either from surgical grafts of dura mater (brain membrane) or from receiving contaminated growth hormones. The tissue of the CJD disease patients showed the expected damage from the prion protein that caused the disease, but it also revealed something unusual—initial signs of amyloid-ß plaques, the same plaques found in Alzheimer's disease. The gray matter of the brains was found to have more deposits of amyloid-ß than usual, though none of the patients' medical history indicated that they had developed Alzheimer's disease. The studies showed evidence that along with the infectious prion, amyloid-ß was also transmitted through the procedures that gave them CJD.

B. Read the questions and choose the best answers.

1. Which paragraph does NOT contain an extended metaphor?
   a. Paragraph 1
   b. Paragraph 3
   c. Paragraph 5
   d. Paragraph 7

2. Which of the following is the author's metaphor for a person afflicted with Alzheimer's disease?
   a. The human body
   b. Insects
   c. A building
   d. Deterioration

3. In the first extended metaphor of the article, what do the termites correspond to?

    a. Destructive aspects of Alzheimer's

    b. Loved ones who watch a patient's decline

    c. Prion diseases that are eventually fatal

    d. Treatments for Alzheimer's that do not help

4. In Paragraph 2, why is an iron gate a better metaphor than a solid door would be?

    a. Because the door could be unlocked more easily than a gate

    b. Because the door would not allow a view of what's inside

    c. Because the door would protect the patient from the disease

    d. Because the "rust" and "vines" of Alzheimer's would not develop on the door

5. In Paragraph 4, what are spoken of as metaphorically like the links in a chain?

    a. Alzheimer's patients

    b. Proteins

    c. Chemical groups

    d. Prion diseases

6. In Paragraph 4, why does the author use the image of scrunching something up in a person's hand?

    a. To explain why proteins have a native shape

    b. To explain why proteins break

    c. To explain that proteins are very strong

    d. To explain how some proteins look

7. In what way is an Alzheimer's plaque similar to a spot of spilled syrup?

    a. It is a layer of a sticky substance.

    b. It is formed from a liquid that has escaped a container.

    c. It contains a large amount of sugar.

    d. It is round and dark brown in color.

8. What does the metaphor of the "bad seed" allow us to strongly infer about amyloid-ß peptides?

    a. They might cause CJD, Parkinson's disease, or Huntington's disease.

    b. They might be found in the brains of some Alzheimer's patients.

    c. They might cause proteins to misfold or break.

    d. They might be removed in order to cure Alzheimer's disease.

C. Think of a detailed process you are familiar with. Then think of a metaphor that conveys the crucial aspects of the process. Review the Characteristics of Extended Metaphors (p. 192). Then write a short passage describing the process, using your metaphor.

D. Share your passage with another student.

Go to **MyEnglishLab** to complete a vocabulary exercise and skill practice, and to join in collaborative activities.

For more about METAPHORS, see |OC| HUMANITIES ②.

LANGUAGE SKILL
IDENTIFYING AND USING EXPRESSIONS OF FUNCTION AND PURPOSE

WHY IT'S USEFUL By learning and familiarizing yourself with expressions that convey functions and purposes, you will understand how they serve to explain the nature of certain things and processes.

In English, a number of phrases serve the purpose of expressing how an entity operates and what its objective is. These phrases are grouped into a category called **language of function and purpose.** While this type of language is found in writing in many academic disciplines, it is especially common in scientific writing. This is because scientific writing frequently involves the explanation of processes, experiments, and research objectives.

The phrases in bold in this example show this language in action:

> Researchers at the Scientific University of Brookland have been tasked with investigating the long-term effects of radiation exposure in individuals who had previously had radiation therapy as a treatment for breast cancer. **The objective of their research is to** determine whether patients who had received more radiation treatments than others were more susceptible to developing cancer a second time. In a report written at the outset of the research, scientists involved explained that **the purpose of radiation therapy is to** annihilate mutated cells that are still present in and around an individual's breast after the person has had surgery. They wrote that **radiation therapy functions as** a "cancer cell killer," **using high-energy rays** to meet this goal. **The end goal is** to reduce the chances that cancer cells will return in the same region in the future.

Phrases Commonly Used to Convey Function or Purpose	
by x [action verb]	X focuses on
the aim of x is	X forms
the end goal is	X functions as
the goal / objective / intent of x is to	X leads to
the purpose of x is to	X operates by / through
the use of x is to	X plays a role
through the use of x	X plays the role of
using x	X produces the result of
X acts to	X seeks to
X aims to	X serves to
	X works to
	X's job is to

EXERCISE 5

A. Read these excerpts from "Cancer: Not One Disease but Several" (an online reading from the section Evaluating Evidence and Argumentation). Without changing the meaning, rewrite each sentence to include a phrase of function or purpose. It may be necessary to change some language or the sentence structure.

1. Subsequent studies in the early 1900s showed that external sources such as carcinogens and viruses were etiologic agents of cancer.

....

....

2. From experiments in 1914 at Tokyo University, researchers concluded that cell mutation was the reason why, after they applied coal tar to the skin of rabbits, the animals developed cancer.

....

....

3. Today, physicians understand that a number of risk factors contribute to a person's likelihood of developing cancer.

....

....

4. A progressively clearer understanding of cancer has ushered in an age of increasingly advanced research.

....

....

5. Today's concept of cancer is that it is a large group of related diseases, all of which begin with a basic disorder of cellular function but proceed along divergent paths.

....

....

6. For example, "individualized chemotherapy" treatments are becoming the norm for chemical treatments; the therapeutic chemical is chosen to fit the genes expressed by an individual tumor.

....

....

B. Compare rephrasings with another student. Has the original language been replaced by a phrase that appropriately and effectively conveys function or purpose?

C. You have read about several cancer-causing agents, such as viruses, cigarette smoke, and genetic mutations; you have also read about types of cancer treatments, like hormone therapy, radiation therapy, and chemotherapy. Choose one of these cancer-causing agents *or* one of these types of cancer treatments and do research on how the agent or treatment functions. Write a short paragraph explaining how it operates, using at least four phrases that help convey function or purpose.

....

....

....

....

....

....

....

Go to **MyEnglishLab** to complete a skill practice.

APPLY YOUR SKILLS

WHY IT'S USEFUL By applying the skills you have learned in this unit, you can successfully read this challenging text and learn about techniques for vaccinating people against certain types of cancer.

BEFORE YOU READ

A. Discuss these questions with one or more students.

1. Vaccines against some cancer-causing viruses are currently in development. Do you know of any cancer-causing viruses? Even if you don't know of any such viruses, imagine the benefits of being able to use vaccines in the fight against cancer. How would that improve the field of cancer treatment?

2. You probably recognize that it's impossible to vaccinate against some diseases. Give two or three examples. Why is it impossible to vaccinate against them? If necessary, do a little research online.

3. Would you ever refuse to be vaccinated against anything? If so why would you refuse? If not, why not? Are you concerned that new, experimental vaccines—especially against life-threatening diseases like cancer—may not be safe?

B. Imagine that you will be participating in a small group discussion about the passage "Vaccinating Against Cancer," which begins on the next page. Your group will be discussing the following questions. Keep these questions in mind as you read the passage.

1. Why are vaccines against HPV of special importance?

2. In what way(s) was the work of Peyton Rous similar to the work of Ludwik Gross?

3. In what way(s) was the hepatitis B vaccine different from any vaccine before it?

4. How are the hepatitis C vaccine and the Eppstein-Barr vaccine similar?

5. What is the difference between a prophylactic vaccine and a therapeutic vaccine?

C. Review the Unit Skills Summary. As you read the passage, apply the skills you learned in this unit.

UNIT SKILLS SUMMARY

Evaluate evidence and argumentation.

- Use your critical thinking skills to assess the value and validity of the arguments and supporting evidence you encounter in a reading.

Identify and evaluate evidence.

- Recognize patterns of evidence used in support of claims. Notice differences in quality among types of evidence so that you can give appropriate weight to various arguments.

Recognize and deal with faulty rhetoric.

- Think critically about the techniques the author uses to support a claim. Be ready to get past faulty arguments and avoid being misled by them.

Understand extended metaphor.

- Use your understanding of extended metaphors to strengthen your command of difficult concepts.

Identify and use the expressions of function and purpose.

- As you encounter expressions of function and purpose, be aware of how they explain the nature of certain things or processes—and how they create interrelated systems.

READ

A. Read the passage, which contains examples of faulty rhetoric. Annotate and take notes as necessary.

Vaccinating Against Cancer

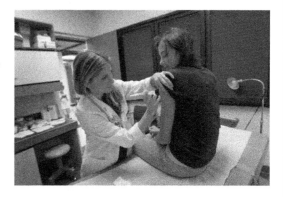

1 Oncogenic viruses, or tumor viruses, cause cells to mutate, which can later lead to tumor growth. Approximately 10 to 20 percent of all cancers are caused by oncogenic viruses, though some scientists suggest this percentage may be higher. In many cases, the onset of cancer occurs long after patients initially contract a tumor virus, sometimes decades later. The vast majority of oncogenic-virus-based cancers are from the human papilloma virus (HPV), a sexually transmitted virus with more than one hundred strains. It is found in a majority of adults in the United States and causes approximately 30,000 cancer cases annually. In 2006, a vaccine became available that works to protect individuals against cervical cancer by guarding against several types of HPV. The development of this vaccine is extremely promising because it means that oncologists may be able to create vaccines that aim to safeguard individuals against other oncogenic viruses as well. If scientists understand how one tumor virus functions—and how to make preventive vaccines for it—they should be able to make vaccines for all.

2 There are a handful of known viruses that are oncogenic in humans, and they possess either RNA or DNA genomes. The DNA viruses include the papilloma, herpes, and hepatitis viruses. The RNA oncogenic viruses include the human T-cell leukemia viruses. A nucleic acid present in all living cells, RNA (ribonucleic acid) conveys instructions from DNA for controlling the synthesis of proteins, and sometimes carries genetic information. RNA viruses, or retroviruses, operate by producing viral DNA after transcribing their RNA into host cells. A retrovirus that is not specifically an oncogenic virus but that plays a role in the development of cancer is the human immunodeficiency virus (HIV). Though not thought to cause cancer directly, it is like the low-level thugs of a gang that has moved into a good neighborhood, weakening the formerly stable immune system and paving the way for a move-in by a criminal kingpin, cancer. It is only the fact that HIV disproportionately affects socially disadvantaged people, including gay people, intravenous drug users, and nonwhites, that prevents the government from seeking to conquer this disease.

HISTORICAL ROOTS

3 The study of tumor viruses began, astonishingly, in the early 20th century before viruses were even fully understood. Zoologist Peyton Rous discovered the later-named avian Rous Sarcoma Virus by injecting healthy hens with tissue from sarcoma-infected hens. The goal of this experiment was to determine whether the healthy hens would then develop sarcoma, which, in fact, is what occurred. Though Rous's findings first proved the theory that a sub-bacterial particle could play a role in causing cancer, virologist Ludwik Gross put the subject on the map in the 1950s when he focused on how oncogenic viruses applied to human cancer pathology. In the period between Rous's work and Gross's, two world wars impaired scientific study in many fields—a clear reminder that we have a choice between research and violence, and we too often make the wrong choice. Gross studied the transmission of leukemia in mice and higher primates and found that in mammals, leukemia could be passed infectiously as well as via heredity. Gross's work moved the field of viral oncology firmly into mainstream cancer research.

Continued

4   In the 1960s, biochemist Baruch Blumberg discovered the hepatitis B virus and later helped develop a vaccine against the virus. He won a Nobel Prize in 1976 for his work. This vaccine was the first of its kind in two ways: It was the first vaccine to tackle a virus that has a role in cancer development—though the virus does not actually cause liver cancer, it does make the liver more prone to cancer—and the first so-called subunit vaccine. While all vaccines prior to the hepatitis B vaccine used whole viruses, the subunit vaccine for hepatitis B uses only particles from the outer protein shell of the virus. After injection of these particles into the body, the immune system works to build antibodies against the virus. While it defends against the real virus, the vaccine does not contain viral genes, so it is not infectious. At about the same time, German physician Harald zur Hausen—who also went on to win the Nobel Prize, in 2008—discovered HPV, which, as alluded to, causes a large proportion of the cases of cervical cancer.

RECENT ADVANCES

5 The field of research in oncogenic viruses has been particularly lively in the past two decades following the cancer breakthroughs of the mid-20th century and the mapping of the human genome in the 1990s. Numerous vaccines against other oncogenic viruses are in development, including vaccines for the hepatitis C virus and for the Epstein-Barr virus. Epstein-Barr, or EBV, is a type of herpes virus that causes mononucleosis and is also believed to cause 200,000 cases of cancer in the United States each year. EBV can cause epithelial cellular malignancies like stomach cancer and cancer of the nose and throat, as well as several kinds of cancers of the lymph nodes, such as Hodgkin's lymphoma. Once a vaccine is made for all oncogenic viruses, scientists will be able to limit the spread of many kinds of cancer.

A NOTE OF CAUTION

6 We noted earlier the great importance of HPV vaccines, and we were correct in our characterization. However, it is also important to note that the use of HPV vaccines does not protect against all strains of the virus. In addition, the vaccine is a prophylactic vaccine, meaning the purpose of it is to prevent the virus, not to provide therapeutic treatment for it. In other words, if a person already has HPV, the vaccine cannot stop cancer from developing. The number of cases of HPV has fallen since doctors began giving the vaccination, as multiple studies show, but the vaccine is unlikely to single-handedly prevent all future cases of cervical cancer—nor may it need to. A number of therapeutic vaccines, which involve using a patient's own immune system to craft vaccines that target and kill specific tumor cells, are in the final stages of clinical trials or entering the market, and excitement about that method of treatment is growing rapidly.

B. Reread the questions in Before You Read, Part B. Is there anything you cannot answer? What reading skills can you use to help you find the answers?

Go to **MyEnglishLab** to read the passage again and answer critical thinking questions.

THINKING CRITICALLY

In "Vaccinating Against Cancer," you read about a relatively recent practice: vaccinating against some types of cancer. Some of the early experiments that established the safety and efficacy of this practice—in the early 20th century—involved injecting hens with cancer-causing material. Later experiments have involved mice and rhesus monkeys, among other animals. Indeed, government regulations in many countries, as well as international standards of medical research, require that prospective medicines be tested in animals before they can be trialed in humans. However, there are many opponents of animal testing. Some oppose all medical experiments on animals. Others attempt to discover and stop testing that they consider cruel and painful to animals. Consider your own attitude toward animal testing of cancer vaccines and other high-stakes medical experimentation. Is it ethical to experiment with animals? Why or why not? If your attitude is that it is sometimes ethical but sometimes not, how can we distinguish between ethical and unethical experimentation? As you craft your argument, be sure to use sound evidence and avoid faulty rhetoric.

THINKING VISUALLY

The graph and its accompanying notes give essential data about cervical cancer in the United States. Using the information in the graph, follow these steps:

1. Summarize the overall trends in cervical cancer incidence and mortality over the time period covered by the graph.

2. What do you expect the future to hold, regarding the incidence and mortality of the disease?

3. Briefly state what you think has been the impact of HPV vaccines.

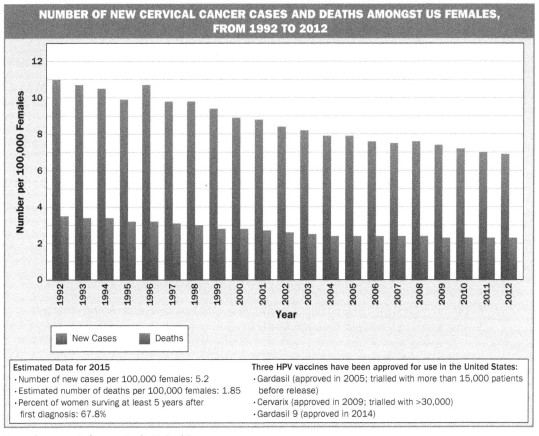

NUMBER OF NEW CERVICAL CANCER CASES AND DEATHS AMONGST US FEMALES, FROM 1992 TO 2012

Legend: New Cases, Deaths

Estimated Data for 2015
- Number of new cases per 100,000 females: 5.2
- Estimated number of deaths per 100,000 females: 1.85
- Percent of women surving at least 5 years after first diagnosis: 67.8%

Three HPV vaccines have been approved for use in the United States:
- Gardasil (approved in 2005; trialled with more than 15,000 patients before release)
- Cervarix (approved in 2009; trialled with >30,000)
- Gardasil 9 (approved in 2014)

Facts about cervical cancer in the United States

THINKING ABOUT LANGUAGE

The reading "Vaccinating Against Cancer" contains a substantial amount of language that conveys function and purpose. Follow these steps:

1. Identify and underline such language in each of the excerpts on the following pages.

2. Use an online corpus (such as Corpus of Contemporary American English) to find one authentic example of the language you underlined in each excerpt.

3. Write the example sentence you find as well as the frequency of the phrase (e.g., the number of instances in which this language appeared in the corpus).

4. If the corpus you use has a "context" or "genre" filter, write whether the phrase appears to be frequently used in scientific speech or publications.

5. Write down as many of the following facts as possible about the source of the example—year, title, author, and journal.

Paragraph 1

1. In 2006, a vaccine became available that <u>works</u> to protect individuals against cervical cancer by guarding against several types of HPV.

   Example: *As the stars move apart, the tidal force drops and each star's gravity works to restore its*

   shape to a sphere.

   Frequency: *1,626*   Context / Genre: *Astronomy (magazine)*

   Source information: *Date: 2015*

   Title: How Astronomers Hear Stellar Heartbeats

   Author: Matthews, Jaymie   Source: Astronomy

2. The development of this vaccine is extremely promising because it means that oncologists may be able to create vaccines that aim to safeguard individuals against other oncogenic viruses as well.

   Example:

   Frequency: Context / Genre:

   Source information:

3. If scientists understand how one tumor virus functions—and how to make preventive vaccines for it—they should be able to make vaccines for all.

   Example:

   Frequency: Context / Genre:

   Source information:

4. RNA viruses, or retroviruses, operate by producing viral DNA after transcribing their RNA into host cells.

   Example: ....

   ....

   Frequency: ....   Context / Genre: ....

   Source information: ....

   ....

5. A retrovirus that is not specifically an oncogenic virus but that plays a role in the development of cancer is the human immunodeficiency virus (HIV).

   Example: ....

   ....

   Frequency: ....   Context / Genre: ....

   Source information: ....

   ....

6. It is only the fact that HIV disproportionately affects socially disadvantaged people, including gay people, intravenous drug users, and nonwhites, that prevents the government from seeking to conquer this disease.

   Example: ....

   ....

   Frequency: ....   Context / Genre: ....

   Source information: ....

   ....

   ....

Paragraph 3

7. The goal of this experiment was to determine whether the healthy hens would then develop sarcoma, which, in fact, is what occurred.

   Example: ....

   ....

   Frequency: ....   Context / Genre: ....

   Source information: ....

   ....

   ....

8. Though Rous's findings first proved the theory that a sub-bacterial particle could play a role in causing cancer, virologist Ludwik Gross put the subject on the map in the 1950s when he focused on how oncogenic viruses applied to human cancer pathology.

   Example: ....

   ....

   Frequency: ....   Context / Genre: ....

   Source information: ....

   ....

   ....

Paragraph 4

9. After injection of these particles into the body, the immune system works to build antibodies against the virus.

   Example: ....

   ....

   Frequency: ....   Context / Genre: ....

   Source information: ....

   ....

   ....

Paragraph 6

10. However, it is also important to note that the use of HPV vaccines does not protect against all strains of the virus.

Example: ....

....

Frequency: .... Context / Genre: ....

Source information: ....

....

....

11. In addition, the vaccine is a prophylactic vaccine, meaning the purpose of it is to prevent the virus, not to provide therapeutic treatment for it.

Example: ....

....

Frequency: .... Context / Genre: ....

Source information: ....

....

....

12. A number of therapeutic vaccines, which involve using a patient's own immune system to craft vaccines that target and kill specific tumor cells, are in the final stages of clinical trials or entering the market, and excitement about that method of treatment is growing rapidly.

Example: ....

....

Frequency: .... Context / Genre: ....

Source information: ....

....

....

▶ Go to **MyEnglishLab** to listen to Professor Siegel and to complete a self-assessment.

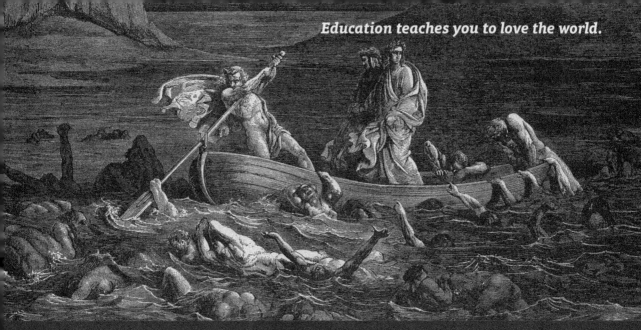

Education teaches you to love the world.

Synthesis of Information

UNIT PROFILE

In this unit, you will consider the subject of humanities—
specifically the perspectives of ancient cultures on life and death.
You will learn about the poetry of Homer, Virgil, and Dante, and
the underworld, including the journey to and from as depicted
above.

Preview the reading "The Hero's Journey" on page 231.
Skim the reading. How many sources are there? How are their
perspectives different on a given topic? Does any source seem
to be more credible than another?

OUTCOMES

- Synthesize information from several sources
- Understand multiple perspectives
- Evaluate the credibility and motives of sources
- Understand and use direct and indirect quotations
- Appreciate hedging

GETTING STARTED

▶ Go to **MyEnglishLab** to listen to Professor Harrison and to complete a self-assessment.

Discuss these questions with a partner or group.

1. English has the phrase "magical thinking." It means believing that one thing results from another
thing even though there is no evidence or solid reasoning to support a link between the two.
Superstition is an example of magical thinking. So is the ancient Greek and Roman tradition of
believing that immortals—from Aphrodite to Zeus—were constantly interfering in human affairs.
Do you or anyone you know engage in magical thinking? What do you believe?

2. Countless stories, from ancient to modern times, feature the idea of communication between the
living and the dead—including Odysseus's visit to the underworld and Hamlet's encounters with the
ghost of his father. What examples can you think of? What is the basis for our fascination with these
exchanges?

For more about **HUMANITIES**, see ① ③. See also Ⓦ and ⓄⒸ **HUMANITIES** ① ② ③.

CRITICAL THINKING SKILL
SYNTHESIZING INFORMATION FROM SEVERAL SOURCES

WHY IT'S USEFUL By learning to synthesize information from several sources, you will be able to build well-rounded conceptions of a topic. You will also be able to place the information from any given source into an overall schema of the facts and opinions about a topic.

Synthesizing—combining different ideas, experiences, or pieces of information to make something new—is a necessary skill for becoming a successful reader. Synthesizing information involves paying close attention to what you are reading with the goal of making connections between ideas. It is important because in academic courses, you will often be asked to read multiple texts about a certain topic—as well as texts in which an author has already synthesized information from several texts—and you will be expected to determine where information from these sources overlaps, conflicts, concentrates on certain lines of reasoning, updates earlier concepts, and so on. In the end, you can make inferences about the work of a given source in relation to the broader field of commentators.

While reading information from several sources about a given topic, you should take into account what you have learned about active reading. Specifically, try to recognize whether information from one source agrees or conflicts with information from another source—for example, if certain aspects of a fact are emphasized in one source but minimized in another—and question the validity of the information being presented. Synthesizing also involves being mindful of differences across sources, including the following:

- Sources may define concepts differently.
- Only one source may provide definitions of terminology that is used in all of the sources.
- One source might make a generalization about a topic, but another may describe it in detail.
- The classification of concepts may differ from source to source.
- One source may be more reliable than another in terms of its recency or the qualifications of the author.

By learning to effectively synthesize information from several sources, you will further develop your active reading and critical thinking skills. You will be able to identify gaps in information when comparing one source with another, consider evidence presented through different lenses, and compare and contrast main ideas. This will help with writing research papers, as you will be better able to identify similarities and discrepancies between information in the research you have gathered.

This unit breaks **synthesizing information from several sources** down into two supporting skills:

- understanding multiple perspectives
- evaluating the credibility and motives of sources

A. Read the passage, which synthesizes the views of three researchers: King, White, and Hall.

DEPICTIONS OF THE UNDERWORLD

1   The portrayal of the underworld in epic tales of ancient Greece, Rome, and medieval Europe reveals each culture's complex and divergent beliefs about the afterlife. The works of King, White, and Hall correspond with one another in that they each conclude that the Greeks viewed the underworld as a realm to which all humans descended after death, regardless of their actions during life. (Romans and many medieval Europeans, on the other hand, largely considered the afterlife a place divided according to a person's behavior in life.) The one exception for the Greeks, King notes, are heroes, who are awarded an intermediary position between mortals and gods, and get a pass from spending eternity in the depths of the underworld. While King gives a succinct, cursory description of this midpoint that the Greeks, and later the Romans, believed in, White writes extensively of the concept in his examination of Dante's *The Divine Comedy*. He notes that the notion of a halfway point—later to be tagged as *purgatory*—underwent expansion in medieval times because it was a central node in the Christian latticework of after-death possibilities.

2   Hall's research, in contrast with King's and White's, is more contemporary, and contains fewer biases in its analysis of pre-Christian concepts of faith and the afterlife. Hall explores the similarities between the hierarchy of the underworld in the *Aeneid* and in *The Divine Comedy*, stating, along with the other two sources, that Virgil's and Dante's images of hell were alike in that there was logic in the way dead souls were assigned transgression-appropriate punishments—for example, how greedy people were forced to push great weights (symbolizing the things they wished to hoard). Unlike King and White, however, Hall offers a significant amount of evidence indicating that Virgil and, later, Dante subjected these souls to torture and misery in various levels of the underworld as much to make a political point as to fall in line with the religious views of their respective societies.

The sources in this passage are fictional.

B. Read the statements about the passage. Then mark each statement as *T* (True) or *F* (False).

.... 1. King, White, and Hall each state that Greeks, Romans, and medieval Europeans shared the belief that all humans reached the underworld after death.

.... 2. King, White, and Hall each point out that heroes are exceptions among Greeks in terms of destiny and the underworld.

.... 3. Of the three experts, White gives the most thorough description of the position of purgatory.

.... 4. Of the work done by the three authors, White's research addresses the most modern notions of the afterlife.

.... 5. King, White, and Hall agree that in the *Aeneid* and *The Divine Comedy*, logical methods are used to group people in the underworld.

.... 6. White and King do not indicate, as Hall does, that Dante's and Virgil's motives for subjecting souls to torture in various levels of the underworld were political and religious.

Go to **MyEnglishLab** to complete a vocabulary exercise and skill practice, and to join in collaborative activities.

SUPPORTING SKILL 1
UNDERSTANDING MULTIPLE PERSPECTIVES

WHY IT'S USEFUL By understanding information from various sources about a given topic, you can build a comprehensive, wide-ranging command of the concept. Recognizing how various sources agree with, disagree with, add to, and update one another gives you a well-rounded feel for the range of opinion among experts.

In academic readings, you will come across texts that are about the same topic, idea, or fact but are presented or understood by their authors in very different ways. You will also be exposed to texts on a given topic that offer information other texts on the same topic do not. This is even common in research—while one researcher may interpret evidence to mean one thing, another might draw a different conclusion.

In order to understand **multiple perspectives**, it is first necessary that you ensure that the sources are discussing the same general idea. For example, the information in a text by Author A about Aristotle's idea of the "golden mean" cannot be synthesized with information in a text by Author B about Aristotle's concept of "syllogism." While they are both ideas propounded by the same philosopher, they do not share the same main idea.

After determining that the texts you are reading are on the same topic, your next task is to recognize the perspectives that are presented by each author. In order to do this, it is helpful to become familiar with language that is used to express a perspective.

Phrase Expressing Perspective	Example
It is generally accepted that …	**It is generally accepted that** historical writings provide clues about a given society.
According to [X person / people] …	**According to Randall**, the textiles were meant to honor the Greek god.
Many / Some / [other noun] believe (that) …	**Researchers believe that** the artifacts are historically significant.
It is considered … [X person / people] consider …	**It is considered** a travesty that some of the ancient texts were damaged. **Baldwin considers** the symbol to be of little significance within the entire context of the poem.
[X person / people] demonstrates …	**Mullins demonstrates** the importance of carefully discerning between fact and fiction in ancient poetry.
[X event / fact / evidence] indicate that …	**Research on ancient Greek artifacts indicates that** jewelry was worn by individuals of high social status.
[X event / fact / evidence] will likely … [X event / fact / evidence] are likely / unlikely to … It is likely that …	**The finding will likely** shed light on recent archaeological discoveries in the same area. **The sculpture is unlikely to** have been the work of an ancient artist. **It is likely that** the artifacts mentioned in the passage were figments of the author's imagination.
[X person / people] maintain that …	**Drake maintains that** historical figures in the poems are entirely fictional.

Continued

Phrase Expressing Perspective	Example
[X event / fact / evidence] reveal ...	**The works of art reveal** that ancient sculptors used quite advanced methods.
[X person / people] emphasize / stress (that) ...	**Highland stresses that** the Trojan War is an event that must not be left out of the narrative.
X suggests (that) ...	**The discovery suggests that** ancient Greeks highly valued works of art.
It is thought that ...	**It is thought that** Homer spoke, not wrote, his legendary stories.
X must / can be viewed ...	**The art can be viewed** as authentic if the research is reliable.

Read the following paragraph. Notice how the language from the chart is woven throughout the paragraph to express the perspectives of the two (fictional) researchers.

VIEWS ON DISCOVERIES OF ANCIENT GREEK SCULPTURES

Two prominent researchers in the field of ancient Greek art history recently penned articles about research conducted on artwork uncovered in Greek ruins. While they both believe **it is likely that** the pieces of artwork discovered date back to the time of Homer, perspectives on some technical features of the artifacts differ between the two experts. **Schmidt**, whose team is credited with the discovery of a variety of sculptures, **maintains that his findings indicate** that the sculptors responsible for creating the pieces used advanced methods far beyond what were previously believed to have been used. However, a different view is held by Thompson, an art historian and professor who specializes in ancient Greek sculptures. **He emphasizes that** while **the works of art discovered by Schmidt indeed reveal** evidence that advanced sculpting techniques were utilized, the existence of such innovative methods was previously known by researchers in his own department. With that said, **he does consider** the discoveries made by Schmidt's team to be of extreme importance, as the sculptures found differ significantly in size, shape, and material from previously known pieces.

Recognizing varying viewpoints is not always as easy as picking out phrases like those above, however. These viewpoints often take the form of longer, complex explanations, so it is up to the reader to first determine whether the information presented by the sources really conflicts—that is, whether the two sets of information are mutually exclusive and cannot both be true—or if the authors present slightly different viewpoints on the same topic, perspectives that are different but may both be true, at least to some degree. If it is the former (conflicting information), you must ask yourself *how* these sources disagree with one other. This could be disagreement about facts, the significance of facts, an idea, or an interpretation of an idea. If it is the latter (different viewpoints), it is important to think about how different the *perspectives* are from one another. Consider the angle from which that information is viewed by each source to determine whether Source A may take one concept into consideration while Source B focuses on another.

EXERCISE 1

A. This reading contains three perspectives on the depiction of art in Homer's epics. As you read each passage, highlight language the author uses to express a certain perspective. Then circle points made by the author that are similar to points made in the other passages. Underline points that stand in contrast to those in the other passages.

How Realistic Were Homeric Descriptions?

Source 1: Painter
Authentic Descriptions of Art in Homer's Epics

1   Homer's epic poems the *Iliad* and the *Odyssey* give vivid descriptions of textiles, decorative battle gear, and architectural elements that should be considered in art history as an authentic depiction of art objects of great importance. Though Homer's work is filled with mystical beasts and mythic lands, historical facts are the basis for his narrative. Modern art historians consider the works Homer describes as cultural art, or "lesser" art, rather than fine art, but these so-called lesser arts were prized in pre-Hellenic ancient Greece. To determine the importance of the art described by Homer, it is essential that he first be compared with Thucydides, who authored a detailed but somewhat lifeless and dry account of the Peloponnesian War in the 5th century BCE. Though Thucydides is widely regarded as a more historical source than Homer, the touch of an artist is noticeably absent in his work. Homer's story, on the other hand, rings with praise of aesthetic works of his time and provides art criticism in the narrative through careful descriptions of objects that were clearly valuable. Homer's artistic eye is what gives the text merit as a resource in the study of art history.

2   Historic records indicate that that Homer lived around 750 BCE. The *Iliad* and the *Odyssey* interweave Greek mythology with historical accounts of war and travel around Asia Minor. Though much of Homer's work is devoted to the influence of the gods on the life of Odysseus and his contemporaries, the myths transmit facts about art. For example, Homer devotes many lines of praise to the artifice of Hephaistos, the god of fire, crafts, and metalworking, but he is merely alluding to the skilled smiths who lived during his time. The clothing that Homer describes his hero or the gods wearing is an accurate description of the woven textiles and battle garb of his time, and further, an indication that textiles were prized as a fine art. Finally, in the examination of Homer's account of Greek architecture, the texts linger poetically on the palaces of Menelaus and Alcinous and their bronze-paneled walls, azure molding, golden doors, silver lintel, and silver sculptures. Though Menelaus and Alcinous are part of Greek mythology and the location of the actual palaces Homer based his narrative on remains uncertain, Homer's accounts likely provide an exceptional window of truth on what existed in the world of ancient architecture.

Source 2: Martínez
The Imaginative Art in Homer's Epics

3   While it may tempting to regard the work of the legendary bard Homer as text that provides a fascinating glimpse into an ancient epoch, the truth is that Homer's accounts of art must be viewed as imaginative poetry, not history. The epic's main focus is on battle, not on documentation of works of art that existed during his time. Homer records the lesser arts, or cultural artifacts like weapons and clothing, and while these are of use for archaeological and historical purposes, they are not fine art. Further, many fine art examples described in the text, such as the famous shield of Achilles, likely did not exist. Art historians and archaeological should use caution when citing artworks as described by Homer, especially fine arts like sculpture, as their historicity is uncertain, and it is difficult to separate fact from fiction in the narrative.

Continued

4   The personhood of Homer himself is unclear as is the provenance of his work, a phenomenon dubbed "The Homeric Question." Many scholars generally believe the Homeric texts were passed down verbally over a thousand-year period dating back to the Trojan Wars in the Bronze Age in the second millennium BCE. The Homeric texts are likely a result of multiple authorships. The poems convey tales from Greek mythology that feature fictional places like the underworld, separating them from the work of historians like Thucydides, whose careful annotations reference clear historical events, places, and persons.

5   The main purpose of the *Iliad* was to dramatize the Trojan War; references to cultural materials like textiles and battle implements are secondary to its main purpose. The process of manufacturing battle gear described in the text testifies to the development of metallurgy in ancient Greece, but the objects themselves are products of Homer's imagination. His descriptions of works of art often include fanciful imagery—metal, for example, is depicted as glowing like the moon. His architectural imagery is equally romantic, prizing beauty over accuracy. He also attributes much of his documentation of art to palaces of figures who may or may not have existed. Homer's quality as a storyteller is superb, but the art described in the Homeric texts should remain in the annals of literary fiction and only be referenced with caution in art history.

Source 3: Evans
Unknown Accuracy of Homer's Account of Arts

6   Homer's ancient texts, born out of oral tradition and transcribed before the classical period of ancient Greece, reveal a glimpse of the art made during the Iron Age in Asia Minor. While some objects are believed to be clearly mythic and fanciful, such as the shield of Achilles, detailed descriptions in Homer's texts of minor artworks and cultural materials like shields, sculptures, chariots, and textiles indicate that similar objects could have actually existed. The detailed descriptions of the pieces of art and the methods used to create them convey important information to historians of ancient art. The actual existence of the art objects—such as the shield—is irrelevant because knowledge of the methods of production of such objects is more important for a discussion of art in ancient cultures.

7   The authorship of the *Iliad* and the *Odyssey* is ascribed to a person who scholars believe lived around 750 BCE, though the stories, communicated through oral tradition, have roots that possibly date back to the Trojan War around the 12th century BCE. Homer's quasi-historic figures had palaces with polished stone and precious metals, they wore soft linens, and they carried golden-studded staffs. These small, rich details give scholars of ancient art important clues as to how the arts flourished in Homer's time. They include jewelry, clothing, weapons, and other works that are often placed in a category of cultural materials, or minor arts, in contrast to the fine, or higher, arts of ceramics, paintings, and sculptures.

8   Homer's story inspired countless black-figure ceramics as well as other types of art in ancient Greece, and it also contains the first instance of *ekphrastic* poetry, a technique that describes the manufacturing process and appearance of a work of art in great detail so that a reader may form a clear picture of the work. This type of poetry is extremely valuable to art historians searching for possible works of art from the Dark Ages and may be used as a reference by art historians. What's more, Homer's descriptions of the process of creating art objects reveal knowledge of metallurgy in ancient times that may assist scholars in identifying pieces of art yet to be discovered.

The sources and quotations in this passage are fictional.

B. Read the questions and choose the best answers.

1. Painter, Martínez, and Evans agree that ....

   a. Homer depicts art accurately in his epic poems.
   b. Homer does not describe art correctly in his epic poems.
   c. it is irrelevant whether Homer depicts art accurately in his epic poems.
   d. Homer's poetry does not always reflect true events or creatures.

2. What do Martínez and Evans agree about in terms of Homer's poetry?

   a. It likely that Homer's tales were originally conveyed orally.
   b. Much is known about Homer's identity.
   c. The characters in the poetry were real people.
   d. It is safe to draw some historical conclusions from Homer's works.

3. Which authors think Homer has merit as a storyteller?

   a. Painter and Evans
   b. Painter, Martínez, and Evans
   c. Martínez and Evans
   d. Painter and Martínez

4. Painter and Martínez agree that Homer describes ....

   a. art that is based on pure fantasy
   b. artifacts that are considered lesser art
   c. art, but is more focused on describing historic wars
   d. fully accurate historical events

5. Unlike the other two sources, Painter believes Homer's work is valuable because it ....

   a. tells stories of fictional lands from which scholars can gain knowledge
   b. describes art that is often overlooked in historical studies today
   c. contains artistically critical descriptions of historic art
   d. is considered more of a historically accurate source than works of Thucydides

6. How does Martínez's perspective of Homer's work differ from the other two sources?

   a. The author believes Homer's stories are boring.
   b. The author believes Homer's stories are unreliable.
   c. The author believes Homer's stories are accurate.
   d. The author believes Homer's stories are delusional.

7. Painter and Evans each imply that Homer's depictions of art ....

   a. are fully accurate representations of art that existed during his time
   b. are indisputably works of pure literature
   c. reflect the fact that art was valued during his time
   d. should not be judged based on their authenticity

8. Which statement about Homer's epic poetry would *all three* sources likely disagree with?

   a. It has merit for the study of art history.
   b. It was written for the purpose of depicting actual artwork of the time.
   c. It was more artistic than that of other writers of Homer's time.
   d. It includes factual events that occurred during his time.

Go to **MyEnglishLab** to complete a vocabulary exercise and skill practice, and to join in collaborative activities.

SUPPORTING SKILL 2
EVALUATING THE CREDIBILITY AND MOTIVES OF SOURCES

WHY IT'S USEFUL In a reading that presents multiple perspectives, some sources are more believable or persuasive than others. By recognizing and evaluating sources' qualifications, present standing in their fields, and possible motivations for their stances, you can better judge whose perspectives are more convincing.

Most of the academic texts you read have been reviewed by experts and editors—at book publishing companies or journals—before you see them. Even online material, if you find it on a reputable site, may have gone through strenuous checks for factuality and **credibility**. You are unlikely to read very many academic pieces that present totally ridiculous ideas from sources who have no credibility at all. However, that does not mean that every claim in every article or chapter is equally believable and convincing. Editors may be screening material before you read it, but they do not necessarily remove every doubtful claim, every self-serving remark, or every controversial point of view. In fact, some authors and their editors think they have an obligation to present views that are not in the mainstream, simply to get their readers to consider issues from a number of viewpoints.

Applying your critical thinking skills is vital when you read material that argues an issue several ways. A source's expertise is the first thing most readers consider. Which of the following sources do you find most credible regarding the portrayal of gold objects in Homer's *Odyssey*?

A. Joseph Novak, professor of mathematics at Harvard University, argues that Homer could not have described golden treasure troves so well unless he had been an occasional guest of Greece's wealthiest families.

B. "Homer's detailed eye for the intricacies of golden plate work," says Dionis Katzanopoulos, "reflects the sensibilities of a visual artist, not just a writer."

C. According to Lara Worth, professor of Greek and Roman history at Baldwin State University, most of the details regarding golden objects were added by "later transcribers of Homer's works," not originated by the bard himself.

Most readers would say that the source cited in Example C probably has the greatest expertise. Greek history is her field. Even though the university she represents is not as illustrious as Harvard (Example A), the Harvard source is a mathematician. He is probably very smart, but from the little bit we know, his profession may not grant him expertise on this subject. The source quoted in Example B is hard to evaluate. He has a Greek-sounding name, but that does not mean he knows very much about ancient Greek golden objects. We simply cannot tell whether he has expertise.

Expertise may derive from several factors:

- a source's present job
- the quality of the organization (university, company, government office, etc.) that employs the source
- a source's past or present research
- the books, articles, movies, and other materials produced by the source
- a source's relationship—via family, friendship, acquaintance—with the person or subject matter under discussion
- a source's firsthand observation of an incident or situation

Besides expertise, **motive** influences a source's credibility and effectiveness. Might the source make unreliable claims because of any of the following?

- a desire to make money
- a desire for attention or fame
- political or religious beliefs
- a personal relationship (good or bad) with someone involved in the subject at hand
- a deterioration in the source's dependability (owing to recent mental or emotional difficulty, etc.)

It may not be easy to know whether one of these factors, such as the desire to promote a religious or political belief, is operating in the source's case, but you may be able to guess by doing an informal online search of the source. If the source writes for general audiences (not just technical specialists), you might also be able to find relevant reviews in newspapers, magazines, blog posts, and so on.

> **CULTURE NOTE**
>
> *Sometimes, a person of great achievement who is considered a highly credible source in one arena becomes a promoter of strange ideas in another. His or her credibility, therefore, becomes, or at least risks becoming, diminished. For example, the American chemist Linus Pauling (1901–1994) won two Nobel Prizes, one in chemistry and the other the Nobel Peace Prize. His early work on molecular structures was groundbreaking, but late in life he developed a belief in the healing power of certain vitamins that was not backed up by generally accepted medical research. This seemingly irrational attachment to unsupported medical / dietary ideas tainted Pauling's reputation. For another example, Henry Ford, the founder of the Ford Motor Company and a revolutionary genius in manufacturing, would certainly have been considered a highly credible source regarding production efficiencies. However, he used his wealth and prominence to promote a range of weird, idiosyncratic ideas about everything from personal diet, to religion, to the supposed danger of putting up tall buildings. (He thought they would make the Earth's surface collapse.) Ultimately, an author must be very discerning when choosing sources and quotes as evidence for an idea, weighing the benefits of expertise against the potential costs of damaged integrity.*

EXERCISE 2

A. Read the passage.

Greek and Roman Funeral Beliefs

1   Ancient Greek and Roman cultures shared similar burial customs and beliefs about how an improper burial could create problems for the soul of the deceased and for surviving family members. The 1950s excavations at Hermelaktia led by Barnard professor Elaine Moore elucidated much about the extreme importance that the Greeks placed on funeral customs. The site yielded not only terracotta panels showing *ekphora* (funeral processions) but also dozens of papyrus manuscripts describing proper funerary procedures. The French philosopher Hector LeBaise, inspired by Moore's work, based a poetic cycle called *L'Hermieuse* on the excavations, speculating that the Greek spirit world interacted with the living world via dreams and mystical experiences—an idea that some of the more rational Greeks may have frowned upon.

2   Later, Theodore Garcia's research, though at times scant on the Roman concept of the afterlife, provided an updated account of archaeological findings in the funerary realm, advancing what Moore had written. As a linguist, rather than as a field archaeologist, Garcia enjoyed a unique perspective afforded by his ability to interpret ancient Greek. Moore's earlier interpretations of several papyri were called into question by Garcia, some quite controversially so. But while it's true that Garcia found references to human sacrifice in the texts, there is no evidence in any of the artistic funeral representations, at Hermelaktia or any other site, that the Greeks themselves practiced it. They simply noted that it occurred elsewhere. As of the early 21st century, there is a general consensus that Moore's evidence trumps Garcia's.

3   The *Iliad* recounts heroic burials that were thought to bring honor to mythic heroes like Patroclus, who was cremated and whose ashes were then placed in a funerary urn and buried. His

Continued

funeral was accompanied by the ritual sacrifice of animals as well as offerings of oil and other precious materials. According to the Edwardian British socialite and amateur archaeologist Sir Beowulf Tate, this was originally an Anatolian heroic burial custom that the Greeks eventually emulated, especially for soldiers who had perished on the battlefield. Whether the Greeks practiced cremation before the Trojan War is a matter of debate. Tate stumbled across various animal bones interred alongside human remains in graves in both Cyprus and Attica—graves that predate the Trojan War across the seas—which has led scholars such as George Kristidis of the Athenian Academy to reluctantly acknowledge a possible connection between the cremation passages in the *Iliad* and burial customs in ancient Greece. Cremation among the Greeks did eventually become somewhat acceptable but never really commonplace.

4   Hundreds of years later, the majority of Roman citizens practiced cremation and burial of the ashes as a funerary tradition, for a while. Tate speculated that cremation proved eventually too unceremonious for what he considered the "grandiosity" of Rome, but he was doing little more than airing prejudices. In reality, as Heather Parenti, professor of religious studies at the University of Corinth, points out, the spread of Christianity and its decriminalization in 313 CE brought the widespread practice of cremation to an end. Garcia and Moore agree that the custom of cremating was eschewed for both religious and practical reasons: Cremation simply consumed too much of an already limited timber crop.

5   In reality, there was an anticremation *geist* in ancient Greek epic poetry, which contained some early references to an unquiet spirit. In the *Odyssey*, in discussing the dead, Homer writes that the fires of cremation destroy the body: " ... life leaves the white bones," he writes, "and the spirit, like a dream, flits away, and hovers to and fro." But doing nothing was not an option, of course. The Greeks, especially by the mid-8th century BCE, believed that the soul of one unburied would continue to trouble the living, according to Moore. Garcia's translations corroborate ideas that Moore first introduced. In *The Art of Death*, Moore devotes a chapter to the discovery of graves in which the inhumed are covered in heavy stones to prevent a zombielike rising and haunting of the living.

6   Romans had similar concepts of the interaction between the living and dead. Like Odysseus, Aeneas interacts in the underworld with unburied friends, who implore the hero to bury them so that they can be at rest. According to Moore, this theme in Virgil's *Aeneid* was a value shared by Roman citizens, who, like the Greeks before them, believed the spirits of the dead could influence living relations, either positively or negatively. This was an idea that the dilettante Tate could sink his amateur teeth into, and did—and even serious scholars have come to the same conclusion: that extensive funerary rites in ancient Roman culture were an attempt to ward off the dead. Along with the body, food was interred in the tomb, and deceased family members were honored on designated days of the year. These kinds of rites, so Romans believed, would protect the living and give peace to the dead.

The sources and source quotations in this passage are fictional.

B. Read each question and write a short answer about sources and their credibility.

1. The author mentions two aspects of Elaine Moore's background that indicate expertise. What are they? ....

....

2. Why would Hector LeBaise probably not be considered a respected source of archaeology?

....

....

3. In what way is Theodore Garcia competent to speak about ancient Greek life? ....

....

4. In what way is Garcia less competent than Elaine Moore in speaking about ancient Greek life?

....

....

5. What is the author's attitude toward the expertise of Sir Beowulf Tate?

....

....

6. What indicator of expertise is shared by George Kristidis and Heather Parenti?

....

....

7. When the author mentions Tate in the last paragraph, he uses two adjectives to indicate that Tate is not a great expert. What is one of them?

....

....

8. What does the author say in the last paragraph, however, that indicates Tate was not always wrong? ....

....

Go to **MyEnglishLab** to complete a vocabulary exercise and skill practice, and to join in collaborative activities.

READING-WRITING CONNECTION
UNDERSTANDING AND USING DIRECT AND INDIRECT QUOTATIONS

WHY IT'S USEFUL By recognizing and evaluating how an author quotes other sources, both directly and indirectly, you can add depth to your understanding of a reading. You not only appreciate the author's efforts to support his or her claims, but you also see how the author is trying to position his or her text within a larger sphere of discourse. By understanding the way an author frames a quote, you can also appreciate nuances of the author's own stance and point of view.

The English physicist and mathematician Sir Isaac Newton once wrote, "If I have seen further, it is because I have stood on the shoulders of giants." This is a remarkable thing for him to say because very few humans have shaped our knowledge of the physical universe as fundamentally as Newton. Yet, the statement expresses his debt to the countless generations of explorers and thinkers who went before him and whose accumulated wisdom made his own discoveries possible. This attitude also explains something basic about academic writing and the authors who engage in it: Great value is placed on knowing what other thinkers have said or written, and your own work gains credibility if you can support it with quotations from other writers or researchers.

Notice that, even in describing the importance of quotations, we used a quotation. It is a **direct quotation** because it reproduces Newton's exact words, as indicated by the set of quotation marks around part of the statement.

We also could have expressed it as an **indirect quotation**, a statement based on his words but not reproducing them exactly (a kind of paraphrase):

> Sir Isaac Newton once commented that, if he could see things that most people couldn't, it was because he was able to make use of the contributions of other great thinkers before him.

Another possibility is a **hybrid statement**, which is partly a direct quote and partly indirect:

> Sir Isaac Newton once commented that if he "saw further" than most people, it was because he "stood on the shoulders of giants."

Direct, indirect, and hybrid quotes are all effective, and all have their place in academic pieces. Here are some factors to note:

- Direct quotations are often preferred if the wording from a source is particularly clever or picturesque. This could be said of Newton's quote. The value of the statement is not just in what he said but in the way he said it.
- This "clever or picturesque" point includes wording that creates an allusion or a metaphor. Consider the passage by Winston Churchill in the CULTURE NOTE. Not only does Churchill's clever phrasing, with its persistent rhythm, justify a direct quote, but his mention of the "beaches" and "landing grounds" (an allusion to recent Nazi victories in France) and his choice of words—all of Old English descent except for "surrender"— also strike a defiantly British tone that no paraphrase could equal.

> **CULTURE NOTE**
> As prime minister of the UK, Winston Churchill (1874–1965) delivered what is perhaps one of the greatest expressions of defiance under pressure. Speaking to the House of Commons in June 1940, a time when World War II seemed to be going entirely the Nazis' way, he said, "We shall fight on the beaches, we shall fight on the landing grounds, we shall fight in the fields and in the streets, we shall fight in the hills; we shall never surrender."

- An indirect quotation may be preferred if the original is too long or not efficiently stated.
- A hybrid quotation may be preferred if part of the original is notably well stated, but the whole quotation is either too long or not consistently well worded.
- Often quotations are **extended**—that is, referred to off and on throughout an entire paragraph or even a set of paragraphs.
- Sometimes, a direct quotation is **inset**—printed with narrower margins than the text around it—not printed within an ordinary text paragraph. If the quotation is inset, there are no quotation marks around it. Typically authors inset a quotation if it is four lines long or longer.

EXERCISE 3

A. Read the passage. Then read the questions on the following page and choose the best answers.

The Norse Underworld

1   Like the Greeks and Romans, the Norse of medieval northern Europe believed in an underworld that awaited people after their death. However, as Professor Bjarni Gorlund puts it, "Our knowledge of the Norse afterlife is a mere inch of thread compared to the elaborate Greek and Roman shrouds we know." These elaborate, well-documented, hero-populated underworlds of the Mediterranean peoples—Gerda Rollins went so far as to call their highly organized strata "rational"—are so fully realized that subsequent writers, viz. Dante Alighieri, could have characters give tours of them. Karl Ramstad characterized the Norse underworld as a "dark basement," which we navigate "without much light from early commentators and certainly no floor plan."

2   Alva Ros Gunnarsdottir, of Iceland's Poetic Trust, notes that the few sources we do have that describe the underworld in Norse mythology—primarily the *Poetic Edda*, the *Prose Edda*, and the *Eglis Saga* of Iceland—are of relatively late provenance. Gunnarsdottir doesn't take at face value the claims these sources make—including the unknown author of the *Eglis Saga*—about being based on earlier works, and indeed she notes that they date from the post-mythological age. Snorri Sturluson is the primary authorial suspect in the literary "whodunnit" surrounding those specifically named works, at least Gunnarsdottir believes so—and Sturluson was writing in the 13th century, after the Norse had been Christianized.

3   Perhaps because a long-prevailing metaphor in English situates the punitive afterlife in hell, which is reflexively understood as being "down," we have given too little attention to directionality in both the Mediterranean and Norse mythic cosmologies. As Gorlund puts it:

> The dead are buried. Downward, below the surface that the living inhabit, is perhaps the most intuitive location for a land of the dead. Since we can only access the depths of the Earth through fearsome places like caves or craters, the entrance to a subterranean underworld—if one ever saw it—would probably be a frightening place, and construing it as guarded by a wizened gatekeeper or a vicious beast seems almost rational, at least according to the spirit-besotted worlds in which ancients lived.

4   Gunnarsdottir has attempted to draw a trail map of the three possible destinations for the soul. The English word *hell* derives from the name of one Norse destination of the dead—Helheim, ruled by the goddess Hel. Gunnarsdottir cautions that Norse sources are unclear and contradictory, but Helheim was not a place of suffering. "It wasn't an especially distinguished place," she says. "It was really a bland default position." Valhalla, perhaps the best known postmortem destination in Norse mythology, was supposedly a gathering place of heroes, chosen by supernatural beings called the Valkyries—although many heroes apparently were not chosen and wound up elsewhere. Finally, Gunnarsdottir mentions Folkvangr ("Field of the People"), ruled by the goddess Freyja. This was another pleasant but unexciting destination—at least as far as one can gather from what Gunnarsdottir calls "a mythical canon that really needed an editor."

The sources and source quotations in this passage are fictional.

1. Which sentence contains a direct, non-hybrid quotation?
   a. Sentence 1
   b. Sentence 2
   c. Sentence 3
   d. Sentence 4

2. Which person is NOT quoted (directly or indirectly) in the first paragraph?
   a. Bjarni Gorlund
   b. Gerda Rollins
   c. Dante Alighieri
   d. Karl Ramstad

3. Which is used in a metaphor in the quotation in Sentence 2?
   a. War
   b. A journey
   c. Cloth
   d. A celebration

4. Which does the pronoun *she* in Sentence 6 refer to?
   a. Gunnarsdottir
   b. *Eglis Saga*
   c. "unknown author"
   d. Snorri Sturluson

5. Which statements are true of Sentences 10 to 12? Choose TWO.
   a. They are a direct quotation.
   b. They contain thoughts by Gunnarsdottir.
   c. They show how Norse myths differ from Roman or Greek.
   d. They are inset because they form a quotation more than four lines long.
   e. They are an extended quotation that's part direct and part indirect.

6. In this reading, there is one extended quotation. Which source is quoted (both directly and indirectly in the same paragraph) in this extended quotation?
   a. Gorlund
   b. Ramstad
   c. Sturluson
   d. Gunnarsdottir

B. Read the article. Notice the various quotations—direct, indirect, and hybrid—within the article.

Virgil as the Guide of Dante

1   The focus on theological matters in Dante Alighieri's *The Divine Comedy* may seem, at first glance, to be representative of the archaic belief system of the late Middle Ages, complete with blazing inferno and eternal damnation. However, Dante's influential text also focuses on individuality, earthly happiness, and classical scholarship, which cemented the epic poem's place in the foundation of neoclassical humanism. Dante wrote in Italian, the common language of the people, rather than in Latin, so that anyone could read his work. He also revealed a deep admiration for Roman and Greek classics, which was a key component of Renaissance thought. "Within his writing about the depths of hell," says Benjamin Cook, professor of medieval literature and culture at Mid-Coast College, "Dante plants a seed that blossoms into the medieval Renaissance" (*Ultra Praescriptum* 2015). What immediately lifts Dante's work out of the realm of simple espousal of medieval beliefs, Cook claims, is the man who Dante chose for his guide at the beginning of his narrative: Virgil, the celebrated Augustan poet of the pre-Christendom Roman Empire, and a pagan in the eyes of the medieval church. In this essay, we will examine why Dante chose Virgil as his guide and what ramifications this choice had for the development of thought in medieval Europe.

2   *The Divine Comedy* has long posed this question for scholars: Why did Dante choose Virgil? Dante did not choose a religious character from the Bible, nor did he choose an anthropomorphized virtue, such as "Faith," to lead his character, as English author John Bunyan later did in *The Pilgrim's Progress*. Rather, Dante chose Virgil, "the pagan," to lead him through hell and purgatory. Some scholars, such as Marguerite Spellman, professor of literature at the University of Reinsdorf (South Africa), have argued that Dante chose Virgil because Virgil's epic poem the *Aeneid* is about the founding of the city of Rome, "a worthy topic" because it is the precursor to the Holy Roman Empire of Dante's time. However, that seems a stretch, and it would provide marginal ecclesiastical immunity at best. "No serious Church censor would be deterred by such weak tea," as Cardinal Avery Billinks puts it. Most scholars agree that the connection Dante has with Virgil goes far beyond geographic ties to the homeland of the Latin poet.

3   Dante wrote *The Divine Comedy* in the 13th century after he had been exiled from his native Florence for political reasons. He completed the poem shortly before his death at age 56, never having returned to his home. His work is both fictional and autobiographical; Dante simultaneously authors the book and becomes the main character in his epic journey through the underworld, purgatory, and paradise. He begins his poem with a famous line that reveals a depth of despair, possibly referring to the author's inner psychological struggle as well as to his character's journey through the underworld:

> Midway upon the journey of our life
> I found myself within a forest dark,
> For the straightforward pathway had
> been lost.

It is just after this passage that Dante meets Virgil, who becomes his guide, his protector, and his father figure as he passes through hell and purgatory. Dante makes the reader aware of Virgil's presence in the story when he rhetorically asks if the character he sees is indeed Virgil, and clues the reader in to the greatness of the Roman poet. Dante refers to Virgil as a fountain, and poetically states that a river of speech flows from the ancient poet. Dante makes his partnership with Virgil in the following stanzas, and names him as his muse:

> Thou art my master, and my author thou,
> Thou art alone the one from whom I took
> The beautiful style that has done honor
> to me.

The praise Dante bestows on Virgil shows Dante's great respect for the Roman poet's writing.

4   Dante's epic poem then follows in the footsteps of Virgil in more ways than one,

Continued

according to Cook. There is the metaphorical following, in which Virgil guides Dante through the darkness of the underworld, and there is the literal pattern in literature, in which Dante follows Virgil by emulating his epic poem about a journey to an underworld. Cook, speculating on how Dante viewed his work, writes that the poet saw *The Divine Comedy* "first and foremost as his literary masterpiece" and believed it would become a classic in the annals of literature. "By choosing his most-admired author," Cook notes, "Dante draws attention to the literary nature of his work." Just as he described Aeneas's geographical meanderings in the *Aeneid*, Virgil explains the various topographical features of hell, even offering details of where various rivers originate. Dante offers lavish praise to Virgil and goes on later in the book to offer similar praise to all his favorite classical authors, whom he meets in the underworld. He imagines himself as a similar, celebrated author in the following stanzas:

> And more of honour still, much more, they did to me,
> In that they made me one of their own band;
> So that the sixth was I, 'mid so much wit.

The other great minds, according to Dante, were Horace, Ovid, Lucan, and Homer. He travels for a short while with the other classical poets and sees many other important figures from ancient Greece and Rome, including Hector and Aeneas, Socrates and Plato, and Euclid and Ptolemy. Cook suggests that it is in these stanzas that Dante helps the reader understand the importance that studying the classics had to him.

5   Dante's bold choice of the secular Virgil as a guide has more modern reverberations as well. The revered (and officially "Blessed," according to the Roman Catholic Church) John Henry Newman echoed Virgil when he wrote, in his *Apologia*

> who can afford to be leisurely and deliberate, while he practises on himself

a cruel operation, the ripping up of old griefs, and the venturing again upon the '*infandum dolorem*' of years, in which the stars of this lower heaven were one by one going out?

"*Infandum dolorem*" (unspeakable pain) is a direct quote from the *Aeneid*, used by Newman in depicting the difficulties of his own spiritual journey. Spellman noticed Newman's affinity for Virgil despite the extreme orthodoxy of his time, and she finds it striking that even in Newman's Victorian milieu, perhaps less experimental than other periods of Christian history, Virgil is an acceptable intellectual trailblazer.

6   This glimpse into Dante's admiration for the classics foretells the neoclassical revival of the Renaissance and, as we see from Newman, sets a sturdy precedent. The medieval church ruled over civic matters as well as "matters of faith and morals"—as the Church's First Vatican Council would put it in 1870, during the height of Newman's career—and it did not stress liberal education. Dante, who believed the Church should focus solely on spiritual matters and leave civic rule to the government, longed for a different, reawakened society, as Cook notes in *Ultra Praescriptum*. "It is not difficult to imagine Dante, the exile, longing for a society like that of ancient Rome or Greece, which placed a priority on scholarship," Cook writes. Dante's work sparked an interest in the Roman and Greek classics, which went on to inspire a revival in classical education, especially after the classics were reprinted and made widely available through the invention of the printing press in the 15th century. From the study of these classics, Cook maintains, the humanist philosophy of the Renaissance emerged from the shadows of Church strictures because Dante, and a few others of his ilk, promoted the belief that moral and ethical issues are a matter for civil society.

Aside from excerpts from Dante's *The Divine Comedy* and Newman's *Apologia*, the sources and source quotations in this passage are fictional.

C. Read the questions and choose the best answers.

1. Which idea is expressed in a direct quotation in Paragraph 1?

   a. Dante meant his work to be understandable by the average person.
   b. Dante's tale of the underworld led to the development of the Renaissance.
   c. Choosing Virgil as his guide is what truly distinguishes Dante's work.
   d. Virgil was a pagan, and as such was not able to enter the realm Christians knew as "hell."

2. In Paragraph 2, the author preserves the source's own words by using a direct quote, which contains a metaphor. What is that metaphor?

   a. That a concept like faith can be spoken of as a person.
   b. That when Dante had Virgil speak of "hell," he meant it to be a reference to the city of Rome.
   c. That a certain idea is so unimpressive that it is like drinking something tasteless.
   d. That Virgil's lack of Christian belief made him like one of the people suffering in hell.

3. In Paragraph 3, the author directly quotes Dante twice. What do the two quotes have in common? Choose TWO.

   a. Both are inset.
   b. Both are hybrids.
   c. Both are explained by the author in the sentence before the quote.
   d. Both are introduced by verbs showing that something is in dispute.
   e. Both involve the voice of Dante speaking to Virgil.

4. Which paragraph involves an extended quote from a single scholarly source?

   a. Paragraph 3
   b. Paragraph 4
   c. Paragraph 5
   d. Paragraph 6

5. According to Paragraph 5, what evidence is given that John Henry Newman appreciated Virgil as an intellectual forebear?

   a. Newman quotes a Latin phrase from Virgil.
   b. Newman is considered "Blessed" by the Catholic Church.
   c. Newman caught the attention of Marguerite Spellman.
   d. Newman was writing during the strict Victorian Era.

6. Which of these ideas are ascribed to Cook in Paragraph 6? Choose TWO.

   a. The Church before the Renaissance got too involved in the affairs of civic life.
   b. Dante probably wished he had lived in earlier times when learning was more widely respected.
   c. Dante's use of Virgil, a figure from classical times, helped usher in the Renaissance.
   d. Newman showed that references to classical figures was a strong technique, usable in nearly any era.

....

Usage Notes The verb an author uses to introduce a direct or indirect quotation indicates a lot about the author's views of the source, what the source said, and how the source said it.

The Source Is ...	Example
saying something neutral, believable, or moderate:	say, write, note, mention, point out, comment, observe, remark, put it, call, characterize
conveying something new or not commonly said:	propose, posit, postulate, put forth, suggest, reveal, announce
engaged in an issue that many others are also commenting on:	add, agree, disagree, answer, admit, deny complain, repeat, confirm
saying something that others might dispute:	claim, argue, insist, maintain, aver

D. **Based on sources and information in "Virgil as the Guide of Dante," create direct, indirect, and hybrid quotes. Follow the prompts. (For ideas, see the TIP: Usage Notes, above.)**

1. Neutral, hybrid quote: *Marguerite Spellman calls Rome "the central actor of an entire millennium" and says that the city defined life even for peoples who had never heard of it.*

2. Neutral, direct quote: ....

   ....

3. New information, direct quote: ....

   ....

4. Information others are commenting on, indirect quote: ....

   ....

5. New information, extended quote, partly direct and partly indirect: ....

   ....

6. Neutral, hybrid quote: ....

   ....

7. New information, hybrid quote: ....

   ....

Go to **MyEnglishLab** to complete a vocabulary exercise and skill practice, and to join in collaborative activities.

For more about QUOTATIONS, see ⟨W⟩ ECONOMICS ②.

LANGUAGE SKILL
APPRECIATING HEDGING

WHY IT'S USEFUL Recognizing hedging language will enable you to understand when a writer is attempting to sound reasonable, strike a moderate tone, or avoid unsupportable extremes, all through the use of cautious language.

Hedging is cautious, vague, or noncommittal language used intentionally by authors in academic writing. It includes language like modal verbs, adjectives of probability, and phrases for generalization, and is employed for several reasons. Identifying hedging language is important because while some may assume that academic writing is wholly based on facts, researchers often have to take a subjective position on a "fact" or a result and the level of certainty they have about the statements they are making.

One reason that a writer might hedge is to express a certain level of precision when presenting information, data, or results of a study. For example, the first sentence—which includes hedging language with the words *Based on the evidence* and *likely*—is much more precise than the second sentence:

> Based on the evidence from our study, it is likely that the Greek text was written by a prominent scholar of ancient times

> Our study demonstrates that the Greek text was written by a prominent scholar of ancient times.

In the first sentence, the writer is being as specific as possible in order to demonstrate the source of the information—the evidence from their study. The writer is also using an adverb that indicates a level of bias and impreciseness (*likely*) to demonstrate that the conclusion was interpreted by the writer, rather than proven by the evidence. The second sentence, on the other hand, leaves a reader wondering *how* the author drew this conclusion, as it lacks the source that led the writer to the conclusion. It also conveys a level of certainty with the word *demonstrates*, which does not accurately capture the level of (un)certainty the author actually has about the conclusion.

Another reason authors hedge is to indicate to readers that while they are confident about the validity of their statements, they recognize that other writers also have valuable information to contribute on the same topic. It also helps them to appear willing to accept other viewpoints and to demonstrate that they do not believe that they possess all knowledge that exists about a given topic.

Writers also may use hedging language in an attempt to decrease the likelihood of other authors arguing with or disputing the information they are writing about.

Hedging Language		Example
Modal verbs	can, may, might, could, should, would	Art pieces described in Virgil's the *Aeneid* **may** represent art that actually existed during his time.
Verbs indicating tentativeness or evaluation	appear, seem, estimate, tend, suggest, assume, speculate, propose, argue, postulate, claim	Some scholars **argue** that Dante and Virgil placed souls in given rings of hell in order to make political points.
Some nouns	possibility, estimate, assumption, suggestion, likelihood	The **possibility** exists that the Greeks viewed the afterlife as something significantly more dreadful than the Romans did.

Continued

Hedging Language		Example
Some adverbs	perhaps, likely / unlikely, possibly, apparently, presumably, approximately, occasionally, somewhat, usually, roughly, frequently, generally, conceivably, necessarily	**Perhaps** art as depicted by Homer was nothing more than a figment of his imagination.
Adjectives of probability	possible, probably, unlikely	It is **possible** that the first instance of ekphrastic poetry was in Homer's epic the *Odyssey*.
Phrases introducing an author's position on a topic	It is my view that, We believe that, To my knowledge	**We believe that** there is little evidence that ancient Romans and Greeks practiced human sacrifice.
Compound hedges	seems likely, may suggest, could assume	It **seems likely** that heroic burial customs existed, as they were recorded in the *Iliad*.
Phrases of attribution	based on, on the basis of, according to, on the evidence of, in the words of	**Based on** University of Sedona's classicist Wei Chen Liu's examination of the aesthetics of Achilles's shield, it is a characterization of everyday life of the aristocracy in ancient Greece.
Language for generalization	mainly, usually, primarily, largely, generally, predominantly, for the most part, to a great extent, most, the majority of, except for, with the exception of, apart from	The underworld in Norse mythology is **primarily** based on the *Poetic Edda*, the *Prose Edda*, and the *Eglis Saga of Iceland*.

Language that writers typically avoid when they are attempting to be cautious in their communication of information includes the following: *undoubtedly, without a doubt, there is no doubt that, clearly, obviously, definitely, certainly, absolutely, always, never, all, every*. This is due to the fact that this language expresses complete certainly, thus leaving no room for error or alternative viewpoints.

EXERCISE 4

A. The following are excerpts from readings in this unit. What hedging language do you see? Identify the words and phrases that hedge and underline them.

1. Virgil's hero Aeneas, like Homer's Odysseus, descends into the underworld to interact with the deceased, but Virgil's portrayal is that the honor due to Aeneas vastly outweighs whatever the reader may owe Odysseus.

2. Different scholars have speculated on various intentions Homer may have had for writing the passage, from simply recording what life looked like during his time to using the beauty of the passage to deepen the scope of the great tragedy about to occur in the poem.

3. Further, many fine art examples described in the text, such as the famous shield of Achilles, likely did not exist.

4. Tate stumbled across various animal bones interred alongside human remains in graves in both Cyprus and Attica—graves that predate the Trojan War across the seas—which has led scholars such as George Kristidis of the Athenian Academy to reluctantly acknowledge a possible connection between the cremation passages in the *Iliad* and burial customs in ancient Greece.

5. The Greeks, especially by the mid-8th century BCE, believed that the soul of one unburied would continue to trouble the living, according to Moore.

6. Romans and many medieval Europeans, on the other hand, largely considered the afterlife a place divided according to a person's behavior in life.

7. Homer's epic poems the *Iliad* and the *Odyssey* give vivid descriptions of textiles, decorative battle gear, and architectural elements that should be considered in art history as an authentic depiction of art objects of great importance.

8. Odysseus heroically longs for his land and his love, and the reader can more easily empathize with him than with the somewhat pompous Roman poetic hero.

B. The information in the following sentences is stated in an overly confident manner. Identify the excessively confident language and then replace it with hedging language. It may be necessary to change word order or grammar. The sentences you write should express the same information as the original sentences but with lesser degrees of certainty.

1. Ancient Greek artifacts depicted in the *Odyssey* and the *Aeneid* were certainly real artistic pieces that existed at the time the epics were written.

2. Ancient Greeks undoubtedly practiced cremation before the Trojan War.

3. It is obvious that Dante wrote in Italian—the common language of the people—rather than in Latin so that his work could be understood by everyone.

4. Dante clearly chose Virgil to be his guide because of Virgil's reputation as a pagan in the eyes of the medieval church.

5. Every scholar disagrees about the authenticity of the art pieces described by Homer and Virgil.

6. Dante's *The Divine Comedy* is absolutely a literary masterpiece of ancient times.

Go to **MyEnglishLab** to complete a skill practice.

APPLY YOUR SKILLS

WHY IT'S USEFUL By applying the skills you have learned in this unit, you can successfully read this thought-provoking text and learn what a hero's journey entails.

BEFORE YOU READ

A. Discuss these questions with one or more students.

   1. Think of a heroic character from a modern book or movie. What type of journey does he or she take to become a hero? Is it linear, or are there many incremental tests and triumphs along the way?

   2. Do you think that most hero stories follow a pattern similar to the example you gave in Question 1? Why or why not, and what do you think the reason for this is?

   3. What do you think makes people relate to stories about heroes even if, on the surface, they seem to have nothing in common with a heroic character?

B. Imagine that you will be participating in a small group discussion about the passage "The Hero's Journey," which begins on the next page. Your group will be discussing the following questions. Keep these questions in mind as you read the passage.

   1. What is a monomyth, and what are some of its key features?

   2. Why are hero stories so easy for average people to identify with, regardless of the culture from which they come?

   3. What is a "collective unconscious," and how does it relate to hero stories?

   4. What do ancient stories of hero journeys like the *Odyssey* have in common with more contemporary works, such as *Star Wars*, *Lord of the Rings*, and *Harry Potter*?

   5. Do readers or viewers have to be able to relate to the time period in which a hero's tale takes place in order to form a connection with the tale? Why or why not?

C. Review the Unit Skills Summary. As you read the passage, apply the skills you learned in this unit.

UNIT SKILLS SUMMARY

Synthesize information from several sources.
- Put together ideas and perspectives from several different sources.

Understand multiple perspectives.
- Recognize how sources agree, disagree, add to one another, and update one another.

Evaluate the credibility and motives of sources.
- Learn to better judge which sources' perspectives are more convincing than others.

Use and understand direct and indirect quotations.
- Understand the author's efforts to support claims and try to recognize the author's attempt to position ideas within a larger sphere of discourse.

Appreciate hedging.
- Appreciate and recognize the author's rhetorical strategies to sound reasonable, strike a moderate tone, avoid unsupportable extremes, and avoid or minimize possible points of controversy.

A. Read the passage. Annotate and take notes as necessary.

The Hero's Journey

1   At first glance, an ancient epic poem like the *Odyssey* may seem wholly disconnected from 21st century life and the modern student. However, the text quickly reveals familiar experiences, including a call to a quest, a yearning for a homeland, a seemingly insurmountable challenge, and a heroic emergence from trials as a wiser and stronger individual. This pattern, known as the "hero's journey," is found in many stories in different cultures, from ancient epic poetry to modern popular fiction. Researchers refer to the concept as a "monomyth" and argue that this archetypal story arises from the inherent human need for understanding and growth through quests for knowledge.

2   The hero's journey archetype contains several identifiable stages. There is a call, motivated by either internal longing or external pressure, for the hero to leave his common world and join a quest, which is followed in the narrative by a reluctance to answer the call. The hero, male or female (but typically male), is persuaded to leave and shortly thereafter finds a mentor. At this point in the narrative, the hero generally meets trials, tests of endurance, and enemies. This individual then undergoes a major struggle, either external or internal, from which he emerges victorious with an earned reward. Following the reward, the hero attempts to complete the journey and must sacrifice something—often his own life—in order to be reborn with a sort of healing power. The last stage, the *apotheosis*, is when the hero experiences self-realization, gained through battling his foe.

3   Gareth Fields, professor of cognitive psychology and author of *The Hero's Journey in the Modern Mind*, postulates that the hero's journey emerges from the human desire to use an external struggle—a story—to mirror psychological difficulties that people must overcome. This hero narrative is evident in one of the first recorded myths found in the

ancient world, the story of the Sumerian goddess Inanna's descent and journey through the underworld, where the goddess is forced to undergo trials that eventually lead to her death and rebirth. Ancient myths portray learning as a journey, Fields writes, and journeys to knowledge are part of the human experience. This is why the modern reader may still find a connection to Inanna's ancient journey. Fields notes that the repetition of the themes in other stories support the theory. Epic poems from the Greeks, the Romans, medieval authors, and many others contain the same prevailing theme of a journey to the underworld and the undertaking of physical and psychological trials along the way. Modern tales contain similar components as well, which we will see later in this essay in a discussion of 20th and 21st century hero quests.

> **CULTURE NOTE**
> The first person to write of the phenomenon of the monomyth was American researcher Joseph Campbell, who studied myths from around the globe and identified familiar patterns, or archetypes, that transcend time and culture. Campbell's book *The Hero with a Thousand Faces*, published in 1949, was popularized in the 1970s and is still studied today in comparative mythology, literature, film, and religion courses. Campbell argues in his work that the human consciousness naturally creates characters who undergo similar journeys. Campbell names each stage of the journey of the hero in his chapters, beginning with the departure, then the initiation, and finally the return of the hero and the keys, or the reward, that the hero earns through his journey. Subsequent writers, scholars, and filmmakers termed this particular pattern "the hero's journey," and a great deal of popular fiction, including *Star Wars*, follows this archetypal story.

4   Fields claims that the hero's journey emerges in every culture because the stories and the trials the characters undergo are a representation of the knowledge growth and character development that occur in our own life stories. This is why we empathize with Homer's character Odysseus as he plummets to literal and metaphorical darkness when facing the underworld, where he must journey to find his way home. The hero Frodo from J.R.R. Tolkien's *The Lord of the Rings* captures a reader's heart, as well, Fields says, because "individuals easily identify with the despair of dealing with

Continued

difficulties and the longing for order and peace in the world." Frodo and his fellow travelers eventually bring about the destruction of the ring, supposedly ridding the world of evil forces, though the effort nearly destroys him. Like Odysseus, Frodo must overcome his trial before emerging with the strength necessary to restore order to his homeland. Fields argues that these two examples, among many, are common and popular in lore because they mirror the way in which humans must prevail over hardship and grow into their potential.

5   While Fields focuses on the draw that myths have because of the way they inspire character growth and help individuals face psychological hurdles, Thaddeus Burns, professor of archaic and classical Greek civilization, looks more closely at the monomyth concept and how humans use the template of myth to express common yearning. Burns addresses how the theories of analytical psychologist Carl Jung influenced the development of the idea of an archetypal story, in particular Jung's theory of the collective unconsciousness. The collective unconscious is, according to Burns, a shared structure of archetypes found in the human unconscious mind. It is part of the foundation of the hero's journey archetype and the reason myths transcend culture and history. It is from this collective unconscious that humans draw common themes. Burns argues that the story of the *Odyssey*—as well as other epic poems that imitate it—uses common tropes to provoke feelings of triumph, despair, and glory that bring about an individual's awareness of the self, which Burns refers to as knowledge acquisition.

6   While the *Odyssey* may not fall into the category of "pleasure reading" for the average student of the mid-2010s, as Boudicca Inez so poignantly expresses in her recent article in *Bolster Magazine*, other tales of heroes who follow the same hero's journey archetype do not necessarily suffer the same fate. Inez's work, though it appears in a popular source rather than a scholarly source, makes valid points that are relevant to the discussion, particularly in the context of pointing out how modern hero journeys resemble ancient texts. Citing heroes from Frodo and Harry Potter to Luke Skywalker and Neo (*The Matrix*), Inez shows that their success as characters lies in their quests and in an audience's desire to see them achieve self-realization through perseverance. Their glory, unlike Odysseus's, is something not just understood, but celebrated. The tale of author J.K. Rowling's hero, Harry Potter, is a "dyed-in-the-wool" example of the hero's journey, Inez writes. The wild success of the story, despite the character living in a magical world completely unlike the real world, is rooted in the main character's journey. Like Odysseus, Harry is called to a quest. During the quest, he gains a mentor, grows through trials, and eventually conquers evil through special powers he wins through sacrifice.

7   Even nonreaders cannot avoid the hero's journey, Inez claims, and that is in no small part due to *Star Wars*. Theaters in 2016 opened to a film that continues one of the classic journeys of a hero—that of Luke Skywalker. Skywalker fits all the tropes of a classic hero, complete with his call to the quest, his sacrifice, and his choice to die—or sacrifice himself—instead of succumb to evil. Skywalker's journey culminates with victory and the salvation of his people. What the story means to viewers, however, represents "much more than just cute Ewoks and victory over the Emperor," says Inez. "It appeals to the human yearning for personal growth through a quest." Jung would likely agree.

The sources and source quotations in this passage are fictional.

B. Reread the questions in Before You Read, Part B. Is there anything you cannot answer? What reading skills can you use to help you find the answers?

Go to MyEnglishLab to read the passage again and answer critical thinking questions.

THINKING CRITICALLY

Follow these steps:

1. Consider the seven stages of a hero's journey:

   1 A call to a journey or quest
   2 Reluctance to answer the call
   3 Persuasion of hero and meeting with mentor
   4 The encountering of tests, trials, or enemies

   5 An internal or external struggle
   6 A sacrifice in order to complete the journey
   7 Victory

2. Then choose the main character (Frodo, Harry Potter, Luke Skywalker, or Neo) from one of the works you just read about OR the main character of a book or movie of your choice.

3. Try to identify each of the seven steps in your chosen character's journey. What occurs in each of these stages? You may have to do some research if you do not know or cannot recall the events of each stage. If any of the stages do not exist, what do you think is the reason for this?

THINKING VISUALLY

You have learned that the collective unconscious is a shared structure of archetypes found in the human unconscious mind and is part of the foundation of the hero's journey.

1. Study the chart, which features archetypes suggested by June Singer, a psychologist and analyst of Carl Jung's work. Do some quick Internet searches to find out the meanings of unfamiliar words or concepts in the chart. You will note that each row presents a pair of opposites (e.g., the Great Mother is the opposite of the Terrible Mother.)

2. Now think of literary and film characters you know well. Which archetypes from the chart do you think these characters represent? Think of specific examples of scenes in which these archetypes manifest themselves. Add their names to the chart. How do these archetypes contribute to the "hero's journey" of this character? Share your chart with another student.

Characteristic	Examples from Film and Literature	Characteristic
Ego		Shadow
Great Mother		Terrible Mother
Old Wise Man		Trickster
Time		Eternity
Light		Darkness

THINKING ABOUT LANGUAGE

Read these excerpts from "The Hero's Journey." What hedging language do you see? Identify the words and phrases and write them on the line. Then rewrite the original sentence, replacing the hedging language with a hedging word or phrase that is similar in meaning.

1. At first glance, an ancient epic poem like the *Odyssey* may seem wholly disconnected from 21st century life and the modern student.

   Words / Phrases: ....

   Rewritten sentence(s): ....

   ....

   ....

2. Researchers refer to the concept as a "monomyth" and argue that this archetypal story arises from the inherent human need for understanding and growth through quests for knowledge.

   Words / Phrases: ....

   Rewritten sentence(s): ....

   ....

   ....

3. At this point in the narrative, the hero generally meets trials, tests of endurance, and enemies.

   Words / Phrases: ....

   Rewritten sentence(s): ....

   ....

4. Gareth Fields, professor of cognitive psychology and author of *The Hero's Journey in the Modern Mind*, postulates that the hero's journey emerges from the human desire to use an external struggle—a story—to mirror psychological difficulties that people must overcome.

   Words / Phrases: ....

   Rewritten sentence(s): ....

   ....

   ....

5. The collective unconscious is, according to Burns, a shared structure of archetypes found in the human unconscious mind.

   Words / Phrases: ....

   Rewritten sentence(s): ....

   ....

   ....

6. Burns argues that the story of the *Odyssey*—as well as other epic poems that imitate it—uses common tropes to provoke feelings of triumph, despair, and glory that bring about an individual's awareness of the self, which Burns refers to as knowledge acquisition.

   Words / Phrases: ....

   Rewritten sentence(s): ....

   ....

   ....

7. While the *Odyssey* may not fall into the category of "pleasure reading" for the average student of the mid-2010s, as Boudicca Inez so poignantly expresses in her recent article in *Bolster Magazine*, other tales of heroes who follow the same hero's journey archetype do not necessarily suffer the same fate.

   Words / Phrases: ....

   Rewritten sentence(s): ....

   ....

   ....

   ....

8. Even nonreaders cannot avoid the hero's journey, Inez claims, and that is in no small part due to *Star Wars*.

   Words / Phrases: ....

   Rewritten sentence(s): ....

   ....

9. Jung would likely agree.

   Words / Phrases: ....

   Rewritten sentence(s): ....

   ....

Go to **MyEnglishLab** to listen to Professor Harrison and to complete a self-assessment.

Sound design creates a healthier world.

ENVIRONMENTAL ENGINEERING

Definitions and Classifications

UNIT PROFILE

In this unit, you will consider the subject of environmental engineering—specifically the issue of air quality inside buildings. You will read about the technical features of heating, air-conditioning, and ventilation (HVAC) systems, and the tricky nature of balancing ventilation needs and energy costs.

Look ahead to the reading "The Impact of Energy-Saving Devices on Indoor Air Quality" on page 257. Scan the reading (run your eyes over it quickly, without actually reading). Note terms in **bold** that are defined. Scan again for classification terms such as *type*, *category*, and *kind*. What do you think will be classified in the reading?

OUTCOMES

• Understand definitions and classifications

• Recognize and understand definitions within a text

• Work with classifications

• Understand and produce references to other sources

• Understand and use clarifiers

GETTING STARTED

▶ Go to MyEnglishLab to listen to Professor Hildemann and to complete a self-assessment.

Discuss these questions with a partner or group.

1. What do you think is done during the construction of a building to guarantee a fresh air environment?

2. In order to ensure clean indoor air, it is sometimes necessary to use devices that consume a significant amount of energy. In which situations do you think it makes sense to employ devices that use a lot of energy?

3. You just learned that most people in America spend up to 90 percent of their time indoors. What percentage of your time do you spend indoors? What impact might this have on your health?

For more about **ENVIRONMENTAL ENGINEERING**, see ① ③. See also W and OC
ENVIRONMENTAL ENGINEERING ① ② ③.

CRITICAL THINKING SKILL
UNDERSTANDING DEFINITIONS AND CLASSIFICATIONS

WHY IT'S USEFUL By working with definitions and classifications, you will broaden your knowledge of specialized terms, improve your general vocabulary in English, and understand relationships among things that are like—or unlike—one another in specific ways.

Definitions and classifications are basic features of most academic writing. Nearly every university course introduces students to the specialized vocabulary of a field. Once concepts are named and learned, academic texts often group them to help articulate similarities and differences.

A key to understanding academic writing within a particular discipline is **understanding definitions and classifications**. This unit breaks the skill down into two supporting skills:

- recognizing and understanding definitions within a text
- working with classifications

NOTICING ACTIVITY

A. As you read the passage, notice the use of vocabulary that is not common in everyday writing but is appropriate for a reading in the field of environmental engineering. Write three such vocabulary items on the lines. (Do not include *organic* or *volatile* as these are addressed in Part C.)

....

INDOOR AIR POLLUTANTS—VOCs

1   Indoor air quality can be dramatically worse than outdoor air quality if proper ventilation is not maintained, resulting in a bottling-up effect that creates in-building air pollution levels two to five times greater than that of outdoor air. People spend the vast majority of their time indoors, so indoor air quality has a dramatic effect on human health simply due to exposure level. Indoor air pollutants can be categorized as mold and other allergens (agents, like dust mite droppings, that cause allergic reactions); bacteria and viruses; tobacco smoke; hazardous gases; harmful older building materials, including lead paint and asbestos (a naturally occurring compound); and volatile organic compounds (VOCs), the broadest category among indoor pollutants.

2   By definition, VOCs are compounds that are classified as "organic" because they contain carbon bonded to hydrogen, and "volatile" because they have high vapor pressure and a low boiling point, meaning they easily "off-gas," or evaporate, at room temperature. VOCs are widely found in common household products and personal products, including fragrances, paint, air fresheners, carpet, and pesticides. Not all harmful gases are VOCs, however. Carbon monoxide, for example, is a colorless, odorless, and highly toxic gas, but it is inorganic. Similarly, radon, a naturally occurring hazardous radioactive gas that must be tested in homes, is chemically classified as a noble gas; therefore it is not a volatile organic compound.

B. Are there definitions in the passage for the three items you found? If so, underline them.

C. The passage names the criteria for belonging to the category of volatile organic compounds (VOCs). To belong, a substance must be both *organic* and *volatile*. Write a definition for each.

organic ....

volatile ....

Go to **MyEnglishLab** to complete a vocabulary exercise and skill practice, and to join in collaborative activities.

SUPPORTING SKILL 1
RECOGNIZING AND UNDERSTANDING DEFINITIONS WITHIN A TEXT

WHY IT'S USEFUL Much of your success as an academic reader depends on understanding new terminology in what you read. By familiarizing yourself with various ways in which writers signal that definitions are being provided, you will be better able to anticipate, identify, and understand new terms.

In academic courses, you will be exposed to numerous new **terms and definitions** through class readings, lecture slide presentations, and your own research. In order to be able to comprehend the meanings of new words, it is essential to be equipped with the skills necessary to recognize that they are being introduced.

Writers employ a variety of signal words, phrases, and punctuation to indicate the introduction of a new term or phrase.

Signal Word, Phrase, or Punctuation Indicating a Definition or Explanation	Example
are those that	HVAC systems **are those that** combine <u>h</u>eating, <u>v</u>entilation, and <u>air</u> conditioning.
by definition	**By definition**, a dehumidifier is a machine that removes water from the air in a building.
can be defined as	A heat exchanger **can be defined as** an apparatus used to transfer heat from one medium to another.
consists of	The respiratory system, which **consists of** anatomical features such as the nose, nasal passages, pharynx, larynx, trachea, bronchi, and lungs, is what makes respiration possible.
entails	Installing an air-conditioning system in your home **entails** selecting the right equipment and then putting it in.
essentially is essentially	Precipitation **is essentially** moisture, often in the form of rain and snow, that falls to the ground.
involves	Air-conditioning is a process that **involves** making the air in a building or vehicle cooler and drier.
is	A heat pump **is** a tool that applies heat energy to an endpoint called a "heat sink."
is characterized by	Sick building syndrome **is characterized by** headaches and respiratory problems.
<u>noun</u> (definition in parentheses)	<u>Emissions</u> (gases or other substances that are sent out into the air) are increasing worldwide.
<u>noun</u>—definition between dashes—	<u>Velocity</u>—the rate at which something moves in a particular direction over a period of time—is an important consideration.
<u>noun</u>, or + <u>noun</u>,	A <u>damper</u>, **or** a <u>valve</u>, can regulate drafts.
<u>noun</u>, which + <u>verb</u>	<u>Ducts</u>, **which** <u>are</u> pipes or tubes for carrying liquids, air, cables, etc., are used in HVAC systems.
refer to <u>noun</u>, which refers to	Pollutants **refer to** substances in air, water, or soil that are harmful to humans and other organisms.
	The <u>respiratory system</u>, **which refers to** the organs and parts of the body that help you to breathe, is one of the nine major organ systems.
which means a term used to mean	He is an environmental engineer, **which means** that he identifies and solves problems related to the environment.
	Residence time, **a term used to mean** the amount of time water is held in a batch reactor, plug flow reactor, etc., relates to wastewater treatment and water treatment.

EXERCISE 1

A. Scan the reading for six signal words, phrases, and punctuation from the chart on the previous page that indicate that a term is being defined. Circle them.

Is Air-Conditioning Necessary?

1   The widespread use of air-conditioning symbolizes, for some, an upwardly mobile population in a growing, productive economy. The concept that the privileged and powerful have greater access to the comfort of cool air is rooted in both history and truth. Powerful ancient civilizations employed air cooling systems prior to the technological advances of the 20th century, and the wealthiest people in such civilizations reaped the benefits. The Romans built aqueducts, which were channels that carried water. The aqueducts piped cool water through brick and stonework to not only provide fresh water to Roman citizens but also to cool down buildings. Ancient Persians invented *windcatchers*, which refers to tunnel-like devices that funneled wind into buildings and ventilated out hot indoor air. Chinese inventor Ding Huan, who lived during the Han Dynasty 2,000 years ago, built a manually operated rotary fan—a precursor of modern fans—that kept courtiers cool. His invention was used later by Emperor Xuanzong of the Tang Dynasty, who constructed a water-powered fan to keep the imperial palace cool.

2   Modern-day air conditioners achieve the same goal but operate quite differently. Consisting of three main parts (a compressor, a condenser, and an evaporator), air conditioners use chemicals called refrigerants that easily convert a liquid to a gas and back to liquid again in a process known as phase transition. Essentially, the refrigerant helps absorb and expel heat outdoors while evaporating and cooling air to release indoors. The United States, one of the wealthiest nations in the world according to the International Monetary Fund's measure of gross domestic product per capita, uses more air-conditioning than all other nations combined, with nearly 90 percent of households using some form of air-conditioning. Other nations are following suit, and studies show that as incomes rise and average temperatures climb, air-conditioning use increases. In Singapore in the early 2000s, officials made air-conditioning mandatory in parts of new housing and commercial developments, citing it as a pivotal invention that modernized the nation and increased workplace productivity. Air-conditioning usage is also on the rise in the populous nations of India and China.

3   Research corroborates the notion that hot weather reduces overall economic growth. According to a study that measured the effects of temperature and precipitation on economic growth over a 50-year period, poor nations that lack air-conditioning experienced reduced economic growth during heat waves. Wealthier nations, where workers are protected from temperature changes, on the other hand, did not see a lag in economic growth. If two scenarios might be imagined, a man on his way to work in a poorer nation on a sweltering day might take a crowded, oven-like public bus and arrive at a workplace with equally oppressive heat. Fatigue would set in by midday, possibly leading to heat exhaustion, which is characterized by dizziness, heavy sweating, and a rapid pulse rate. Productivity would naturally drop. In contrast, on a hot day in a richer nation, a man would travel in an air-conditioned car to a cool workplace and experience little to no drop in productivity, thanks to the comparably more comfortable environment.

4   The American proclivity to crank up the air conditioner the second the temperature rises, however, is not necessarily a desirable behavior to emulate. This profligate use of energy-hungry air conditioners increases the release of greenhouse gases (which cause the atmosphere to retain heat). Notably, not all developed nations flock to air-conditioning. In Germany, for example, air-conditioning is rare in homes, and officials urge individuals to use simpler measures, such as turning on a fan or wearing more weather-appropriate clothing to alleviate the discomforts brought on by heat.

B. The following questions ask about some of the words that are defined in the reading. Write a short answer to each question.

1. What are aqueducts? ....

   ....

   ....

TIP
....
In a reading, notice when there is a list of examples that define and classify. Such a list could be used to make a definition clearer. It could also be used to clarify the nature of items within a group or class.

2. What are windcatchers? ....

   ....

   ....

3. Explain what air conditioners are made up of and what they use to function. ....

   ....

   ....

4. How do refrigerants function? ....

   ....

   ....

5. Explain what some symptoms of heat exhaustion are. ....

   ....

   ....

6. What do greenhouse gases do? ....

   ....

C. How does understanding the meaning of each of the terms in Part B contribute to your comprehension of the reading overall? Which sections of the reading would not have made sense if you did not know these definitions? Refer back to the reading, and then discuss with a partner.

Go to **MyEnglishLab** to complete a vocabulary exercise and skill practice, and to join in collaborative activities.

SUPPORTING SKILL 2
WORKING WITH CLASSIFICATIONS

WHY IT'S USEFUL By understanding classifications in a text, you can comprehend some of the most basic relationships among specialized information in a field of study: which elements are similar or equal to one another, or in entirely different categories, and why.

Classifications help reveal patterns. By grouping similar things together—and articulating the way(s) in which they are similar—academic authors make complicated systems or processes easier to understand. For example, one of the best ways to understand chemical elements is to group them according to their structure, their properties, their uses, or some other feature. (See the CULTURE NOTE on p. 243 about the periodic table of elements.)

Fundamental Characteristics of a Good Classification
- There is only one basis of classification (sometimes also called "organizing principle").
- The basis of classification is clear (perhaps by means of in-text definitions).
- The classes are meaningful—that is, the grouping shows significant similarities among items.
- If necessary, the author provides examples of members of classes.

A BASIS FOR CLASSIFICATION
For most sets of information, many different classifications are possible. It all depends on the basis of classification. Take, for example, the following set of polluting substances, which are arranged alphabetically:

POLLUTING SUBSTANCES	
cold viruses	insect droppings
dust	mold
engine oil	radon gas
fumes from gasoline	small bits of metal
fungus	waterborne bacteria
human skin	

If your basis of classification were "How a substance is mostly taken into the body," you might classify them into two groups—by breathing and by drinking. In that case, your classification might look like this:

POLLUTING SUBSTANCES	
Taken in Mostly by Breathing	**Taken in Mostly by Drinking**
cold viruses	engine oil
dust	human skin
fumes from gasoline	small bits of metal
fungus	waterborne bacteria
insect droppings	
mold	
radon gas	

Notice that the classification has been carefully worded so that
- every item fits into a class.
- every item fits into only one class.

Sometimes authors build classification schemes that include a "both" or "neither" group—for items that either do not fit into the classification system or could be in either category. This is not a good approach; it is a sign of weak categories. When you see this in a reading, try to think of ways that the author could adjust the classification scheme to avoid these problems. For example, in the classification on the previous page, the author avoided weak categories by including the word *mostly* in the name of each class. So, while an item like a cold virus could sometimes be taken in by drinking, it is not *mostly* taken in that way.

If your basis of classification were something else, you could get a totally different classification. For example, you'd get the following if your basis were "Whether a substance is living":

POLLUTING SUBSTANCES	
Living	**Nonliving**
cold viruses	dust
fungus	engine oil
mold	fumes from gasoline
waterborne bacteria	human skin
	insect droppings
	radon gas
	small bits of metal

When you read a passage that includes classifications, understanding the basis of classification is extremely important. The author may clarify the basis by using definitions, such as "By *living*, we mean 'currently alive.' We do not include items that were formerly alive but no longer are, such as human skin."

Even when an author draws up categories that have a strong, well-defined basis, some readers may disagree with the classification. For example, someone might argue that insect droppings should be considered alive because they contain living bacteria. Or someone may argue that viruses are not really alive (which actually is a matter of debate among biologists). Such disagreements are fine. Academic life is full of them, and they motivate a lot of research and progress in various fields.

The important thing is for any classification to have a clear basis and to have just one at a time. A classification gets confused if a writer tries to organize data according to two criteria at the same time. If both criteria are important, they can both be applied, but they should be applied separately, in two different schemes of classification. After both schemes have been independently, cleanly created, you can look for how items may fall into more than one category across the schemes.

CLASSES AND SUBCLASSES

Many academic readings create classes of information and then create smaller classes—subclasses— within them. For example, an author may want to break down the "Nonliving" class of substances in our earlier classification according to the source of substance (the basis) and create two classes, "From natural sources" and "From industrial sources":

NONLIVING POLLUTING SUBSTANCES	
From Natural Sources	**From Industrial Sources**
dust	engine oil
human skin	fumes from gasoline
insect droppings	small bits of metal
radon gas	

In a long reading, this can result in an inverted tree of classes and subclasses:

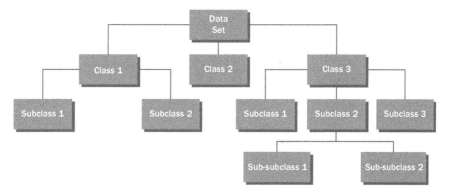

CULTURE NOTE

The Periodic Table of Elements *First published in 1869 by Dmitry Mendeleev, the periodic table has been refined and updated to reflect new knowledge in physics and chemistry, but its classification system was so strong that the basic table is still of use. This amazing longevity is due to the rock-solid bases for classification that Mendeleev chose. The fundamental principle for arranging elements is their atomic number, which is determined by the number of protons in an atom. Mendeleev, however, was operating in a time before protons were even known. His strategy of ordering most elements by the weight of one atom proved to be farsighted, and his order was, for the most part, maintained even after subatomic particles were discovered. Mendeleev's first strategy for organizing the table was to arrange elements into rows called* periods*. Then, by adjusting the number of elements in each period, Mendeleev could create columns (called* groups*) of elements that had similar properties. For example, the table is arranged so the noble gases—elements 2, 10, 18, 36, 54, 86, and 118—all appear in a single column. This reflects several real-world similarities among these elements, such as their gaseous form at room temperature and the unlikelihood that any of them will chemically react with other elements.*

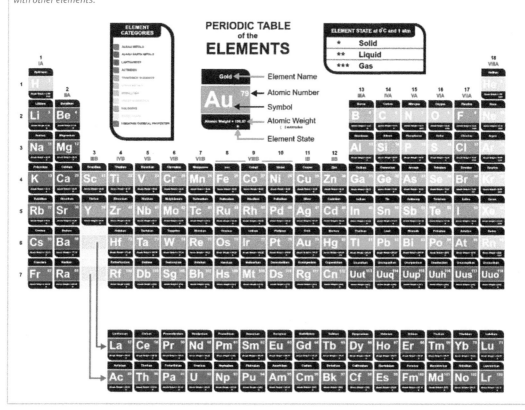

A. Read the passage.

CLASSES OF MOLDS THAT GROW INDOORS

1   An internationally recognized classification system exists for molds that grow inside commercial buildings and houses. Molds are placed into one of three classes—Hazard Class A, B, or C—depending on how harmful they may be to people breathing in the spores of the mold. By the term *mold*, health professionals mean "any type of fungus that grows as threadlike filaments, usually in moist environments." There are other fungi—mushrooms, yeasts, and so on—but they rarely grow in homes or offices and thus don't usually constitute an indoor-air health hazard.

2   Hazard Class A molds are extremely harmful. A person breathing in the spores of such a mold, or perhaps eating the mold itself if it grows on food, may experience severe health problems immediately and may even die. Molds produce poisons called mycotoxins, many of which can induce blindness, heart problems, or malfunctions of the nervous system. In the early 1990s, the mold *Stachybotrys atra* (aka *S. chartarum*, black mold) was blamed for inducing severe bleeding in the lungs of infants at a facility in Cleveland, Ohio. One afflicted child died. Since then, research has brought into question the links between this mold and cases like the one in Ohio. But there is no doubt that molds of Hazard Class A are very dangerous. At the first sign of any such mold, the area of growth should be sealed, if possible, behind an impermeable barrier of plastic sheeting, foam, or some other material until the mold can be removed.

3   Molds of Hazard Class B require less stringent sequestration. They can induce serious symptoms in some people who breathe the spores or ingest the mold itself, but usually only as a matter of allergic reaction. Furthermore, health problems generally are not acute (as they are in Class A molds) but, instead, are apparent only after a period of long exposure. Class B molds pose no health problems for people who are not allergic to them. This is not to downplay their undesirability. Someone highly allergic to *Aureobasidium* molds, for example, can react quite severely indeed, with considerable breathing difficulty.

4   Molds of Hazard Class C pose no health risks at all to humans. They are undesirable mostly because they are ugly, may smell bad, and may even weaken the building materials (such as wood or drywall) on which they grow. *Ulocladium botrytis* is one example. It is present in many bathrooms, visible as unsightly dark patches on painted surfaces.

B. Complete the chart, based on the information in the passage.

Things Being Classified	molds that grow inside structures		
Basis of Classification			
Names of Classes			Hazard Class C
Criterion for Inclusion in the Class			The mold does not cause any human health problems
Example		Aureobasidium	

C. Read the passage.

Indoor Air Pollutants and Health

1   Health problems ranging from a mild headache to severe cognitive impairment can result from exposure to indoor air pollution. US health and environmental agencies have established category distinctions for health professionals to use in identifying a patient's symptoms and the causal relationship of the symptoms to a particular polluting agent. A pollutant's capacity to affect health depends on many factors, such as proximity of the person to the pollutant, level of toxicity of the pollutant, age of the person exposed, and duration of his or her exposure. Reactions to pollutants vary among individuals, but patterns of ill health—particularly when experienced by an entire family in a home or by multiple workers in an office building—may be an aid in diagnosing the condition and resolving the problem. However, the phenomenon of "sick building syndrome" (in which a large number of workers or residents report symptoms like headaches or sore throats but no physical cause can be found) shows that diagnosis is not always easy or even possible.

2   According to the categories established for diagnostic evaluation by the American Lung Association, the American Medical Association, the US Consumer Product Safety Commission, and the US Environmental Protection Agency, indoor air pollutants can be classified into the following groups: combustion products (including tobacco smoke), biological pollutants (including molds and bacteria), volatile organic compounds (including benzene), and heavy metals (such as lead and mercury). Any of these categories could be further broken down according to several bases. For example, biological pollutants could be classified according to their pathogenicity—their likelihood of causing disease, regardless of whether or not the disease is significantly uncomfortable. What matters most to both the classifying agencies and the public, however, is the overall effect of the entire suite of pollutants on the health of people exposed to them.

3   Each group of pollutants is associated with particular adverse health symptoms, which can be further sorted into categories of respiratory or nonrespiratory conditions. Lung health is most affected by indoor air pollution, and the category of "respiratory symptoms" deals specifically with issues related to lung pathology. Though air pollutants enter the body through the respiratory system, some of the health effects they cause are not classified as respiratory issues. For example, breathing in cigarette smoke may cause headaches, but that ailment is not considered a respiratory symptom because it does not deal directly with lung health and function. Wheezing and asthma aggravation, however, which are also precipitated by exposure to cigarette smoke, fall under the category of respiratory symptoms. Respiratory symptoms include the subcategories of nose conditions (rhinitis and epistaxis), throat conditions (pharyngitis and aggravated asthma), and overall lung function (dyspnea and severe lung disease).

4   Nonrespiratory symptoms resulting from exposure to air pollutants include conjunctival irritation, nausea, headache, malaise, rashes, fever, hearing loss, tachycardia, retinal hemorrhage, myalgia, and cognitive impairment. Some of the most severe health effects, such as cognitive impairment, rapid heartbeat (tachycardia), and retinal hemorrhage are associated with exposure to carbon monoxide. Relatively less acute symptoms, such as headache, nasal congestion, cough, eye irritation, and malaise, can be associated with exposure to all or nearly all of the categories of pollutants, and in fact may result from exposure to multiple contaminants at once.

SKILL TIP

In some complicated classification readings, you may have trouble keeping track of the names of classes, subclasses, and examples. One easy way to keep things straight is to make an outline or a graphic organizer that shows these various levels of organization. For more about outlines and graphic organizers, see the section Using Outlines and Graphic Organizers (p. 60).

D. Read the questions and choose the best answers.

1. Which best completes this definition of sick building syndrome?

   Sick building syndrome is a condition in which many occupants of a building .... *but no physical cause can be discovered.*

   a. display similar symptoms
   b. work in places with poor ventilation
   c. pass infections like colds to one another
   d. are unhappy with their jobs

2. The organizations named in Paragraph 2 recognize four classes of indoor air pollutants. Which are NOT among those four? (Circle TWO.)

   a. substances produced by burning
   b. tobacco smoke
   c. living things that cause disease
   d. volatile organic compounds
   e. the suite of pollutants
   f. heavy metals

3. What is the basis of classification for the grouping of indoor air pollutants in Paragraph 2?

   a. The type of the material
   b. The source of the material
   c. The toxicity of the material
   d. The weight of the material

4. What is the best definition of *pathogenicity*?

   a. how much pain an illness can cause
   b. how likely a biological agent is to cause illness
   c. how quickly a disease is passed among people
   d. how hard it is to fight the symptoms of a disease

5. What is the basis for the classification, detailed throughout Paragraph 3, of symptoms caused by poor air quality?

   a. whether they indicate a serious health problem
   b. whether they come from nature or are human-made
   c. whether they are breathed in or not
   d. whether they have negative effects on the lungs or not

6. What is the basis for classifying respiratory symptoms into three subclasses?

   a. whether they affect the respiratory system
   b. how severe the symptoms are
   c. in which body part symptoms are apparent
   d. which kind of medicine each requires

Go to **MyEnglishLab** to complete a vocabulary exercise and skill practice, and to join in collaborative activities.

READING-WRITING CONNECTION
UNDERSTANDING AND PRODUCING REFERENCES TO OTHER SOURCES

WHY IT'S USEFUL By understanding references to other sources, you can get an overall understanding of how the piece you are reading fits in with other work in the field. You can see which topics have been important to writers in the field over several years, and you can appreciate the questions that still remain to be answered.

Most research papers published in professional journals follow a standard structure:

- Abstract
- Introduction
- Literature review
- Method

- Results
- Discussion
- Conclusion
- Reference list

The first two components (abstract, introduction) are short. The **literature review** is the first section that occupies more than one or two paragraphs. It is also where you'll see the highest concentration of references to the works of other writers. Similar references are scattered throughout other sections. In the last section (reference list), you'll find full publication information about the works referred to in short form throughout the text.

No matter where they occur, in-text references to other sources follow a special kind of shorthand. They are also framed in special language that you should learn to understand and use.

The following paragraph, which is excerpted from a literature review, contains some of the techniques used in referring to other sources. Notice the labeled features. (Sources and information are fictional, for demonstration purposes only.)

A generalization about the topic of studies to be cited in this paragraph

A summary of the findings in the cited work. This establishes its place in the thread of research.

A notation in parentheses giving the names of the researchers. (Parentheses are used because the authors' names do not have a grammatical role in the sentence.) Et al. means "and others." It indicates that, besides DeVries, there were at least four more authors of the study.

(1) Various factors besides temperature in the workplace environment have been well researched. (2) Danvers and Gopal (1991) researched the effects of relative humidity in office air—both in concert with temperature and as an independent factor—and (3) found a direct correlation between high humidity and reduced productivity. (4) A team at Scotus College (5) (DeVries et al.) replicated the Danvers-Gopal work and reached similar conclusions, but with the caveat that a threshold of 46 percent relative humidity applies—that is, the correlation is strong only when the relative humidity of office air is 46 percent or higher. The effects of office lighting have also been investigated (6) (Barneveld, Lodi, and Verona 1997; Bassett 2001; Carsten and Leow 2014). In nearly every study, fluorescent lighting has been found to limit workplace productivity as compared to incandescent or LED lighting. This effect may be stronger with female workers than with males (Vanderpool 2011). Researchers at Watervliet Polytechnic (Cardozo, Plinth, and Baxter 2013) examined the effect of dust mites—nearly invisible arachnids that feed on scales of dead skin falling from workers throughout the day—on productivity and found a negligible effect on most workers but a pronounced effect on those workers (about 10 percent of the general population) who are allergic to dust mite excrement. They recommend using floor surfaces other than carpeting to minimize the environment in which dust mites thrive.

*The **names of these researchers** have a grammatical role in the sentence (the subject of the verbs researched and found) so they are not in parentheses. Only the **date** of the study is parenthetical.*

A remark about or reference to the institution (college, university, or other organization) where the researchers worked. This helps give credibility to the study.

A reference to three studies all together in one set of parentheses. This means all three studies dealt with the same topic—in this case, the effects of lighting.

A. Read the passage. Paragraph 2 functions as a literature review. (Note: Sources referred to in the reading are fictional.)

Sick Building Syndrome

1   In certain buildings, a large number of individuals report symptoms ranging from dry eyes and itchy skin to headaches and fatigue. The symptoms appear associated with the building itself, but investigators cannot determine the source of the problem, and doctors treating the afflicted persons cannot find a clear diagnosis. This vague condition is known by the equally fuzzy term *sick building syndrome*. Sick building syndrome can be temporary or long-lasting and is often associated with poor air quality that results from inadequate ventilation, biological contaminants, volatile organic compounds (VOCs), and other pollutants. If a specific pollutant is identified and a clear diagnosis becomes apparent, the condition is known instead as a *building-related illness*. Studies show that a psychosomatic factor is sometimes present in cases of sick building syndrome, meaning that an individual's physical symptoms are sometimes caused by or notably influenced by his or her psychological state, and some studies (e.g., Trask and Haverman 2011) show that a higher proportion of individuals with neurosis report symptoms than those without neurosis. A stressful working environment contributes to the psycho-generative factor because it creates poor psychosocial conditions among workers.

2   Sick building syndrome as an illness is a relatively new phenomenon. The term came into common use in the medical field after a 1984 World Health Organization report (Geister et al.) stated that up to 30 percent of new and remodeled buildings worldwide might be subject to "excessive" complaints about indoor air quality. This was the first in a flurry of reports that debated the nature and even the very existence of the syndrome. DeLuria and Fulton (1989) speculate that the illness arose because of poor air circulation in offices and other workplaces in buildings that were constructed in the 1970s. A comprehensive review of American building standards (Leow, Burns, and VerHage 1991) notes that they were altered in the early 1970s to save energy as a reaction to the 1973 oil embargo, and the minimum required amount of outdoor air ventilation, which had been 15 cubic feet of outdoor air per minute for each building occupant, was reduced to 5 cubic feet per minute. The rate has since been increased to its previous standards, but many buildings constructed in the 1970s and 1980s are stuffy and unevenly heated and cooled. Sick building syndrome complaints are made primarily by women, and the reason for this is not fully understood. A number of possible factors have been outlined (e.g., Castleman 1992; Devlin and O'Meara 1996; DeVilliers 2001). Some point out a selection factor, in that jobs predominantly done by women are inordinately concentrated

in buildings of the type that draw sick-building complaints. A social structure in which women are more prone than men to discuss health effects has also been blamed by some (e.g., Putnam 1992) but has been dismissed by Princeton University's John Matheson and others as an unjust generalization about women.

3   To appreciate a typical case of sick building syndrome, imagine a building constructed in the 1980s that serves as a workplace for 50-some individuals. Over a ten-year period, anywhere from 30 to 70 percent of the workers complain about skin problems, fatigue, and other symptoms occurring after they spend significant time in the building (Diffen 2000; Roth 2004). Their symptoms disappear when they leave the premises. Even after maintenance personnel have replaced parts of the building's ventilation system, flooring, and eventually the entire ventilation system itself, symptoms persist. Multiple tests conducted over the years show no clear causative reason for the ill health effects. The relationship between the workers and the building management sours to the point where it creates a toxic culture of stress and hypersensitivity to health symptoms in the workplace (American Clerical League 2003).

4   Several general causes are associated with sick building syndrome. These causes include inadequate ventilation, either through building design or failures in the ventilation system itself, and chemical contamination from indoor sources, which include VOCs found in adhesives, upholstery, carpeting, pesticides, cleaning agents, and other building materials. An example of one such chemical is formaldehyde, a carcinogenic material. Tobacco smoke, too, is considered an indoor pollution source, though nowadays smoking is prohibited in most workplaces in the United States. Indoor contaminants also come from respirable particulate matter and other toxic compounds. Biological contaminants, such as molds and bacteria that grow in stagnant water in cooling systems, can cause sick building syndrome as well. Radon and asbestos, both of which cause long-term diseases, are not, however, included as causes for sick building syndrome. Why are

they exempt? Primarily because they lack the immediacy in physical reaction the other causes are known to induce. Another source thought to cause sick building syndrome is chemical contaminants from outdoor sources. The reason for this seemingly paradoxical inclusion is that outdoor air eventually ends up indoors. Extensive outdoor pollution from motor vehicle exhaust and industrial emissions is not limited by barriers such as a building's walls and will seep into a structure and influence indoor air quality.

5   Determining causes of indoor air pollution can be a thorny process. A simple sampling of specific air pollutants typically does not yield answers because individual pollutants rarely exceed level requirements. Regular maintenance of ventilation systems and replacement of building materials like carpeting, on the other hand, have been found to be effective at mitigating sick building syndrome complaints. In addition, encouraging more "green" design elements such as low-VOC paints, nontoxic pesticides, and high-efficiency air filters can help overall indoor air quality.

6   Sometimes, if suspected causes are addressed in a given case, workers' reported symptoms may lessen or disappear. However, other times, despite mitigation efforts, sick building syndrome symptoms persist. The degree to which psychosomatic symptoms cause sick building syndrome is unknown. Health professionals have proven that emotions can influence physical symptoms, and several studies suggest this may be as important a causal factor as any of the other causes for sick building syndrome. If the working environment grows strained and tense, it can provoke stress, which in turn can cause an individual to have a heightened awareness of his or her environment, and in some cases spark psychological mechanisms in the body that trigger symptoms. Much as a "placebo effect" produces expected positive results, or adverse side effects, a stressful environment is thought to influence sick building symptoms. However, it should be noted that psychosomatic and psychosocial factors of sick building syndrome do not mean the illness is not real. Sick building syndrome is multilayered, and the reasons and causes for the symptoms are complex.

B. The right-hand column of the chart describes features found in Paragraph 2 of "Sick Building Syndrome." Use the Paragraph 2 excerpts from the box to complete the chart.

> (e.g., Castleman 1992; Devlin and O'Meara 1996; DeVilliers 2001)
>
> et al.
>
> DeLuria and Fulton
>
> (Leow, Burns, and VerHage, 1991)
>
> Princeton University's John Matheson
>
> The illness arose because of poor air circulation in offices and other workplaces in buildings that were constructed in the 1970s.
>
> This was the first in a flurry of reports that debated the nature and even the very existence of the syndrome.

	Element from "Sick Building Syndrome"	Feature of Reference to Other Sources
1		An expression that means "and others"
2		The names of these researchers have a grammatical role in the sentence, so they are not in parentheses.
3		A generalization about the topic of studies to be cited in this paragraph
4		A summary of the findings in the cited work
5		A notation in parentheses giving the names of the researchers and the year the research was published
6		A reference to three studies all together in one set of parentheses. This means all three studies dealt with the same topic—in this case, sick building syndrome and women.
7		A remark about the college (or university, or other organization) where the researcher worked, which helps give credibility to the study

C. Read the questions and choose the best answers.

1. What attitude does the author express in Paragraph 1 about people who claim to have sick building syndrome?

   a. If they saw doctors, they would find out they have some other condition.

   b. They are being dishonest because the symptoms they report don't actually exist.

   c. In reality, they have building-related illness, not sick building syndrome.

   d. They are truly sick, even if the building itself is not the verifiable cause.

2. According to Paragraph 2, what relationship exists between indoor air quality and energy policies of the 1970s and 1980s?

   a. The policies encouraged the burning of dirty fuels, which pollute indoor air.

   b. Policies meant to save energy reduced buildings' airflow too much.

   c. Air-conditioning saved energy but introduced poisonous chemicals into buildings.

   d. Saving energy meant keeping buildings either too hot or too cold.

3. Near the end of Paragraph 3, the word *toxic* is used to refer to ....

   a. chemicals in the original construction of the building

   b. materials used in trying to fix the building

   c. the relationships among people in the building

   d. the effect of the company's problems on a whole city

4. In Paragraph 4, the author mentions where mold and bacteria grow. Why is this location significant?

   a. It explains how the contaminants could affect the whole building.

   b. It shows how outside contaminants can move indoors.

   c. It indicates why those contaminants are not really a problem.

   d. It demonstrates why those contaminants can't be removed.

5. The author doesn't classify radon and asbestos among the possible causes of sick building syndrome. Why not?

   a. They are naturally occurring substances.

   b. They don't have an immediate impact.

   c. They don't actually make anyone sick.

   d. They are no longer present in modern buildings.

6. According to Paragraph 6, which relationship exists?

   a. Stress can take away symptoms of sick building syndrome.

   b. A heightened environmental awareness can lead to psychosomatic reactions.

   c. A workplace full of sick people can become tension-filled.

   d. Psychosomatic symptoms can cause an individual to get sick.

> **ACADEMIC CULTURE NOTE**
>
> *Academic researchers treat each other with respect. Even if you strongly disagree with someone, you should refer to that person's work in polite terms without implying that the other person's work is unimportant or not valuable. In the literature reviews you read, you may see statements like the following:* Smith and Jones investigated X, but
> - the sample size was restricted.
> - the research method did not take into account …
> - there was a possibility of rater bias.
> - their conclusions assume that X, and this is questionable.
> - it leaves several questions unanswered.
>
> *There are hundreds of such statements that can be used to express polite disagreement. Notice that the statements almost always refer to technical aspects of the study or the report. They should never refer to the researchers personally.*

D. Read the passages, each of which includes all necessary publication information about the source. Then complete each reference using the information from the passage. Not every piece of publication information will be used in every reference.

> "Of all the molds common in residential buildings, so-called 'black mold'—usually a shorthand term for *Stachybotrys atra* (also known as *Stachybotrys chartarum*)—is the most dreaded. Successful lawsuits by tenants exposed to black mold have cost landlords and their insurers millions of dollars in the United States, so the very term is anathema in such circles."
> From: William Soltys and Vineet Ratham, "The Particular Tragedy of Black Mold." Published in the July 2014 issue of *Property Management* magazine.

1. _Soltys and Ratham (2014)_ note that landlords and insurance companies hate to hear any reference to black mold.

> "Strictly speaking, *S. atra* itself is not toxic. The toxicity of molds comes from chemicals they produce, called mycotoxins. This may seem like an unimportant distinction, but it has vital implications for the methods one might employ in dealing with the discovery of black mold inside a building."
> From: The American Air Quality Association, "Black Mold." Published in 2007 online at www.amaqa.org.

2. Knowing that the real danger in black mold is from mycotoxins—chemicals produced by the organism—can guide people in dealing with a mold infestation ....

> "Bioaerosols are biological substances (or substances produced by biological agents) that remain suspended in air and are easily spread via wind, ventilation system currents, and other air movements."
> From: Howard Bailey and several other authors, *Air and Health*, a textbook published in 2015 by Borchert Press, Brooklyn, NY.

3. Bailey et al. (..), in the book .... , define the term *bioaerosol* as ....

> "Spores of *S. atra* can grow on a number of surfaces, but they are by far most common on materials rich in cellulose that are chronically damp. Wooden trim in a wet basement provides the mold colony a perfect mix of darkness, humidity, and nutrients for growth."
> From: "Damp and Dangerous: Before You Clean the Basement." No author is named. It is dated Summer 2013. The article is found at www.customcare.biz.

TIP

When No Author Is Given Especially with sources found online, there may be no author listed. How do you refer to such a source? 1) If you can see the name of a company or organization that operates the site—e.g., the National Bricklayers' Association, the Huffington Post—use that as the "author." 2) If you do not even have that much information, use the main part of the URL—e.g., nba.org, huffingtonpost.com.

NOTE: Sometimes it's acceptable to use such authorless material, if you trust the publishing source. However, material without authors may not be dependable in all cases. Use your judgment.

4. Basements are perfect places for mold growth, especially if they are wet and have wood in them. ....

"*S. Atra* can have serious health effects on pets as well as humans. A dog that suddenly loses all energy, refuses to eat, or starts bleeding at the mouth or nose may have been poisoned via contact with the toxins produced by black mold."

From: Marisol V. Ortega and Frances Gardette, "Veterinary Concerns with Black Mold." It was posted online in November 2001 to the site PetsAtHome, which is at www. petsathome.biz.

"Dogs more than cats fall victim to mycotoxin poisoning. Often, a dog is drawn to an infested area by the smell of a food morsel dropped on the floor and inadvertently kicked into a moldy corner."

From: James DeHaan, "Pet Safety in Moldy Homes," published in 2009 in the magazine *Home Quality*.

"Despite their keen sense of smell, dogs are surprisingly vulnerable to mold exposure. Indeed, it is the dog's habit of vigorous sniffing that sets up this particular danger."

From: Jamie Wilson, published online in 2011 as "Clean Dogs in Dirty Houses." Available at www.doggdomicile.com.

5. Pets, especially dogs, are frequent victims of exposure to black mold and the mycotoxins it produces ....

(NOTE: Your completion should indicate that the information comes from three sources.)

"Our survey covered claims to insurance companies of black-mold infestations in the Indianapolis metropolitan area from July 2012 to September 2013. Each of the 89 claims was followed to its resolution. Significantly, about one-third (35%) of the claims were found, on further examination, to be erroneous in that the reported substance was not, in fact, any species of *Stachybotrys*."

From: John F. P. Kolenda, Marian Corzine, and Colin Gretsch, who are researchers at Dane University. Their results were published in December 2016 as "Claims and Resolutions in Black-Mold Cases" in the *Journal of Health Coverage*.

6. A study conducted .... shows that more than a third of black-mold insurance claims ....

"Mold fighters worldwide can take a lesson from the traditional Japanese practice of airing out one's futons—if possible, in direct sunlight—nearly every day. Molds of all sorts are killed off by fresh dry air and the sun's rays."

From: Taro Harada, "Lessons in Fighting Mold," an article in *Honshu Homes* magazine, published in December 1998.

7. Referencing the Japanese custom of putting futons outside for some air, ... reminds us that molds can't take sunlight or dryness.

Go to **MyEnglishLab** to complete a vocabulary exercise and skill practice, and to join in collaborative activities.

For more about REFERENCES TO OTHER SOURCES, see |OC| ENVIRONMENTAL ENGINEERING .

LANGUAGE SKILL
UNDERSTANDING AND USING CLARIFIERS

WHY IT'S USEFUL By recognizing and understanding expressions that clarify and provide more information about a topic, you can more efficiently grasp the scope of an author's statements.

In scholarly material and academic settings, you will often encounter sequences of words that indicate an author's intent to clarify a passage. These **clarifiers** are signposts for further explanations or additional information or details about a certain topic. Recognizing and understanding the meanings and uses of clarifiers is essential in order to function at a high level in university courses.

Clarifier	Example
to clarify	The data demonstrated that there was a correlation between the employees' perception of the appropriateness of office temperature and their levels of productivity. **To clarify**, the more an employee believed that the office space was appropriately heated and cooled, the more work he or she got done in a given period of time.
should be clear that	It is important that large buildings with many residents are equipped with ventilation devices. With that said, we **should be clear that** this is not a "one-size-fits-all" situation." Each building should be assessed and ventilation devices compared to determine the best one for a given building.
to be perfectly clear	The way in which the sickness spread was through contamination of the city's water system. **To be perfectly clear**, bacteria from water drawn from a polluted source grew and was delivered to every unfortunate soul who drank tap water.
this means that	The business is one of the strongest performing companies in the region. **This means that** it reports higher profits than the majority of companies in the area.
in other words	It was concluded last year that the rate of occurrence of asthma among children increased substantially over the last 25 years. **In other words**, the number of children affected by this condition went up a lot during that time period.
i.e.	System failures, **i.e.**, unexplained complete shutdowns of a system, can be caused by human error or technical problems.
that is	Employees who had reported symptoms of sick building syndrome—**that is**, a situation in which building occupants report a variety of health problems that seem to be linked to the indoor environment—were awarded settlements.
that is to say	In terms of funding, the charity receives most of its money from private donations; **that is to say**, almost all of the funds that flow in come from individual citizens or companies.
to put it another way	Given the size of its engine, the truck is extremely powerful. **To put it another way**, it could outrun pretty much every other vehicle on the road.
this becomes readily apparent	Customer-generated electricity (through solar panels, small wind-turbines, etc.) is a burgeoning factor in the energy market. **This becomes readily apparent** when we consider that rooftop solar generation carries more than 30 percent of the grid load in some locations.
this becomes all the more evident	Faulty ventilation systems can cause the air quality in buildings to be inadequately regulated. **This becomes all the more evident** upon reviewing studies that blame such systems for more than 20 percent of air-quality complaints in workplace settings.
this bears some explanation	As demonstrated in Figure 4, the building envelope is characterized by several breaches. **This bears some explanation**. Because the building is not well sealed—due to cracks in the structure and small gaps around doors and windows—a significant amount of outside air enters it every hour.

| to further explain | Many opposed the recycling policy. **To further explain**, their opposition was due to the hefty fine incurred if they didn't participate. |
| in simpler / clearer terms | The findings were deemed to be profoundly impactful on a local scale and deeply resonant globally. **In simpler terms**, the results were significant. |

EXERCISE 4

Complete the sentences. Use the clarifiers from the chart. There may be more than one correct answer possible in some cases, although punctuation may need to be modified.

1. Steps are being taken to ensure that no violence comes about as a result of the conflict with the neighboring country. .... government officials from both countries are working together to devise elaborate plans to keep peace between the dissident groups.

2. Study abroad is often the main reason a student's language skills develop. .... when a student is later able to discuss complex topics.

3. The engineers who examined the new model for the mechanical system were amazed by it. ...., it contained sophisticated components and mechanisms that they had never seen—or worked with—before. This would be a challenge.

4. While it is clear that we understand the symptoms of sick building syndrome, we must work to analyze the entire problem; ...., we must conduct extensive research on its possible causes and find out how to best treat its wide variety of symptoms.

5. The installation of the HVAC system led to remarkable savings. ...., it cut energy expenses in half.

6. While some schools have protocols for when ventilation systems fail, the majority lack such procedures. ...., it is likely no one will know what to do.

EXERCISE 5

Complete the chart. Use an online corpus, dictionary, or Internet browser to investigate how the clarifiers are used in academic writing. Compare answers with a partner.

		Where in a Sentence Does the Expression Typically Appear?	Which Parts of Speech Often Precede or Follow the Expression?	In Which Contexts Does the Expression Typically Appear?
1	to clarify			
2	to be perfectly clear			
3	this bears some explanation			
4	this becomes all the more evident			
5	should be clear that			
6	in simpler / clearer terms			

Go to **MyEnglishLab** to complete a skill practice.

APPLY YOUR SKILLS

WHY IT'S USEFUL By applying the skills you have learned in this unit, you can gain a deep understanding of this challenging reading about the impact that various energy-saving devices have on indoor air quality.

BEFORE YOU READ

A. Discuss these questions with one or more students.

1. How concerned are you about saving energy? What do you do to be more energy efficient?

2. Many homes and buildings are equipped with ventilation systems. Do you know if the building where you live or work has one? If it does, do you think it has any effect on your comfort while you are inside the building? Explain why or why not.

3. Look at the title of the reading on the following page. What specific topics do you think you might encounter? Think about what you already know about energy-saving devices and indoor air quality.

B. Imagine that you will be participating in a small group discussion about the passage "The Impact of Energy-Saving Devices on Indoor Air Quality," which begins on the next page. Your group will be discussing the following questions. Keep these questions in mind as you read the passage.

1. What are some causes of poor indoor air quality?

2. Why are stand-alone dehumidifiers not discussed in depth in this reading?

3. What do turnstiles or permanent infrared sensors allow demand-controlled ventilation systems to do?

4. Energy-saving devices were installed in a building in the Upper Peninsula of Michigan. How did the system that was installed function? How did the building benefit from the installation?

5. Why is ventilation extremely important for net-zero energy buildings?

C. Review the Unit Skills Summary. As you read the passage, apply the skills you learned in this unit.

UNIT SKILLS SUMMARY

Understand definitions and classifications.
- Expand your knowledge of both specialized terms and general vocabulary, and understand relationships between similar and dissimilar things.

Recognize and understand definitions within a text.
- Identify and comprehend expressions the writer uses to signify the definition of a term.

Work with classifications.
- Understand the most fundamental relationships between pieces of information.

Understand and produce references to other sources.
- Gain an understanding of how information in the reading fits in with the work of other writers in the same field.

Understand and use clarifiers.
- Familiarize yourself with expressions that frequently appear in academic writing to clarify and provide more information about a topic.

A. Read the passage. Annotate and take notes as necessary.

The Impact of Energy-Saving Devices on Indoor Air Quality

1 Fresh, clean indoor air is a necessary condition for human health. The energy required to achieve unpolluted, high quality indoor air, however, often comes at a high cost, both in dollars and to the planet. Out of a desire to find a balance between maintaining a healthy indoor environment and lowering energy consumption, people are increasingly constructing new buildings with environmentally conscious features and relying on energy-efficient devices that can either be installed in new buildings or retrofitted to older buildings. Such devices provide energy efficiency primarily in the form of **heating, ventilation, and air-conditioning (HVAC) systems,** which regulate indoor air quality. Since these systems consume the most energy in a structure, any increment of efficiency can have a significant effect on the building's operational costs.

2 Indoor environmental quality, or to put it in clearer terms, the healthfulness of a building, is influenced by many factors including a building's lighting, moisture level, and chiefly, its air quality. Poor indoor air quality can result from various classes of contaminants, including mold, airborne chemicals, and dangerous gases like radon. Indoor air contaminants bring about a number of different kinds of maladies—including skin irritation, respiratory issues, headaches, and fatigue. Pollution can cause more serious problems as well, in both the short and long term. The difficulty of maintaining clean indoor air is compounded if there is inward leaking, that is, if outdoor air pollution from fuel emissions and industrial processes seeps into homes, schools, and other structures. Many people spend up to 90 percent of their time indoors (Boorstein, 2011), and pollution quickly builds up in closed spaces, much as smoke accumulates in a glass jar if it is placed over a burning stick

of incense. The more airtight the building, the greater the need for mechanical ventilation.

3 Building laws require certain amounts of ventilation and access to fresh air, but as Patterson (2015) notes, this too presents a problem when considering the cost and emissions from HVAC systems. In a world that is facing climbing global temperatures due to emissions from human activities such as the heating and cooling of structures, using more energy to improve air quality—and, not incidentally, increasing carbon emissions—can be a hard sell. Of course, the extent to which individuals employ energy-saving measures such as simply turning off the air conditioner in the summer, opening the windows, and wearing appropriate clothing is worth considering, as these types of modifications would cut monthly bills and save energy. However, in many cases—if it is exceedingly hot, if an office building or school has no easily accessible windows, or if an individual's asthma is worsened by outdoor air—people feel they must turn to mechanical ventilation.

4 The key to a balance of energy consumption and air quality lies in using energy-saving devices that can be installed in new buildings or retrofitted into existing structures. These systems fit under the umbrella of HVAC-related machines and consist of three main devices: demand-controlled ventilation systems, variable frequency drives, and energy recovery systems. While we should be clear that other devices, such as a standalone dehumidifier, undoubtedly improve indoor air quality by reducing moisture and mold growth, they are not included in the discussion because they are not components of a building's complex and energy-consuming HVAC system.

5 Demand-controlled ventilation systems rely on a control system that calculates occupancy levels by sensors that most commonly detect **carbon dioxide**, which is a colorless, odorless gas exhaled by humans. The more people in a room, the higher the level of carbon dioxide. The system also uses other occupancy-counting

Continued

measures such as turnstiles or sensors. With these sensors, the demand-controlled HVAC system mechanically adjusts the volume of air—typically by opening the **damper**, or valve—based on how many people are in the building. A demand-controlled ventilation system acts as the shutoff switch in an HVAC system, regulating indoor air according to occupancy of the building. Studies show that such ventilation systems save energy, reduce power consumption, and can pay for themselves in a relatively short amount of time. In the absence of such systems, a building's energy plant might work unnecessarily hard at an unnecessary cost.

6   Demand-controlled ventilation systems often use variable frequency drives, which are also known by the terms "variable speed drives," "adjustable drives," or simply "drives." A variable-frequency drive refers to a control device for the motor of an HVAC system. It adjusts the speed of the fans in the motor when the unit is not needed to operate at full capacity. To further explain, like a carbon dioxide sensor, a drive can be programmed to allow the motor to operate at full capacity during times when the occupancy level is high, such as during a school day, and to slow the system down during lower-occupancy times, like nighttime. A variable drive is often connected to the sensors of a demand-controlled ventilation system.

7   Another energy-saving device for HVAC systems is known as an "energy recovery ventilation" system, which serves regions with extreme climates particularly well in terms of energy conservation. This system exchanges heat between the outgoing air and the air being ventilated into a building, thus using less energy for heating. In one example where such a system has benefited occupants of a building, school officials retrofitted—that is, completely overhauled the HVAC of—a 1960s building in the frigid Upper Peninsula of Michigan (Heikkila 2015). The building was unevenly heated with an aging HVAC system that was both inefficient and costly. School leaders installed an energy recovery system in addition to a demand-controlled ventilation system composed of carbon dioxide sensors and variable speed drives. These systems, along with several other energy-saving devices, generated $48,000 annually in energy savings.

8   Some school districts, homeowners, and other commercial building developers are going a step further in terms of energy efficiency. In addition to using the three aforementioned HVAC-related devices, many builders are installing onsite solar panels to achieve a net-zero or nearly **net-zero energy building**. To put it another way, the building meets all of its energy needs through renewable resources. The approach depends on which category the structure falls in: new construction versus existing. In new buildings, architectural elements can help achieve net-zero energy environments. Ventilation is a key component of keeping the air healthy in such structures because net-zero energy homes and buildings are typically airtight. In older buildings, near net-zero energy can only be achieved through renovating the structure and retrofitting the devices. Increasingly, school officials and other commercial building developers are working toward this goal by installing HVAC energy-efficient systems first and leaving space for solar panels to be installed at a later time.

9   Research shows that HVAC system improvements result in measurable reductions in energy consumption. Indoor air quality is a significant part of the equation and cannot be disregarded on the basis of the desire to construct ever-more efficient buildings. In other words, "airtight" is a good feature only if the air inside is good. Energy-saving devices like demand-controlled ventilation, variable frequency drives, and energy recovery ventilation systems all supply healthy indoor air and can work either together or individually to help owners lower energy costs and breathe easy.

B. **Reread the discussion questions in Before You Read, Part B. Is there anything you cannot answer? Which of the reading skills you have learned in this unit can you use to find the answers?**

Go to **MyEnglishLab** to read the passage again and answer critical thinking questions.

THINKING CRITICALLY

You just read about the many benefits of installing energy-saving devices in buildings, including improved air quality and energy savings over the long term. If a country's government were to attempt to pass a law requiring all educational buildings to be equipped with devices like energy recovery ventilation systems and demand-controlled ventilation systems, would you support it? Why or why not? In your deliberation, consider whether any points were left out of the reading and if there would be any disadvantages to passing a law like this. Explain your ideas to another student.

THINKING VISUALLY

The graph depicts US energy consumption by type, from 2004 through 2014. Carefully analyze the changes in consumption over this period. Consider what was taking place during these years as well as what you have read about in this unit. What factors do you think could explain the trends seen? Explain your thoughts to another student.

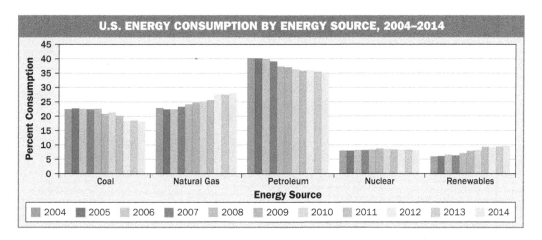

THINKING ABOUT LANGUAGE

Read these excerpts from "The Impact of Energy-Saving Devices on Indoor Air Quality." Underline the clarifiers. How does the presence of each contribute to the meaning of the sentence?

1. Indoor environmental quality, or to put it in clearer terms, the healthfulness of a building, is influenced by many factors including a building's lighting, moisture level, and chiefly, its air quality.

2. The difficulty of maintaining clean indoor air is compounded if there is inward leaking, that is, if outdoor air pollution from fuel emissions and industrial processes seeps into homes, schools, and other structures.

3. While we should be clear that other devices, such as a standalone dehumidifier, undoubtedly improve indoor air quality by reducing moisture and mold growth, they are not included in the discussion because they are not components of a building's complex and energy-consuming HVAC system.

4. To further explain, like a carbon dioxide sensor, a drive can be programmed to allow the motor to operate at full capacity during times when the occupancy level is high, such as during a school day, and to slow the system down during lower-occupancy times, like nighttime.

5. In one example where such a system has benefited occupants of a building, school officials retrofitted—that is, completely overhauled the HVAC of—a 1960s building in the frigid Upper Peninsula of Michigan (Heikkila 2015).

6. To put it another way, the building meets all of its energy needs through renewable resources.

7. In other words, "airtight" is a good feature only if the air inside is good.

 Go to **MyEnglishLab** to listen to Professor Hildemann and to complete a self-assessment.

Part 3 presents authentic content written by university professors. Academically rigorous application and assessment activities allow for a synthesis of the skills developed in Parts 1 and 2.

Struggle influences social change.

SOCIOLOGY

The Art of Strategy

UNIT PROFILE

In this unit, you will read about strategy, illustrated through the concepts of investment, leverage, and war to show how it plays out in real-world decision-making. In the online extended reading, you will see strategy in action in the form of a civil rights campaign. As a capstone to the unit, you will research people who have invested in social change and present your findings.

EXTENDED READING

BEFORE YOU READ

Discuss these questions with another student.

1. What comes to mind when you hear or see the word *strategy*? Do you have strategies for achieving personal, financial, social, academic, or career goals? If so, what are they? If not, explain what you know—or can speculate—about the strategies of a company, organization, or person you know well.

2. Imagine you're on a sports team that has made it all the way to the Olympics. What actions might you take prior to as well as during the championship game to ensure victory?

3. What do you know about financial investments? Do you (or someone you know) invest in the stock market? If so, explain what you invest in, how you make decisions, how you calculate potential gains and losses, and so on. If not: Would you ever consider investing? What would you have to do to prepare for making investments?

4. Imagine you are a high-ranking military official and your country is at war. You have to come up with strategies for defeating the enemy and winning the war. What factors would you take into consideration in developing a strategic plan?

READ

Read the passage. Then answer the questions after each section.

PART 3

Thinking About Strategy

INTRODUCTION

1 What is strategy and why is it important to think about it? How can thinking analytically about strategy enable you to develop better, more effective strategies for any organization to which you belong?

2   This essay ventures to tackle these questions, providing a brief introduction to this field of intellectual and moral inquiry.[1] It may be surprising to talk about the idea of "strategy" in this way since we implicitly and instinctively develop and implement strategies every day. For example, we take x approach rather than y approach to solving one of our problems. But this essay suggests that thinking about strategy in greater depth opens up a rich and useful field of analysis and reflection, one with a deep intellectual history. Moreover, thinking about strategy is a moral inquiry because it is necessary for first designing effective plans for action, and then implementing those plans effectively to make a better world. The question of what makes a better world is a moral question, a question that each person must answer for himself or

herself in alignment with personal values, ethics, and aspirations. I cannot tell you whether your vision of a better world has more or less merit as compared with someone else's vision. But I can tell you that thinking carefully and deeply about strategy will increase your ability to succeed in turning that vision into reality.

3   For purposes of this essay, I will discuss the concept of strategy as it applies to organizations and teams. These include governments, business enterprises, nonprofit organizations, philanthropic foundations, and teams of any kind.

WHAT IS STRATEGY?

4 Speaking of teams, let's talk about sports, specifically, a game hundreds of millions of people all over the world know and love. In nearly every country, this sport is called football (in the United States, it is referred to as "soccer.") Imagine you are playing on a football team. What is your purpose? As a player, your immediate problem is how to be excellent in your position. Excellence in your position is defined by the extent to which you are able to take actions on the field in support of the team's collaborative efforts to get the ball into the net.

5   What is the team's purpose in the game? To get the ball into the net as many times as possible? While this might galvanize the highest level of team motivation for the players, this is not the answer. The team's purpose in a given game is simply to win the game. The definition of victory in football is very simple: for your team to get the ball into the right net at least once more than the opposing team is able to do so in the opposite net.

6   Imagine now that you are the coach of a football team. What is your purpose? To maximize total goals across a season? No. Your purpose is for your team to win as many games as possible throughout a season to achieve the highest comparative ranking vis-à-vis the other teams in the league. Over the course of multiple

Continued

---

[1] The author of the essay wishes to acknowledge the important work of Sir Lawrence Freedman, and his book Strategy: A History (Oxford 2013), which has significantly informed the analysis set out in this essay, especially in the section FRAMEWORK #3: The Metaphor of War.

seasons, the mission is to sustain the highest possible ranking year after year. But perhaps this may not be your full purpose. Your purpose is actually for your team to win as many games as necessary—and especially the priority games—to enable it to emerge as the top team in your league. At the highest level, your purpose is to win the World Cup.

7   But, of course, you likely have a wide variety of additional goals as a coach. One might be to build comradeship—loyalty and lifelong friendships between the members of your team. Another might be to encourage the growth of your players in skill, competence, and commitment. Yet another goal might be to mobilize the community to support your team emotionally and financially. Evidently, a coach can have a wide variety of goals that could be motivating the person in his or her job.

8   Which of these goals is more important than the other? The first answer to this question is, *I can't tell you.* That is because the selection of a goal or purpose is primarily a matter of values, and values are neither objective nor empirical. Therefore, a first, critically important step a team should take is hiring a coach whose fundamental values align with those of the team members.

9   For example, my son is on a sports team that is looking for a coach. There are several excellent coaches available in our community. But as a matter of values, we have decided that we will not hire a coach who yells at the kids on the team under any circumstances. Even if that coach has an outstanding record of pushing previous teams to victory. As parents who are involved with our children's team, it is more important for us to have a coach who cares more about the physical, emotional, and moral development of our children—and who is able to motivate kids to take responsibility and learn discipline, sportsmanship, and teamwork—than to have a coach who comes with an impressive record of winning but who cares less about the personal growth of the kids. Even if we could find the "best" coach in the world (when it comes to a track record of victories), we would not hire that person if we believed that he or she might not care about nurturing and encouraging our children.

10   Again I ask, which goal is most important? The second answer to this question is one word, *success*. For the parents of children on my son's team, success means personal development, and, in fact, we prioritize it over victory in any particular game as well as throughout the season overall. But for a football team at the highest level of performance, when we consider *success*, it is defined much more simply by the team's achievements on the field. A coach who fails to deliver—in the sense of winning as many games as possible given the team's assets (capacity, skill, and resources)—will very likely not be retained. From this discussion, we can see that the mission of a coach should be aligned with the mission of a team.

CHECK WHAT YOU'VE LEARNED (Paragraphs 1–10)

Think about what you have just read. Answer each question. Then continue to the next part of the reading.

1. The author says that "thinking about strategy is a moral inquiry." What does he mean by that?

   ....

   ....

2. How does the author define the objectives of a soccer player and a soccer team? In what ways do these goals differ from those of a soccer coach?

   ....

   ....

3. In Paragraphs 9 and 10, what is the author's reason for discussing his son's sports team and the parents' search for a coach?

   ....

   ....

4. In the last sentence of Paragraph 9, the author indicates that he and the other parents are looking for a coach who cares about "nurturing and encouraging" their children. What connotations do these words carry? How would the tone of the sentence change if the author had instead written that they were seeking a coach who would not be "hostile and abusive" toward their children?

   ....

   ....

5. How would you describe the author's tone in this section? Cite specific examples from the reading in your explanation. ....

   ....

"Thinking About Strategy," *continued*

11 Now we have come to the first step in our analysis of strategy: the difference between *mission* and *strategy*. **Mission** is the overarching goal or purpose you are trying to achieve. **Strategy**, on the other hand, is the plan you will develop and implement to achieve your fundamental objectives. In the lexicon of corporations, foundations, and nonprofit organizations, *strategy* refers to a coordinated set of decisions and actions designed to enable the organization to achieve its mission. Strategic plans are instrumental for any organization; they define in a detailed, systematic way *how* the organization seeks to achieve its fundamental goals—by what means, according to what criteria, in what sequence, and with which partners.

12   Thinking analytically and comprehensively about strategy increases the likelihood that your organization will develop a good strategy. This is extremely important because without a good strategy, prospects for achieving the organization's mission are significantly reduced. This raises the following question: What is a good strategy? The answer depends on a wide variety of factors. The simple answer is that the measure

Continued

of the worth of a strategy is its **effectiveness**. But it turns out that thinking about the effectiveness of a strategy is also complicated, especially because we cannot know in advance whether Plan A will be more or less effective than Plan B. This is because all strategic decisions, by definition, occur under circumstances of uncertainty, competition, scarcity, and other contingencies and obstacles.

13   If we had a crystal ball that allowed us to learn the consequences of various strategic choices, we would be in an excellent position to select the best of the competing alternative paths available to us. But no such crystal ball exists. This is why it can be illuminating to take a step back and think about the implications of various conceptual frameworks for understanding how strategy works. Toward this goal, scholars and practitioners have used a variety of metaphors to help illustrate the role of strategy in political campaigns, business corporations, nonprofit organizations, and philanthropic foundations. In this essay, I highlight three metaphors: 1) the metaphor of *investment*, 2) the metaphor of *leverage*, and 3) the metaphor of *war*.

FRAMEWORK #1:
The Metaphor of *Investment*

14 Strategy always requires decisions about the optimal investment of scarce organizational

assets. These include time, money, energy, and effort. As a starting place for understanding this metaphor, think about a professional investor in the stock market. Should the investor purchase stock *x* or *y*? What mix of stocks and bonds would create an optimal portfolio? How can this portfolio enable the investor to optimally diversify and manage risks in a given market environment? To what extent and how should the investor invest his or her own time and resources in the process of due diligence to investigate and analyze data in order to enable empirically sound decision making?

15   Assume that the fundamental goal of the investor is to achieve the highest possible expected return on the underlying investment. This requires cost/benefit analysis, including an analysis of the **opportunity cost** of the investment even when there is a positive expected return. Thus, in retroactively assessing the investment decision-making process, it is necessary but not sufficient to ensure that the process aligns closely with the mission and strategy of the investor (as an individual or organization). Nor is it sufficient to simply determine that application of the decision-making criteria in a given case—say, to purchase stock in Apple rather than GM—has generated a profit. Rather, it is necessary to go one step further and compare what is with what *could have been*—i.e., to compare the investment

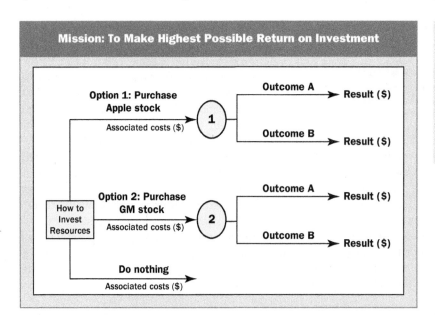

Mission: To Make Highest Possible Return on Investment

Option 1: Purchase Apple stock
Associated costs ($)
1
Outcome A → Result ($)
Outcome B → Result ($)

How to Invest Resources

Option 2: Purchase GM stock
Associated costs ($)
2
Outcome A → Result ($)
Outcome B → Result ($)

Do nothing
Associated costs ($)

> **TIP**
> The abbreviations i.e. and e.g. are often confused. The abbreviation i.e. is used to mean "in other words," whereas e.g. means "for example." Notice i.e. used in Paragraph 15 as well as in Paragraphs 18 and 20. The abbreviation e.g. is employed in Paragraph 31.

outcome of that Apple stock purchase with what would have resulted from a GM stock purchase, had it been made.

16   Keeping with our example, if the profit on the GM stock turns out to be greater than the profit on the Apple stock, then the optimal investment was not made. This does not necessarily mean that the criteria and procedures used to make the investment decision were incorrect or that they require revision. For example, the strategy might be to achieve long-term gains over the short term, or to prefer moderate gains from lower-risk investments as compared to higher-risk alternatives with more dramatic upside potential and downside risk. However, it does mean that the decision-making criteria need to be evaluated and refined to accurately assess the opportunity costs in past decisions so that the investor can increase the likelihood that future decisions will yield better results.

17   The metaphor of investment enables organizations to think about strategic decisions as investments of scarce assets. This metaphor suggests that, in each instance, these decisions should be made in close alignment with a clear, well-researched, and well-designed strategic plan and in accordance with a comprehensive and well-executed cost-benefit analysis, properly taking into account the opportunity costs of all decisions. It also suggests that strategic decisions should be made with a realistic and accurate assessment of a variety of factors including the following: internal organizational capacity and human resources; financial assets, fundraising capability, and comparative investment choices; competitive pressures; external partners and alliances that might facilitate increased performance; and last but not least, likelihood of success.

FRAMEWORK #2:
The Metaphor of *Leverage*

18 Most of us are involved in relatively small organizations and teams in contrast to the "big players" in the world socioeconomic system. How can we move the world? We can't do it—at least not by ourselves. But maybe it is possible with a little help from our friends, with the added strength and resources of partnering organizations, with the application of tools, instruments, and technologies, and most importantly, with the power of creative strategy based on the principle of value multiplication, i.e., *leverage*. Leverage is a strategy related to the laws of physics, in which a lever—a bar made of wood or another firm, rigid material—is used to augment the strength of an actor seeking to lift a heavy weight or pry something open. Archimedes (c. 287–212 BCE) emphasized the extraordinary capacity-enhancing power of leverage in his quote, "Give me a lever and a fulcrum, and I will move the world." Here, the iconic Greek mathematician emphasized the extraordinary capacity-enhancing power of leverage.

19   Imagine a stone blocking a road that people need for travel, or closing a cave that people need to enter. People have failed to lift or move the stone by the force of their own strength. Struggling with this problem, ancient Greek scientists discovered the lever, a tool to significantly augment the power of the human body. However, in and of itself, a lever provides little if any additional assistance. It must be utilized in conjunction with a fulcrum, the support upon which the lever balances and moves in order to generate the necessary increased force. Without a fulcrum, the lever is useless.

20   The large stone in the picture represents a burden to be lifted—an obstacle to be overcome. The size and weight of the stone corresponds to the size and complexity of the problem as well as the level of difficulty of lifting it. A heavier stone makes for a tougher, more complex problem to solve. The amount of force required to move the stone on a lever depends upon the *leverage point* (i.e., where the fulcrum is situated in relation to the lever). Unless it is balanced on the fulcrum on the correct leverage point along the bar, the lever's value will be reduced, and it may fail to work. The effectiveness of a lever can only be assessed in terms of a particular use. If the purpose (mission) of the lever is to lift stone x to height y, then it is effective only if it does so.

Continued

21 This is a fine science lesson, but how does it apply to our discussion? The stone represents a problem for which an individual or organization is seeking to produce a solution. A stone is heavier and harder to lift considering the extent to which the problem has been perceived to be difficult to manage; the urgency of the need to lift the stone corresponds to the degree of social cost, harm, and suffering the problem continues to generate. Actors trying to lift the stone are the stakeholders, decision makers, and thought leaders in the field. Their inability to lift the stone at a certain point in time is caused by many factors, including their geographic dispersion and lack of coordination; it by no means indicates a lack of urgent necessity to lift it, nor does it prove whether or not the stone can be lifted using a different, better strategy.

22 In its figurative sense, **leverage** is the ability to apply limited influence to harness significantly greater influence; to apply limited power to harness and coordinate significantly greater power; to make small *investments* to mobilize large investments by others—and thus powerfully magnify an organization's limited capacity.

CHECK WHAT YOU'VE LEARNED (Paragraphs 11–22)

Think about what you have just read. Answer each question. Then continue to the next part of the reading.

6. Describe the difference between *mission* and *strategy*. Use your own words.

   ....

   ....

7. By what criteria is strategy measured? Why is achieving this tricky for decision makers?

   ....

   ....

8. The terms *upside potential* and *downside risk* are used in Paragraph 16 but are not explicitly defined. Using what you know, define these in your own words.

   ....

   ....

9. What are some factors that should be taken into consideration when making a strategic decision?

   ....

   ....

10. What do the figurative applications of the word *leverage* share with the physics definition of the word?

   ....

   ....

"Thinking About Strategy" continued

FRAMEWORK #3:
The Metaphor of *War*

23 Sir Lawrence Freedman, professor of war studies at King's College London, argues that it is impossible to understand the concept of "strategy" without thinking deeply about war. This is because the origins of strategy are military. The word comes from the Greek strategos ("the art of the general.") For Freedman, strategy is a creative art form and the medium is power. Strategic planning enables an organization to fare better in a situation than the odds-makers would have predicted.[2] Strategic decision making by political, policy, and business leaders is intimately connected with strategic decision making at the highest rank of the armed forces. Executives routinely speak of *deploying assets, initiating campaigns, mobilizing resources,* and *capturing market share.* Institutes of "strategic studies" are found in elite military training facilities such as the US Army War College and research centers dedicated to international security. What lessons does the war metaphor offer? I suggest the following:

Lesson #1: Tactics ≠ Strategy

24 *Tactic* is not equal to *strategy.* The importance of this distinction is a recurring theme among strategic thinkers, Western and Eastern alike, throughout history. Beyond taxonomy, the two are unique. Cautionary warning: If you confuse the two, you will suffer great casualties and eventually defeat. **Tactics** are operational decisions and actions taken to implement a comprehensive strategic plan. In contrast, writes the most renowned Western thinker about strategy, Prussian General Carl von Clausewitz, "Strategy is the employment of the battle to gain the end of the War." As it frames all components of military action into an integrated whole, "strategy forms the plan of the War, and to this end it links together the series of acts which

are to lead to the final decision, that is to say, it makes the plans for the separate campaigns and regulates the combats to be fought in each."[3]

25 Clausewitz goes on to make it clear that strategic planning is not only much more important than tactical decision making on the field but is also more difficult, even agonizing. "It may sound strange, but for all who know War in this respect it is a fact beyond doubt that *much more strength of will is required to make an important decision in Strategy than in tactics.*"[4] With the phrase "it may sound strange," Clausewitz highlights the counterintuitive nature of his insight. Why is it more painfully challenging for a general to make decisions at the strategic command post than for

> **TIP**
> ....
> *Authors use* italics *for a variety of reasons—to express new terms, expressions, and words in other languages. Another reason is to emphasize certain language and ideas which is why italics are used in part of the quote in Paragraph 25. In this case, the author includes the full quote, but uses italics to draw the reader's attention to the specific part of it that he believes to be especially important.*

Continued

---

[2] Lawrence Freeman, *Strategy: A History* (Oxford 2013), p. xii
[3] Carl von Clausewitz, *On War,* Book III, Chapter 1.
[4] Ibid, italics added.

a commanding officer in the bloody field of war? Clausewitz answers this question, writing:

> In the latter we are hurried on with the moment; a Commander feels himself borne along in a strong current, against which he durst not contend without the most destructive consequences, he suppresses the rising fears, and boldly ventures further. In Strategy, where all goes on at a slower rate, there is more room allowed for our own apprehensions and those of others, for objections and remonstrances ... everything must be conjectured and assumed ...[5]

26 In other words, while a commander in the field makes quick tactical decisions on the spot, a general making strategic decisions prior to engaging in battle is "blessed" with ample time to take into consideration myriad options and outcomes, examining all potential pros and cons of each decision. While the general has more time to make decisions, he or she unfortunately also has more time to second-guess each one of them. Clausewitz warns that the cost of postponing the hard task of comprehensive strategic planning can be very high, and eventually fatal.

Lesson #2: Strategy Has Only One Purpose—Victory

27 At what point can a strategy be deemed successful? Only when it has led to victory. What, then, does "victory" mean, and how is it measured? For Clausewitz, victory meant nothing less than the defeat or unconditional surrender of the enemy. Woe to anyone who declares victory (or "Mission accomplished!") with any lesser result. But organizations do precisely that all the time. This is the product of confusing strategy with tactics, and battles with wars. For the strategic decision-maker, only the final objective matters; the intermediate achievements are meaningless if the final identified strategic goal is not achieved. Thus generals hold themselves and subordinates accountable to a disciplined, unified strategic plan aimed only at this final result.

28 What, then, is our "enemy"? Our enemy is the underlying substantive problem the strategy is designed to solve, or an obstacle that we are trying to overcome. For Doctors Without Borders, for example, the enemy is the lack of medical care available to civilians in conflict zones. For Amnesty International, the enemy is the persistent abuse of human rights by governmental authorities throughout the world. For the Intergovernmental Panel on Climate Change (IPCC), the enemy is the pervasive ignorance of policymakers in rich and poor nations alike concerning the risks and harms of human-made climate change and measures required to manage those risks and counteract those harms. Note that the war metaphor provides a useful framework to think about strategy for each of these Nobel Peace Prize recipients.

29 If we define strategic success using this framework, all that matters is the end result. By this analysis, the *starting point* of program decision making should be to identify very clearly *what social or environmental harm, national or international, we seek to eliminate or*

[5] Ibid.

reduce, and how we seek to achieve this goal by the strategic deployment of the physical, technological, network, and intellectual assets in our arsenal.

30 In *The Art of War*, an archetypal Eastern treatise on strategy, the Chinese general and philosopher Sun Tzu writes that such a strategic focus requires great and constant "method and discipline" at every stage of decision making and activity, and that this focus is more important than the most vigorous, brilliant fighting. It is disastrous to be lured into a battle when it is better to refrain from military involvement. "Hence to fight and conquer in all your battles is not supreme excellence; supreme excellence consists of breaking the enemy's resistance without fighting."[6]

Lesson #3: Lesser Capacity Demands Greater and More Creative Strategy

31 Understanding that victory is the only viable strategic goal produces several corollary insights. A nation (or organization) should not engage in military intervention (in any kind of strategic campaign) unless it has the capacity and will to achieve victory. What if a nation (or organization) faces an enemy but does not have the capacity to mobilize necessary force against it, as measured, for example, by the size and strength of the enemy army? That nation must either a) refrain from battle, and thus fail to meet its strategic needs, b) invest enormous resources in a massive crash program to bolster its forces (e.g., Britain's rearmament policy in the face of Hitler's aggression in the years prior to World War II), or c) somehow come up with a new, creative strategy that promotes the attainment of victory, notwithstanding its insufficient military resources and capacity.

32 Best practice in the area of strategy mobilizes an internal process to draft a strategic plan. Thus developing "good strategy" is expensive in financial, time-allocation, and human resource terms. But the war analogy suggests that investing in strategic planning is much less expensive than not doing so.

CONCLUSION

33 I hope that this essay has helped you to see the critical importance of strategy, in many areas of life, and in your work with organizations of all kinds. I also hope that it has given you some analytical tools for thinking about strategy more deeply, and more effectively as well. Remember that designing and implementing strategy is a *process*, a process relevant or even necessary to achieving your personal or group goals. Moreover, it is a *creative* process, or at least it can be, and that creativity can not only be fulfilling but also make the difference between success and failure. Sir Lawrence Freedman emphasizes that reaching out to partners and allies (and, under certain circumstances, even adversaries) to augment capacity or solve problems that cannot otherwise be successfully addressed is a strategy whose odds of success can only be bolstered by creative thinking. As Freedman rightfully observes, collaborating with other people is often the smartest strategy of all. By any standard, conjuring creative strategies is an art form: It is an art to persuade others to cooperate even when they are motivated by self-interest, not benevolence. It takes an artist to convince others, and even yourself, to do what you say. And just as each of us has personal goals, within each of us is the artistic potential for creating strategies to achieve those goals.

---

6 Sun Tzu, *The Art of War*, Chapter III, paragraph 2, available at http://classics.mit.edu/Tzu/artwar.html, accessed July 13, 2015.

CHECK WHAT YOU'VE LEARNED (Paragraphs 23–34)

Think about what you have just read. Answer each question.

11. Why might being a general in charge of strategic planning be more challenging than serving as a commander on the field?

....

....

12. When considering what you have learned about the difference between tactics and strategy, what is most important to a strategic decision maker? Why?

....

....

13. In Paragraph 27, the author reports the following opinion held by Clausewitz: that victory means nothing less than the defeat or unconditional surrender of the enemy. This opinion is followed by the exclamation, "Woe to anyone who declares victory (or "Mission accomplished!") with any lesser result." Based on the information in the paragraph, do you think the author agrees or disagrees with Clausewitz's opinion? Why?

....

....

14. How does the allusion to Sun Tzu in Paragraph 30 contribute to the discussion of strategy?

....

....

15. The following sentences from Paragraph 33 contain both facts and opinions. Identify them. Why do you think the author decided to combine these particular facts and opinions? For what purpose?

> Remember that designing and implementing strategy is a *process*, a process relevant or even necessary to achieving your personal or group goals. Moreover, it is a *creative* process, or at least it can be, and that creativity can not only be fulfilling but also make the difference between success and failure. Sir Lawrence Freedman emphasizes that reaching out to partners and allies (and, under certain circumstances, even adversaries) to augment capacity or solve problems that cannot otherwise be successfully addressed is a strategy whose odds of success can only be bolstered by creative thinking.

....

....

THINKING CRITICALLY

Consider each situation in light of what you read in "Thinking About Strategy." By yourself or with a partner, apply what you know about strategy to address each situation.

Situation 1 A "heavy stone to lift" for many graduating university students is securing a well-paying job with good benefits in their field of study. Consider the factors that make this situation challenging. Then identify the stakeholders, decision makers, and thought leaders who could help to "lift this stone." Using the notion of leverage, outline specific steps that could be taken to address the situation.

Situation 2 Imagine that you are a business consultant with a client who owns a bakery. You design a marketing campaign that includes buying online ads and hosting a grand reopening, and a strategic business plan that outlines long-term strategies for bringing in new customers and increasing annual profits by 40 percent. After you present your plan to the client, she says she will advertise and loves the grand reopening idea, but has decided not to devote resources to strategic planning. Think back to what you read. What is the problem with your approach? What is the problem with the client's response? What are some solutions to these problems?

Go to **MyEnglishLab** to complete a critical thinking exercise.

THINKING VISUALLY

A. Look back at the "Framework #1" section of the reading (p. 266). With the examples of Apple versus GM in mind, use your own examples and ideas to complete the diagram with options, costs, outcomes, and results.

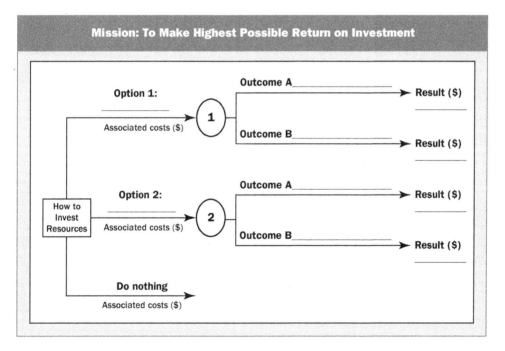

B. The following information represents a brainstorming session for developing a strategic plan. Choose one of the tactics that you think would be effective, or come up with one of your own, and show in graphic form the steps involved in fully executing the tactic, including decisions made along the way.

Goal	Strategy	Possible Tactics	Opportunity Costs / Considerations
Convince university and its students to reduce water consumption by 30 percent	Launch a campus-wide awareness campaign to change people's water consumption behaviors	Host open forums featuring water conservation experts	Rent space? Pay speaker?
		Multimedia advertising campaign featuring facts and anecdotes about water shortages	Costs? Time to research campus water consumption / costs?
		Partner / share resources with like-minded groups	Time / ability to track down data?
		Find "success story" to demonstrate rewards of conservation	How to publicize? How to connect with?
		Organize protest on campus lawn during scheduled watering times	Could anger some
		Develop list of changes: timed showers for dorms; xeriscaping campus; replace campus fountains with sculptures ...	How to prioritize?
		Interview focus groups about their water usage	How to get participants and compensate for time?

THINKING ABOUT LANGUAGE

USING DICTIONARIES TO STRENGTHEN VOCABULARY

A. Read these excerpts from the essay. Complete the task indicated for each item.

1. Identify the collocations:

   For example, we take *x* approach rather than *y* approach to solving one of our problems.

   ....

2. Identify the phrasal verb(s). Then provide a definition for each one.

   But this essay suggests that thinking about strategy in greater depth opens up a rich and useful field of analysis and reflection, one with a deep intellectual history.

   ....

   ....

   ....

3. Identify the idiom. What does it mean?

   But I can tell you that thinking carefully and deeply about strategy will increase your ability to succeed in turning that vision into reality.

   ....

4. What two words are an example of a multiword unit, specifically, a compound noun?

The definition of victory in football is very simple: for your team to get the ball into the right net at least once more than the opposing team is able to do so in the opposite net.

....

5. Of the following dictionary definitions, which is the best definition for the word *mission* in this sentence?

Over the course of multiple seasons, the **mission** is to sustain the highest possible ranking year after year.

a. an important job that involves traveling somewhere, done by a member of the air force, army, etc.
b. a group of important people who are sent by their government to another country to discuss something or collect information
c. the purpose or the most important aim of an organization
d. a duty or service that you have chosen to do and be responsible for

6. Which two pair of words most strongly collocate?

But, of course, you likely have a wide variety of additional goals as a coach.

....

7. What words are an example of a multiword unit, specifically, a complex preposition?

But as a matter of values, we have decided that we will not hire a coach who yells at the kids on the team.

....

8. What is the best definition for the word *deliver*? Consult a dictionary to view multiple definitions for the word and then write the most appropriate one.

A coach who fails to deliver—in the sense of winning as many games as possible given the team's assets (capacity, skill, and resources)—will very likely not be retained.

....

9. What words are an example of a multiword unit, specifically, a complex adverbial?

Strategy, on the other hand, is the plan you will develop and implement to achieve your fundamental objectives.

....

10. Identify the phrasal verb.

Leverage is a strategy related to the laws of physics, in which a lever—a bar made of wood or another firm, rigid material—is used to augment the strength of an actor seeking to lift a heavy weight or pry something open.

....

UNDERSTANDING SIGNPOST EXPRESSIONS THAT LIMIT OR DEFINE

B. Read these excerpts from the essay. Underline the signpost expressions that limit or define.

1. Speaking of teams, let's talk about sports, specifically, a game hundreds of millions of people all over the world know and love.

2. As a player, your immediate problem is how to be excellent in your position. Excellence in your position is defined by the extent to which you are able to take actions on the field in support of the team's collaborative efforts to get the ball into the net.

3. Even if we could find the "best" coach in the world (when it comes to a track record of victories), we would not hire that person if we believed that he or she might not care about nurturing and encouraging our children.

4. But for a football team at the highest level of performance, when we consider *success*, it is defined much more simply—by the team's achievements on the field.

5. A coach who fails to deliver—in the sense of winning as many games as possible given the team's assets (capacity, skill, and resources)—will very likely not be retained.

6. The effectiveness of a lever can only be assessed in terms of a particular use.

7. A stone is heavier and harder to lift considering the extent to which the problem has been perceived to be difficult to manage; the urgency of the need to lift the stone corresponds to the degree of social cost, harm, and suffering the problem continues to generate.

8. If we define strategic success using this framework, all that matters is the end result.

9. Best practice in the area of strategy mobilizes an internal process to draft a strategic plan.

10. By any standard, conjuring creative strategies is an art form: It is an art to persuade others to cooperate even when they are motivated by self-interest, not benevolence.

Go to **MyEnglishLab** for more practice reading an extended text and using your reading skills.

RESEARCH PROJECT

The essay in this unit touches on some of the many factors investors consider when deciding on investments to make. By doing research, you can learn about the decision-making process of individuals who have invested in social change.

A. The following is a list of figures who are notable for their "investment" in change movements. Choose and research one figure, or two or more that have something important in common.

- Chetna Sinha, women's economic empowerment activist
- Sara Blakely, billionaire philanthropist
- Ingrid E. Newkirk, president of People for the Ethical Treatment of Animals (PETA)
- Lin-Manuel Miranda, composer and community activist
- Micah M. White, a leader of Occupy Wall Street
- Muna AbuSulayman, women's rights proponent

B. Conduct your research. As you read about your subject, formulate a thesis. Gather information that supports your thesis. Use the following questions to help guide you:

- What has been the person's strategy for effecting change?
- What features of the person's strategies have been praised? Criticized?
- What historic movement has the person modeled his or her strategies on?
- How do the person's strategies compare to those of other leaders in the same movement?

C. Choose a presentation style from the box, or use your own idea, and present your research to the class.

> interview (role-play with a partner)   informative speech   slideshow

Go to **MyEnglishLab** to complete a collaborative activity

Individual choices impact the global economy.

ECONOMICS

Supply and Demand in the Marketplace

UNIT PROFILE

In this unit, you will read about the dynamics of market economies—specifically the principles of supply and demand. In the online extended reading, you will read about how, like products and services, the labor market adheres to the supply-demand model. In these discussions, you will consider government attempts to control prices. As a capstone to the unit, you will research an example of such government intervention and present your findings.

EXTENDED READING

BEFORE YOU READ

Discuss these questions with another student.

1. Think of the things you buy during the course of an average day—perhaps coffee, snacks, clothes, bottled water, and bus tickets. Does the price of such things vary from place to place? If so, why do you think the price varies? If not, why do you the price is the same everywhere?

2. Is there anything that you really want to buy that is just too expensive for you? Why do you think it's so expensive? How much would the price have to be lowered in order for you to buy it? Do you think there's a chance the price might ever decline that much? Why or why not?

3. Of all your expenses—food, shelter, transportation, entertainment, and so on—which are the most necessary? Is there anything you could do without? If you suddenly found yourself very short of money, which things would you have to give up?

4. In every country there exists an economically poor and disadvantaged population, people who can't afford some of life's necessities. Should government intervene in the markets to make sure certain things—such as housing, food, and health care—are affordable to everyone, including the very poor? Why or why not?

READ

Read the passage. Then answer the questions after each section.

Markets, Prices, and Price Controls

ABSTRACT

This essay describes the concepts of supply and demand and elaborates on their relationship in a competitive market. It details how the willingness of consumers to buy and of sellers to sell is dependent on price. The equilibrium price is introduced, and it is shown to occupy a special point in market movement, the point at which supply matches demand.

The essay also examines attempts by governments to intervene in markets, usually to relieve the price pressure faced by lower-income consumers as they try to secure essentials like housing, food, and hygiene products. The example is given of price controls imposed by the Venezuelan government on toilet paper. The essay concludes with the contention that the Venezuelan government's price-control attempts were unsuccessful, generating market dynamics that were harmful to both consumers and producers. The author generalizes from this case and contends that markets should be left alone to reach price points through the natural interplay of supply and demand.

1 Take a look around you at the kinds of products and services you usually consume. Focus on the clothes you are wearing, the food you had for lunch, the phone you communicate with, and the computer you write assignments or play video games on. Chances are that the vast majority of these goods and services were purchased in several markets.

2 What is a **market**? A market is a gathering of people. This gathering allows producers of a good or service to find buyers who are interested in their good or service. A market can be local, such as your neighborhood mall or town farmers' market, or much larger, such as global markets for different types of clothing, which involve sellers and buyers from all over the world. A market can be physical, like a brick-and-mortar grocery store, or virtual, such as a website where you buy books or an online broker service through which you purchase stocks and bonds.

3 Markets have existed for thousands of years, ever since humans discovered the advantages of specialization and trade beyond their family unit or small tribe. **Specialization** means someone spends much of his or her time producing a good or service that he or she is particularly proficient at creating. The next step in specialization is **trade**—finding someone who wants that product or service. As the number of such specialties becomes larger and societies become more complex, markets become more elaborate mechanisms for facilitating multi-party trade among potential buyers and sellers. This complexity is far from just a modern phenomenon, and there are notable examples in ancient civilizations of trade networks stretching thousands of miles and involving scores of middlemen. Today's myriad markets both differ from and are remarkably similar to those of earlier exchanges, in scale and sophistication.

Continued

4   A lack of complete self-sufficiency may seem like a weakness, but in fact it's not. Almost no one in a modern economy is even close to being self-sufficient. To understand why, imagine what would happen if you had to create from scratch everything that you consume. Imagine that you had to sew the fabric to get the shirt that you wear, and you also had to weave cotton to create that fabric, and furthermore you had to plant and harvest the cotton that would eventually be part of your shirt. Imagine that you had to create your phone from scratch, from the plastic or metal casing to the delicate electronic components inside, and the smooth and delicate piece of glass that covers the screen. No single human being can produce the variety of goods we enjoy today. Under a regime of self-sufficiency, one's pursuits would be incredibly narrow and even the most basic subsistence would be difficult. We have achieved our current level of consumption and economic well-being through specialization and trade.

5   In this essay we will focus on how markets facilitate trade and let all of us—consumers and producers, society overall—achieve better economic outcomes. A market attracts producers and buyers of a certain good or service. Within a market, each producer is trying to maximize revenue from selling a product while each buyer is trying to pay as little as possible for a product. Out of all market transactions, two critical numbers emerge. First, the number of units sold within a certain period of time—for example, the number of cars sold in your hometown in a month or the pounds of tomatoes sold in your local farmers' market in a day. The second important number is the price at which these transactions occurred. Prices may fluctuate across sellers and with time, but at each point in time, the price of a good tends to converge to a certain value. The resulting price—when the quantity supplied equals the quantity demanded—is called the **equilibrium price**.

6 Modern markets are very complex institutions, sometimes with millions of consumers and tens of thousands of sellers in a single market, producing intricate behavioral patterns. As all scientists normally do, economists take this complex, real-life situation and represent it with a model that captures the main features and allows us to understand what is going on and make useful predictions. In this essay, we will focus on competitive markets— those with several sellers and buyers, all trading the same product.

7 Economists represent the behavior of consumers in a competitive market through the **demand curve**, which states that when the price of a product increases, consumers will buy fewer units (if nothing else changes simultaneously). For example, let us say we are studying the market for medium-quality bicycles, and ten million bicycles are purchased when the price is $250. If the price doubles to $500, then economists would expect to observe a decrease in the quantity demanded (e.g., to 8 million). Graphically, the demand is a downward-sloping curve (Figure 1). Another way of interpreting the demand curve is that at each point, it shows how much the last consumer was willing to pay for the last unit purchased. For example, the customer who bought the very last bike that was sold at a price of $250 (bike number ten million) was also willing to pay exactly $250. Consumers higher on the demand curve have a higher **willingness to pay** (WTP) and thus would be willing to pay more than the market price of $250. Consumers lower on the demand curve have a willingness to pay less than the market price of $250, and as a result, do not buy a bike.

8 In a competitive market, producers are willing to sell more units of the good when its price increases. That behavior is summarized by an upward-sloping supply curve (Figure 2). In our bicycle-market example, with ten million bicycles being sold at a price of $250, if the price of a bike doubles, then we would expect more bikes being offered in this market as more producers enter the market. Just as consumers' willingness to pay is represented on the demand curve, the producers' **willingness to sell** (also called reservation price) is represented on the supply curve. The producer's willingness to sell

is based on the minimum value he or she will accept in order to sell a good.

9 Given these representations of the fundamentals of the behavior of buyers (demand) and sellers (supply), economists analyze their impact on the market dynamics. In essence, economists superimpose a supply curve on a demand curve to find the point where the two intersect. If the price is high— above the intersection of demand and supply (as represented in Figure 3)—sellers are offering more bicycles (Qs) than consumers are

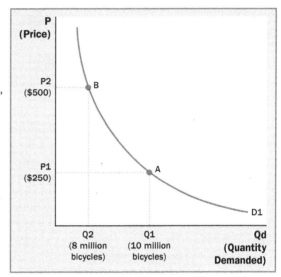

Figure 1 Demand curve

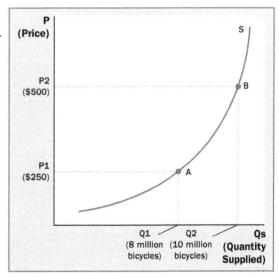

Figure 2 Supply curve

Continued

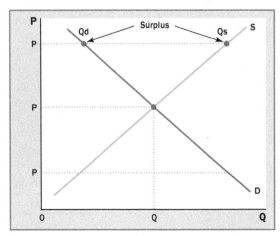

Figure 3 Surplus

willing to buy (Qd), resulting in a **surplus**. That surplus or excess supply of bicycles means that bicycles are piling up in stores, and to get rid of them, sellers are willing to lower the price to attract more consumers. As the price falls, the quantity of bicycles demanded increases, but at the same time, sellers are willing to sell fewer units. Prices will continue to fall only as long as the quantity supplied exceeds the quantity demanded. This movement will stop when the price reaches the intersection of demand and supply, where the quantity demanded and the quantity supplied are equal.

10 Similarly, if the price is low (below the intersection of demand and supply, as represented in Figure 4), consumers would

like to buy many bicycles (perhaps multiple units per household), but sellers are willing to supply fewer bikes. That creates a **shortage** of—or excess demand for—bicycles. Some of those potential buyers who would like to have a bike but could not get one will be willing to bid up the price to buy a bike despite the shortage. As the price of bicycles increases, producers will be willing to put more bikes on the market, and some consumers will decide not to buy any at the higher price, reducing the shortage. The increase in prices will continue as long as there is a shortage, that is, until the price reaches the intersection of demand and supply.

11 As you can see, whether the price is too high and there are too many bikes or the price is too low and there are not enough bikes to satisfy the demand, the combined behavior of consumers and producers will push the price of a bicycle toward the intersection of demand and supply. At that point there is no further incentive to change the price, and we have reached the **market equilibrium** (Figure 5). The competitive market model predicts two specific numbers (the equilibrium price and the equilibrium quantity) that we can test against a real market to see whether the outcome of our simplified representation is close enough to real life.

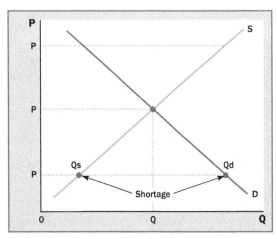

Figure 4 Shortage

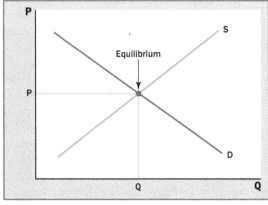

Figure 5 Market equilibrium

12   Note that for all but the last unit sold at the market equilibrium, the willingness to pay (represented by the demand curve) exceeds the market price. For example, if I use a bicycle to go to work as well as to exercise and I am willing to pay $700 for the bike, but I only end up paying the market price of $250, then I gain $450 (WTP $700 – Price $250) in the transaction. **Consumer surplus** is the difference between what a consumer is willing to pay and what he or she actually pays. The aggregate gains for all consumers in this market are represented by the area between the demand curve and the market price, as shown in Figure 6. Likewise, producers enjoy similar gains because the market price exceeds their willingness to sell for all but the last unit sold at the market equilibrium. **Producer surplus** is the benefit that a producer receives by getting more for his or her product than the minimum he or she was willing to accept. The aggregate difference between market price and willingness to sell is shown in Figure 7.

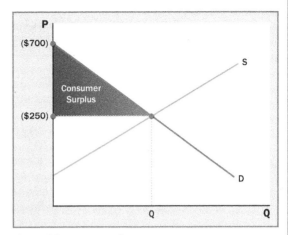

Figure 6 Consumer surplus

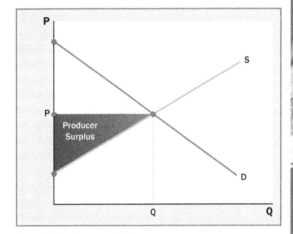

Figure 7 Producer surplus

CHECK WHAT YOU'VE LEARNED (Paragraphs 1–12)

Think about what you have just read. Answer each question. Then continue to the next part of the reading.

1. In Paragraph 4, the author implies that there would be big problems in a system that depended on self-sufficiency. What would these problems be?

   ....

   ....

2. In Paragraph 6, the author mentions how economists create models to make "useful predictions." Think about recent economic events. What's an example of an economic event that could have been predicted by an economist studying people's behavioral patterns?

   ....

   ....

3. Using the author's example of bicycles, explain the situation in the market at the point where the supply curve and the demand curve intersect. At that point, what is the relationship between consumers' willingness to buy bicycles and sellers' willingness to sell them?

   ....

   ....

4. Who benefits from a producer surplus? Explain.

   ....

   ....

5. This section portrays market equilibrium as a good thing. Yet markets almost never stay in equilibrium once they reach it. Why? Use reason and what you know to guess.

   ....

   ....

"Markets, Prices, and Price Controls," *continued*

13　A fascinating aspect of competitive markets is that consumers and producers individually need very little information to reach the market equilibrium. In fact, a person may be completely ignorant about what others are doing as long as he or she has two pieces of information: his or her own willingness to pay (for consumers) or willingness to sell (for producers) and the market price. The market price serves as a very accurate summary of the aggregate actions of all buyers and sellers in the market, and that information, coupled with the individual, self-interested behavior of buyers and sellers, yields three results that are good for society.

14　First, consumer surplus and producer surplus are maximized at the market equilibrium. How do we prove that? Imagine a dictator who prevents market participants from selling—and therefore buying—as many units as in equilibrium. Because of this, some buyers with willingness to pay above the market price will be prevented from buying the good (thus reducing consumer surplus), and some producers with willingness to sell below the market price will not be able to sell their product (thus reducing producer surplus). So reducing the quantity of goods to below the equilibrium quantity hurts both consumers and producers.

15　Conversely, if the dictator forces consumers and producers to buy and sell more units, for each unit beyond the equilibrium quantity, some consumers will be forced to pay more than they are actually willing to pay (thus reducing consumer surplus), and some sellers will be forced to sell at a price below their willingness (thus reducing producer surplus). Taking those two scenarios together, if a forced decrease in quantity and a forced increase in quantity both result in a reduction in consumer and producer surplus, we can infer that the equilibrium quantity maximizes consumer and producer surplus. This is an extremely important conclusion. It implies that a competitive market (remember: many buyers and sellers) will make consumers and

producers as well off as they can be, and that no amount of tinkering with the total quantity or the price will improve this outcome.

16　But is there any way to leave the market quantity untouched and just change the allocation among consumers or producers, and increase the consumer or producer surplus? Let's tackle that question for consumers first. Each and every consumer has the incentive to continue buying as long as the market price is less than or equal to his or her willingness to pay, so the willingness to pay for the very last unit purchased by each consumer will be equal to or close to the market price. Each consumer makes this decision independently, without knowing anyone else's willingness to pay; knowing just the market price and one's own willingness to pay is enough. However, the combined result of these actions is that the willingness to pay of *every* consumer is equal to or close to the market price, which also means that without any conscious coordination, everyone has about the same willingness to pay for the last unit consumed. That, in turn, means that if you were to take one unit from one consumer (thus hurting that person) to improve the welfare of another consumer (by adding one more unit to that person's consumption at a lower willingness to pay), then you will hurt the first consumer more than you benefit the second one, thus reducing consumer surplus. For example, let's say Jane and Paul are each buying two cups of coffee a day for $2 per cup, in equilibrium. So both of them have the same willingness to pay the same amount for that second cup—$2. If you now forcefully take one cup of coffee from Jane and give it to Paul for free, Jane loses her second cup (worth $2 to her) while Paul gains a third cup—which will be worth less than his second cup of coffee, thus less than $2. The competitive market equilibrium automatically guarantees that there is no way to improve the welfare of any consumer without hurting others even more, a situation that economists describe as an **efficient allocation of goods across consumers**.

17　Similarly, each and every producer has the incentive to continue selling as long as the market price is higher than or equal to the willingness to sell, so the willingness to sell the very last unit created by each producer will be equal to or close to the market price

Continued

and therefore close to every other producer's willingness to sell. If you attempt to improve overall welfare by reallocating production across firms, you will hurt some firms who end up producing at a point where the market price is below their willingness to sell. So a competitive market also results in an automatic **efficient allocation of goods across producers**.

18   Let's recap: If anyone messes with the total quantity transacted in a competitive market, or if anyone messes with the allocation of goods across consumers and producers in a competitive market, the result will be lower consumer and producer surplus. No central planner can improve on the equilibrium outcome of a competitive market. The one critical piece of information that allows this almost-magical result to happen over and over again across all competitive markets is the equilibrium price. The price conveys to all consumers and producers essential information that allows them to reach maximum consumer and producer surplus without central coordination.

19   Are all markets competitive? No. For several reasons, in some markets you may observe just one or two sellers, or one or two buyers—for example, markets with goods that have relatively high fixed costs, like pharmaceutical products and electricity. And the competitive markets' results may not apply to some special types of goods. But by and large, competitive markets are efficient, resulting in the best allocation of goods and resources, maximizing consumer and producer surplus.

CHECK WHAT YOU'VE LEARNED (Paragraphs 13–19)

Think about what you have just read. Answer each question. Then continue to the next part of the reading.

6. In Paragraph 13, the author talks about the information needed by consumers and producers to function in the market. Of course, producers and consumers both need to know the market price of a product or service. But this is not enough. Why does a consumer need to know his or her own willingness to buy, and why does a producer need to know his or her own willingness to sell? ....

....

7. Reread Paragraph 14. Imagine a dictator who declared, "Cars are bad for the environment. Only five thousand cars may be produced this year." How would that hurt consumers? How would it hurt producers? ....

....

8. In Paragraph 15, the author states, "if a forced decrease in quantity and a forced increase in quantity both result in a reduction in consumer and producer surplus, we can infer that the equilibrium quantity maximizes consumer and producer surplus." He calls that inference an "extremely important conclusion." In your own words, explain why this is so important.

....

....

9. Paragraphs 16 and 17 are about the efficient allocation of goods, across consumers and across producers, respectively. What does "efficient allocation" mean?

....

....

10. In Paragraph 19, the author indicates that there are exceptional cases in some markets. Which markets are those? How might such cases arise? ....

....

"Markets, Prices, and Price Controls," *continued*

20   Despite the critical role of prices in competitive markets, sometimes governments prevent the price of a good or a service from reaching its equilibrium, thus interfering with the information communicated across buyers and sellers. There are two basic types of **price controls**: the maximum price or **price ceiling**, and the minimum price or **price floor**. The minimum wage and the prices of raisins, milk, and some other agricultural products are all examples of price floors. At this point in our discussion, we will focus our analysis on price ceilings, which include some notable examples, such as controlled rent and the prices of some goods deemed to be necessities in a given location at a given point in history.

21   Price ceilings are meant to facilitate access to basic goods. For example, at this point in history, rent control laws in New York City and San Francisco are politically important as city leaders try to make housing accessible to low-income households. Similarly, the current government of Venezuela enforces price ceilings on coffee, bread, toilet paper, and other basic items in an attempt to keep these goods relatively cheap despite the rampant rate of price increases throughout the country.

22   Inexpensive goods for everyone! What could be better? But do price ceilings actually achieve their goal? Furthermore, how do price ceilings affect consumer and producer surplus? Can price ceilings beat the market outcome without intervention?

23   Let's analyze price ceilings with our competitive market model. Figure 8 shows a competitive market reaching equilibrium at (Pe, Qe). Let's say this is the market for toilet paper in Venezuela, and the government imposes a price ceiling at Pmax. At this lower price, the quantity demanded increases and more consumers would be happy to get toilet paper. However, producers would only be willing to sell a limited quantity of toilet paper at this lower price. What does our model predict? A shortage of toilet paper. There will indeed be some lucky consumers who will be able to buy toilet paper at the low price. But the limited supply will soon run out, and many consumers will be left without toilet paper. In the absence of government intervention, the price of toilet paper would increase until the shortage disappears. But raising the price of toilet paper is illegal in Venezuela, and anyone who attempts to get around this regulation risks imprisonment. The net result is not at all what the government intended.

24   So we are stuck with a price ceiling for toilet paper. What are the consequences? First, since the quantity of toilet paper produced and consumed is lower than in equilibrium, the total surplus for society (consumer plus producer surplus) is smaller—the Venezuelan society is worse off, a noticeable and unfortunate effect of the price ceiling. When loss of economic efficiency occurs because equilibrium is not achieved, the result is **deadweight loss**. The shaded triangle in Figure 9 represents this loss.

25   Note that producer surplus is certainly smaller. On the other hand, the effect on consumer surplus is ambiguous: some

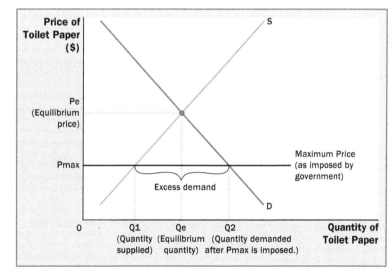

Figure 8 Price ceiling

Continued

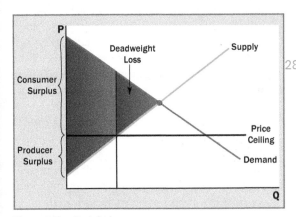

Figure 9 Deadweight loss

consumers benefit from the lower price, though only those who are able to buy toilet paper. But even for those consumers who got to purchase some toilet paper, is the artificially low price their only cost? Unfortunately not. Those consumers were able to buy toilet paper by waiting in line for hours, trying to be one of the first people to enter supermarkets as soon as they opened to be one of the few who could get their hands on a pack of toilet paper before the shelves were emptied. Figure 9 does not explicitly show the cost of lining up and the uncertainty of getting toilet paper, but it is undoubtedly another disadvantage of setting a price ceiling.

26   Producers who see their ability to charge higher prices curtailed may resort to reducing their cost by lowering the quality of their product. In the case of toilet paper, we should expect the high-quality toilet paper to be displaced by thin and rough toilet paper.

27   Last but not least, who gets the toilet paper? In a competitive market, those buyers who value toilet paper the most would get it—everyone with a willingness to pay above the market price. But the introduction of the price ceiling means that many people who would be willing to pay the price will not get toilet paper, and those who do get it are not necessarily the consumers who value toilet paper the most. The price ceiling has cost us not just our overall efficiency (the maximum total surplus for society) but also

the efficiency in allocation across consumers. The combined loss is much larger than the deadweight loss represented in Figure 9.

28   Did the predictions of economists play out in Venezuela? They certainly did. However, this phenomenon is not exclusive to the price ceiling of toilet paper in Venezuela. It is observed in any competitive market with a price ceiling below the equilibrium price. In some markets, like housing subject to rent control, beyond the short-term shortage and misallocation of resources, the prospect of permanently lower future rents reduces investment in housing, resulting in poor maintenance and long-term shortages of good-quality housing in rent-controlled areas. Governments may introduce additional regulation trying to lessen the negative impacts of price ceilings, but the only truly successful solution is the elimination of price controls.

29   In a nutshell, the argument against price controls is that they result in fewer people getting the products or jobs they want. So are economists who dislike them saying that we should abandon the goal of access to basic goods to all people? Not at all. If that is indeed the societal goal, there are better, less costly ways of achieving it. Examples include a direct subsidy for low-income people or better subsidized education that improves the opportunities of low-income people.

30   Why then do price controls exist at all? Because those who benefit, benefit in not insignificant ways and therefore tend to fight hard to keep them. The few who can work at a higher wage, buy a good at a lower price, or sell a product at a higher price may, for example, actively lobby government to keep the status quo. This occurs despite the harm caused to the many others who, in the absence of such price controls, would also be able to work or buy or sell goods. In other words, price controls create very visible, empowered winners—those who earn the higher wage, pay the lower rent, sell the more expensive product—and this empowerment greases the gears of the political process that leads to price controls.

CHECK WHAT YOU'VE LEARNED (Paragraphs 20–30)

Think about what you have just read. Answer each question.

11. Based on the examples given in this section, what relationship does the author suggest exists between time, place, politics, and price controls?

....

....

12. Who bears the brunt of deadweight loss? How? What are some hidden costs of deadweight loss?

....

....

13. The price controls on toilet paper in Venezuela caused problems for both consumers and producers. Explain how the price-control system may have harmed consumers and demotivated producers.

....

....

14. The author does not reject the idea of government ensuring access to necessities. However, he favors alternatives to price controls. What alternatives does he mention?

....

....

15. According to the author, why are price ceilings put in place even though they are, overall, not good for an economy?

....

....

THINKING CRITICALLY

Consider each situation in light of what you have read in "Markets, Prices, and Price Controls." By yourself or with a partner, apply what you know about competitive markets to address each situation.

Situation 1 You are the mayor of San Francisco—a beautiful, highly desirable city with scores of top-quality employers who pay their high-level employees very well. These highly paid workers have been buying up or renting all the desirable housing at high prices. People with lower-income jobs (e.g., salespeople in stores, restaurant workers, taxi drivers, maintenance workers, low-level medical workers) are being priced out

of the city. Their pay is not high enough for them to compete for good housing. In turn, they now have to live in outlying communities far from their jobs and have to spend huge amounts of time commuting to work. It is also bad for the city in many ways. For example, it is in danger of becoming less interesting and vibrant as its cultural diversity is being weakened and low-paid creative people (artists, writers, thinkers, etc.) have to flee to more affordable locations. In what ways should you, the mayor, respond to this situation?

Situation 2 You are the head of an airline company. Of course your company is the producer of a service sold to general consumers—a service considered a necessity by some and therefore possibly subject to price controls. Make a list of some of the factors you have to consider in setting ticket prices—not only your costs but also factors that affect consumer demand for your services. Is there anything your company can do to reduce volatility in pricing?

Go to **MyEnglishLab** to complete a critical thinking exercise.

THINKING VISUALLY

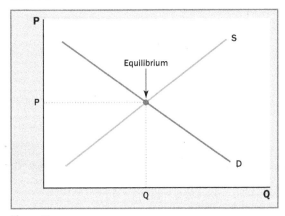

Figure 5

A. Review the information represented in Figure 5, taken from the essay (p. 282). Describe the concepts represented in the graph. Why is this graph essential to the discussion in the reading?

....

....

....

....

B. The following information represents the average rental price per month of a two-bedroom apartment in various cities in the United States. Figures are in US dollars. Review these figures and create a graph that best communicates the information.

City	Average Rental, April 2014	Average Rental, April 2016	Average Rental, April 2018 (projected)
New Blenheim, NY	$4,670	$4,880	$5,026
Foreston, MO	$4,510	$4,645	$4,675
Los Padres, NM	$3,225	$3,113	$3,051
Parker, CA	$3,127	$3,291	$3,406
San Junipero, CA	$2,732	$2,862	$2,976
Bareford, MA	$2,648	$2,731	$4,812
Temple, IL	$2,036	$1,952	$1,874

Cities and rental prices are fictional, for practice purposes only.

THINKING ABOUT LANGUAGE

ANALYZING MEANING USING WORD PARTS

A. The chart lists ten vocabulary items from the essay that are important to understanding the economic concepts presented in this unit. Find the word in the reading and read it in context. Then complete the information in the chart.

When finished, review the essay and select five additional vocabulary items that you found necessary to understand the content. Find the necessary information to complete the chart by using the reading, your dictionary, or an online search tool, or by asking classmates or peers.

	Vocabulary Item	Paragraph	Word Parts: Prefix, Root, Suffix	Prefix, Root, Suffix Meaning	Word Meaning
1	interplay (n)	Abstract	Prefix: *inter* Root: *play* Suffix: None	"between" "movement"	action that takes place involving two or more people or actors
2	proficient (adj)	3			
3	potential (adj)	3			
4	outcome (n)	5			
5	transaction (n)	5			
6	fluctuate (v)	5			
7	superimpose (v)	9			
8	welfare (n)	16			
9	intervention (n)	22			
10	ambiguous (adj)	25			
11					
12					
13					
14					
15					

B. Find each phrase in the essay and read it in context. Then, from your own knowledge of English, write a word or phrase that is an equivalent or near-equivalent expression to show the meaning of the item.

	Expression	Paragraph	Equivalent or Near-Equivalent Expression
1	the vast majority of	1	
2	a modern phenomenon	3	
3	from scratch	4	
4	real life	11	
5	self-interested behavior	13	
6	in turn	16	
7	in the absence of	23	
8	get their hands on	25	

Go to MyEnglishLab for more practice reading an extended text and using your reading skills.

RESEARCH PROJECT

The reading in this unit explores supply and demand in the competitive marketplace, and the pros and cons of government intervention. By doing research, you can learn more about the impacts of price controls on trade.

A. The following list features goods and services that have been subject to government price controls or government attempts to control supply. Choose one to research.

- cigarettes
- wine
- gasoline
- water
- gold
- guns
- health care

B. Conduct your research. As you read about your subject, formulate a thesis. Gather information that supports your thesis. Use the following questions to help guide you:

- Why did government step in to control pricing / supply?
- What was the impact of government intervention?
- What would have happened if government had not intervened?
- Are there examples of other governments taking similar or different actions on a similar good or service? What was the outcome?

C. Choose a presentation style from the box, or use your own idea, and present your research to the class.

> short video documentary   model debate with another student   persuasive speech

Go to MyEnglishLab to complete a collaborative activity.

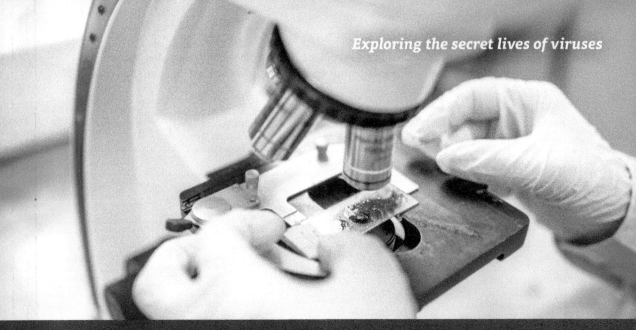
Exploring the secret lives of viruses

BIOLOGY

A Study of Deadly Diseases

UNIT PROFILE

In this unit, you will read about a group of diseases that has attracted a lot of research: prion diseases. The more researchers learn about these ailments, the odder they seem—being generated not on the cellular level but via anomalies in proteins. In the online extended reading, you will learn about new treatments for certain cancers and how a greater understanding of them has led to the development of some preventive vaccines. As a capstone to the unit, you will research one aspect of the physiology of prion diseases.

EXTENDED READING

BEFORE YOU READ

Discuss these questions with another student.

1. What do you know about proteins? Why are they necessary in our diets?

2. Even in cultures where eating meat is normal and generally considered healthy, there are limits to which parts of animals are normally consumed. Think of a meat-eating culture you know well. Which parts of animals are not normally eaten? Why?

3. The study of biology often requires that we think about terrible and greatly feared diseases. Without such thought, people cannot understand diseases well enough to eventually treat them. In your opinion, which are the three most dreaded diseases? Why are they especially feared?

4. Human experience over the past half century or so has shown that the treatment for a disease—like some cancers—may be very unpleasant and painful. Some treatments even pose health risks of their own. Based on what you know, how can treatments for cancer and other such diseases be improved? How could medical practices change so that the treatment is no longer as bad as, or worse than, the disease?

Read the passage. Then answer the questions after each section.

Cows, Cannibals, and Crystals—Explaining the Mechanism of Prion Diseases

Prion Disease	Distribution
Creutzfeldt-Jakob disease (CJD)	worldwide including some familial forms
Gerstmann-Straussler-Scheinker syndrome (GSS)	familial
kuru	Papua New Guinea
fatal familial insomnia (FFI)	familial
bovine spongiform encephalopathy (BSE)	primarily Great Britain

Table 1

ABSTRACT

Prion diseases are most unusual. Our current understanding suggests that these diseases occur when proteins from our body act to form crystal-like structures that can damage and kill cells in the brain. Once this process starts, it appears to be relentless, resulting in the death of the individual. Even more frightening is the fact that, under the right conditions, these afflictions may be passed from one individual to another. This essay will focus on how these prional structures form and suggest some possible avenues for future therapy and prophylaxis.

1 This essay is about one of the most bizarre groups of diseases in the world. These diseases are known as **prion diseases** because they are caused by pathologic agents known as **prions**. Over the years, a great deal has been learned about these diseases, and many perplexing questions have been answered. However, the answers have been surprising and have given rise to even more questions.

2 One thing that distinguishes prion diseases from others is that they are the deadliest known diseases. Not one single person has ever survived. This makes prion diseases deadlier than Ebola, even deadlier than rabies. Table 1 lists the known prion diseases in humans.

3 Another unusual aspect of prion diseases is the way in which they arise. This is known as the **pathogenesis** of disease. In prion diseases, a particular protein that is normally found in everyone turns against its host and starts to ravage the brain. The protein is called PrP, which stands for *prion protein*. PrP was discovered by studying prion diseases, so the

protein was named after the disease rather than the other way around. The way in which PrP contributes to pathogenesis is by forming large aggregates that lead to the death of cells and the spread of these protein aggregates to adjacent cells.

HISTORY

4 The first clinical descriptions of these diseases in animals date back hundreds of years. These descriptions involved a wasting disease of sheep known as scrapie. For many years scrapie was the best animal model for these diseases. Table 2 lists several prion diseases in animals.

Prion Disease	Host Species
scrapie	sheep
bovine spongiform encephalopathy (BSE)	cows
transmissible mink encephalopathy	mink
chronic wasting disease (CWD)	cervids: deer and elk
experimental models	rodents and others

Table 2

5 Icelandic researcher Björn Sigurðsson greatly increased our understanding of prion diseases through his studies of scrapie in sheep. Sigurðsson introduced the concept of the "slow viral infection." Sigurðsson characterized these diseases as having a long incubation period, a protracted clinical course often terminating in death, and species specificity. Sigurðsson also

Continued

did pioneering work on Maedi / Visna, another disease of sheep that was subsequently shown to be an HIV-like retroviral disease. Unfortunately, sheep are large animals and prion diseases progress very slowly. Because of this, for many years it was difficult to get a clear understanding of the underlying pathogenesis or underlying mechanism that gives rise to prion diseases.

HUMAN PRION DISEASES

6 The first clinical description of a prion disease in humans dates back to 1920. Referred to as Creutzfeldt-Jakob disease, or CJD, the name pays homage to the researchers who published these first reports. While this field of research may seem somewhat obscure, two Nobel Prizes have been given for work on prion diseases. In 1976, Baruch Blumberg and D. Carleton Gajdusek shared the Nobel Prize in Physiology or Medicine "for their discoveries concerning new mechanisms for the origin and dissemination of infectious diseases." Gajdusek was the first to show that prion diseases could be transferred from humans to an animal model. This was accomplished by inoculating material from the brains of individuals who had died of a disease named kuru into the brains of three female chimpanzees: Georgette, Daisy, and Joanne. These animals went on to develop a syndrome that was essentially indistinguishable from kuru. A similar experiment carried out earlier by Cuillé and Chelle in 1936 showed that scrapie could be transmitted between sheep.

7 Gajdusek's familiarity with kuru came from work he had done in Papua New Guinea. He was introduced by Vincent Zigas, a government medical officer, to the existence of the disease—a bizarre neurological malady among the Fore tribes. Symptoms associated with kuru include incoordination, difficulty walking, shivering, tremors, aberrant eye movements, fixed gaze, muscular rigidity, and progressive wasting. These were inevitably followed by immobility, coma, and death.

8 Anthropological research by Shirley Lindenbaum and others showed that kuru first arose in the early decades of the 20th century and subsequently spread widely throughout the region of the Fore language group. Gajdusek asserted that this disease was spread by cannibalistic rituals practiced when relatives and other members of a village died. In effect, these practices amplified the disease as the pathogen that caused the death of one individual with kuru was spread to others in the area in a continuously spreading ring. Because of the slow natural history of this disease, it often took many years for exposed individuals to fall ill. Furthermore, the seemingly capricious and deadly nature of this disease led the local inhabitants to attribute the affliction to sorcery. With the cessation of cannibalistic practices, kuru eventually disappeared, but sporadic cases continued to appear for many decades after Gajdusek's initial work. Health officials are not entirely sure, however, whether the disease has truly been eradicated or its slow, unnoticed development currently goes on within some individual somewhere.

9 In 1997, Stanley Prusiner won a solo Nobel Prize in Physiology or Medicine "for his discovery of prions—a new biological principle of infection." It was Prusiner who helped to characterize these agents as protein aggregates devoid of genetic information. And Prusiner was the person who coined the term "prion" for these "proteinaceous infectious agents." Prusiner also developed a rodent model for studying prions, and this served to greatly speed up the pace of research, opening many new avenues of investigation, including the possibility of testing potential therapies.

> **TIP**
> It is common for scientific articles to contain passages about the history of discoveries. For example, in this reading, discoveries going back to the work of Björn Sigurðsson are discussed. In such passages, pay special attention to the work of anyone who—like Blumberg and Gajdusek, or Prusiner—has won a Nobel Prize. Such awards are rare and extremely prestigious, so the work recognized by them is usually considered highly valuable.

THE CENTRAL DOGMA OF BIOLOGY

10 In order to understand prion diseases and how they arise, it is necessary to consider how human cells function at the molecular level. It is useful to begin with the flow of biological information within every cell. The normal flow of biological information is known as the **central dogma of biology**. See Figure 1.

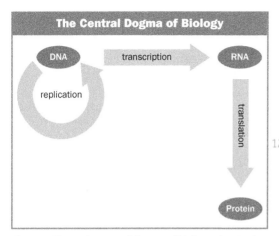

The Central Dogma of Biology

DNA → transcription → RNA

replication

translation

Protein

Figure 1 Shows the central dogma of biology, that is, the replication of DNA (deoxyribonucleic acid, the complex nucleic molecule that carries genetic information); the transcription of that information from DNA to RNA (the nucleic molecule ribonucleic acid, which sometimes carries genetic information); and RNA's translation of that information, to control the synthesis of proteins

11   Virtually every human cell carries the full set of genetic instructions for making that individual. This information is known as the **human genome**. The human genome differs slightly from one person to another and a bit more as we look at the genomes of our closest relatives, the great apes. Though the human genome contains the complete set of instructions, only small amounts of that information are expressed at any given time, depending on the function of each type of cell. The information that is expressed differs over time and from one cell to another.

12   The individual units of information within the genome are known as **genes**. Each gene's job is to express the information for making a single protein. Each protein consists of a linear string with a sequence of chemical building blocks called amino acids. The sequence of amino acids is determined by the sequence of DNA letters in the gene. After it is constructed, each protein folds into a three-dimensional shape. To a large extent, the amino acid sequence determines how the protein will fold, and the shape of the folded protein will determine the function of that protein.

PrP

13 Within the human genome, every human carries the gene for making PrP. This gene is expressed in the brain, among other places, and the protein is produced in cells that reside there. Not only is PrP

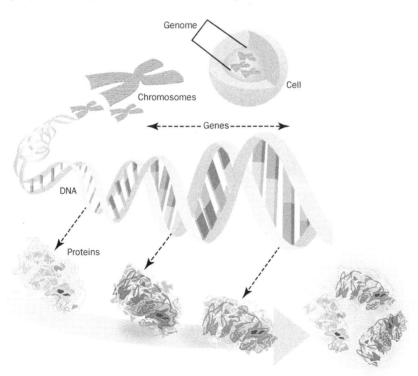

Genome

Cell

Chromosomes

Genes

DNA

Proteins

Figure 2

Continued

found in humans, it is also found in the brains of every mammal, differing slightly from one species to the next. It appears that all mammals may be susceptible to these bizarre diseases.

PRIONS AND CANCER

14 As we see in cancer, in prion diseases, our own biology turns against us. If we compare prion disease and cancer, there are some other interesting similarities and differences. One similarity is that both groups of diseases involve aberrant proteins that are expressed within the human genome. A second important similarity is that both types of disease can be familial, infectious, or spontaneous—at least insofar as no cause is easily identified. Important differences include the types of damage we see in cells and tissues, and the mechanisms by which that damage occurs.

CHECK WHAT YOU'VE LEARNED (Paragraphs 1–14)

Think about what you have just read. Answer each question. Then continue to the next part of the reading.

1. One result of the fact that prion diseases progress very slowly is that it was hard for Björn Sigurðsson and others to identify the pathological mechanism in scrapie. Another result of prion diseases' slow progression is that _____ .

    a. prion diseases often lead to cancer
    b. the disease cannot pass from one live animal to another
    c. the host rarely dies from the prion disease
    d. we can't be sure yet whether kuru has truly disappeared

2. What was the main contribution of D. Carleton Gajdusek to medical knowledge of prion diseases? Answer in one or two original sentences.

    ....

    ....

3. Stanley Prusiner won a Nobel Prize more than 20 years after Blumberg and Gajdusek. Name one or two of Prusiner's main contributions to the field. Answer in one or two original sentences.

    ....

    ....

4. The author spends several paragraphs discussing genetic mechanisms. Why? What is the connection between genetics and PrP?

    ....

    ....

5. What similarity between prion diseases and cancers is mentioned in Paragraph 14?

    ....

    ....

"Cows, Cannibals, and Crystals— Explaining the Mechanism of Prion Diseases," *continued*

PrP^C is a normal protein

PrP^C
is a normal protein

PrP^{Sc}
the disease-causing form of the prion protein

Figure 3

A PATHOGENIC MODEL

15 We can think of the prion protein PrP as existing in two forms: a normal, functional form and an abnormal, pathologic form. In the normal form, PrP exists as an individual globular-shaped protein in solution, and it is characterized by a series of helical substructures. The normal form of PrP is also called PrP-C, for cellular or alpha PrP because the helical regions are known as alpha helices.

16 The PrP-Sc form—for scrapie—has sticky regions made up of wavy substructures called beta pleated sheets. In the beta form, the proteins can bind together to form large crystal-like fibrils. When stained, aggregations of these fibrils form dark regions called amyloid plaques within the brains of infected individuals. Patricia Merz took high-resolution electron micrographic images of these plaques, showing that they are composed of individual fibrils. While the exact way in which these fibrils cause disease is under debate, it is clear that these fibrils are important in causing disease and, ultimately, the death of the host.

FORMATION OF A SEED FIBRIL

17 In the presence of a small fibril, which can be thought of as a seed fibril, the aggregation will continue to expand like a growing ice crystal.

The subunits for the fibril are the normally occurring PrP-C in the cell. Remarkably, the abnormal PrP-Sc in the fibril is able to transform the normal PrP-C into PrP-Sc and recruit it into the growing fibril. In a *Star Wars* analogy, these once-normal proteins are recruited over to "the dark side."

18 There are two theories for how this conversion occurs. In one model, the abnormal protein acts like an enzyme to actively alter the protein. This seems unlikely, as enzymes are typically honed by millions of years of evolution into their precise function. In addition, this model suggests that the disease would follow a much more explosive course of development as one enzyme begets many more enzymes, and so on.

19 The second model suggests that PrP has the ability to flip-flop between the PrP-C and the PrP-Sc forms. In this model, PrP spends vastly more time in the PrP-C form, and when it does assume the PrP-Sc sticky form, it will rapidly shift back to the PrP-C form. The exception occurs when two or more PrPs in close proximity happen to switch to the PrP-Sc form at the same time. This allows the proteins to stick together and stabilizes them in the PrP-Sc form. If there are only two PrPs together, they may shift back, but at a certain critical number, they will form a stable fibril seed. **Polymerization**, or binding between

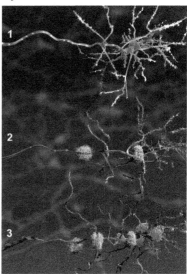

> **TIP**
> ....
> *In this section of the essay, the author has chosen to boldface only one word, polymerization. This is an extremely strong signal that the concept of polymerization is vital to the diseases discussed. In fact, this is borne out later in the reading, where we learn that not only prion diseases but also other maladies are characterized by abnormal polymerization.*

Continued

PrP molecules, leads to stabilization of an otherwise unfavorable conformation. This fibril seed can then go on to recruit any additional PrPs in the area that happen to flip to the PrP-Sc form, and the crystal will begin to grow. This polymerization of PrP is essential to the development of disease.

20   The growth of these pathogenic fibrils is limited by several factors. The first is the difficulty of forming the initial seed fibril. Although this process could potentially play out in anyone, the probability is extremely low, making prion diseases quite rare. Even after the initial seed fibril forms, the growth of the seed can only occur when a rare flip-flopping PrP protein encounters a fibril. It is further limited by the rate of PrP-C within the cell. Because of these factors, spontaneous CJD is rarely seen in individuals less than 50 years of age. Prion disease in younger individuals suggests either environmental exposure or genetic predisposition.

21   It is worth noting that cells also make use of nonpathogenic fibrils to make up the structural components of the cell. However, these normal fibrils are all highly regulated in terms of their polymerization, building up and breaking down at appropriate times. Curiously, researchers have synthesized nonfunctional proteins with random strings of amino acids. These nonfunctional proteins will often form protein polymers, leading to the conclusion that during the evolutionary process, most functional proteins in living cells have been selected for their inability to polymerize spontaneously.

DURABILITY

22 These fibrils are very, very durable and resistant to destruction by chemical or physical means. They can retain their infectivity outside the body over the course of years. This means that instruments used on individuals with prion disease may transmit infection to other patients or health care workers, even if the instruments are carefully cleaned using standard methods.

PATHOLOGY

23 In addition to amyloid plaques, several other types of pathology or abnormal findings are found in the brains of individuals afflicted with a prion disease.

- Cell loss: There is a decrease in the number of neurons due to cell death.
- Astrocytosis: There is a proliferation of particular star-shaped neuronal cells called astrocytes.
- Spongiform changes: The affected regions of the brain take on a sponge-like appearance with holes. This has led to the term *spongiform encephalopathy* to describe these diseases. In most cases, the terms *spongiform encephalopathy* and *prion disease* are used interchangeably.

HUMAN GROWTH HORMONE (hGH) AND IATROGENIC TRANSMISSION

24 Iatrogenic—or health-care-associated—transmission has been well documented. Table 3 lists some of the documented examples of health-care–associated transmission of prions.

Corneal transplantation
Cortical electrode implantation
Dura mater grafting
Human growth hormone therapy
Neurosurgical and neuropathological procedures

Table 3 Procedures with documented occurrences of prion transmission

25   One striking example involves the human growth hormone (hGH). The use of this hormone is to treat growth disorders. hGH was initially derived from large numbers of human pituitary glands obtained from cadavers. This was the only source since the protein hormone could not be synthesized and animal-derived growth hormone was slightly different and did not work in humans. What was not realized at the time was that a single pituitary from an individual with CJD might contaminate the entire batch, and all the children who were recipients might go on to develop a fatal neurological disease. This link was first made by an astute endocrinologist who saw a young patient dying of such a disease. He quickly notified health authorities. The use of the cadaver-derived hormone was stopped in 1985, but not before at least 160 children had been infected. They all went on to die. What is not widely recognized is that this cohort is around the same size as the number of people who have died of the much more widely publicized mad cow disease epidemic.

Also in the mid-1980s, a company called Genentech offered the first commercially available hGH produced using recombinant technology and free from the possibility of prion contamination. As a side note, a dispute over the ownership of the hGH, patent led to a lawsuit in which the University of California at San Francisco (UCSF) sued Genentech. The settlement of this suit included a $50 million payment by the company toward establishing the Mission Bay campus at UCSF.

CHECK WHAT YOU'VE LEARNED (Paragraphs 15–25)

Think about what you have just read. Answer each question. Then continue to the next part of the reading.

6. Paragraphs 15–17 describe a process of going to "the dark side." What does this phrase mean?

   a. A normal, harmless chemical in the body suddenly changes into something harmful.
   b. Laboratory results show dark traces where harmful chemicals exist.
   c. A protein that is easy to understand suddenly becomes too complex to analyze.
   d. Researchers have to go deep into hard-to-reach regions.

7. Describe how polymerization involving PrP can lead to the development of disease. Write one or two original sentences.

   ....

   ....

8. Reread Paragraphs 21 and 22. Which of the following claims is made?

   a. Polymerization changes nonfunctional proteins into functional ones.
   b. It is natural for protein fibrils to keep building up without breaking down.
   c. In healthy cells, fibrils can occur, but their growth is controlled.
   d. Fortunately, polymerized proteins cannot survive for very long on medical tools.

9. What does *spongiform encephalopathy* mean?

   ....

   ....

10. What can be most strongly inferred from Paragraph 25?

    a. Infection through hGH administration gave the children CJD.
    b. This is another case of disease being passed from the dead to the living.
    c. Prion disease from hGH treatment has killed more people than any other prion disease.
    d. Animal-derived growth hormone has been shown to cause no problems.

"Cows, Cannibals, and Crystals— Explaining the Mechanism of Prion Diseases," *continued*

MULTIPLE FORMS

26 One of the most confusing aspects of prion diseases in humans is the fact that they exist in multiple forms. These forms differ somewhat in their clinical symptoms, their primary locus in the brain, their aggressiveness, their physical and chemical properties, and their epidemiology. At present, the best explanation for this is the possibility that in each of these diseases, PrP-Sc differs slightly, like different crystal forms of ice. And just like different crystal forms of ice, the newly recruited molecules will conform to the structure of the existing crystal.

MAD COW DISEASE

27 The advent of **bovine spongiform encephalopathy** (BSE, or more colloquially, mad cow disease) conforms well to this model of prion disease. In 1986, a new prion disease in cows was first reported in England. The incidence of this disease began to rise exponentially, peaking in the early 1990s. This disease appeared to have a similar pattern to kuru. In this case, through the use of diseased cows not suitable for human consumption for cattle feed, the cattle industry turned these cows into cannibals. Although cows are herbivores, the addition of cow-derived proteins in their feed can increase their growth rate. With the realization of what was happening, this practice was discontinued. In addition, the detection of BSE within an individual cow often led to culling the entire herd. The animals were burned in large bonfires; the goal of this was to destroy the causative agent. Despite these efforts, the long incubation period of BSE meant that cases continued to arise through the 1990s.

HUMAN BSE

28 In May 1995, the first human case of BSE was detected in a 19-year-old named Stephen Churchill. British tabloids immediately made the connection to BSE. However, the scientific community hesitated to link this new disease to the earlier mad cow epidemic. They cautiously referred to it as variant CJD (vCJD). Unlike scrapie, BSE has managed to jump species. Experimental studies show that it was possible to transmit the disease to a variety of different animals.

29 Because of the longer incubation period in humans and because the mechanism of transmission to humans had never been established, dire predictions were made regarding the number of people who might become infected and die. This was intensified by the fact that both BSE in cows and in humans appeared in several counties in England and then across the globe.

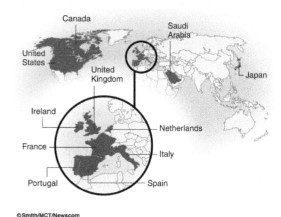

Figure 4 Occurrences of BSE

30 Although it was initially thought that BSE emerged when scrapie jumped species from sheep to cows, it now seems more likely that BSE arose spontaneously and was subsequently amplified by existing farm practices. Once again, this is analogous to the situation with kuru. This model suggests that the ban against such feeding practices should remain in place as novel forms of prion diseases can arise *de novo*. However, the story of mad cow disease also emphasizes the possibility that prion diseases may jump species.

IMPLICATIONS

31 This pathogenic model has important implications. Using this model, we can now go back and understand how prion diseases can be genetic, infectious, and spontaneous. The genetic version of this disease arises in individuals who

have a mutation in the PrP gene. Such mutations make PrP more likely to form the initial seed that gives rise to fibril formation and subsequently to clinical disease. Perhaps the mutant PrP is simply a bit more likely to flip into the PrP-Sc form, or maybe the cell makes just a little bit more PrP so that the randomly formed PrP-Sc proteins are more likely to bump into each other, or perhaps PrP-Sc is a bit more likely to stay in the PrP-Sc form before it flips back to PrP-C. While familial forms of prion disease are quite rare, naturally occurring variants in the PrP gene are far more common, including alternative sequences, deletions, and insertions. Some of these variants appear to be more susceptible to both the infectious and spontaneous forms of disease.

> **TIP**
>
> *A large majority of scientific articles employ abbreviations of some sort—such as PrP-C and PrP-Sc in this article. Notice the pattern of capitalization in the abbreviation. In this case, we have a small r between two capital Ps. That is because the r does not stand for a separate word, only for the second letter in the word* prion. *The same logic explains why in PrP-Sc the c is lowercase; it is the second letter in the word* scrapie.

32   The infectious form occurs when a person or animal is exposed to a preformed seed from another affected individual. This greatly facilitates the probability and speed of progression because it bypasses the difficulty of the seed fibril formation step. The spontaneous form occurs in the unlikely and unlucky event that several individual beta-form proteins bump into each other and form an initial seed.

33   A second implication of this model suggests some testable hypotheses. For example, it implies that animals that lack PrP completely should not be able to develop these diseases. The problem is that PrP is highly conserved in evolution, suggesting that the protein plays a critical role. It seemed that animals that lacked this gene would not survive until birth. The experiment was first carried out in mice. To everyone's surprise, not only did the animals survive, but they also appeared to be perfectly normal. True to predictions, however, they were completely resistant to the development of prion diseases. What if all cows intended for human consumption in any form were bred with the PrP deleted?

TREATMENT?

34   Another prediction from this model involves the treatment and prevention of these diseases. While it is hard to fathom that a disease that is currently 100 percent fatal could be effectively treated, this model suggests the possibility of designing small molecules that could bind to the aberrant form of PrP and prevent it from any further polymerization. Such a treatment could not repair any cellular brain damage that has already occurred, but it could prevent any further damage. If these drugs were safe enough, it might be possible to take them on a daily basis to prevent the initial occurrence of prion disease. This would be similar to the way that millions of people take a baby aspirin every day to prevent heart disease. Some polymerase blockers are being tested, but so far none are safe or effective enough for use by humans.

35   While PrP deletion seems to have little impact on the health of mice, we do not know how important this normal protein is to the health of humans. With the advent of new, facile techniques for gene editing, there will surely be debates over the possibility of creating prion-disease-free humans.

36   If we think of prion diseases more generally as diseases of abnormal polymerization (DAPs), it appears they are not as unique as was initially believed. Several important neurological diseases including Alzheimer's disease, amyotrophic lateral sclerosis (ALS, or Lou Gehrig's disease), and even Parkinson's disease fit this pattern. Nonneurological diseases like sickle cell anemia and amyloidosis may also fit this pattern. Each of these diseases involves a different protein leading to other key differences. However, this model does raise important questions. For example, under the right conditions, could Alzheimer's disease have a contagious component when someone is exposed to a seed fibril or crystal?

37   Initially, prion diseases seem to be rare but fascinating disorders. However, a deeper understanding of this class of diseases provides insights into protein function, into what it means to be infectious, and into broader issues of health and disease.

CHECK WHAT YOU'VE LEARNED (Paragraphs 26–37)

Think about what you have just read. Answer each question.

11. Why does the author make a comparison to crystals of ice in Paragraph 26?

   ....

   ....

12. Which idea does the author imply in Paragraphs 28–30?

   a. Journalists unnecessarily scared the public by irresponsibly claiming humans had come down with BSE.
   b. Scientists were being too cautious by failing to acknowledge that BSE had spread to humans.
   c. BSE is actually not a separate disease but is a type of scrapie that cows get.
   d. England was the only country where BSE occurred in both cows and humans.

13. Complete the chart.

How Prion Diseases Develop	
genetically	By ....
infectiously	By ....
spontaneously	By "bad luck" when two ....

14. What "hope for the future" is expressed in Paragraph 33?

   ....

   ....

15. What similarity does the author point to among diseases as various as prion diseases, Alzheimer's disease, and sickle cell anemia?

   a. They are all prion diseases.
   b. They are all neurological diseases.
   c. They all involve abnormal polymerization.
   d. They can all be passed from one human to another.

THINKING CRITICALLY

Consider each situation in light of what you have read in "Cows, Cannibals, and Crystals—Explaining the Mechanism of Prion Diseases." By yourself or with a partner, apply what you know about diseases to address each situation.

Situation 1 You are an official with the local public health agency. A very disturbing event has occurred: Tests on some sick cattle from a few local farms have come back positive for mad cow disease (BSE). Cattle farming is big business in your area. This disease could have tragic consequences. How should you and your staff proceed? What can you do to protect public health while trying to minimize damage to the local economy?

Situation 2 You are a doctor. A female patient in her 60s comes in, complaining of a variety of symptoms including difficulty walking, tremors, muscular rigidity, and forgetfulness. In conversing with her, you learn that she was a humanitarian worker in Papua New Guinea in the 1970s. She has also spent time in Great Britain. You also learn that her mother suffered from Alzheimer's. How do you go about making your diagnosis? What is your diagnosis? And what do you base your diagnosis on?

THINKING VISUALLY

A. In the reading, Figure 1 (p. 297) gives a symbolic interpretation of "the central dogma of biology." Based on the figure and the associated text, what is that dogma? State it in your own words, but make it sound like a natural law—a statement of the way things are in nature.

....

....

....

....

B. Look back at Figure 4 (the map on p. 302) in the reading and at the example map below. Build a map of your own to show the occurrence of Alzheimer's disease—like BSE, a disease of abnormal polymerization—in a country that you know well. This will require some online research to get data about the incidence of the disease in the country you choose. For most countries, you can find a blank map online that you can then customize by hand (or with drawing software).

Your map might show any of the following, on a place-by-place basis, for example:

- The number of Alzheimer's cases reported in given locations
- The rate of increase in Alzheimer's cases in given locations
- The number of people (per 100,000 or per 1 million) dying of Alzheimer's in given locations

Your choice of which map to produce will depend on what kind of data you can find.

Example

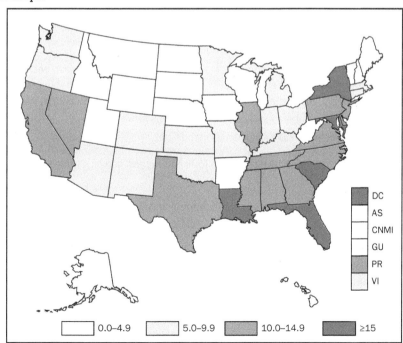

Rates per 100,000 population of diagnosed HIV cases in US in 2012

THINKING ABOUT LANGUAGE

RECOGNIZING COLLOCATIONS

A. Read these excerpts from the essay. Each excerpt contains an underlined set of words that represents a collocation. Circle at least one other collocation in each sentence. Some excerpts will have more than one. Use an online corpus, a dictionary with a collocations feature, and your own intuition to assist you in answering the questions.

1. Even more frightening is the fact that, <u>under the right conditions</u>, these afflictions may be passed from one individual to another.

2. Over the years, a great deal has been learned about these diseases and many <u>perplexing questions</u> have been answered.

3. Another <u>unusual aspect</u> of prion diseases is the way in which they arise.

4. Referred to as Creutzfeldt-Jakob disease, or CJD, the name <u>pays homage to</u> the researchers who published these first reports.

5. Though the human genome contains the complete <u>set of instructions</u>, only small amounts of that information are expressed at any given time, depending on the function of each type of cell.

6. <u>As we see in</u> cancer, in prion diseases, our own biology turns against us.

7. In the normal form, PrP exists as an individual globular-shaped protein in solution, and it <u>is characterized by</u> a series of helical substructures.

8. While the exact <u>way in which</u> these fibrils cause disease is under debate, it is clear that these fibrils are important in causing disease and, ultimately, the death of the host.

9. The exception occurs when two or more PrPs in close proximity happen to switch to the PrP-Sc form <u>at the same time</u>.

10. It <u>is worth noting</u> that cells also make use of nonpathogenic fibrils to make up the structural components of the cell.

IDENTIFYING AND USING EXPRESSIONS OF FUNCTION AND PURPOSE

B. Read these excerpts from the essay. Circle one expression of function or purpose in each sentence. Then replace the expression with another expression of function and purpose, making sure not to change the original meaning. It may be necessary to change the sentence structure in some cases.

1. Our current understanding suggests that these diseases occur when proteins from our body act to form crystal-like structures that can damage and kill cells in the brain.

2. This essay will focus on how these prional structures form and suggest some possible avenues for future therapy and prophylaxis.

3. The way in which PrP contributes to pathogenesis is by forming large aggregates that lead to the death of cells and the spread of these protein aggregates to adjacent cells.

4. Prusiner also developed a rodent model for studying prions, and this served to greatly speed up the pace of research, opening many new avenues of investigation, including the possibility of testing potential therapies.

5. Each gene's job is to express the information for making a single protein.

6. This means that instruments used on individuals with prion disease may transmit infection to other patients or health care workers, even if the instruments are carefully cleaned using standard methods.

7. The use of this hormone is to treat growth disorders.

8. In this case, through the use of diseased cows not suitable for human consumption for cattle feed, the cattle industry turned these cows into cannibals.

9. The animals were burned in large bonfires; the goal of this was to destroy the causative agent.

10. The problem is that PrP is highly conserved in evolution, suggesting that the protein plays a critical role.

Go to **MyEnglishLab** for more practice reading an extended text and using your reading skills.

RESEARCH PROJECT

The essay in this unit discusses various prion diseases and their mechanisms. By doing research, you can learn more about the prion proteins associated with the diseases and how they operate, how the diseases were discovered, how they are contracted, what symptoms accompany them, and whether there is currently a large outbreak of any of them in any region of the world.

A. The following is a list of the prion diseases discussed in the reading. Choose and research one or two or more that form a group—like diseases in humans or diseases in animals.

- bovine spongiform encephalopathy (BSE)
- kuru
- Creutzfeldt-Jakob disease (CJD)
- fatal familial insomnia (FFI)
- Gerstmann-Straussler-Scheinker syndrome (GSS)
- scrapie
- transmissible mink encephalopathy
- chronic wasting disease (CWD)

B. Conduct your research. As you read about your subject, formulate a thesis. Gather information that supports your thesis. Use the following ideas to help guide you:

- Focus on classifying the disease(s) you chose.
- Compare and contrast the symptoms of one disease with another.
- Create a demographic profile of the victims.

C. Choose a presentation style from the box, or use your own idea, and present your research to the class.

| recorded interview | speech using metaphors | slideshow |

Go to **MyEnglishLab** to complete a collaborative activity.

Education teaches you to love the world.

Cultivation of the Educated Person

UNIT PROFILE

In this unit, you will read about education as a process of cultivation, similar to the tending of a garden. In the online extended reading, you will explore ways in which classical and Renaissance writers and philosophers supposedly gained knowledge through conversations with the dead. As a capstone to the unit, you will research an educational philosopher or theorist and present your findings.

EXTENDED READING

BEFORE YOU READ

Discuss these questions with another student.

1. Look at the image above, which features the Pavilion Gardens at the University of Virginia. Think about the physical environment of the schools you've attended. Were any physical environments more suitable for learning than the others? Describe why such environment(s) were especially suitable for your learning style.

2. In the United States, university campuses display certain typical styles of building design, landscaping, and physical layout. Think of campuses you've seen outside of the United States. Describe them and how they compare to US campuses in design.

3. The essay you are about to read speaks about higher education as a process of nurturing a student's talents and curiosity just as one might tend a garden. Do you think most of your former teachers held this attitude? Explain.

4. From your experience so far in higher education (college, university, an intensive-English program) do you think the cultures of ancient Greece and Rome are still influential in academia? How so?

Read the passage. Then answer the questions after each section.

The Cultivation of Higher Learning

ABSTRACT

This paper explores education as a process of cultivation, like the tending of a garden. The sometimes park-like nature of college campuses is a natural correlative of the university's mission as an agent of cultivation. The essay examines classical application of not only the metaphorical gardening involved in education but also the literal placing of the process in cultivational settings like the Garden of Epicurus (named after its founder, the Greek philosopher Epicurus, 341–270 BCE). Disquisitions by Socrates through Plato, and by Plato writing in his own voice, support the concept that the self is tended like soil so that seeds of knowledge planted there can bear fruit. The paper considers whether the fundamental role of research in modern education may objectify knowledge and move education away from its cultivational realm. In the end, however, the British and US university tradition is portrayed as strongly legitimate and true to its classical roots as a protected "garden" in which the learning potential of the self is tended and intellectual pursuits bear fruit.

1 The verdant environments of most US campuses have the feel of expansive, well-manicured gardens. This is not by chance. Institutions of higher learning have a long history of association with such bucolic settings. Think of the "college gardens" of famous British universities (Oxford has some 30 colleges, each with its own distinctive garden). Think of the Italian garden academies of the Renaissance (the Platonic Academy outside Florence, for example, founded by the ruler of Florence, Cosimo de' Medici in the 15th century); or of the bowers of Sainte-Geneviève, near Paris, where the first medieval universities sprang up; or of the ancient country villas where much of the tutoring of upper-class Roman youths would take place. Finally, think of the groves and gardens of the most famous Greek schools (Epicurus's school

was known as the *kepidion*, or little garden; Plato's Academy was located in an ancient grove of plane trees, and then planted with olive trees grown from slips of the sacred olive of the Erechtheum temple, built on the Acropolis).

2 In this essay I will argue that the garden like environments of these educational institutions provide more than just a congenial setting for the learning to which those institutions are devoted. If one views education as a rarefied form of gardening, as I do, then one sees in these settings an **objective correlative** of the distinctly human activity that takes place within them. I mean the activity of cultivation.

3 Cultivation presupposes a potential that nature itself does not fulfill on its own. As it progresses from infancy to adulthood, the human body matures according to the biological laws that hold sway over physical development. The same cannot be said of a person's mental, emotional, and moral development, which depend in large part on various modes of cultural transmission. Most of what makes humans exceptional in the natural order—our capacity for knowledge, acquired skills, moral virtue, and historical understanding—we owe to education in one form or another. Education is an unnatural agent that augments nature. In the same way that a garden does not come into being spontaneously but by cultivation of the soil's potential for flourishing, so too the cultural burgeoning brought about by education comes from a sustained cultivation of our human potential for growth of a second order (i.e., cultural and not merely biological growth).

4 The Czech modernist writer and democratic activist Karel Čapek (1890–1938), who was a passionate gardener, authored in the 1920s a beautiful little book called *The Gardener's Year*, in which he provides an eloquent definition of a gardener. In this description the value of a gardener is not in the act of planting seeds and helping flowers to grow; rather, his value lies in maintaining the soil that allows a seed to mature and grow into a healthy plant. The gardener helps actualize the vital potential of the soil to

Continued

sustain and nourish that which takes root in it. As described by Čapek, it is through the work of the gardener that a flower is allowed to mature successfully from a seed to a plant, avoiding potential dangers like overgrowth from weeds or lack of nutrition. Čapek's flower here stands for all that thrives through human care and cultivation, above all the cultural maturity that education, especially in its higher forms, makes possible.

5   If culture is the fruit of cultivation, as the word itself suggests, we can understand why education has long been associated with tilling, tending, and gardening. The association goes as far back as Confucius (551–479 BCE) and Plato (470–399 BCE). The former taught that virtue germinates in thought—that virtue is the organic outgrowth of meditation. Thought requires knowledge, which in turn requires education. That is why the cultivation of knowledge through education is a prime directive of yi, or righteousness. Yi consists not merely of following rules of behavior but of understanding the intrinsic goodness of the positive virtues. It is, in every respect, the flower of a genuine education.

Figure 1 Plato's Academy

6   The cultivation of the self through knowledge was a prime directive also for Plato, who founded the first institution of higher learning in the ancient world—the so-called Academy, located just outside the walls of Athens, in an enclosed park that contained a sacred grove linked to a local hero named Academos. The degree to which Plato saw education as analogous to or even connatural with husbandry and gardening becomes evident in a famous passage of the *Phaedrus*, where Socrates attempts to convince his interlocutor that *paideia*, or a formative education, is better served through the live verbal interchange between teacher and student than through the dead words of writing. Socrates to Phaedrus:

> And now may I be allowed to ask you a question: Would a husbandman, who is a man of sense, take the seeds, which he values and which he wishes to bear fruit, and in sober seriousness plant them during the heat of summer, in some garden of Adonis, that he may rejoice when he sees them in eight days appearing in beauty? At least he would do so, if at all, only for the sake of amusement and pastime. But when he is in earnest he sows in fitting soil, and practises husbandry, and is satisfied if in eight months the seeds which he has sown arrive at perfection? … And can we suppose that he who knows the just and good and honourable has less understanding, than the husbandman, about his own seeds? … Then he will not seriously incline to 'write' his thoughts 'in water' with pen and ink, sowing words which can neither speak for themselves nor teach the truth adequately to others? … No, that is not likely—in the garden of letters he will sow and plant, but only for the sake of recreation and amusement; he will write them down as memorials to be treasured against the forgetfulness of old age, by himself, or by any other old man who is treading the same path. He will rejoice in beholding their tender growth; and while others are refreshing their souls with banqueting and the like, this will be the pastime in which his days are spent.[1]

7   Adonis, beloved by Aphrodite, died young, and on his festival day (the *Adone*), the ancient Greeks engaged in the strange ritual of casting potted plants out of their windows. These bowls or boxes, which Socrates

TIP

A long discourse attributed to Socrates gives you a chance to speculate: What personality is imputed to Socrates via this quote? Does it indicate anything about the thought processes that Plato wants to attribute to him?

---

[1] Plato. *Phaedrus*. Trans. by Benjamin Jowett. Oxford, 1892

calls "gardens," contained newly sprouting plants that had not yet produced seeds. By comparing writing to these seedless "gardens of Adonis," Plato (through his spokesman Socrates) implicitly declares that writing is a sterile form of knowledge, as opposed to living intercourse (of the sort that presumably took place at the Academy), which is likened to the seeds (*sperma*) that the judicious farmer sows in fertile soil.

8   This analogy becomes fully explicit when Socrates goes on to declare that the highest form of education takes place when a worthy teacher employs the art of dialectic, and, fastening upon a suitable soul, plants and sows in it truths accompanied by knowledge. Such truths can defend themselves as well as the man who planted them; they are not sterile but contain a seed from which fresh truths spring up in other minds; in this way, they secure immortality for it and confer upon the man who possesses it the highest happiness possible for a human being to enjoy.[2]

CHECK WHAT YOU'VE LEARNED (Paragraphs 1–8)

Think about what you have just read. Answer each question. Then continue to the next part of the reading.

1. In Paragraph 2, the author says of park-like university campuses, "one sees in these settings an objective correlative of the distinctly human activity that takes place within them." What do you think this statement means?

   ....

   ....

2. In Paragraph 3, the author makes the point that education is unnatural, but he means this in a good way. In your own words, paraphrase the author's reasoning in calling education "unnatural."

   ....

   ....

3. The author references an observation by Karel Čapek (Paragraph 4) that a gardener cultivates the soil, not the eventual plant. This is meant as a metaphor for the way humans are educated. In the process of education, what might the soil metaphorically correspond to?

   ....

   ....

4. Why does the author mention an "enclosed park" and a "sacred grove" in Paragraph 6?

   ....

   ....

5. As mentioned in the long quote from the *Phaedrus* and explicated in Paragraph 7, what is a "garden of Adonis"? Why, in the quote from Plato, does Socrates mention them?

   ....

   ....

---

[2] Plato, Complete Works, ed. John M. Cooper (Indianapolis: Hackett Publishing Company, 1997). Page 99.

"The Cultivation of Higher Learning," *continued*

9   In the long passage from the *Phaedrus*, which understands education as a veritable "seminar," that is a sowing of seeds in the student's soul, Plato renders explicit something we tend to assume but fail to appreciate sufficiently, namely that soul and soil share a natural affinity. By that I mean that both lend themselves to cultivation in their potential for new life—vegetal life in one case, intellectual and spiritual life in the other. This is another way of saying that human beings possess a "humic" soul-substance, as it were—where ideas, virtues, and skills can take root and grow. The analogy between soul and soil goes beyond mere metaphor, for the unitary phenomenon of life envelops them both, each in its own way. Viewed from that perspective, education, when it remains true to its highest calling, is akin to Čapek's "real gardener," who cultivates the soil rather than flowers.

10   Plato was by no means alone in believing that education had to do primarily with "care of the self"—in Greek, *epimeleia heautou*; in Latin, *cura sui*. Whether one was a Platonist, a Stoic, an Epicurean, or a Christian, education took the form of cultivating various spiritual, intellectual, and moral capacities within the self. Self-care was not only an idea but a practice. It required following a fixed curriculum or protocol based on a guiding philosophy of the *summum bonum*, or highest good. The philosophies in question may have differed from one another, but they had in common the assumption that education fulfilled its vocation in self-care.[3]

11   The other intimately related assumption the philosophies had in common was that, for the individual, the goal of education is happiness. All of the philosophies aimed for happiness, but they believed that only one kind of philosophy—or one form of self-care—could lead to it. For the Platonists, the way to true happiness lay in contemplation of the super-sensate realm of ideas. For the Stoics, it lay in the dispassionate wisdom that enables a person to "live in accordance with divine nature." The Epicureans considered the pleasures of earthly life the essential core of happiness. For the Christians, monastic discipline and learning aimed to purify the soul and ready it for the ultimate happiness, namely salvation. However divergent the philosophies were from one another, the schools that were founded on them conceived of their mission as an extended cultivation of the art of living based on a deep understanding of the ultimate nature of reality.

12   Consider the Epicurean schools that flourished all around the Mediterranean world for 700 years after Epicurus founded, in 306 BCE outside the Dipylon Gate of Athens, his Garden School—so-named because it had a house and a small garden where instruction and various forms of conviviality took place, and where the disciples would grow vegetables and fruits that would find their way on to the communal dining tables. Epicurus taught that the *summum bonum*, or highest good, was neither citizenship, nor wisdom, nor Stoic detachment, but an earthly, pleasure-based happiness. Fear of death—of death's unknown—constitutes a major impediment to happiness since it keeps us in a state of constant anxiety about what awaits us after we die. To overcome this dread was one of the primary goals of Epicurean self-care. To that end Epicurus recommended an in-depth, comprehensive study of his doctrinal philosophy in all its various dimensions—scientific, metaphysical, and moral.

13   To overcome the fear of death, one must start by understanding the nature of the "void," which requires that one understand the atomic nature of reality. Once one understands that even the soul is made up of atoms, its intrinsic mortality becomes manifest, and one realizes that the soul is born and dies with the body. By the same means one realizes that the gods (whose existence Epicurus did not deny) remain supremely indifferent to human affairs. While these insights into the nature of reality may unsettle at first, they ultimately have

---

[3] On self-care traditions in Greek and Roman antiquity, see Michel Foucault's *The History of Sexuality*, vol 3: *The Care of the Self* (Vintage: Reprint edition, New York, 1998).

a liberating effect on the Epicurean. Earthly happiness for Epicurus requires *ataraxia*, a state of mind free from perturbation and compulsion. Inner serenity is not the default condition of human beings; it is attained through assiduous cultivation, training, and discipline. Epicurean ataraxia could be called a garden of the psyche. Just as a garden can quickly revert to a more wild state when neglected by its caretakers, so too ataraxia, once achieved, can easily lose its composure under stress and give way to the more "natural" state of anxiety.

14 Ataraxia makes the human soul ready for, or receptive to, the earthly pleasures that make for human happiness. These pleasures have nothing to do with the gratification of appetite. They consist instead of a series of cultivated virtues. Pleasure and virtue are bound together inextricably in Epicurus's philosophy. Take the supreme Epicurean virtue of friendship. Like most of his fellow Greeks, Epicurus believed that happiness is impossible without it. Friendship, however, requires constant cultivation—not only of one's friends but above all, of oneself. Since the better part of friendship consists in *conversation*, one must develop the verbal, intellectual, and social skills to become the sort of interlocutor who can give pleasure to one's friends, expecting them to do the same for you. This means, or so taught Epicurus, that one must study philosophy, especially the Epicurean philosophy, for nothing enhances the pleasure of conversation as much as an intelligent, thoughtful exchange of ideas. To that same end, one should become fluent in poetry and eloquence, learning to use one's voice the way musicians learn to play instruments. The Epicurean should also cultivate graceful demeanor and appearance—all by way of rendering oneself more pleasing to one's friends. In this same vein Epicurus urged the cultivation of three supreme social virtues: *epikeia*, or courtesy; *parresia*, or honesty and candor in one's

speech; and *suavitas*, "a certain agreeableness of speech and manners." He also advocated the more traditional virtues of prudence, moderation, and justice.

15 In addition to these social virtues, Epicurus also recommended cultivating what we might call the psychological dispositions of gratitude, patience, and hope. These dispositions relate to the three temporal dimensions of past, present, and future. Toward the present we should adopt an attitude of patience; toward the past, gratitude; toward the future, hope. These dispositions do not come naturally. By nature we tend to be more greedy than grateful, more impulsive than patient, and more heavy-hearted than hopeful. Gratitude, patience, and hope require an inward transformation of attitude toward time in its finite generosity. All three virtues are indispensable ingredients of the earthly human happiness that Epicurus considered not only possible but also readily attainable for those who followed his teachings.

16 The Epicurean school placed more emphasis on persona, social, and spiritual virtues than on civic and moral virtues, for, unlike Plato's Academy, the Garden School did not seek to prepare its adherents for political leadership. Yet both schools conceived of their missions as self-curation. The same was true of Aristotle's Lyceum, the Stoa of the Stoics, and even the early Christian institutions of higher learning, all of which directed their efforts toward an organic cultivation of the *whole* person (mind, body, and soul). They conceived of happiness not so much as a reward for the labor of self-care but as the measure, or natural outgrowth, of a person's actualization of his or her human potential.

TIP

Where the author inserts words from other languages, did you try to relate them to English words that may be related? For example, did you recognize a similarity between summum and the word summit?

CHECK WHAT YOU'VE LEARNED (Paragraphs 9–16)

Think about what you have just read. Answer each question. Then continue to the next part of the reading.

6. This section contains a number of Latin and Greek expressions and terms (in italics). The author could certainly have written these paragraphs without them, but their inclusion adds a dimension to the presentation. What function do you think these foreign phrases serve?

....

....

7. Why does the author devote, in Paragraph 11, a sentence to each of four different philosophical / religious traditions? What point does the author make about each of them?

....

....

8. In Paragraphs 12–14, the author stresses that Epicurean philosophy expected a virtuous person to exert significant effort and exercise a substantial level of discipline to cultivate a certain attitude. What is this attitude, and why is it important to a person?

....

....

9. To Epicurus, attaining the virtue of friendship required considerable education. What was a virtuous person expected to cultivate in order to be a good friend?

....

....

10. Many modern psychologists have pointed to a process called "self-actualization" as one of the highest achievements in the development of one's personality. Self-actualization involves fulfilling one's personal potential. How does this modern concept relate to the classically valued processes described in Paragraphs 15 and 16?

....

....

"The Cultivation of Higher Learning," *continued*

17   Our modern universities and colleges differ in many respects from the ancient schools, while in other respects they have inherited and incorporated some of the latter's most important legacies. Nowadays most universities do not represent distinct schools of philosophical thought. Nor are most of them based any longer on explicitly Christian foundations, as was the case when most of our modern universities first came into being in continental Europe, England, and the United States. Now science determines the institutional organization of the university. Science requires neither a philosophical nor a theological foundation but only "academic freedom" to pursue research. The doctrine of academic freedom serves as one of the foundations of our institutions of higher learning today—at least at public colleges and universities and private ones that are not strongly religious.

18   Academic freedom is not a philosophy but a structural principle, a form of institutional protection for research and discourse, especially in the sciences. Until relatively recently, scientific research was under scrutiny and even threat from authorities of church and state. The principle of academic freedom arose as a way of limiting the reach of these erstwhile supervising authorities. Appealing to the need for autonomy and objectivity in scientific inquiry, the principle holds that external, nonexpert authority of any sort has no place in the sciences, that science functions properly only where it is free to posit its own methodological criteria for establishing truth and matters of fact, without fear of repercussion. Science's successful push for autonomy has influenced or even created analogous research-based activities in the humanities as well as the social sciences. Every university department now pursues research of some type. Today freedom of research, rather than any school of philosophy, unifies the university.

19   For better or worse, schools of philosophy fostered ideas, attitudes, and principles that were meant to take root and germinate within the "subject" of knowledge, leading to a new maturation process within the individual. Research, by contrast, de-emphasizes the subject and remains focused on its object; and objective knowledge—be it of nature, society, history, or art—remains the goal across its diverse fields and departments. This is idiosyncratically modern. From a historical point of view, this discounting of the student's subjective engagement in the pursuit of knowledge—and through it, of wisdom, happiness, or transcendence—remains exceptional. For the philosophical schools, knowledge meant, first and foremost, self-knowledge by way of self-cultivation. The eliding of the self in modern-day research—the objective discounting of the subject of knowledge in his or her existential commitment—redefines the very conception, and with it the vocation, of higher learning.

Figure 2 Modern campus life

20   Despite this fundamental difference, however, the ancient schools of thought continue to inform and animate to varying degrees the traditional universities and colleges of England and the United States, if only through the organization of their campus life. These campuses are semi-unworldly sites where students spend formative years not only in classrooms but also in dormitories, cafeterias, sports fields, music halls, theaters, and various other places of organized activity and congregation. In its ideal, undergraduate education still aims, if only implicitly, to foster conditions that would enable self-transformation in the expansive second-order nursery of the campus. In the final analysis the campus remains a place where an intellectual, social, and civic flowering among its students is intended to take place under optimal conditions.

21   In that respect, the garden-like environments of the traditional US and British campus still reflect or symbolize, in their curated aspects, the ancient vocation of education, namely self-care and self-cultivation. Why else would the vast majority of commencement speakers at US graduation ceremonies speak directly to the moral, existential, and civic core of the students' selfhood, emphasizing this flowering of the whole person that a university education is intended to provide?

22   In my view, what is most needed today is an infusion of new life in the latent legacies that still tenuously bind our institutions of higher education to their ancient predecessors as places where a higher form of cultivation takes place—the cultivation of the humic soul-substance that defines the human potential for new life and new cultural forms of maturation. To render universities not merely as places for the acquisition of skills, expertise, or specialized knowledge alone, but as institutions that render students more fit for life—fit to live it, sustain it, and enhance its potential for happiness.

23   At Stanford University, where I teach, there is a place called the Community Garden that occupies half an acre of land on the margins of the campus. Students, faculty, and staff may apply for a little plot to cultivate. All of the designated plots are claimed, and most sprout various fruits and vegetables. It is a place of lively community and conviviality. I dream of a university that would put aside a few acres of land for a wide open communal garden where every student, upon entering the university, would be assigned his or her patch of earth to cultivate. This ritual of caring for one's own plot would serve to foster a deeper understanding of nature's cycles of birth and decay, of life's intrinsic mortality, and of the basics of sustaining life. It would also offer fundamental insights into what education, in its most essential vocation, consists of. In addition, it would give a fuller, more expansive meaning to the famous phrase that brings Voltaire's novel *Candide* to its conclusion: "*Il faut cultiver notre jardin*"—we must cultivate our garden. If higher education has anything truly "practical" to teach students, it's that the world we share in common is always *our* garden, and that its continued existence depends on our learning to become its caretakers. That in turn depends on the student's learning to cultivate his or her potential for care.

CHECK WHAT YOU'VE LEARNED (Paragraphs 17–23)

Think about what you have just read. Answer each question.

11. The author says (Paragraph 17), "Science requires neither a philosophical nor a theological foundation but only 'academic freedom' to pursue research." Some people reading this passage might say that science actually *does* have a philosophical foundation—that part of that foundation is the belief that researchers should be free to express whatever their supposedly objective research discovers. In your view, is science truly free of philosophy, or not?

12. In Paragraph 18, it is significant that the author speaks about the religious and governmental "supervisors" that formerly interfered with universities as being "external." In what way were they external? Why do you think this undermined their claims to authority?

13. In Paragraph 19, the author makes special use of the terms *subject* and *object*. As used in this paragraph, what is a "subject"? What is an "object"?

14. In Paragraph 20, the author writes, "In its ideal, undergraduate education still aims, if only implicitly, to foster conditions that would enable self-transformation in the expansive second-order nursery of the campus." Read the paragraph again. In what sense is a campus a "second-order nursery"?

15. The author concludes the essay by harking back to the garden-related classical references earlier in the essay and by introducing a garden-related "dream" of his own. What is that dream? Why does he think it would be a good thing for students at educational institutions?

THINKING CRITICALLY

Consider each situation in light of what you have read in "The Cultivation of Higher Learning." By yourself or with a partner, apply what you know about education as a process of cultivation to address each situation.

Situation 1 You are the parent of two school-aged children. You and your family are moving to a new city and your kids will have to enroll in schools there. You go online and do some searches to get an idea of which schools would be best. As you take notes and form your ideas about where best to send your kids, what factors will be most important to you? What good things are you looking for that might distinguish the best schools from the others? What undesirable factors are you trying to discover so that you can avoid bad schools?

Situation 2 You are the newly hired principal of a troubled high school. In fact, it has such serious problems that you wonder whether you can really do anything to turn this school around and make it a functioning educational institution. The school building is a mess, with graffiti on the walls, broken plumbing in the restrooms, broken windows in the classrooms, bugs in the cafeteria, and so on. On any given day, the proportion of students absent from school is close to 20 percent. Violence on the school grounds is common; the police are called to the school at least twice a week. But you took the job because you want to make a difference, and you are determined to try. What will be your first steps? How can you best begin to make a difference? Which conditions in the school, the neighborhood, and the city will you try to change or influence, as first steps?

Go to **MyEnglishLab** to complete a critical thinking exercise.

THINKING VISUALLY

A. Take a moment to study the image on page 308 (the Pavilion Gardens at the University of Virginia) and the image in Figure 2 of the reading (p. 315). The images say a lot about the US ideal of a campus setting. Describe three or four notable features. What does each feature indicate about the ideal of a college campus?

B. The reading mentions that many US colleges have spacious, park-like campuses. The following information shows the size of a few selected colleges / universities. Also shown is the number of students taking classes on campus (students in online programs not included). Review these figures and create a chart or graph that best communicates the information. You may want to go further to calculate the number of acres per student and add that to your visual. (NOTE: An acre is a measure of land area. Approximately 2.5 acres = 1 hectare.)

College / University	Acres	Number of Students
Berry College (Mount Berry, GA)	27,000	2,254
Kenyon College (Gambier, OH)	1,200	1,662
Liberty University (Lynchburg, VA)	6,819	13,800
Michigan State University (East Lansing, MI)	5,200	50,085
Stanford University (Stanford, CA)	8,180	16,136
University of Connecticut (Storrs, CT)	4,313	31,119
University of Wisconsin — Platteville (Platteville, WI)	8,967	820

THINKING ABOUT LANGUAGE

UNDERSTANDING NOMINALIZATION

A. Read these excerpts from the essay. Each is accompanied by two paraphrases of the excerpt. Both paraphrases are grammatical and basically accurate—so neither paraphrase is "wrong." However, native and highly proficient speakers of English might consider one more "sophisticated" than the other. Check (✓) the paraphrase you think is at a higher level of sophistication. Then discuss your choices with one or more students. Try to articulate to your partner(s) why you preferred one or the other. Consider nominalization as you explain your answers. Is your preferred version more highly nominalized?

	Excerpt	Paraphrases
1	As it progresses from infancy to adulthood, the human body matures according to the biological laws that hold sway over physical development. (Paragraph 3)	□ a. Biological laws determine human maturation from infancy to adulthood. □ b. The human body obeys physical laws as it matures from infancy to adulthood.
2	Čapek's flower here stands for all that thrives through human care and cultivation, above all the cultural maturity that education, especially in its higher forms, makes possible. (Paragraph 4)	□ a. Čapek's flower is, metaphorically, every object of human nurture, especially education and especially higher education. □ b. All things that humans take care of, especially higher education, are symbolized by Čapek's flower.
3	Adonis, beloved by Aphrodite, died young, and on his festival day (the *Adone*), the ancient Greeks engaged in the strange ritual of casting potted plants out of their windows. (Paragraph 7)	□ a. Adonis, Aphrodite's lover, died young and was remembered on the festival of *Adone* by the casting out of potted plants. □ b. On *Adone*, the festival of Aphrodite's lover Adonis, Greeks commemorated his early death with a ritual of throwing potted plants out of windows.
4	Such truths can defend themselves as well as the man who planted them. (Paragraph 8)	□ a. Such truths are strong. □ b. Such truths defend both themselves and their planter.

Continued

	Excerpt	Paraphrases
5	Since the better part of friendship consists in *conversation*, one must develop the verbal, intellectual, and social skills to become the sort of interlocutor who can give pleasure to one's friends, expecting them to do the same for you. (Paragraph 14)	☐ a. A responsible friend becomes a skilled conversationalist. ☐ b. To be a good friend, you have to develop excellent communication skills, enough to interest your friends.
6	Appealing to the need for autonomy and objectivity in scientific inquiry, the principle [of academic freedom] holds that external, nonexpert authority of any sort has no place in the sciences, that science functions properly only where it is free to posit its own methodological criteria for establishing truth and matters of fact, without fear of repercussion. (Paragraph 18)	☐ a. Academic freedom demands that science reject outside authorities and take responsibility itself for determining whether a research methodology is good or bad. ☐ b. By the principle of academic freedom, science itself, not any outside authority, determines the validity of any research plan.
7	In its ideal, undergraduate education still aims, if only implicitly, to foster conditions that would enable self-transformation in the expansive second-order nursery of the campus. (Paragraph 20)	☐ a. Ideally, undergraduate education provides nursery-like protection for self-development. ☐ b. The self develops, as it would in a nursery, during the process of undergraduate education.
8	If higher education has anything truly "practical" to teach students, it's that the world we share in common is always *our* garden, and that its continued existence depends on our learning to become its caretakers. (Paragraph 23)	☐ a. Higher education is very practical in that it teaches us to take responsibility for the garden where our education is cultivated. ☐ b. The practical lesson of higher education is that the health of the garden depends on us.

APPRECIATING HEDGING

B. Answer the questions about hedging language in "The Cultivation of Higher Learning."

1. What verb of tentativeness is used in the first sentence of Paragraph 5?

   ....

2. In this excerpt, why and how does the author express certainty?

   > Yi consists not merely of following rules of behavior but of understanding the intrinsic goodness of the positive virtues. It is, in every respect, the flower of a genuine education.

   ....

3. What phrase indicating the author's perspective appears near the start of Paragraph 22?

   ....

   ....

4. In this excerpt, underline a phrase that limits a claim about reality by saying whose opinion it is:

   > This means, or so taught Epicurus, that one must study philosophy, especially the Epicurean philosophy, for nothing enhances the pleasure of conversation as much as an intelligent, thoughtful exchange of ideas.

5. In the first few sentences of Paragraph 17, what "generalization word" appears three times to limit the claims about modern universities? Hint: It is a "quantity" word.

....

....

Go to **MyEnglishLab** for more practice reading an extended text and using your reading skills.

RESEARCH PROJECT

The reading in this unit portrays education as a process of nurturing and eliciting the potential in a student. Few educational theorists would dispute such a portrayal, but the history of educational philosophy shows enormous variation in beliefs about how to accomplish this. By doing research, you can learn more about about the variety of philosophies and theories in education today.

A. The following list features some notable educational philosophers and theorists of the past 150 years or so. Choose one to research.

- John Dewey
- Maria Montessori
- Paulo Freire
- Rudolf Steiner
- Erik Erikson
- Madeline Cheek Hunter

B. Conduct your research. As you read about the person you have chosen, formulate a thesis. Gather information that supports your thesis. Use the following questions to help guide you:

- Is one of the philosophies, such as the curiosity-focused learning philosophy of Montessori schools, superior to others? How?
- What enduring impact has the person had on philosophy or educational theory?
- Is there anything controversial about the person's point of view? What criticisms are valid?

C. Choose a presentation style from the box, or use your own idea, and present your research to the class.

biographical portrayal	model debate	persuasive speech

Go to **MyEnglishLab** to complete a collaborative activity.

Sound design creates a healthier world.

In Pursuit of Clean Air

UNIT PROFILE

In this unit, you will read about sources of indoor air pollutants, factors affecting pollution levels, and implications of indoor versus outdoor sources. In the online extended reading, you will learn about the challenges associated with energy-efficient ventilation. As a capstone to the unit, you will research the health effects of exposure to pollution and present your findings.

EXTENDED READING

BEFORE YOU READ

Discuss these questions with another student.

1. Some populations of people eat, work, and sleep outdoors. Others spend the vast majority of their time inside structures. Consider indoor and outdoor air pollution sources. Which population faces a greater health risk? Why?

2. Most people think of pollution as something that comes only from outside of the home, but a variety of pollutants originate inside the home. What would you guess some might be? Support your ideas.

3. Think about the house or apartment you live in and the building(s) where you work or study. Which one do you think has better ventilation? Why? Consider the size of the structure, its age, its construction, and whether it has a mechanical ventilation system.

4. Think of a major air pollution source near your home or work or other place you often go. What could you do to mitigate its potential effects on air quality and your health? Discuss tactics and strategies for doing so.

Read the passage. Then answer the questions after each section.

Sources of Indoor Air Pollutants

INTRODUCTION

1 In developed countries such as the United States, the average adult spends 69 percent of his or her time at home and 18 percent in other indoor locations. Most people like to think of their home as a healthy environment, but unfortunately this is not always the case. The causes are twofold: Ventilation brings outdoor air pollutants inside—a significant concern in locations where outdoor air pollution levels are high—and indoor sources frequently emit air pollutants.

HEALTH EFFECTS OF AIR POLLUTANTS

2 Some of the major indoor air pollutants of concern are presented in Table 1, along with their health effects. Laws regulate the release

of many, but not all, of these pollutants into outdoor air. Ozone and pollen (a bioaerosol) enter the indoor environment mainly from outdoors; they do not typically have important indoor sources. However, the other pollutants listed can come from emissions from both outdoor air and indoor sources.

3 The pollutants listed in the first group in Table 1 are gaseous. They can dissolve into liquids, such as the mucus that lines the respiratory tract. Some, such as NO_2, VOCs, and O_3, irritate the tissues in the respiratory tract. While CO is not an irritant, it readily passes into the bloodstream where it interferes with the ability of the blood to carry oxygen.

4 The pollutants listed in the second group—particulate matter—are airborne particles, which can come in the form of a solid or a liquid. PM larger than 10μm is captured with 100 percent efficiency in the nose and throat,

MAJOR INDOOR AIR POLLUTANTS			
	Regulated Outdoors?	Composition / Description	Health Effects
GASEOUS POLLUTANTS			
Carbon monoxide (CO)	x	Binds with hemoglobin in blood	Causes oxygen deprivation that can lead to headaches, nausea, etc.
Nitrogen dioxide (NO_2)	x	Diffuses into fluid lining the respiratory tract	Irritates eyes and upper respiratory tract
Volatile organic compounds (VOCs)	x	A category of gaseous pollutant that includes hundreds of different organics	Causes eye and throat irritation and headaches. Some are neurotoxins / suspected of causing cancer
Ozone (O_3)	x	Created from VOCs and NO / NO_2 (in the presence of sunlight)	Associated with eye and respiratory tract irritation
PARTICULATE MATTER (PM)			
Respirable PM (PM_{10})	x	PM that is 10 μm or smaller in diameter	Deposits in nose, throat, and lungs, causing irritation. Body flushes out PM from the nose and throat within a few hours
Fine PM ($PM_{2.5}$)	x	PM that is 2.5 μm or smaller in diameter	Can deposit deep in lungs, causing irritation and inflammation, taking several weeks or longer to be removed
Bioaerosols		PM that is biological in origin, such as pollen, molds, bacteria, pet allergens	Can cause allergy and asthma symptoms

Table 1 Indoor air pollutants of concern

Continued

so it is not able to reach the lungs. However, the collection efficiency of the nose and throat decreases for PM < 10 μm. Thus, the smaller the size of the particle, the more easily it can penetrate deep into the lungs and deposit in the pulmonary region. To clarify the significance of this, we should note that the body cannot quickly remove particles from the pulmonary region, so smaller particles can remain deposited in the respiratory tract for weeks or longer.

CATEGORIES OF INDOOR AIR POLLUTANTS

5 Any air pollutants present outdoors can be carried into the indoor environment via ventilation. In addition, many indoor sources of pollutants exist, and these can cause the concentration of certain air pollutants to be substantially higher indoors than outdoors.

6   There are three major categories of indoor air pollution, the first of which is **indoor combustion**. Examples include combustion from stoves, cigarettes, incense, and candles. Under perfect, complete combustion of a hydrocarbon fuel, such as fuel oil, the hydrogen and carbon in the fuel should become completely oxidized, and emissions should consist entirely of CO_2 and H_2O. However, the mixing of fuel and air is never perfect, so combustion is never 100 percent complete. As a result of this imperfection, incompletely oxidized gaseous products such as CO and VOCs, along with smoke ($PM_{2.5}$) are emitted. In addition, under hot combustion temperatures, the nitrogen and oxygen molecules present in the air can chemically react to form nitrogen oxides (NO and NO_2). Cooking also contributes. To be perfectly clear, cooking itself does not involve actual combustion of food, but the heating process involved in cooking can release VOCs from the food into the air. It can also volatilize

fats and oils, which will quickly recondense onto existing airborne particles, adding to the mass of indoor PM.

7   The second category is **materials and consumer products** used indoors, such as paint, wallpaper, carpeting, flooring, furniture, cleaning products, and cosmetics. These materials and products typically emit VOCs. Materials such as furniture, flooring, and paint tend to have the highest VOC emission rates when they are newly installed. Cleaning and cosmetic products—such as furniture polish, sunscreen, deodorant, and hairspray—are of concern because many utilize sprays in which a solvent is used to deliver a nonvolatile product to a surface. The solvent evaporates from both the surface and any spray droplets remaining in the air, adding to the indoor VOC concentrations. After evaporation, any nonvolatile product in the spray droplets is left floating in the air, adding to the airborne $PM_{2.5}$.

8   **Human activities** indoors, such as walking and cleaning, make up the third category of indoor air pollution sources. The movement of humans (and their pets) in the indoor environment can resuspend dust from the floors, furniture, and other surfaces. These dust particles include small amounts of $PM_{2.5}$ and a much larger amount of PM_{10}, including bioaerosols. Carpeting and fabric-covered furniture contain large reservoirs of settled PM because they are much more difficult to thoroughly clean than wood flooring or wood or vinyl furniture. Thus, walking on a carpeted floor, even one that has recently been vacuumed, can resuspend twice as much dust as walking on a wood or vinyl floor. And three people walking on indoor carpeting can generate as much PM_5 (particulate matter of 5 μm or smaller) per minute as someone smoking a cigarette.

CHECK WHAT YOU'VE LEARNED (Paragraphs 1–8)

Think about what you have just read. Answer each question. Then continue to the next part of the reading.

1. In the following sentence from Paragraph 2, the author uses the word *important* to describe indoor sources of ozone and pollen. Which of the following is the best definition in this context?

   Ozone and pollen (a bioaerosol) enter the indoor environment mainly from outdoors; they do not typically have **important** indoor sources.

   a. imperative
   b. significant
   c. profound
   d. vital

2. Table 1 is included in order to _____ indoor air pollutants.

   a. define all major types of
   b. give specific examples of
   c. detail the biological composition of
   d. summarize two categories of

3. Which statements based on the reading does Table 1 support? Choose TWO.

   a. Particulate matter bigger than 10μm is unable to make it to the lungs.
   b. Airborne particles can be in either liquid or solid form.
   c. It takes some weeks to rid the pulmonary region of small particles.
   d. The collection efficiency of the nose and throat decreases for PM 10 μm or smaller.

4. According to the reading, which statement is true about indoor combustion?

   a. In the situation of perfect combustion of a hydrocarbon fuel like fuel oil, the emissions should be made up of CO, CO_2, and H_2O.
   b. Combustion never totally finishes due to the fact that air and fuel do not mix perfectly.
   c. The cause of combustion is the emission of incompletely oxidized gaseous products and smoke.
   d. When combustion temperatures are high, nitrogen and carbon molecules chemically react.

5. In Paragraph 8, what is the author's reason for comparing walking on indoor carpeting with smoking a cigarette?

   ....

   ....

"Sources of Indoor Air Pollutants," *continued*

INDOOR VENTILATION

9 Small buildings tend to be naturally ventilated. Windows and doors are opened to allow the outdoor air to move inside. When the wind is blowing, this natural ventilation rate can be quite high. However, even with the windows and doors closed, outdoor air still enters the building via small openings found in door and window frames and other small cracks and openings present in the exterior of the building (the building "envelope"). Because older buildings tend to have more of these small cracks, they also tend to have higher natural ventilation rates.

10 Many large buildings have a mechanical ventilation system, where a large fan or blower delivers air via ductwork into individual rooms. Often a filter is used to capture large dust particles so they do not damage the fan or blower. But the filter used in a mechanical ventilation system is typically low efficiency, capturing <10 percent of the fine ($PM_{2.5}$) particles in the air. In addition, filters have no effect on gaseous pollutants, such as carbon monoxide and nitrogen dioxide.

11 Indoor pollution levels can be greatly influenced by the ventilation rate in a building. This ventilation rate can be quantified as the volume of air per time flowing through the indoors (Q). To standardize for the different sizes of rooms, Q can be divided by the volume of the room (V). This measure is called the **air exchange rate** (I, with units of inverse time—inverse time meaning 1 divided by time). This measure is represented by this equation:

$$I = Q/V \qquad \textbf{Equation 1}$$

12 The air exchange rate represents how many "roomfuls" of air per unit of time leave (or enter) the room, due to ventilation. For example, an air exchange rate of 2/hr. indicates that two roomfuls of air per hour pass through the room. The higher the air exchange rate, the more rapidly

indoor pollutants leave the room. The average time a molecule of air spends inside a well-mixed room can be calculated by simply taking the reciprocal of I (that is, 1/I). So, for I = 2/hr., the average air molecule spends 0.5 hours (30 minutes) inside the room. The typical air exchange rate for homes ranges from 0.4/hr. to 4/hr.

FACTORS AFFECTING INDOOR AIR POLLUTION LEVELS: OUTDOOR AIR AS A SOURCE

13 To conduct an engineering analysis of how pollutants accumulate and are removed from the indoor environment, let us consider a single room, with ventilation bringing polluted outdoor air into the room. For this case, it will be assumed that all the indoor air pollutants originate from outdoors; there are no indoor pollution sources.

14 The flow of an air pollutant out of a room due to ventilation (F_{out}, in mass per time) will depend on the volumetric flow rate (Q) and the concentration of pollutant indoors (C_{in}, in mass/ volume). This is represented in this equation:

$$F_{out} = QC_{in} = IVC_{in} \qquad \textbf{Equation 2}$$

15 The mass of pollutant inside this room is its concentration indoors (C_{in}) times the volume of the room (V). So, as is shown in Equation 2, F_{out} can be represented as the air exchange rate (I) times the mass of pollutant inside the room ($V C_{in}$).

16 An equal flow rate (Q) of air is entering the room. However, some outdoor pollutants are removed during passage into the building as air travels through the ventilation system or the building envelope.

17 The **penetration factor**, p, quantifies what fraction of an outdoor pollutant is carried indoors via ventilation. Having p = 0.8, for example, means that 20 percent of the pollutant gets removed as it moves from outdoors to indoors; the other 80 percent makes it inside. Examples of penetration losses would include airborne particles depositing or settling inside narrow openings or ventilation ducts, or gaseous pollutants being taken up by (or reacting with) surfaces present inside the duct or opening. Thus, the flow of outdoor pollutants into the room (F_{in}) due to ventilation will depend on p as well as on the ventilation rate (Q) and the outdoor ("**ambient**") pollutant concentration (C_{amb}):

$$F_{in} = pQ C_{amb} = pIV C_{amb} \qquad \textbf{Equation 3}$$

18   Pathways for removing air pollutants in the indoor environment exist in the form of sinks. Examples of indoor sinks include the floor of a room (on which particles might settle), the walls of a room (to which gaseous particles might bind), and ambient chemicals in the air and on surfaces (with which gaseous pollutants might react, thereby being destroyed). Often, the rate of pollutant removal (F_{rem}) varies with the mass of pollutant present indoors, with a proportionality constant k:

$$F_{rem} = kVC_{in}$$ **Equation 4**

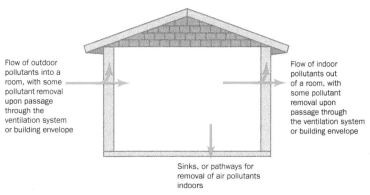

Flow of outdoor pollutants into a room, with some pollutant removal upon passage through the ventilation system or building envelope

Flow of indoor pollutants out of a room, with some pollutant removal upon passage through the ventilation system or building envelope

Sinks, or pathways for removal of air pollutants indoors

Figure 1 Flows of an air pollutant in and out of a room, for the case where outdoor air pollution is the only important source

19   For a situation where the only source of indoor pollutants is from outdoors, these three flows of pollutants in and out of the room will influence the indoor concentration, C_{in}, as shown in Figure 1.

Note that the equation for F_{out} is not multiplied by the penetration factor, p. Because air pollutants are lost inside the building envelope when air flows out of the room, the total removal from the room will be the sum of what is lost in the envelope plus what goes back outside. This means that the magnitude of p does not influence F_{out}.

CHECK WHAT YOU'VE LEARNED (Paragraphs 8–19)

Think about what you have just read. Answer each question. Then continue to the next part of the reading.

6. How are smaller buildings normally ventilated? Contrast this with how larger buildings are typically ventilated. Why do you think they are ventilated differently?

....

....

7. In your own words, explain the term *air exchange rate* and how it can be calculated.

....

....

8. What is the meaning of the term *penetration factor*? Based on what you know about ventilation systems and pollutants, inside which structure would having p = 0.95 be more likely—a well-built modern home or an old factory?

....

....

9. Based on the information in Paragraph 18, how would you define a *sink*?

....

10. Paraphrase the following sentence: Because air pollutants are lost inside the building envelope when air flows out of the room, the total removal from the room will be the sum of what is lost in the envelope plus what goes back outside.

....

....

"Sources of Indoor Air Pollutants," *continued*

20 We can evaluate how the steady-state—or unvarying—indoor concentration compares with the outdoor concentration by setting the flows of pollutants into the room equal to the pollutant-removal pathways for the room:

$$F_{in} = F_{out} + F_{rem} \qquad \textbf{Equation 5}$$

21   In the absence of indoor sources, the indoor pollutant concentration will always be less than or equal to the outdoor concentration. If there is 100 percent penetration ($p = 1$), and there are no removal pathways indoors ($k = 0$), then the pollution concentration will be the same indoors as outdoors. This is shown in Figure 2. But if $p < 1$, then the indoor concentration will be lower than outdoors. And if $k > 0$, the indoor concentration will also be lower than outdoors. However, in this case, how much lower it is will depend on the magnitude of the removal rate *compared with* the ventilation rate; that is, the ratio k/I. As is shown in Figure 2, the larger k/I is, the lower the indoor pollutant concentration is, as compared with outdoors. This bears some explanation. This trend can be conceptually understood by

22 considering an air pollutant with a set indoor removal rate, k. The lower the air exchange rate (I) is, the longer this pollutant spends indoors, so the more time there is for removal pathways to act on the pollutant.

22   The penetration factor p will vary with the pollutant as well as with the building design and its ventilation. The indoor removal rate k will vary with the pollutant and may also vary with factors like temperature, materials present indoors, and the concentrations of other indoor air pollutants. The indoor / outdoor ratio, I/O, is often used to measure how important penetration and/or indoor sink losses are for a given pollutant. In general, in the absence of indoor sources, I/O is very close to 1 for CO, indicating that penetration losses and indoor removal sinks are negligible. I/O ratios in the absence of indoor sources tend to be around 0.7–0.95 for $PM_{2.5}$, 0.5–0.8 for PM_{10}, and 0.4–0.7 for NO_2. O_3, which is strongly reactive with surfaces, undergoes substantial penetration losses and significant removal indoors, with typical I/O ratios of 0.2–0.4.

$$I/O = \frac{C_{in}}{C_{amb}} = \frac{p}{1 + k/I} \qquad \textbf{Equation 6}$$

Looking at Equation 6, you should remember that p is always less than or equal to 1, since p tells you what fraction of the pollutants successfully penetrate the building envelope. In addition, you can see that the denominator will always be > or = 1, since k and I are always positive numbers. Thus, the only way to get an I/O value close to 1 (as opposed to much less than 1) is if a) the denominator is as close to 1 as possible, which will only happen if the k/I term is very close to 0, meaning that the indoor removal sink term (k) must be close to 0; and b) p is as close to 1 as possible (because a p value < 1 will also cause I/O to be less than 1).

FACTORS AFFECTING INDOOR AIR POLLUTION LEVELS: INDOOR SOURCE EMISSIONS

23 In the case of a single room where the major source of an air pollutant is an indoor source, it will be assumed that outdoor levels of this air pollutant are negligible (that is, $F_{in} = 0$). The flows

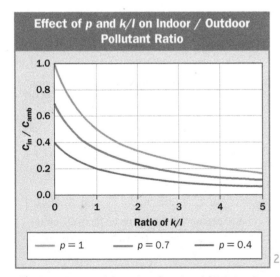

Effect of p and k/I on Indoor / Outdoor Pollutant Ratio

- $p = 1$
- $p = 0.7$
- $p = 0.4$

(y-axis: C_{in} / C_{amb}; x-axis: Ratio of k/I)

Figure 2 Variation of the indoor / outdoor (I/O) ratio of an air pollutant with k/I, and with p, for the case with no indoor air pollution sources

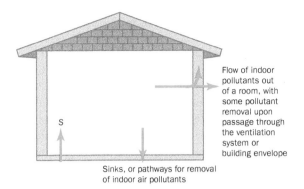

Flow of indoor pollutants out of a room, with some pollutant removal upon passage through the ventilation system or building envelope

S

Sinks, or pathways for removal of indoor air pollutants

Figure 3 Flows of an air pollutant in and out of a room for the case where an indoor source is the major contributor and outdoor air pollution is negligible

in and out of the room for this case can be seen in Figure 3. The flow from the indoor source is shown as S (in mass/time).

24   For this case, we can again set the flows in equal to the flows out, deriving an equation that shows, under steady-state, how the indoor concentration, C_{in}, depends on the other variables:

Substituting in: $S = F_{rem} + F_{out}$ **Equation 7**

$S = kVC_{in} + IVC_{in}$ **Equation 8**

Rearranging Eqn. (8) gives: $C_{in} = \dfrac{S/V}{k + I}$ **Equation 9**

25   For this case where an indoor source dominates, in addition to the air exchange rate (I) and the decay rate (k), the indoor concentration also depends on the volume of the room, V. For example, suppose you wanted to calculate the steady-state concentration of formaldehyde in a room of volume V and air exchange rate I, where a person was constantly smoking. The emission rate, S, of formaldehyde from a cigarette can be assumed to be 5 mg/hr., and the indoor removal of formaldehyde (via chemical degradation) can be approximated as $k = 0.4$/hr.

IMPLICATIONS FOR OUTDOOR AIR POLLUTION AS A SOURCE

26 If outdoor air pollution is the major source of indoor air pollutants in a home, then there are three factors that determine how the steady-state indoor pollutant concentration compares with the outdoor concentration:

1. The first factor is the penetration fraction, p. This penetration fraction will vary from pollutant to pollutant. It also depends on the construction of a home, including the materials used, the prevalence of

narrow openings and cracks (e.g., around a window frame), and the frequency with which windows are opened or closed.

2. The second factor is the air exchange rate, I. The larger the air exchange rate is, the shorter the amount of time a molecule of pollutant spends indoors. Air exchange rate can be influenced by the opening of windows as well as a higher wind speed, which causes more air to flow in and out of a home via the narrow openings and cracks. An older home with a building envelope that is not as well sealed experiences a higher air exchange rate under windy conditions than when the air is calm. However, the air exchange rate only matters if there are significant removal pathways indoors. If $k = 0$, then the magnitude of I is unimportant.

3. The third factor consists of pollutant removal pathways indoors. Natural indoor removal pathways include particles settling onto the floor, gaseous pollutants being destroyed via chemical reactions, and gases binding to indoor surfaces. Portable indoor filters can also act as a removal pathway for PM. The longer the amount of time a pollutant spends indoors, the more effective these removal pathways will be. However, the importance of a removal pathway is determined by comparing it with the ventilation rate. If the rate of removal is faster than or roughly comparable to the rate of air exchange, then indoor pollutant levels will be significantly reduced. But if the air exchange timescale is 100 times faster than the removal timescale, then the impact of the removal pathway on indoor pollutant concentrations will be negligible (<1%).

27   Thus, if there are no penetration losses, and the pollutant removal rate indoors is negligible compared with the air exchange rate, then the indoor pollutant concentration will be the same as the outdoor concentration. But if $p < 1$, or there is a significant removal pathway, then the indoor pollutant concentration will be less than the outdoor level, as shown in Figure 2. A way of increasing the removal of outdoor pollutants

Continued

in the indoor environment is to decrease the air exchange rate. This allows the removal pathways more time to remove the pollutants that have penetrated indoors.

IMPLICATIONS FOR INDOOR SOURCES

28 For the case where indoor emissions are the major source of indoor air pollutants, the larger the emission rate is, the higher the indoor pollutant concentration will be. The other factors that determine the magnitude of the steady-state indoor pollutant concentration are as follows:

1. The volume of the room, V. The larger the volume of the room, the more dilution of the emissions can occur.

2. The ventilation rate, I. In this case, ventilation will carry the indoor emissions back outdoors. So the higher the ventilation rate, the more quickly the polluted air will be carried back outside and replaced with cleaner outdoor air. In this case, the ventilation rate is important even if $k = 0$.

3. The removal rate, k. Like ventilation, removal pathways help lower the indoor pollutant concentration. But this type of removal only has a noticeable effect if it is significant in magnitude compared with ventilation.

29   The above mathematical analyses assume the indoor air pollutants are at steady-state, and are well mixed—that is, that any indoor emissions are instantaneously mixed throughout the entire room. However, indoor mixing processes are not instantaneous; it typically takes 10 to 20 minutes for just-released indoor emissions to mix fairly uniformly (to within +/– 10%) throughout a room. Before this time, pollutant levels are higher close to the source, and much lower far away from the source. This becomes readily apparent if you imagine yourself in a room with someone who is smoking. If you are sitting or standing close to this actively-emitting indoor source, you will be exposed to much higher pollutant concentrations than if you were in a far corner. This is called the **proximity effect**. Breathing within 0.5 meters of an active emission source can cause a person to inhale pollutant concentrations that are, on average, 7 to 20 times as high as what would be predicted using the well-mixed room assumption. Thus, in addition to the mitigation strategies mentioned above, residents should also avoid being in close proximity to active indoor emission sources whenever possible.

30   In summary, if the source of pollution is indoors, increasing the room's ventilation rate helps reduce indoor pollution concentrations. But if the source of pollution is from outdoors, then the opposite is true—the ventilation rate should be decreased to allow more time for indoor removal processes to reduce indoor pollutant levels.

CHECK WHAT YOU'VE LEARNED (Paragraphs 20–30)

Think about what you have just read. Answer each question.

11. Where no indoor air pollution sources exist, what is the relationship between the air exchange rate and the amount of time a pollutant stays inside?

   ....

   ....

12. What factors affect the indoor removal rate (k)?

   ....

   ....

13. In Figure 3, what does S represent?

   ....

   ....

14. When considering pollutant removal pathways, what is the relationship between the rate of removal and indoor pollutant levels?

   ....

   ....

15. What is the *proximity effect*? Why do you think the author includes a discussion of this?

   ....

   ....

THINKING CRITICALLY

Consider each situation in light of what you have read in "Sources of Indoor Air Pollutants." By yourself or with a partner, apply what you know about indoor air pollutants to address each situation.

Situation 1 You are a homeowner and share your house with your immediate family and two dogs. You are looking to decrease pollution caused by indoor sources in order to provide your family with a healthier living environment. What specific changes can you make to your surroundings and to activities in the home to do this? Consider what you read about the three major categories of indoor air pollution sources—indoor combustion sources, materials and consumer products, and human activities.

Situation 2 You are in the process of building a new home in a nice neighborhood. Your lot is right on the edge of the neighborhood, which you like, because you won't have neighbors too close to your home. There is a large building in the near distance, however, that you just learned is an industrial facility. From your past studies, you know that such facilities can produce nitrogen dioxide emissions, which can be harmful to your health. Based on the smoke visible in the air above the building, you guess that the facility also emits particulate matter. What actions can you take—both while building your home and when you begin living in it—to minimize the amount of pollutants that make their way into your home? Consider what you read about penetration factor, air exchange rate, and pollutant removal pathways.

Go to **MyEnglishLab** to complete a critical thinking exercise.

A. Look at the plot point, added to the graph from the reading (p. 328). Reread Paragraph 21 and answer the questions.

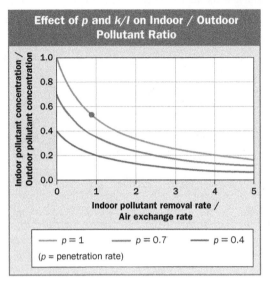

Effect of p and k/l on Indoor / Outdoor Pollutant Ratio

Indoor pollutant concentration / Outdoor pollutant concentration

Indoor pollutant removal rate / Air exchange rate

— $p = 1$ — $p = 0.7$ — $p = 0.4$

(p = penetration rate)

1. Any building on the blue line has a penetration of 100 percent because that line is for buildings where $p = 1$. But at the plot point, the indoor concentration of a pollutant is lower than the outdoor concentration. Why?

....

....

....

2. A penetration rate of 100 percent is very high. What is one type of building that might have such a rate?

....

B. Review what you read about proximity effect. Then create a graphic that demonstrates it.

THINKING ABOUT LANGUAGE

RECOGNIZING AND LEARNING MULTIWORD VOCABULARY ITEMS

A. Read these excerpts from the essay. Complete the task indicated for each item.

1. Identify the compound nouns.

   Ventilation brings outdoor air pollutants inside—a significant concern in locations where outdoor air pollution levels are high—and indoor sources frequently emit air pollutants.

   ....

2. Refer back to Paragraph 2. What is the multiword unit that refers to a visual?

   ....

3. Look at the Health Effects column for Respirable PM in Table 1. What phrasal verb can you identify?

   ....

4. Paragraph 3 contains a multiword unit that refers to a visual. What is it?

   ....

5. Identify the multiword units.

   There are three major categories of indoor air pollution, the first of which is indoor combustion.

   ....

6. Identify the compound noun.

   Materials such as furniture, flooring, and paint tend to have the highest VOC emission rates when they are newly installed.

   ....

7. Look back to Paragraphs 14 and 15. What two multiword units refer to a visual (in this case, an equation)?

   ....

8. Identify the phrasal verbs.

   Examples of indoor sinks include the floor of a room (on which particles might settle), the walls of a room (to which gaseous particles might bind), and ambient chemicals in the air and on surfaces (with which gaseous pollutants might react, thereby being destroyed).

   ....

9. Paragraph 23 contains two multiword units that refer to a visual. What are they?

   ....

10. What are the compound nouns?

    But if the source of pollution is from outdoors, then the opposite is true—the ventilation rate should be decreased to allow more time for indoor removal processes to reduce indoor pollutant levels.

    ....

UNDERSTANDING AND USING CLARIFIERS

B. Read these excerpts from the essay. Identify the clarifiers.

1. To clarify the significance of this, we should note that the body cannot quickly remove particles from the pulmonary region, so smaller particles can remain deposited in the respiratory tract for weeks or longer.

   ....

2. Cooking also contributes. To be perfectly clear, cooking itself does not involve actual combustion of food, but the heating process involved in cooking can release VOCs from the food into the air.

   ....

3. This means that the magnitude of p does not influence F_{out}.

   ....

4. This bears some explanation. This trend can be conceptually understood by considering an air pollutant with a set indoor removal rate, k. The lower the air exchange rate (l) is, the longer this pollutant spends indoors, so the more time there is for removal pathways to act on the pollutant.

....

5. This becomes readily apparent if you imagine yourself in a room with someone who is smoking. If you are sitting or standing close to this actively emitting indoor source, you will be exposed to much higher pollutant concentrations than if you were in a far corner.

....

Go to MyEnglishLab for more practice reading an extended text and using your reading skills.

RESEARCH PROJECT

The reading in this unit discusses the sources of indoor air pollutants and health effects associated with them. By doing research, you can learn more about the ways in which gaseous pollutants and particulate matter detrimentally affect individuals' health.

A. The following is a list of gaseous pollutants and types of particulate matter. Choose and research either 1) one pollutant, 2) one of the two categories of pollutants, OR 3) one pollutant from each category.

Gaseous Pollutant
- carbon monoxide (CO)
- nitrogen dioxide (NO_2)
- volatile organic compounds (VOCs)
- ozone (O_3)

Particulate Matter
- respirable PM (PM_{10})
- fine PM ($PM_{2.5}$)
- bioaerosols

B. Conduct your research. As you read about your subject, formulate a thesis. Gather information that supports your thesis. Use the following ideas to help guide you:

- Compare and contrast a gaseous pollutant with a type of particulate matter.
- Explain the process by which one pollutant is emitted and subsequently affects human health.
- Find a trend and consider its implications for the future.

C. Create a list of discussion questions about interesting points related to your topic. Choose a presentation style from the box, or use your own idea, and present your research to the class. Then pose the questions to the class and have a group discussion.

> a short audio documentary a slideshow a short lecture

Go to MyEnglishLab to complete a collaborative activity.

Text Credits

Pages 16, 17, 18, 67, 68, 69, 70, 125: Dictionary entries from the *Longman Advanced American Dictionary*, Third Edition.

Photo Credits

Front Cover: Roman Babakin/Shutterstock; Part and unit openers (multi use): Budai Romeo Gabor/Fotolia (gold coins), Nik_Merkulov/Fotolia (leaf with water droplets), Scisetti Alfio/Fotolia (old letter), Vichly4thai/Fotolia (red molecule dna cell), Tobkatrina/123RF (children's hands holding earth), orelphoto/Fotolia (background texture). Page 2: Gannet77/Getty Images; 5: Courtesy of Jefferson Singer; 12: Everett Historical/Shutterstock; 13 (top, bottom): Peter Hermes Furian/Fotolia; 14: duncan1890/Getty Images; 23: Oleksandr Molotkovych/Shutterstock; 24: Sergey Novikov/Shutterstock; 34: National Geographic Creative/Alamy Stock Photo; 46: Guschenkova/Shutterstock; 63: Banaras Khan/AFP/Getty Images; 76: Martin Shields/Alamy Stock Photo; 81: Martin Shields/Alamy Stock Photo (detail); 104: Jeremy Horner/Alamy Stock Photo; 105 (top): Oxford Designers & Illustrators Ltd/Pearson Education Ltd; 105 (bottom): Pearson Education Ltd; 106 (top): surfupvector/Fotolia; 106 (bottom): Designua/Shutterstock; 107 (top): Alila Medical Media/Shutterstock; 107 (center): Blamb/Shutterstock; 107 (bottom): Steve Gschmeissner/ Getty Images; 110: Encyclopaedia Britannica/UIG/Getty Images; 118: HL Studios/Pearson Education Ltd; 120 (top, left): Ezume Images/Fotolia; 120 (bottom): Shivendu Jauhari/iStock/Thinkstock/Getty Images; 121 (top): NASA Goddard's Scientific Visualization Studio/T. Schindler; 121 (bottom): NASA Goddard's Scientific Visualization Studio/T. Schindler; 129 (left): Inok/Fotolia; 129 (right): Gang/Fotolia; 130 (left): Javier Larrea/age fotostock/Alamy Stock Photo; 134: Everett Collection Inc/Alamy Stock Photo; 138: Everett Collection/Newscom; 151: Derek Cattani/ REX/Newscom; 154: Everett Historical/Shutterstock; 156 (bottom): Zack Frank/Shutterstock; 156 (center): Wynnter/ Getty Images; 156 (top, left): lesniewski/Fotolia; 156 (top, right): Valzan/Shutterstock; 158: Tina Manley/Alamy Stock Photo; 169: Alexandere17/123RF; 176: Elena Elisseeva/Shutterstock; 180: Sciepro/Science Photo Library/Getty Images; 185: Cancer cells: Shebeko/Shutterstock; 201: Joe Raedle/Getty Images News/Getty Images; 208: Stefano Bianchetti/Corbis Historical/Getty Images; 236: Craig Wilson Kite Aerial Photography/Moment/Getty Images; 243: udaix/Shutterstock; 248: Donvictori0/Fotolia; 262: Guillermo Legaria/AFP/Getty Images; 263: erhui1979/ DigitalVision Vectors/Getty Images; 264: Anilakkus/Getty Images; 267: Arsgera/Shutterstock; 269: P. Spiro/ Alamy Stock Photo; 270: BPTU/Shutterstock; 278: Miscellaneoustock/Alamy Stock Photo; 279: Lasse Kristensen/ Shutterstock; 280: Stuart Monk/Shutterstock; 290 (top): Dell/Fotolia; 290 (bottom): Blend Images/Shutterstock; 294: Bogdanhoda/Shutterstock; 299 (top, left): Designua/Shutterstock; 299 (right): Juan Gaertner/Shutterstock; 302: Smith/MCT/Newscom; 305: Al/Fotolia; 308: Andrew Shurtleff/Alamy Stock Photo; 310: Incamerastock/Alamy Stock Photo; 315: William Perugini/Shutterstock; 322: Zoonar GmbH/Alamy Stock Photo.

Index

Page numbers in bold refer to visuals (tables and figures).
Page numbers in italics refer to terms found in audio
referenced on those pages.

opinion, statements of, 136
   author purpose, 138
   bias, 136
   connotation, 136
   features of, 136
   recognizing and interpreting, 136
   signal phrases, 137
   source, 138
   tone, 136
opportunity cost, 266
Orwell, George, 92
outline, 60–61
Ovid, 224
Oxford, 309

pace, 79
Pakistan, polio vaccinations and, 63–64
The Paper Chase (movie), 91
paragraph, 25
   basic elements of, 25
   beginning connector, 25
   end connector, 25
   main idea, 25
   set-up sentence, 25
   support and nonsupport sentences in, 14
   supporting details, 25
   topic sentence, 25
paraphrase, 168
   characteristics of, 168
   writing, 168
Park Jongwoo, 21
Parkinson's disease, 196
particulate matter (PM), **323**
   national trends in concentrations of 2000–2014, *123*
"Patriotic Purchasing" (economics reading), 29–30
Pauling, Linus, 217
Peloponnesian War, 213
penetration factor, 327
"Perceptions of the Civil Rights Movement" (sociology
   reading), 135
Periodic Table of Elements, 243
Persia, ancient, 239
Persig, Robert, 85
Petrobras, 43
Phaedrus (Plato), 310–311
Philip II, King of Macedonia, 80
photographs, 105
The Pilgrim's Progress (Bunyan), 223
plagiarism, US culture and, 168
Plato, 78, 91, 310, 312
   Allegory of the Cave, 87
   Phaedrus , 310–311
   "Plato's Academy" (humanities reading), 86–87
   Republic, 86–87
   theory of forms, 86–87
Platonic Academy, 309
Platonists, 312

Plato's Academy, 86–87, 91, 309, 310
"Plato's Academy" (humanities reading), 86–87
Poetic Edda, 221
Poliakoff, Michael B., 15
polio, 63–64
   epidemic in United States, 63
   eradication efforts, 63, 65
   Global Polio Eradication Initiative, 65
   Nigeria and, 64
   vaccinations in Afghanistan, 63–64
   vaccinations in Pakistan, 63–64
"Political Conditions for African Americans" (sociology
   reading), 149
"Pollutants and the Respiratory System" (environmental
   engineering reading), 107
polluting substances
   nonliving, 242
   ways of classifying, 241–242
pollution. *see also* air quality
   athletics and, 114
   Chile and, 114
   China and, 114
   distribution of US 2010 total emission estimates by
      source category, 131
   in Eastern US in 2005 (satellite image), **121**
   in Eastern US in 2011 (satellite image), **121**
   Fairbanks, Alaska, 123
   global emissions from fossil fuels, **118**
   health and, 245–246
   impact of energy-saving devices on, 257–258
   in India, 110
   indoor air and, 237–238, 245–246
   internal combustion engines and, 109–111
   particulate matter, national trends in concentrations
      of 2000-2014, **123**
   Phoenix, Arizona, 123
   Reno, Nevada, 123
   respiratory system and, 108
   San Francisco area, 123
   sick building syndrome, 248–249
   in United States, 110, 119, 121, 123, 131
   Visalia, California, 123
   volatile organic compounds (VOCs), 237–238
   wealth of country and, 131
   Yakima, Washington, 123
polymerization, 301
Portugal, trade with Britain, 36–37
potlatch, 34
prefix, 38
prereading, 10, 26, 41, 71, 175, 230, 256, 262, 294,
   308, 322–334
   discussion questions, 278
   questions, 20, 200
previewing, 26
price ceiling, **287**, 287
price controls, 287
price floor, 287

prion diseases, 195–196
    Alzheimer's disease and, 195–196
    cannibalism and, 296
    "Cows, Cannibals, and Crystals—Explaining the Mechanism of Prion Disease", 302–303
    Creutzfeldt-Jakob disease (CJD), 196
prion diseases
    distribution and, **295**
    formation of seed fibril, 299
    history of, 295
    host species and, **295**
    human BSE, 302
    human growth hormone (hGH) and Iatrogenic transmission, 300
    human prion disease, 296
    multiple forms, 301
    occurrences of BSE (map), **302**
    pathogenic model, 299
    pathology, 300
    polymerization, 300
    prions and cancers, 298
    procedures with documented occurrences of prion transmission, **300**
    PrP, 298, 300, 302
prions, 295
PRNP gene, 196
problem/solution, 50, 52
    language used with, 52
processes, descriptions of, 48
producer surplus, **283**, 283
Prohibition, 165
Prose Edda, 221
protectionism, 29–30, 42–43
proximity effect, 330, 332
Prusiner, Stanley, 296
public goods, 176
    culturally significant sites and, 177
"Public Goods vs. Private Gain" (economics reading), 176–178

Qin Dynasty, 101
quotation, direct, 220
    verbs introducing, 226
quotation, indirect, 220
    verbs introducing, 226
quotation, inset, 220

race relations. *see also* civil rights; King, Martin Luther Jr.
    in Jim Crow South, 135
    in United States, 12, 135
reading skills, fundamental
    active reading, 3–10
    cohesion, 46–75
    fluency 76–103
    visuals, 104–132
    main ideas and supporting details, 22–45

reading speed, 79
reading-writing connection
    annotating and taking notes, 11–15
    critiques, 143–145
    direct and indirect quotation, 219, 220–226
    extended metaphor, 192–193
    outlines and graphic organizers, 60
    paraphrasing, 168
    recognizing and using rhetorical techniques, 89–90
    references to other sources, 247–248
    referring to visual data, 117
    summarizing, 34
reasoning by anecdote, **188**
reasoning by question, **188**
Reconstruction Era, 145
references to other sources, 250–251
    date of study, 247
    et al., 247
    generalization about the topic, 247
    names of researchers, 247
    parentheses and, 247
    plagiarism, US culture and, 168
    publication information, 252
    techniques for using, 247
    understanding and producing, 247–248
    when no author is given, 252
refrigerants, 239
relationship words, 48
rent controls, 287
rental costs, average in US cities, **291**
Republic (Plato), 86–87
research, 16
research paper
    literature review, 247
    structure of, 247
research project (biology)
    choose a presentation style, 307
    choose topic, 307
    conduct research and formulate a thesis, 307
    prion diseases, 307
research project (economics)
    choose presentation style and present, 293
    choose topic, 293
    conduct research, 293
research project (environmental engineering), 334
    choose topic, 334
    conduct research and formulate a thesis, 334
    presentation, 334
research project (humanities)
    presentation, 321
    research, 321
    select topic for, 321
research project (sociology)
    choose presentation style, 277
    choose topic, 277
    formulate thesis and gather support, 277